NEW WOMAN FICTION, 1881–1899

CONTENTS OF THE EDITION

NEW WOMAN FICTION, 1881–1899

General Editor
Carolyn W. de la L. Oulton

Volume 9
Mary Cholmondeley, *Red Pottage* (1899)

Edited by
Carolyn W. de la L. Oulton

Routledge
Taylor & Francis Group

LONDON AND NEW YORK

First published 2011 by Pickering & Chatto (Publishers) Limited

2 Park Square, Milton Park, Abingdon, Oxon OX14 4RN
711 Third Avenue, New York, NY 10017, USA

First issued in paperback 2017

Routledge is an imprint of the Taylor & Francis Group, an informa business

BRITISH LIBRARY CATALOGUING IN PUBLICATION DATA

New woman fiction, 1881–1899.
Part 3, Volumes 7–9.
1. Women – Social conditions – Fiction.
I. Ouida, 1839–1908. Massarenes. II. Egerton, George, 1859–1945. Wheel of
God. III. Cholmondeley, Mary, 1859–1925. Red pottage. IV. King, Andrew,
1957– V. March-Russell, Paul. VI. Oulton, Carolyn, 1972–
823.8'08-dc22

ISBN-13: 978-1-85196-643-1 (set)
ISBN-13: 978-1-1387-5559-8 (hbk)
ISBN-13: 978-1-138-11320-6 (pbk)

Typeset by Pickering & Chatto (Publishers) Limited

CONTENTS

ACKNOWLEDGEMENTS

Thanks are due to those shadowy figures the anonymous readers, for their enthusiastic reception of this project and their constructive advice on the initial proposal; to Canterbury Christ Church University for a term's research leave; to members of the Victoria list who were generous with their time and expertise; and at the other end of the process to Julie Wilson for her painstaking (as ever) proofreading. The volume editors alone know how much this series owes to their dedication and unassailable good humour. It is a genuine pleasure to thank them again here.

INTRODUCTION

This introduction necessarily refers to details of the plot of the novel and first-time readers may therefore prefer to read it afterwards.

After Mary Cholmondeley's death in 1925, her friend and first biographer Percy Lubbock recalled with glee a story of her hosting a meeting of literary ladies, all of whom had trooped in with compliments on *Red Pottage*. Responding with a standard 'Thanks, thanks, I'm so glad you liked it', Cholmondeley was suddenly confronted by an irate woman crying 'But I didn't like it at all. I thought it an abominable book!' By the spring of 1900 she had received a number of abusive letters, as well as many congratulations.[1]

While the novel was an instant bestseller its claims to be taken seriously as a work of literature have taken over a century to process. Like Annie E. Holdsworth's *The Years that the Locust Hath Eaten*, Cholmondeley's novel confronts the position of vulnerable middle-class women living on a low income in East London and, like Holdsworth, her fictional woman writer directly addresses the forbidden knowledge that this life in the city brings. Hester Gresley's ironically titled *An Idyll of East London*, discussed by some of the central characters in an early chapter, is seen as a shockingly candid work for a well-connected woman to have written. Apart from anything else, it is later made clear to the reader that her novel includes sexual fall in its portrayal of a ruthless economic framework. In *Red Pottage* itself one of the two main plots concerns the scandalous liaison between Hugh Scarlett and the married Lady Newhaven, for which neither initially appears to feel even a modicum of guilt.

Nonetheless the scandal caused by *Red Pottage* on its first publication in October 1899 is surprising given that it was written in the wake of far more obviously daring New Woman novels such as Sarah Grand's *The Heavenly Twins* (1893) and Grant Allen's *The Woman Who Did* (1895),[2] to name but two. Ironically it was not the treatment of illicit sexual relations but Cholmondeley's satire of provincial churchmen that caused the most extreme reactions among readers, including the assurance from one anonymous correspondent that as he was faithfully religious he felt it his duty to burn at least one copy of her book.[3] In fact, as a few early reviewers pointed out, the narrator is notably sympathetic to the Gresleys' plight even when satirizing their failures of comprehension. James Gresley is 'both fanatic and saint' (below, p. 37), while his wife is presented as both laughable and heroic in her dealings with 'the real difficulties of life, its butcher's bills, its monthly nurses, its constant watchfulness over delicate children, its long, long strain at two ends which won't meet' (below, p. 63).

The Bishop of Stepney proved a powerful ally, and the only critic of Gresley whom Cholmondeley declared to be entirely in sympathy with her aim, to create a character 'who is to every clergyman who reads [the novel] a standing self-examination'.[4] Nonetheless his public support from the pulpit of St Paul's did little to stem the tide of indignation from more conservative readers and the *Bookman* was stating a simple fact when it described Gresley as 'one of the most discussed figures in recent fiction'.[5] In a classic confutation of fact with fiction, one reader went so far as to suggest that Cholmondeley must have been jilted by a clergyman in order to display his faults with such evident relish.[6]

Speculation aside, little was known of Cholmondeley's private life outside her own literary circle, but what readers did know was that she was the daughter of a retired rector, which can only have added zest to the controversy. Now living in London, Cholmondeley had been born in the small village of Hodnet, Shropshire, in 1859, the third child and eldest daughter of Rev. Richard Hugh Cholmondeley and his wife Emily. After the birth of their youngest child Hester in 1869 Emily was left partially paralysed, and by the spring of 1876 this and her neurasthenic symptoms left her unable to cope with the housekeeping, a role which by default was delegated to the sixteen-year-old Mary, herself a chronic asthmatic since the age of seven. This domestic responsibility was one that Cholmondeley came increasingly to resent as she grew older, not least because it interfered with her writing as well as curtailing her formal education.

This sense of resentment was no doubt increased by her suspicion, felt for many years to come, that no one in her own county circle took her work particularly seriously. She admitted to George Bentley that she had been forced to contend with the prejudice against her wanting to write at all, and so join the ranks of professional 'scribblers'.[7] As Percy Lubbock later put it:

> Everybody was kind to a young woman, pleased with her and proud of her, no doubt; but other people were there first, they had occupied the ground, and the young woman was welcome to her fancies, but she couldn't expect to upset the world in order to make room for them.[8]

To add to her troubles, although she was always too loyal to blame her father, the expectations of her as the eldest daughter of the Rev. Cholmondeley caused a constant conflict between what she termed 'parish duties' and her own work as an increasingly renowned writer. As a woman who wrote without the excuse of financial necessity, and at a time when women's writing was paradoxically more widely accepted but also under particularly intense scrutiny, Cholmondeley inevitably reveals both bitterness and anxiety about her status.

Red Pottage is metatextual in ways that none of Cholmondeley's other novels attempt, and in its repeated exploration of reader response it reveals an acute awareness of current literary debates. In an early chapter Hester Gresley's book is attacked in her absence as ephemeral; the absurdity of James Gresley's pronouncements tend to occlude the sense in which his hostility may be representative of a provincial but important reading public. While the narrator deftly guides the reader to admire Hester's achievement, Gresley's literalism, as he alters metaphors and reverses paradoxes in the manuscript, is suggestive of contemporary attacks on the New Woman's stylistic experiments. As Galia Ofek argues, late Victorian women writers were engaged in a highly conscious attempt to renegotiate the literary canon, as 'advocacy of an elite circle of literary critics who would banish New Woman or other novels became increasingly complicated and problematic as the century drew to an end'.[9]

The question of who has the authority publicly to pronounce on new works of literature permeates *Red Pottage*. But equally the novel is concerned with the private experience of the writer, whose opportunities are circumscribed at the most practical level by her own family circle. Hester, whose work is celebrated in London and virtually unknown in the country, captures the woman writer's sense of mingled self-doubt and frustration in her response to Rachel's questions about her work, 'If you call it working. I used to call it so once, but I never do now'. When a horrified Rachel demands, 'surely you told the Gresleys when first you came that you must not be interrupted at certain hours?' she can only answer, 'I did. I did. But of course – it is very natural – they think that rather self-important and silly' (below, p. 54). In this conversation Hester can be seen carefully internalizing the language of the household in which she has come to live. However in her climactic assault on Regie towards the end of the novel, she also stands as a warning to the upholders of the repressive patriarchal regime represented by James Gresley.

Cholmondeley was in fact luckier than her fictional writer in having the support of both mother and sisters, who could be relied on to give honest criticism of her manuscript drafts, which she seems to have begun showing them from 1877[10] (strikingly there are no extant references to her having shown her early work to her brothers, although she did seek advice from a male cousin at various points). Several of her novels would be dedicated to her sisters, in testament to this crucially supportive relationship.

She would also benefit from periodic visits to her maternal grandmother, Mrs Legard, who was able to introduce her to distinguished literary and artistic circles in the 1880s. Cholmondeley, who had suffered from acute shyness as a girl, quickly learned the importance of 'networking' at every opportunity. Having published a number of short stories, including the still disturbing 'Geoffrey's Wife' in the *Graphic* in 1885, she began her career as a novelist under the guidance of Anne Thackeray Ritchie and her husband in London. On their advice she sought an introduction to George Bentley, through a family friend and fellow author, Rhoda Broughton. Bentley was suitably impressed and *The Danvers Jewels* was published by the firm in 1887 following serialization in *Temple Bar*, as were *Sir Charles Danvers* (1889) and *Diana Tempest* (1893). It was during the writing of this, her most accomplished work to date, that Cholmondeley's twenty-two-year-old sister Hester, who had also planned to make her name as a writer, died of congestion of the lungs. Their mother was to die only three years later in 1895, followed by her publisher and mentor George Bentley in the same year.

These catastrophic events made no discernible mark on Cholmondeley's fourth novel. *A Devotee: An Episode in the Life of a Butterfly* was duly serialized in *Temple Bar* in 1896, and published in one volume by Edward Arnold the following year, in what may well have been a knee-jerk reaction to the sale of the Bentley firm to Macmillan.[11] This little-known work is important chiefly for its introduction of Sybell and Doll Loftus, and James Gresley, who Cholmondeley soon realized was too good to throw away in the bit part he is given in *A Devotee*. But in *Red Pottage* (originally titled *Tomorrow We Die*), begun in 1896 and published by Arnold in 1899, Cholmondeley notably gives her writer heroine the name of Hester, and despite the constant hints that hers will not be a long life, intervenes in the final pages to save her from what seems an inevitable decline. Of course Hester, despite the name and some recognizably biographical characterization (*Under One Roof*, published in 1918, makes this more than clear), is not simply a revivification of a beloved sister. Cholmondeley admitted to Broughton that she had accorded to the fictional author many of her own ideas about writing,[12] as would surely have been obvious to any old friend from the sheer determination Hester displays to finish her book at whatever cost to her health.

The novel is autobiographical in other ways too. Internal evidence, such as the view of Welsh hills from Beaumere, suggest that for Middleshire we can safely read Shropshire. Gresley's insistence on hanging up a card reading 'How dreadful is this place. This is none other than the house of God' is carefully referenced with the information that Cholmondeley spotted the text in a real country churchyard in 1898 (below, p. 46). What she does not say is that she only left London in this year to pay a series of visits to old friends in her home county. One would give much to be able to identify the church in question.

Red Pottage, with its merciless scrutiny of country life, was in fact the first of Cholmondeley's novels to be written after her long dreamed of move to London with her father and sisters Diana and Victoria on the former's retirement in 1896. In this sense her experience exactly reverses that of Hester, who finds sympathy and acclamation in the capital only to be plunged into obscurity in the parochial world of Warpington, where her brother attempts to hide the fact that she has written a novel at all, 'for we all keep our domestic skeletons in their cupboards' (below, p. 172). In an extraordinary comment on this situation that nonetheless echoes Cholmondeley's expressed conviction about her own imaginative process, the Bishop declares that Hester actually benefits from opposition, as it stimulates her own resolve, and presumably prevents her from becoming complacent.

Cholmondeley's own novel was written over a period of roughly three years, for much of which time she was, like the fictional Hester, seriously ill (it is no coincidence that during this period she began to suffer increasing dependence on the drug morphia, prescribed for her during her more severe attacks of asthma). In an uncanny re-enactment of Hester Gresley's breakdown at the end of the novel, Cholmondeley literally collapsed on sending the manuscript to her publisher, and was forced to correct proofs in the intervals of lucidity left to her by asthma and morphia. Not surprisingly the first edition of the novel contains a number of errors (an early reviewer observed that she was 'a correct writer – though she does stagger us in the very first line of her book by giving Sterne's starling to Swift'),[13] most of which were corrected for the second edition as soon as she was well enough to attend to them.

Despite her growing apprehension as the publication date came closer, the novel sold at an extraordinary rate on both sides of the Atlantic, and to Cholmondeley's consternation she was assumed to be raking in a huge profit from her work.[14] In fact her contract made no provision for US rights, and although the novel was still in print with Harper Brothers in 1913, she herself never saw more than £2,000 from the entire proceeds.[15] As Curtis Brown, who later became her agent, dryly recalled years later, 'Miss Cholmondeley left [Arnold] as soon as she could, and the story got about among the authors'.[16] Over the next year Cholmondeley was obliged to refuse a number of lucrative offers for her next work, on the grounds of ill health. There was even talk of putting *Red Pottage* on the stage, a scheme that ultimately fell through.[17] However, she would never write another novel to equal this one, artistically or in terms of sales.

Throughout 1900 Cholmondeley's work was still being vigorously debated, but the nature of her achievement was at this stage unclear. That such a novel had been written by the spinster daughter of a retired country rector was in itself a talking point, as of course was the treatment of the High Church vicar James Gresley. *Judy*, with little respect for offended religious sensibilities, quickly parodied it as *Red Cabbage*: 'Woppingham was in the middle of an epidemic of suicide, mainly due to the shocking bad sermons of the Reverend Josephus Grizzly', and enjoyed itself hugely with Hester's dilemma, 'She was old enough to be wise and young enough to be beautiful. Her brother, the Vicar, was quite an ordinary person, who thought he could write but was wrong, so there now!'[18]

Cholmondeley was particularly pleased to learn that she was being read by soldiers engaged in the Boer War, among whom Hester was a great favourite. Gratifying too was the reaction of the *Spectator*, which in the world of the novel devotes leading articles to Hester's *Idyll*, and now described Hester herself as 'a most fascinating specimen of the emancipated modern woman',[19] one of the earliest explicit associations of the novel with the controversial New Woman writing of the 1880s and '90s.

If both Rachel and Hester can claim to be identifiable as New Women, the shaping of Cholmondeley's text is not wholly derived from the feminist debates of the last years of the century. Linda Peterson has argued for the novel as a presentation of the female experience in the realist tradition of George Eliot, as it 'concentrates on the intellectual and artistic development of the woman writer, struggling with domestic repression, separating herself from provincial life and mores'.[20] The influence of Eliot is everywhere apparent in the novel, in the boorish pronouncements of James Gresley, who like Eliot's Mr Brooke[21] has already 'threshed out' any subject under discussion, no less than in the chapter epigraphs.

Equally the sensational influence of Wilkie Collins is apparent, not just in the dramatic suicide plot, but in the violation of the female writer's manuscript – as Count Fosco hijacks Marian Halcomb's diary in *The Woman in White* (1860), so the reader is forced to participate in Gresley's unsanctioned reading of his sister's book, and to watch helplessly as he first alters and then destroys it. Hester's furious response to this incident reminds the reader, while it fails to convince Gresley, that the woman writer is entitled to privacy – the control of her text – as much as to publicity.

If the fictional writer is passionate, even aggressive in her protection of her work and the way it will be read, her creator was notably more oblique. Tamara Wagner has recently argued in relation to the earlier novel *Diana Tempest* that Cholmondeley deliberately deploys and interrogates the imperatives of both sensational and realist fiction in her own writing.[22] But whether strategically or otherwise, by placing her New Woman figures, Rachel and Hester, within sensational and realist plots respectively, the narrator places them within an established literary tradition at a time when New Woman writing was under close scrutiny as a threatening and subversive new genre.

As in Netta Syrett's *Nobody's Fault* one of the key relationships in the novel is the romantic friendship between Hester and Rachel, that is significantly capable of withstanding differences of class and situation, even outright opposition from Hester's aunt Lady Susan. While these characters are presented as complementary rather than similar, the narrator subtly indicates their affinity through a series of parallels. Rachel, although not a writer like Hester, transforms economic deprivation into subversive independence when she keeps on her room in Museum Buildings and so asserts her right to 'a room of her own' after her accession to wealth. Notably she is described as '*spending* herself and part of her colossal fortune in the East End' (below, p. 139; emphasis added) just as Hester literally spends herself on her book. Towards the end of the novel each will suffer the loss of what she values most, Hester her unpublished masterpiece and Rachel her lover.

The friendship between these two New Women is variously tested and parodied, most visibly in the posturing of Lady Newhaven with Rachel, to whom she declares:

> I loved you from the first moment I saw you ... I don't take fancies to people, you know. I am not that kind of person. I am very difficult to please, and I never speak of what concerns myself. I am *most* reserved. (below, p. 32)

This pseudo-friendship conceals a growing hostility on Rachel's part which flares up into open competition when Lady Newhaven learns of the relationship between Rachel and Hugh. In another parallel between the New Woman heroines, Hester's dramatic final confrontation with her brother over her right to a public voice foreshadows the intensity of Rachel's condemnation of Hugh and its catastrophic results.

At the end of the novel, Rachel and Hester save each other through acts of love, notably made possible only by the death of the man who would come between them. During Hester's illness, Rachel admits to herself that 'A year ago if Hester had died I should have had nothing left to live for ... Now this newcomer, this man whom I have known barely six months, fills my whole life' (below, p. 224). This admission both acknowledges the limits of female friendship and signs Hugh's death warrant; more importantly yet, it gives Hester a motive to live in tending to her heartbroken friend after Hugh's death by drowning. Cholmondeley had read Ethel Arnold's *Platonics* (1894), in which a friendship between women is destroyed by their mutual love for a man, only to be restored by the death of one of the women and her posthumous assurance that 'looking forward I seem to see the radiance of a coming day'.[23] In her own formulation of this dilemma, a second, less threatening lover will be substituted for the first, but Dick does not make the mistake of becoming jealous of the women's friendship. The importance of this triangular relationship is emphasized in the postscript to the novel, where the female characters appear centre stage as in one of Lady Newhaven's parodic *tableaux*, with Dick as a slightly hazy figure in the background.

Nonetheless the allegiance of Hester and Rachel to the figure of the New Woman is complex and often subtextual, as SueAnn Schatz has pointed out: 'By examining the positioning of this duo against the stereotypical bad New Woman [Miss Barker], Cholmondeley's "double vision" is both conservative and liberal, but ultimately a product of practical idealism'.[24] While protecting her characters from immediate identification with the 'bad New Woman', Cholmondeley nonetheless links them to several identifiable strands of New Woman thought. The Bishop's comment that as Hester grows older she will become 'passive, contemplative' (below, p. 61) is reminiscent of Sarah Grand's ideal feminist, figured as 'sitting apart in silent contemplation'.[25] Again like Grand's heroines Rachel is a social purist. Zsuzsa Berend comments that: 'In much European romanticism love ... was seen as a potentially subversive emotion, with a tendency to disregard the world and a potential for disaster. Themes of love and death were intimately connected.'[26] It is on precisely this discourse of romantic love that Lady Newhaven bases her claim to Hugh; Rachel herself refuses to accept either the discourse or the claim. Having rejected her own would-be seducer Mr Tristram (who officially proposes after her rescue from poverty, and considers her prosaic for failing to fall in with his half-remembered quotations from various love poems), she goes on to deplore the sins of her lover Hugh with Lady Newhaven:

> I had to choke down my jealousy when he kissed me. He had kissed her first. He had made that side of his love common and profane; but the other side remained. I clung to that ... that supported me and enabled me to forgive him, though men don't know what that forgiveness costs us. Only the walls of our rooms know that. (below, p. 230)

Hester shares Rachel's abhorrence of sexual immorality; in an echo of Sarah Grand's defence of *The Heavenly Twins* (1893) she angrily answers her brother's accusation of deliberate prurience in her writing, 'that if she introduced improprieties into her book in order to make money, in her opinion she deserved to be whipped in the public streets' (below, p. 170).

This focus on sexual immorality and the appropriate female response to it creates a further, and perhaps surprising parallel, between Hugh and Hester (whose liking for her friend's lover is in this instance at odds with the narrator's rising contempt). Each is denounced for a supposed failure of integrity, although Gresley's ironic approval of Hugh as a moral character underscores the falsity of his own judgement, as he insists that the pure-minded Hester has written a 'profane, immoral book' (below, p. 170).

Despite their differences, Hugh will become, in the words of Rainwater and Scheck, 'a good reader like Hester and Rachel, and not a bad reader like James'.[27] His early appreciation of Hester's *Idyll* can be seen in these terms as a 'readable' symbol of his transformative potential, a potential that is acknowledged by Hester even as she expresses reservations about him as a suitable husband for her friend. Throughout the novel these characters are repeatedly linked through the image of fire as either punitive or purifying – in the early chapters Hester's unrealized writing vocation is 'an unlit fire in her soul' (below, p. 24); Gresley's later anger towards her is described as 'the rage that in bygone days found expression in stake and faggot' (below, p. 106), while the fire lit in her bedroom at Warpington on her return from the Palace is an ironically loving gesture given that her manuscript is at that moment smouldering on a bonfire. Hugh meanwhile wavers like 'the flame of a candle' (below, p. 235) in his confrontation with Lord Newhaven; he is later enveloped in his own weaker nature as in 'a shirt of fire' (below, p. 152), is 'consumed by the smouldering flame of his self-contempt' (below, p. 160) having failed to honour the suicide pact, but is finally redeemed when he tells the truth to Rachel as 'a sudden passion of anger shot up and enveloped him as in one flame from head to foot' (below, p. 204). Just as Rachel's friendship for Hester is the catalyst for the latter's first attempt at writing, so her love for Hugh is transformative and redemptive for him.

In line with orthodox Victorian religion, the Bishop will subsequently berate Rachel for her failure to save Hugh at the moment of his final confession, 'God will require his soul at your hands. Scarlett gave it into your keeping, and you took it. You had no business to take it if you meant to throw it away' (below, p. 232). Zsuzsa Berend has argued that religious belief not only governs choice, but 'provides an idiom in which choices are conceived, framed and pondered'.[28] In relocating responsibility for Hugh's salvation onto Rachel herself, the Bishop ironically divests him of the moral autonomy that justifies his being forgiven; nonetheless it is Rachel whose religious status is jeopardized according to the ideal of womanhood she herself endorses. Her adherence to such a moral framework ensures that the Bishop's arguments will ultimately prevail, signalling Rachel's own attainment of sanctity; but having once forgiven Hugh his supposed cowardice and his more serious crime of dishonesty, she can be permitted to marry the more suitable Dick, who is himself related to Hester. If the climax of the novel sees her preparing to embrace the traditional role of angelic saviour, she is saved by a watchful narrator to find ultimate fulfilment as a New Woman. In what may or may not be a reworking of the last lines of Arnold's *Platonics*, Cholmondeley ends her novel with a vision of her female friends escaping death and walking together 'in the growing light towards the Perfect Day' (below, p. 243).

Notes

1. P. Lubbock, *Mary Cholmondeley: A Sketch from Memory* (Jonathan Cape: London, 1928), p. 24.
2. Galia Ofek points out that Cholmondeley's titles references a line in Allen's novel. See '"Reviewing the Rites Proper to Canonisation": New Woman Novels and New Conceptualizations of Canonicity', *Victorian Literature and Culture*, 38 (2010), pp. 165–86, on p. 168.

3. E. H. Williams, 'The Reader: Mary Cholmondeley', *Bookman*, 18 (May 1900) pp. 40–7, on p. 41.
4. Sermon preached in St Paul's Cathedral, cited in ibid., p. 45.
5. Williams, 'The Reader', p. 44.
6. *Guardian*, 11 April 1900, p. 528.
7. Letter of Mary Cholmondeley to George Bentley, 24 July 1894, Bentley Archive, Mic.B.53/177 L46, British Library.
8. Lubbock, *Mary Cholmondeley*, pp. 51–2.
9. Ofek, '"Reviewing the Rites Proper to Canonisation"', p. 172.
10. M. Cholmondeley, MS diary, 16 May 1877, private archive.
11. Cholmondeley's relations with Bentley had been close and her choice of Edward Arnold seems particularly odd given that he published a relatively small amount of fiction.
12. Letter of Mary Cholmondeley to Rhoda Broughton, 30 October 1899, Box M, Delves Broughton Collection, DDB/M/C/2/1, Cheshire Records Office.
13. 'Fiction', *Literature*, 5 (1899), p. 495. This mistake was rectified in the second edition and is silently corrected here.
14. Williams, 'The Reader', pp. 45–6.
15. The final figure taken from Cholmondeley's personal record book, private archive.
16. C. Brown, 'Bargaining with Writers: Random Notes of an Authors' Agent', *Harper's Magazine*, 171 (June–November 1935), pp. 26–35, on p. 27.
17. For the history of Cholmondeley's stage adaptations, see C. W. de la L. Oulton, *Let the Flowers Go: A Life of Mary Cholmondeley* (London: Pickering & Chatto, 2009), pp. 118–19, 123, 148–9.
18. 'Red Cabbage', *Judy* (17 January 1900), p. 27.
19. *Spectator* (8 October 1899), pp. 612–13.
20. L. Peterson, *Traditions of Victorian Women's Autobiography: The Poetics and Politics of Life Writing* (Charlottesville, VA: University Press of Virginia, 1999), p. 174.
21. The uncle of the heroine Dorothea in *Middlemarch* (1870).
22. See T. Wagner, '"Social Suicide – Yes": Sensational Legacies in *Diana Tempest*', in C. W. de la L. Oulton and S. Schatz (eds), *Mary Cholmondeley Reconsidered* (London: Pickering & Chatto, 2009), pp. 11–23.
23. E. Arnold, *Platonics* (Bristol: Thoemmes Press, 1995), p. 128.
24. S. Schatz, 'How to be Feminist without Saying So: The New Woman and the New Man in *Red Pottage*', in Oulton and Schatz (eds), *Mary Cholmondeley Reconsidered*, pp. 25–36, on pp. 27–8.
25. S. Grand, 'The New Aspect of the Woman Question', in C. Nelson (ed.), *A New Woman Reader* (Hertfordshire: Broadview 2001), pp. 141–6, on p. 142. The article first appeared in *North American Review*, 158 (March 1894), pp. 270–6.
26. Z. Berend, '"The Best or None!": Spinsterhood in Nineteenth-Century New England', *Journal of Social History*, 33:4 (Summer 2000), pp. 935–57, on p. 937.
27. C. Rainwater and W. J. Scheick, 'Aliens in the Garden: The Re-Vision of Mary Cholmondeley's *Red Pottage*', *Philological Quarterly*, 71:1 (1992), pp. 101–19, on p. 112.
28. Berend, '"The Best or None!"', p. 947.

BIBLIOGRAPHY

Anon., 'Fiction', *Literature*, 5 (1899), p. 495.

—, 'Red Cabbage', *Judy* (17 January 1900), p. 27.

Arnold, E., *Platonics* (Bristol: Thoemmes Press, 1995).

Berend, Z., '"The Best or None!": Spinsterhood in Nineteenth-Century New England', *Journal of Social History*, 33:4 (Summer 2000), pp. 935–57.

Brown, C., 'Bargaining with Writers: Random Notes of an Authors' Agent', *Harper's Magazine*, 171 (June–November 1935), pp. 26–35.

Cholmondeley, M., *Under One Roof: A Family Memoir* (London: J. Murray, 1918).

Grand, S., 'The New Aspect of the Woman Question', in C. Nelson (ed.), *A New Woman Reader* (Hertfordshire: Broadview 2001), pp. 141–6.

Lubbock, P., *Mary Cholmondeley: A Sketch from Memory* (Jonathan Cape: London, 1928).

Ofek, G., '"Reviewing the Rites Proper to Canonisation": New Woman Novels and New Conceptualizations of Canonicity', *Victorian Literature and Culture*, 38 (2010), pp. 165–86.

Oulton, C. W. de la L., *Let the Flowers Go: A Life of Mary Cholmondeley* (London: Pickering & Chatto, 2009).

Oulton, C. W. de la L., and S. Schatz (eds), *Mary Cholmondeley Reconsidered* (London: Pickering & Chatto, 2009).

Peterson, L., *Traditions of Victorian Women's Autobiography: The Poetics and Politics of Life Writing* (Charlottesville, VA: University Press of Virginia, 1999).

Rainwater, C., and W. J. Scheick, 'Aliens in the Garden: The Re-Vision of Mary Cholmondeley's *Red Pottage*', *Philological Quarterly*, 71:1 (1992), pp. 101–19.

Schatz, S., 'How to be Feminist without Saying So: The New Woman and the New Man in *Red Pottage*', in Oulton and Schatz (eds), *Mary Cholmondeley Reconsidered*, pp. 25–36.

Wagner, T., '"Social Suicide – Yes": Sensational Legacies in *Diana Tempest*', in Oulton and Schatz (eds), *Mary Cholmondeley Reconsidered*, pp. 11–23.

Williams, E. H., 'The Reader: Mary Cholmondeley', *Bookman*, 18 (May 1900) pp. 40–7.

Willis, C., '"Heaven Defend me from Political or Highly Educated Women!": Packaging the New Woman for Mass Consumption', in A. Richardson and C. Willis (eds), *The New Woman in Fiction and in Fact: Fin de Siècle Feminisms* (Basingstoke: Palgrave Macmillan, 2002), pp. 53–65.

CHRONOLOGY OF EVENTS IN
MARY CHOLMONDELEY'S LIFE

Year	Events
1859	8 June: Mary Cholmondeley born to Richard Hugh and Emily Cholmondeley, probably at Hodnet Rectory, Hodnet, Shropshire.
c. 1861	The family move to Farnborough, Warwickshire.
1861	Essex Cholmondeley born.
1862	Richard Cholmondeley born.
1863	Diana Cholmondeley born.
1865	The family move to Leaton, Shropshire.
1869	Hester Cholmondeley born.
1870	Victoria Cholmondeley born.
1874	Family moves to Hodnet Rectory on Richard Hugh Cholmondeley's appointment as rector.
1877	December: Cholmondeley takes over running the house due to her mother's illness.
1885	Cholmondeley's first stories appear in the *Graphic*.
1886	Essex Cholmondeley marries Ralph Benson (they will be the parents of Stella Benson, the modernist writer).
1887	January–March: *The Danvers Jewels* serialized in *Temple Bar*. *The Danvers Jewels* published by Bentley & Son.
1889	May–December: *Sir Charles Danvers* serialized in *Temple Bar*. *Sir Charles Danvers* published by Bentley & Son.
1892	Hester Cholmondeley dies from congestion of the lungs.
1893	January–December: *Diana Tempest* serialized in *Temple Bar*. *Diana Tempest* published by Bentley & Son.
1895	Emily Cholmondeley dies
1896	August–October: *A Devotee: An Episode in the Life of a Butterfly* serialized in *Temple Bar*. Richard Hugh Cholmondeley retires and moves to Albert Gate Mansions, 219 Knightsbridge, London with Mary, Diana and Victoria.
1897	*A Devotee: An Episode in the Life of a Butterfly* published by Edward Arnold.
1899	*Red Pottage* published by Edward Arnold.
1902	*Moth and Rust* published by John Murray.
1905–6	November 1905–October 1906: *Prisoners (Fast Bound in Misery and Iron)* serialized in *Lady's Realm*.

Year	Events
1906	*Prisoners (Fast Bound in Misery and Iron)* published by Hutchinson. Ralph Benson leaves Essex and their children.
1907	Cholmondeley leases and starts to renovate a house in Ufford, Suffolk.
1913	*Notwithstanding* published by John Murray.
1908	*The Lowest Rung* (collection of short stories) published by John Murray.
1910	Richard Hugh Cholmondeley dies; Cholmondeley moves to 2 Leonard Place with Victoria.
1917–19	Cholmondeley works for Lady Ridley's hospital at 10 Carlton House Terrace (now the British Academy).
1918	*Under One Roof: A Family Record* published by John Murray.
1919	Cholmondeley moves to 4 Argyll Road, Kensington with Victoria.
1921	*The Romance of His Life and Other Romances* (collection of short stories) published by John Murray.
1925	15 July: Cholmondeley dies in London following a series of illnesses.

RED POTTAGE

By

Mary Cholmondeley

Author of 'Diana Tempest'[a]

"After the Red Pottage comes the exceeding bitter cry"[1]

TO
VICTORIA
Good things have not kept aloof,
* * * * *

I have not lack'd thy mild reproof,
Nor golden largesse of thy praise.[2]

RED POTTAGE

CHAPTER I

In tragic life, God wot,
No villain need be! Passions spin the plot:
We are betray'd by what is false within.

GEORGE MEREDITH.[3]

'I CAN'T get out,' said Sterne's starling,[a] looking through the bars of his cage.[4]

'I will get out,' said Hugh Scarlett to himself, seeing no bars, but half conscious of a cage. 'I will get out,' he repeated, as his hansom[5] took him swiftly from the house in Portman Square, where he had been dining, towards that other house in Carlton House Terrace, whither his thoughts had travelled on before him, outdistancing the Trip-Clip-Clop, Trip-Clip-Clop of the horse.

It was a hot night in June. Hugh had thrown back his overcoat, and the throng of passers-by in the street could see, if they cared to see, 'the glass of fashion'[6] in the shape of white waistcoat and shirt front, surmounted by the handsome, irritated face of their owner, leaning back with his hat tilted over his eyes.

Trip-Clip-Clop went the horse.

A great deal of thinking may be compressed into a quarter of an hour, especially if it has been long eluded.

'I will get out,' he said again to himself with an impatient movement. It was beginning to weary him, this commonplace intrigue which had been so new and alluring a year ago. He did not own it to himself, but he was tired of it. Perhaps the reason why good resolutions have earned for themselves such an evil repute as paving stones is because they are often the result, not of repentance, but of the restlessness that dogs an evaporating pleasure. This *liaison*[7] had been alternately his pride and his shame for many months. But now it was becoming something more, which it had been all the time, only he had not noticed it till lately – a fetter, a clog, something irksome, to be cast off and pushed out of sight. Decidedly the moment for the good resolution had arrived.

'I will break it off,' he said again. 'Thank heaven not a soul has ever guessed it.'

How could any one have guessed it?

He remembered the day when he had first met her a year ago, and had looked upon her as merely a pretty woman. He remembered other days, and the gradual building up between them of a fairy palace. He had added a stone here, she a stone there, until suddenly it became – a prison. Had he been tempter or tempted? He did not know. He did not care. He wanted only to be out of it. His better feelings and his conscience had been awakened by the first touch of weariness. His brief infatuation had run its course. His judgment had been whirled – he told himself it had been whirled, but it had really only been tweaked – from its centre, had performed its giddy orbit, and now the check-string had brought it back to the point from whence it had set out, namely, that she was merely a pretty woman.

'I will break with her gradually,' he said, like the tyro he was, and he pictured to himself the wretched scenes in which she would abuse him, reproach him, probably compromise herself, the letters she would write to him. At any rate he need not read them. Oh! how tired he was of the whole thing beforehand. Why had he been such a fool? He looked at the termination of the *liaison* as a bad sailor looks at an inevitable sea passage at the end of a journey. It must be gone through, but the prospect of undergoing it filled him with disgust.

A brougham[8] passed him swiftly on noiseless wheels, and the woman in it caught a glimpse of the high-bred clean-shaved face, half savage, half sullen in the hansom.

'Anger, impatience and remorse,' she said to herself, and finished buttoning her gloves.

'Thank heaven not a soul has ever guessed it,' repeated Hugh fervently, as the hansom came suddenly to a standstill.

In another moment he was taking Lady Newhaven's hand as she stood at the entrance of her amber drawing-room beside a grove of pink orchids.

He chatted a moment, greeted Lord Newhaven, and passed on into the crowded rooms. How could any one have guessed it? No breath of scandal had ever touched Lady Newhaven. She stood beside her pink orchids, near her fatigued-looking, gentle-mannered husband, a very pretty woman in white satin and diamonds. Perhaps her blonde hair was a shade darker at the roots than in its waved coils; perhaps her blue eyes did not look quite in harmony with their blue-black lashes; but the whole effect had the delicate conventional perfection of a cleverly touched-up chromo-lithograph.[9] Of course tastes differ. Some people like chromo-lithographs, others don't. But even those who do are apt to become estranged. They may inspire love, admiration, but never fidelity. Most of us have in our time hammered nails into our walls, which, though they now decorously support the engravings and etchings of our maturer years, were nevertheless originally driven in to uphold the cherished, the long since discarded chromos of our foolish youth.

The diamond sun upon Lady Newhaven's breast quivered a little, a very little, as Hugh greeted her, and she turned to offer the same small smile and gloved hand to the next comer, whose name was leaping before him from one footman to another.

'Mr. Richard Vernon.'

Lady Newhaven's wide blue eyes looked vague. Her hand hesitated. This strongly built, ill-dressed man, with his keen brown deeply scarred face and crooked mouth, was unknown to her.

Lord Newhaven darted forward.

'Dick!' he exclaimed, and Dick shot forth an immense mahogany hand, and shook Lord Newhaven's warmly.

'Well,' he said, after Lord Newhaven had introduced him to his wife, 'I'm dashed if I knew who either of you were. But I found your invitation at my club when I landed yesterday, so I decided to come and have a look at you. And so it is only you, Cackles, after all' – (Lord Newhaven's habit of silence had earned for him the *sobriquet*[10] of 'Cackles') – 'I quite thought I was going into – well, ahem! – into society. I did not know you had got a handle to your name. How did you find out I was in England?'

'My dear fellow, I didn't,' said Lord Newhaven, gently drawing Dick aside, whose back was serenely blocking a stream of new arrivals. 'I fancy – in fact, I'm simply delighted to see you. How is the wine getting on? But I suppose there must be other Dick Vernons on my wife's list. Have you the card with you?'

'Rather,' said Dick, 'always take the card with me since I was kicked out of a miner's hop at Broken Hill because I forgot it. 'No gentleman will be admitted in a paper shirt' was mentioned on it, I remember. A concertina and candles in bottles. Ripping while it lasted. I wish you had been there.'

'I wish I had.' Lord Newhaven's tired, half-closed eye opened a little. 'But the end seems to have been unfortunate.'

'Not at all,' said Dick, watching the new arrivals with his head thrown back. 'Fine girl that; I'll take a look at the whole mob of them directly. They came round next day to say it had been a mistake, but there were four or five cripples who found that out the night before. Here is the card.'

Lord Newhaven glanced at it attentively, and then laughed.

'It is four years old,' he said; 'I must have put you on my mother's list, not knowing you had left London. It is in her writing.'

'I'm rather late,' said Dick composedly, 'but I am here at last. Now, Cack – Newhaven, if that's your noble name – as I am here, trot out a few heiresses, would you? I want to take one or two back with me. I say, ought I to put my gloves on?'[11]

'No, no. Clutch them in your great fist as you are doing now.'

'Thanks. I suppose, old chap, I'm all right? Not had on an evening-coat for four years.'

Dick's trousers were too short for him, and he had tied his white tie with a waist to it. Lord Newhaven had seen both details before he recognised him.

'Quite right,' he said hastily. 'Now, who is to be the happy woman?'

Dick's hawk-eye promenaded over the crowd in the second room, in the doorway of which he was standing.

'That one,' he said, 'the tall girl in the green gown talking to the Bishop.'

'You have a wonderful eye for heiresses. You have picked out the greatest in London. That is Miss Rachel West. You say you want two.'

'One at a time, thanks. I shall take her down to supper. I suppose – er – there *is* supper at this sort of thing, isn't there?'

'Of a kind. You need not be afraid of the claret; it isn't yours.'

'Catch you giving your best at a crush,' retorted Dick. 'The Bishop's moving. Hurry up.'

CHAPTER II

But as he groped against the wall, two hands upon him fell,
The King behind his shoulder spake: 'Dead man, thou dost not well.'
RUDYARD KIPLING.[12]

HUGH had gone through the first room, and, after a quarter of an hour, found himself in the doorway of the second. He had arrived late, and the rooms were already thinning.

A woman in a pale green gown was standing near the open window, her white profile outlined against the framed darkness, as she listened with evident amusement to the tall, ill-dressed man beside her.

Hugh's eyes lost the veiled scorn with which it was their wont to look at society and the indulgent patronage which lurked in them for pretty women.

Rachel West slowly turned her face towards him without seeing him, and his heart leaped. She was not beautiful except with the beauty of health, and a certain dignity of carriage which is the outcome of a head and hands and body that are at unity with each other, and with a mind absolutely unconscious of self. She had not the long nose which so frequently usurps more than its share of the faces of the well bred, nor had she, alas! the short upper lip which redeems everything. Her features were as insignificant as her colouring. People rarely noticed that Rachel's hair was brown, and that her deep-set eyes were grey. But upon her grave face the word 'Helper' was plainly written: and something else. What was it?

Just as in the faces of seamen we trace the onslaught of storm and sun and brine, and the puckering of the skin round the eyes that comes of long watching in half lights, so in some faces, calm and pure as Rachel's, on which the sun and rain have never beaten, there is an expression betokening strong resistance from within of the brunt of a whirlwind from without. The marks of conflict and endurance on a young face – who shall see them unmoved! The Mother of Jesus must have noticed a great difference in her Son when she first saw Him again after the temptation in the wilderness.[13]

Rachel's grave amused glance fell upon Hugh. Their eyes met, and he instantly perceived to his astonishment that she recognised him. But she did not bow, and a moment later left the nearly empty rooms with the man who was talking to her.

Hugh was excited out of recognition of his former half-scornful, half-*blasé*[14] self. That woman must be his wife. She would save him from himself, this cynical restless self which never remained in one stay. The half acknowledged weakness in his nature unconsciously flung itself upon her strength, a strength which had been tried. She would love him, and uphold him. There would be no more yielding to circumstances if that pure strong soul were close beside him. He would lean upon her, and the ugly bypaths of these last years would know him no more. Her presence would leaven his whole life. In the momentary insanity, which was perhaps after all only a prophetic intuition, he had no fears, no misgivings. He thought that with that face it was not possible that she could be so wicked as to refuse him.

'She will marry me,' he said to himself. 'She must.'

Lady Newhaven touched him gently on the arm.

'I dared not speak to you before,' she said, 'Nearly every one has gone. Will you take me down to supper? I am tired out.'

He stared at her, not recognising her.

'Have I vexed you?' she faltered.

And with a sudden horrible revulsion of feeling he remembered. The poor chromo had fallen violently from its nail. But the nail remained – ready. He took her into the supper room and got her a glass of champagne. She subsided on to a sofa beside another woman, vaguely suspecting trouble in the air. He felt thankful that Rachel had already gone. Dick, nearly the last, was putting on his coat, arranging to meet Lord Newhaven the following morning at his club. They had been in Australia together, and were evidently old friends.

Lord Newhaven's listless manner returned as Dick marched out. Hugh had got one arm in his coat. An instinct of flight possessed him, a vague horror of the woman in diamonds furtively watching him under her lowered eyelids through the open door.

'Oh, Scarlett!' said Lord Newhaven, detaining him languidly, 'I want three minutes of your valuable time. Come into my study.'

'Another crossbow for Westhope Abbey?' said Hugh, trying to speak unconcernedly, as he followed his host to a back room on the ground floor. Lord Newhaven was collecting arms for the hall of his country house.

'No! much simpler than those elaborate machines,' said the older man, turning on the electric light. Hugh went in, and Lord Newhaven closed the door.

Over the mantel-shelf were hung a few old Japanese inlaid carbines,[15] and beneath them an array of pistols.

'Useless now,' said Lord Newhaven, touching them affectionately. 'But,' he added, with a shade more listlessness than before, 'Society has become accustomed to do without them, and does ill without them, but we must conform to her.' Hugh started slightly, and then remained motionless. 'You observe these two paper lighters, Scarlett? One is an inch shorter than the other. They have been waiting on the mantel-shelf for the last month, till I had an opportunity of drawing your attention to them. I am sure we perfectly understand each other. No name need be mentioned. All scandal is avoided. I feel confident you will not hesitate to make me the only reparation one man can make another in the somewhat hackneyed circumstances in which we find ourselves.'

Lord Newhaven took the lighters out of the glass. He glanced suddenly at Hugh's stunned face, and went on:

'I am sorry the idea is not my own. I read it in a magazine. Though comparatively modern it promises soon to become as customary as the much to be regretted pistols for two and coffee for four.[16] I hold the lighters thus, and you draw. Whoever draws or keeps the short one is pledged to leave this world within four months, or shall we say five, on account of the pheasant shooting?[17] Five be it. Is it agreed? Just so! Will you draw?'

A swift spasm passed over Hugh's face, and a tiger glint leapt into Lord Newhaven's eyes, fixed intently upon him.

There was a brief second in which Hugh's mind wavered, as the flame of a candle wavers in a sudden draught. Lord Newhaven's eyes glittered. He advanced the lighters an inch nearer.

If he had not advanced them that inch Hugh thought afterwards that he would have refused to draw.

He backed against the mantel-piece, and then put out his hand suddenly and drew. It seemed the only way of escape.

The two men measured the lighters on the table under the electric light.

Lord Newhaven laughed.

Hugh stood a moment, and then went out.

CHAPTER III

Is it well with thee? Is it well with thy husband?

WHEN Lady Newhaven slipped out of the supper-room after her husband and Hugh, and lingered at the door of the study, she did not follow them with the deliberate intention of eavesdropping, but from a vague impulse of suspicious anxiety. Yet she crouched in her white satin gown against the door listening intently.

Neither man moved within. Only one spoke. There was no other sound to deaden her husband's distinct low voice. The silence that followed his last word 'Will you draw?' was broken by his laugh, and she had barely time to throw herself back from the door into a dark recess under the staircase before Hugh came out. He almost touched her as he passed. He must have seen her if he had been capable of seeing anything, but he went straight on unheeding. And as she stole a few steps to gaze after him, she saw him cross the hall and go out into the night without his hat and coat, the amazed servants staring after him.

She drew back to go upstairs, and met her husband coming slowly out of the study. He looked steadily at her, as she clung trembling to the banisters. There was no alteration in his glance, and she suddenly perceived that what he knew now he had always known. She put her hand to her head.

'You look tired,' he said, in the level voice to which she was accustomed. 'You had better go to bed.'

She stumbled swiftly upstairs, catching at the banisters, and went into her own room.

Her maid was waiting for her by the dressing-table with its shaded electric lights. And she remembered that she had given a party, and that she had on her diamonds.

It would take a long time to unfasten them. She pulled at the diamond sun on her breast with a shaking hand. Her husband had given it to her when her eldest son was born. Her maid took the tiara gently out of her hair, and cut the threads that sewed the diamonds on her breast and shoulders. Would it never end? The lace of her gown cautiously withdrawn through its hundred eyelet-holes knotted itself.

'Cut it,' she said impatiently. 'Cut it.'

At last she was in her dressing-gown and alone. She flung herself face downwards on the sofa. Her attitude had the touch of artificiality which was natural to her.

The deluge had arrived, and unconsciously she met it as she would have made a heroine meet it had she been a novelist, in a white dressing-gown and pink ribbons in a stereotyped attitude of despair on a divan.

Conscience is supposed to make cowards of us all, but it is a matter of common experience that the unimaginative are made cowards of only by being found out.

Had David qualms of conscience when Uriah fell before the besieged city? Surely if he had he would have winced at the obvious parallel of the prophet's story about the ewe lamb.[18] But apparently he remained serenely obtuse till the indignant author's 'Thou art the man'[19] unexpectedly nailed him to the cross of his sin.

And so it was with Lady Newhaven. She had gone through the twenty-seven years of her life believing herself to be a religious and virtuous person. She was so accustomed to the idea that it had become a habit, and now the whole of her self-respect was in one wrench torn from her. The events of the last year had not worn it down to its last shred, had not even worn the nap off. It was dragged from her intact, and the shock left her faint and shuddering.

The thought that her husband knew, and had thought fit to conceal his knowledge, had never entered her mind, any more than the probability that she had been seen by some of the servants kneeling listening at a keyhole. The mistake which all unobservant people make is to assume that others are as unobservant as themselves.

By what frightful accident, she asked herself, had this catastrophe come about. She thought of all the obvious incidents which would have revealed the secret to herself; the dropped letter, the altered countenance, the badly arranged lie. No. She was convinced her secret had been guarded with minute, with scrupulous care. The only thing she had forgotten in her calculations was her husband's character, if, indeed, she could be said to have forgotten that which she had never known.

Lord Newhaven was in his wife's eyes a very quiet man of few words. That his few words did not represent the whole of him had never occurred to her. She had often told her friends that he walked through life with his eyes shut. He had a trick of half shutting his eyes which confirmed her in this opinion. When she came across persons who were, after a time, discovered to have affections and interests of which they had not spoken she described them as 'cunning.' She had never thought Edward 'cunning' till to-night. How had he of all men discovered this – this. – She had no words ready to call her conduct by, though words would not have failed her had she been denouncing the same conduct in another wife and mother.

Gradually 'the whole horror of her situation,' to borrow from her own vocabulary, forced itself upon her mind like damp through a gay wall-paper. What did it matter how the discovery had been made! It was made, and she was ruined. She repeated the words between little gasps for breath. Ruined! Her reputation lost! Hers – Violet Newhaven's. It was a sheer impossibility that such a thing could have happened to a woman like her. It was some vile slander which Edward must see to. He was good at that sort of thing. But no, Edward would not help her. She had committed -. She flung out her hands panic-stricken, as if to ward off a blow. The deed had brought with it no shame, but the word – the word wounded her like a sword.

Her feeble mind, momentarily stunned, pursued its groping way.

He would divorce her. It would be in the papers. But no. What was that he had said to Hugh – 'No names to be mentioned; all scandal avoided.'

She shivered and drew in her breath. It was to be settled some other way. Her mind became an entire blank. Another way! What way? She remembered now, and an inarticulate cry broke from her. They had drawn lots.

Which had drawn the short lighter?

Her husband had laughed. But then he laughed at everything. He was never really serious, always shallow and heartless. He would have laughed if he had drawn it himself. Perhaps he had. Yes, he certainly had drawn it. But Hugh? She saw again the white set face as he passed her. No, it must be Hugh who had drawn it – Hugh whom she loved. She wrung her hands and moaned, half-aloud:

'Which? Which?'

There was a slight movement in the next room, the door was opened, and Lord Newhaven appeared in the doorway. He was still in evening dress.

'Did you call?' he said quietly. 'Are you ill?' He came and stood beside her.

'No,' she said hoarsely, and she sat up and gazed fixedly at him. Despair and suspense were in her eyes. There was no change in his, and she remembered that she had never seen him angry. Perhaps she had not known when he was angry.

He was turning away, but she stopped him.

'Wait,' she said, and he returned, his cold attentive eye upon her. There was no contempt, no indignation in his bearing. If those feelings had shaken him it must have been some time ago. If they had been met and vanquished in secret that also must have been some time ago. He took up an 'Imitation of Christ,'[20] bound in the peculiar shade of lilac which at that moment prevailed, and turned it in his hand.

'You are overwrought,' he said, after a moment's pause, 'and I particularly dislike a scene.'

She did not heed him.

'I listened at the door,' she said in a harsh, unnatural voice.

'I am perfectly aware of it.'

A sort of horror seemed to have enveloped the familiar room. The very furniture looked like well-known words arranged suddenly in some new and dreadful meaning.

'You never loved me,' she said.

He did not answer, but he looked gravely at her for a moment, and she was ashamed.

'Why don't you divorce me if you think me so wicked?'

'For the sake of the children,' he said, with a slight change of voice.

Teddy, the eldest, had been born in this room. Did either remember that grey morning six years ago?

There was a silence that might be felt.

'Who drew the short lighter?' she whispered, before she knew that she had spoken.

'I am not here to answer questions,' he replied. 'And I have asked none. Neither, you will observe, have I blamed you. But I desire that you will never again allude to this subject, and that you will keep in mind that I do not intend to discuss it with you.'

He laid down the 'Imitation,' and moved towards his own room.

With a sudden movement she flung herself upon her knees before him and caught his arm. The attitude suggested an amateur.

'Which drew the short lighter?' she gasped, her small upturned face white and convulsed.

'You will know in five months' time,' he said. Then he extricated himself from her trembling clasp and left the room, closing the door quietly behind him.

CHAPTER IV

For the sin ye do by two and two ye must pay for one by one!

RUDYARD KIPLING.[21]

WHEN Hugh awoke the morning after Lady Newhaven's party the day was already far advanced. A hot day had succeeded to a hot night. For a few seconds he lay like one emerging from the influence of morphia, who feels his racked body still painlessly afloat on a sea of rest, but is conscious that it is drifting back to the bitter shores of pain, and who stirs neither hand nor foot for fear of hastening the touch of the encircling aching sands on which he is so soon to be cast in agony once more.

His mind cleared a little. Rachel's grave face stood out against a dark background – a background darker surely than that of the summer night. He remembered with self-contempt the extravagant emotion which she had aroused in him.

'Absurd,' Hugh said to himself, with the distrust of all sudden springs of pure emotion which those who have misused them rarely escape. And then another remembrance, which only a sleeping draught had kept at bay, darted upon him like a panther on its prey.

He had drawn the short lighter.

He started violently, and then fell back trembling.

'Oh, my God!' he said involuntarily.

He lay still, telling himself that this dreadful nightmare would pass, would fade in the light of common day.

His servant came in noiselessly with a cup of coffee and a little sheaf of letters.

He pretended to be asleep; but when the man had gone he put out his shaking hand for the coffee and drank it.

The mist before his mind gradually lifted. Gradually, too, the horror on his face whitened to despair, as a twilight meadow whitens beneath the evening frost. He had drawn the short lighter. Nothing in heaven or earth could alter that fact.

He did not stop to wonder how Lord Newhaven had become aware of his own dishonour, or at the strange weapon with which he had avenged himself. He went over every detail of his encounter with him in the study. His hand had been forced. He had been thrust into a vile position. He ought to have refused to draw. He did not agree to draw. Nevertheless he had drawn. And Hugh knew that if it had to be done again, he should again have been compelled to draw by the iron will before which his was as straw. He could not have met the scorn of those terrible half-closed eyes if he had refused.

'There was no help for it,' said Hugh, half aloud. And yet to die by his own hand within five months! It was incredible, It was preposterous.

'I never agreed to it,' he said, passionately.

Nevertheless he had drawn. The remembrance ever returned to lay its cold hand upon his heart, and with it came the grim conviction that if Lord Newhaven had drawn the short lighter he would have carried out the agreement to the letter. Whether it was extravagant, unchristian, whatever might have been truly said of that unholy compact, Lord Newhaven would have stood by it.

'I suppose I must stand by it, too,' said Hugh to himself, the cold sweat breaking on his forehead. 'I suppose I am bound in honour to stand by it, too.'

He suffered his mind to regard the alternative.

To wrong a man as deeply as he had wronged Lord Newhaven; to tacitly accept. – That was where his mistake had been. Another man, that mahogany-faced fellow with the colonial accent, would have refused to draw, and would have knocked Lord Newhaven down and half killed him, or would have been knocked down and half killed by him. But to tacitly accept a means by which the injured man risked his life to avenge his honour, and then afterwards to shirk the fate which a perfectly even chance had thrown upon him instead of on his antagonist! It was too mean, too despicable. Hugh's pale cheek burned.

'I am bound,' he said slowly to himself over and over again. There was no way of escape.

Yesterday evening, with some intuition of coming peril, he had said 'I will get out.' The way of retreat had been open behind him. Now by one slight movement he was cut off from it for ever.

'I can't get out,' said the starling, the feathers on its breast worn away with beating against the bars.

'I can't get out,' said Hugh, coming for the first time in contact with the bars which he was to know so well, the bars of the prison that he had made with his own hands.

He looked into the future with blank eyes. He had no future now. He stared vacantly in front of him like a man who looks through his window at the wide expanse of meadow and waving wood and distant hill which has met his eye every morning of his life, and finds it – gone. It was incredible. He turned giddy. His reeling mind, shrinking back from the abyss, struck against a fixed point, and clutching it came violently to a standstill.

His mother!

His mother was a widow and he was her only son. If he died by his own hand it would break her heart. Hugh groaned and thrust the thought from him. It was too sharp. He could not suffer it.

His sin, not worse than that of many another man, had found him out. He had done wrong. He admitted it, but this monstrous judgment on him was out of all proportion to his offence. And like some malignant infectious disease retribution would fall, not on him alone, but on those nearest him, on his innocent mother and sister. It was unjust, unjust, unjust.

A very bitter look came into his face. Hugh had never so far hated any one, but now something very like hatred welled up in his heart against Lady Newhaven. She had lured him to his destruction. She had tempted him. This was undoubtedly true, though not probably the view which her guardian angel would take of the matter.

Among the letters which the servant had brought him he suddenly recognised that the topmost was in Lady Newhaven's handwriting. Anger and repulsion seized him. No doubt it was the first of a series. 'Why was he so altered? What had she done to offend him?' &c. &c. He knew the contents beforehand, or thought he knew them. He got up deliberately, threw the unopened note into the empty fireplace, and put a match to it. He watched it burn.

It was his first overt act of rebellion against her yoke, the first step along the nearest of the many well-worn paths that a man takes at random to leave a woman. It did not occur to him that Lady Newhaven might have written to him about his encounter with her husband. He knew Lord Newhaven well enough to be absolutely certain that he would mention the subject to no living creature, least of all to his wife.

'Neither will I,' he said to himself; 'and as for her, I will break with her from this day forward.'

The little pink notes with the dashing twirly handwriting persisted for a week or two and then ceased.

Hugh was a man of many social engagements. His first impulse, when later in the day he remembered them, was to throw them all up and leave London. But Lord Newhaven would hear of his departure, and would smile. He decided to remain and to go on as if nothing had happened. When the evening came he dressed with his usual care, verified the hour of his engagement, and went out to dine with the Loftuses.

CHAPTER V

What the *Bandar-log* think now the jungle will think later.
Maxim of the Bandar-log – RUDYARD KIPLING.[22]

IT was Sybell Loftus's first season in London since her second marriage with Mr. Doll Loftus. After a very brief sojourn in that city of frivolity she had the acumen to discover that London society was hopelessly worldly and mercenary, that people only met to eat and to abuse each other, that the law of cutlet for cutlet was universal, that young men, especially those in the Guards, were garrisoned by a full complement of devils, that London girls lived only for dress and the excitement of husband-hunting. In short, to use her own expression, she 'turned London society inside out.'

London bore the process with equanimity, and presently Sybell determined to raise the art of dinner-giving from the low estate to which she avowed it had fallen to a higher level. She was young, she was pretty, she was well born, she was rich. All the social doors were open to her. But one discovery is often only the prelude to another. She soon made the further one that in order to raise the tone of social gatherings it is absolutely necessary to infuse into them a leaven of 'clever people.' Further light on this interesting subject showed her that most of the really 'clever people' did not belong to her set. The discovery which all who love adulation quickly make – namely, that the truly appreciative and sympathetic and gifted are for the greater part to be found in a class below their own – was duly made and registered by Sybell. She avowed that class differences were nothing to her with the enthusiasm of all those who since the world began have preferred to be first in the society which they gather round them.

Fortunately for Sybell she was not troubled by doubts respecting the clearness of her own judgment. Eccentricity was in her eyes originality; a wholesale

contradiction of established facts was a new view. She had not the horrid perception of difference between the real and the imitation which spoils the lives of
many. She was equally delighted with both, and remained in blissful ignorance
of the fact that her 'deep' conversation was felt to be exhaustingly superficial if by
chance she came across the real artist or thinker instead of his counterfeit.

Consequently to her house came the *raté*[23] in all his most virulent develop-
ments; the 'new woman'[24] with stupendous lopsided opinions on difficult Old
Testament subjects; the 'lady authoress' with a mission to show up the vices
of a society which she knew only by hearsay. Hither came unwittingly simple-
minded Church dignitaries, who, Sybell hoped, might influence for his good
the young agnostic[25] poet who had written a sonnet on her muff-chain,[26] a very
daring sonnet, which Doll, who did not care for poetry, had not been shown.
Hither, by mistake, thinking it was an ordinary dinner-party, came Hugh, whom
Sybell said she had discovered, and who was not aware that he was in need of
discovery. And hither also on this particular evening came Rachel West, whom
Sybell had pronounced to be very intelligent a few days before, and who was
serenely unconscious that she was present on her probation, and that if she did
not say something striking she would never be asked again.

Doll Loftus, Sybell's husband, was standing by Rachel when Hugh came
in. He felt drawn towards her because she was not 'clever' as far as her appearance went. At any rate, she had not the touzled, ill-groomed hair which he had
learned to associate with female genius.

'This sort of thing is beyond me,' he said mournfully to Rachel, his eyes travelling over the assembly gathered round his wife, whose remarks were calling forth
admiring laughter. 'I don't understand half they say, and when I do I sometimes
wish I didn't. But I suppose,' tentatively, 'you go in for all this sort of thing?'

'I!' said Rachel astonished. 'I don't go in for anything. But what sort of thing
do you mean?'

'There is Scarlett,' said Doll with relief, who hated definitions, and felt the
conversation was on the slippery verge of becoming deep. 'Do you know him?
Looks as if he'd seen a ghost, doesn't he?'

Rachel's interest, never a heavy sleeper, was instantly awakened as she saw
Sybell piloting Hugh towards her. She recognised him – the man she had seen
last night in the hansom and afterwards at the Newhavens. A glance showed her
that his trouble, whatever it might be, had pierced beyond the surface feelings of
anger and impatience, and had reached the quick of his heart. The young man,
pallid and heavy-eyed, bore himself well, and Rachel respected him for his quiet
demeanour and a certain dignity, which, for the moment, obliterated the slight
indecision of his face, and gave his mouth the firmness which it lacked. It seemed
to Rachel as if he had but now stood by a deathbed, and had brought with him
into the crowded room the shadow of an inexorable fate.

The others only perceived that he had a headache. Hugh did not deny it. He complained of the great heat to Sybell, but not to Rachel. Something in her clear eyes told him, as they told many others, that small lies and petty deceits might be laid aside with impunity in dealing with her. He felt no surprise at seeing her, no return of the sudden violent emotion of the night before. He had never spoken to her till this moment, but yet he felt that her eyes were old friends, tried to the uttermost and found faithful in some forgotten past. Rachel's eyes had a certain calm fixity in them that comes not of natural temperament but of past conflict, long waged, and barely but irrevocably won. A faint ray of comfort stole across the desolation of his mind as he looked at her. He did not notice whether she was handsome or ugly, any more than we do when we look at the dear familiar faces which were with us in their childhood and ours, which have grown up beside us under the same roof, which have rejoiced with us and wept with us, and without which heaven itself could never be a home.

In a few minutes he was taking her in to dinner. He had imagined that she was a woman of few words, but after a faint attempt at conversation he found that he had relapsed into silence, and that it was she who was talking. Presently the heavy cloud upon his brain lifted. His strained face relaxed. She glanced at him, and continued her little monologue. Her face had brightened.

He had dreaded this dinner party, this first essay to preserve his balance in public with his frightful invisible burden, but he was getting through it better than he had expected.

'I have come back to what is called society,' Rachel was saying, 'after nearly seven years of an exile something like Nebuchadnezzar's,[27] and there are two things which I find as difficult as Kipling's 'silly sailors' found their harps 'which they twanged unhandily.'[28]

'Is small talk one of them?' asked Hugh. 'It has always been a difficulty to me.'

'On the contrary,' said Rachel. 'I plume myself on that. Surely my present sample is not so much below the average that you need ask me that.'

'I did not recognise that it *was* small talk,' said Hugh with a faint smile. 'If it really is I can only say I shall have brain fever if you pass on to what *you* might call conversation.'

It was to him as if a miniature wavelet of a great ocean somewhere in the distance had crept up to laugh and break at his feet. He did not recognise that this tiniest runlet which fell back at once was of the same element as the tidal wave which had swept over him yesternight.

'But are you aware,' said Rachel, dropping her voice a little, 'it is beginning to dawn upon me, that this evening's gathering is met together for exalted conversation, and perhaps we ought to be practising a little. I feel certain that after dinner you will be 'drawn through the clefts of confession' by Miss Barker, the woman in the high dinner gown with orange velvet sleeves. Mrs. Loftus introduced her to me when I arrived as the "apostle of humanity."'

'Why should you fix on that particular apostle for me?' said Hugh, looking resentfully at a large-faced woman, who was talking in an 'intense' manner to a slightly bewildered Bishop.

'It is a prophetic instinct, nothing more.'

'I will have a prophetic instinct, too, then,' said Hugh, helping himself at last to the dish which was presented to him, to Rachel's relief. 'I shall give you the –' looking slowly down the table.

'The Bishop?'

'Certainly not, after your disposal of me.'

'Well, then, the poet? I am sure he is a poet because his tie is uneven and his hair is so long. Why do literary men wear their hair long, and literary women wear it short? I should *like* the poet.'

'You shall not have him,' said Hugh with decision. 'I am hesitating between the bald young man with the fat hand and the immense ring, and the old professor who is drawing plans on the tablecloth.'

'The apostle told me with bated breath that the young man with the ring is Mr. Harvey, the author of "Unashamed."'

Hugh looked at his plate to conceal his disgust.

There was a pause in the buzz of conversation, and into it fell straightway the voice of the apostle like a brick through a skylight.

'The need of the present age is the realisation of our brotherhood with sin and suffering and poverty. West London in satin and diamonds does not hear her sister East London in rags calling to her to deliver her. The voice of East London has been drowned in the dance-music of the West End.'

Sybell gazed with awed admiration at the apostle.

'What a beautiful thought,' she said.

'Miss Gresley's "Idyll of East London,"' said Hugh, 'is a voice which, at any rate, has been fully heard.'

The apostle put up a pince-nez[29] on a bone leg and looked at Hugh.

'I entirely disapprove of that little book,' she said. 'It is misleading and wilfully one-sided.'

'Hester Gresley is a dear friend of mine,' said Sybell, 'and I must stand up for her. She is the sister of our clergyman, who is a very clever man. In fact, I am not sure he isn't the cleverest of the two. She and I have great talks. We have so much in common. How strange it seems that she who lives in the depths of the country should have written a story of the East End.'

'That is always so,' said the author of 'Unashamed,' in a sonorous voice. 'The novel has of late been dwarfed to the scope of the young English girl (he pronounced it gurl) who writes from her imagination and not from her experience. What true art requires of us is a faithful rendering of a great experience.'

He looked round, as if challenging the world to say that 'Unashamed' was not a lurid personal reminiscence.

Sybell was charmed. She felt that none of her previous dinner-parties had reached such a high level as this one.

'A faithful rendering of a great experience,' she repeated. 'How I wish Hester were here to hear that. I often tell her she ought to see life, and cultivated society would do so much for her. I found her out a year ago, and I'm always begging people to read her book, and I simply long to introduce her to clever people and oblige the world to recognise her talent.'

'I agree with you it is not yet fully recognised,' said Hugh in a level voice; 'but if 'The Idyll' received only partial recognition, it was at any rate enthusiastic. And it is not forgotten.'

Sybell felt vaguely uncomfortable, and conceived a faint dislike of Hugh as an uncongenial person.

The apostle and the poet began to speak simultaneously, but the female key was the highest and prevailed.

'We all agree in admiring Miss Gresley's delicate piece of workmanship,' said the apostle, both elbows on the table after the manner of her kind, 'but it is a misfortune to the cause of suffering humanity – to *our* cause – when the books which pretend to set forth certain phases of its existence are written by persons entirely ignorant of the life they describe.'

'How true,' said Sybell. 'I have often thought it, but I never could put it into words as you do. Oh! how I agree with you and Mr. Harvey. As I often say to Hester, 'How can you describe anything if you don't go anywhere or see anything; I can't give you my experience. No one can.' I said that to her only a month ago, when she refused to come up to London with me.'

Rachel's white face and neck had taken on them the pink transparent colour that generally dwelt only in the curves of her small ears.

'Why do you think Miss Gresley is ignorant of the life she describes?' she said, addressing the apostle.

The author and the apostle both opened their mouths at the same moment, only to register a second triumph of the female tongue.

Miss Barker was in her element. The whole table was listening. She shrugged her orange-velvet shoulders.

'Those who have cast in their lot with the poor,' she said, sententiously, 'would recognise at once the impossibility of Miss Gresley's characters and situations.'

'To me they seem real,' said Rachel.

'Ah, my dear Miss West, you will excuse me, but a young lady like yourself, nursed in the lap of luxury, can hardly be expected to look at life with the same eyes as a poor waif like myself, who has penetrated to the very core of the city, and who has heard the stifled sigh of a vast perishing humanity.'

'I lived in the midst of it for six years,' said Rachel. 'I did not cast in my lot with the poor, for I was one of them, and earned my bread among them. Miss Gresley's book may not be palatable in some respects, the district visitor[30] and the woman missionary are certainly treated with harshness, but as far as my experience goes, the 'Idyll' is a true word from first to last.'

There was in Rachel's voice a restrained force that vaguely stirred all the occupants of the room. Every one looked at her, and for a moment no one spoke. She became quite colourless.

'Very striking. Just what I should have said in her place,' said Sybell to herself. 'I will ask her again.'

'I can hear it raining,' said Doll's voice from the head of the table to the company in general. 'If it will only go on for a week without stopping there may be some hope of the crops yet.'

The conversation buzzed up again, and Rachel turned instantly to Hugh, before Mr. Harvey, leaning forward with his ring, had time to address her.

Hugh alone saw what a superhuman effort it had been to her to overcome her shrinking from mentioning, not her previous poverty, but her personal experience. She had sacrificed her natural reserve, which he could see was great; she had even set good taste at defiance to defend Hester Gresley's book. Hugh had shuddered as he heard her speak. He felt that he could not have obtruded himself on so mixed an assembly. Yet he saw that it had cost her more to do so than it would have cost him.

He began to remember having heard people speak of an ironmaster's daughter, whose father had failed and died, and who, after several years of dire poverty, had lately inherited a vast fortune from her father's partner. It had been talked about at the time, a few months ago. This must be she.

'You have a great affection for Miss Gresley,' he said in a low voice.

'I have,' said Rachel, her lip still quivering. 'But if I disliked her I hope I should have said the same. Surely it is not necessary to love the writer in order to defend the book.'

Hugh was silent. He looked at her, and wished that she might always be on his side.

'About two courses ago I was going to tell you,' said Rachael smiling, 'of one of my chief difficulties on my return to the civilised world and 'Society.' But now you have had an example of it. I am trying to cure myself of the trick of becoming interested in conversation. I must learn to use words as counters, not as coins. I need not disbelieve what I say, but I must not speak of anything to which I attach value. I perceive that to do this is an art and a means of defence from invasion. But I, on the contrary, become interested, as you have just seen. I forget that I am only playing a game, and I rush into a subject like a bull into a china shop, and knock about all the crockery until – as I am not opposed by my native pitchfork – I suddenly return to my senses, and discover that I have mistaken a game for real earnest.'

'We were all in earnest five minutes ago,' said Hugh, 'at least, I was. I could not bear to hear Miss Gresley patronised by all these failures and amateurs. But unless I am very much mistaken you will find several pitchforks laid up for you in the drawing-room.'

'I don't mean to smash any more china,' said Rachel.

Another wavelet skimmed in and broke a little further up the sand. A sense of freshness, of expectation was in the air. The great gathered ocean was stirring itself in the distance. Hugh had forgotten his trouble.

He turned the conversation back to Hester Gresley and her writing. He spoke of her with sympathy and appreciation, and presently detected a softness in Rachel's eyes which made him jealous of Hester.

By the time the evening was over the imperceptible travelling of the summer sea had reached as far as the tidal wave.

Hugh left when Rachel did, accompanying her to her carriage. At the door were the darkness and the rain. At the door with them the horror and despair of the morning were in wait for him, and laid hold upon him. Hugh shuddered, and turned instinctively to Rachel.

She was holding out her hand to him. He took it and held it tightly in his sudden fear and desolation.

'When shall I meet you again?' he said hoarsely.

A long look passed between them. Hugh's tortured soul full of passionate entreaty leaped to his eyes. Hers, sad and steadfast, met the appeal in his, and recognised it as a claim. There was no surprise in her quiet face.

'I ride early in the Row,' she said. 'You can join me there if you wish. Good-night.'

She took her hand with great gentleness out of his, and drove away.

And the darkness shut down again on Hugh's heart.

CHAPTER VI

Içi bas tous les hommes pleurent
Leurs amitiés et leurs amours.
BOURGET.[31]

MANY sarcastic but true words have been said by man, and in no jealous spirit, concerning woman's friendship for woman. The passing judgment of the majority of men on such devotion might be summed up in the words, 'Occupy till

I come.' It does occupy till they do come.[a] And if they don't come the hastily improvised friendship may hold together for years, like an unseaworthy boat in a harbour, which looks like a boat but never goes out to sea.

But nevertheless here and there among its numberless counterfeits a friendship rises up between two women which sustains the life of both, which is still young when life is waning, which man's love and motherhood cannot displace nor death annihilate; a friendship which is not the solitary affection of an empty heart nor the deepest affection of a full one, but which nevertheless lightens the burdens of this world and lays its pure hand upon the next.

Such a friendship, very deep, very tender, existed between Rachel West and Hester Gresley. It dated back from the nursery days, when Hester and Rachel solemnly eyed each other, and then made acquaintance in the dark gardens of Portman Square, into which Hester introduced a fortified castle with a captive princess in it and a rescuing prince and a dragon, and several other ingredients of romance, to the awed amazement of Rachel – stolid, solid, silent Rachel – who loved all two- and four-legged creatures, but who never made them talk to each other as Hester did. And Hester, in blue serge, told Rachel, in crimson velvet,[32] as they walked hand in hand in front of their nursery-maids, what the London sparrows said to each other in the gutters, and how they considered the gravel-path in the square was a deep river suitable to bathe in. And when the spring was coming, and the prince had rescued the princess so often from the dungeon in the laurel-bushes that Hester was tired of it, she told Rachel how the elms were always sighing because they were shut up in town, and how they went out every night with their roots into the green country to see their friends, and came back oh! so early in the morning, before any one was awake to miss them. And Rachel's heart yearned after Hester, and she gave her her red horse and the tin duck and magnet, and Hester made stories about them all.

At last the day came when Rachel's mother, who had long viewed the intimacy with complacency, presented her compliments, in a note-sheet with two immense gilt crests on it, to Hester's aunt, and requested that her little niece might be allowed to come to tea with her little daughter. And Lady Susan Gresley, who had never met the rich ironmaster's wife in this world, and would probably be equally exclusive in the next, was about to refuse, when Hester, who up to that moment had apparently taken no interest in the matter, suddenly cast herself on the floor in a paroxysm of despair and beat her head against the carpet. The tearful entreaties of her aunt gradually elicited the explanation, riddled by sobs, that Hester could never take an interest in life again, could never raise herself even to a sitting position, nor dry her eyes on her aunt's handkerchief, unless she were allowed to go to tea with Rachel and see her dormouse.

Lady Susan, much upset herself, and convinced that these outbursts were prejudicial to Hester's health, gave way at once, and a few days later Hester, pale, shy, in a white muffler, escorted by Mademoiselle, went to tea in the magnificent house on the other side of the square, and saw Rachel's round head without a feathered hat on it, and both children were consumed by shyness until the two Mademoiselles withdrew into another room, and Rachel showed Hester the dormouse which she had found in the woods in the country, and which ate out of her hand. And Hester made a little poem on it, beginning:

There was a mouse in Portman Square.

And so, with many breaks, the friendship attained a surer footing, and the intimacy grew with their growth, in spite of the fact that Lady Susan had felt unable (notwithstanding the marked advances of Mrs. West, possibly because of them) to enlarge her visiting list, in spite of many other difficulties which were only in the end surmounted by the simplicity of character which Rachel had not inherited from her parents.

And then, after both girls had danced through one London season in different ball-rooms, Rachel's parents died, her mother first, and then – by accident – her father, leaving behind him an avalanche of unsuspected money difficulties, in which even his vast fortune was engulphed.

Hard years followed for Rachel. She ate the bread of carefulness in the houses of poor relations not of high degree, with whom her parents had quarrelled when they had made their money and began to entertain social ambitions. She learned what it was to be the person of least importance in families of no importance. She essayed to teach and failed. She had no real education. She made desperate struggles for independence, and learned how others failed besides herself. She left her relations and their bitter bread and came to London, and struggled with those who struggled, and saw how Temptation spreads her net for bleeding feet. Because she loved Hester she accepted from her half her slender pin-money. Hester had said, 'If I were poor, Rachel, how would you bear it if I would not let you help me?' And Rachel had wept slow difficult tears, and had given Hester the comfort of helping her. The greater generosity was with Rachel, and Hester knew it.

And as Rachel's fortunes sank, Hester's rose. Lady Susan Gresley had one talent, and she did not lay it up in a napkin. She had the art of attracting people to her house, that house to which Mrs. West had never forced an entrance. Hester was thrown from the first into a society which her clergyman brother, who had never seen it, pronounced to be frivolous, worldly, profane, but which no one has called dull. There were many facets in Hester's character, and Lady Susan had managed to place her where they caught the light. Was she witty? Was she attractive? Who shall say. Man is wisely averse to 'cleverness' in a woman, but if he possesses any armour wherewith to steel himself against wit it is certain that he seldom puts it on. She refused several offers, one so brilliant that no woman ever believed that it was really made.

Lady Susan saw that her niece, without a fortune, with little beauty save that of high breeding, with weak health, was becoming a personage. 'What will she become?' people said. And in the meanwhile Hester did nothing beyond dressing extremely well. And everything she saw and every person she met added fuel to an unlit fire in her soul.

At last Rachel was able to earn a meagre living by typewriting, and for four years, happy by contrast with those when despair and failure had confronted her, she lived by the work of her hands among those poor as herself. Gradually she had lost sight of all her acquaintances. She had been out of the schoolroom for too short a time to make friends. And alas! in the set in which she had been launched poverty was a crime; no, perhaps not quite that, but as much a bar to intercourse as in another class a want of the letter H is found to be.

It was while Rachel was still struggling for a livelihood that the event happened which changed the bias of her character, as a geranium transplanted from the garden changes its attitude in a cottage window.

On one of the early days of her despair she met on the dreary stairs of the great rabbit warren in which she had a room, a man with whom she had been acquainted in the short year of her social life before the collapse of her fortunes. He had paid her considerable attention, and she had thought once or twice with momentary bitterness that, like the rest, he had not cared to find out what had become of her. She greeted him with shy but evident pleasure. She took for granted he had come to see her, and he allowed her to remain under that delusion. In reality he had been hunting up an old model whom he wanted for his next picture, and who had silently left Museum Buildings some months before without leaving his address. He had genuinely admired her though he had forgotten her, and he was unaffectedly delighted to see her again.

That one chance meeting was the first of many. Flowers came to Rachel's little room, and romance came with them. Rachel's proud tender heart struggled and then gave way before this radiant first love blossoming in the midst of her loneliness. At last on a March afternoon when the low sun caught the daffodils he had brought her he told her he loved her.

Days followed, exquisite days, which have none like them in later life whatever later life may bring. That year the spring came early, and they went often together into the country. And that year when all the world was white with blossom the snow came, and laid upon earth's bridal veil a white shroud. Every cup of May blossom, every petal of hawthorn bent beneath its burden of snow. And so it was in the full springtide of Rachel's heart. The snow came down upon it. She discovered at last that though he loved her he did not wish to marry her; that even from the time of that first meeting he had never intended to marry her. That discovery was a shroud. She wrapped her dead love in it, and would fain have buried it out of her sight.

But only after a year of conflict was she suffered to bury it; after a year during which the ghost of her dead ever came back and came back to importune her vainly with its love. Rachel's poor neighbours grew accustomed to see the tall handsome waiting figure which always returned and returned, but which at last after one dreadful day was seen no more in Museum Buildings. Rachel had laid the ghost at last. But the conflict remained graven in her face.

On a certain cold winter morning Hester darted across the wet pavement from the brougham to the untidy entrance of Museum Buildings where Rachel still lived. It was a miserable day. The streets and bare trees looked as if they had been drawn in in ink, and the whole carelessly blotted before it was dry. All the outlines were confused, blurred. The cold penetrated to the very bones of the shivering city.

Rachel had just come in wet and tired, bringing with her a roll of manuscript to be transcribed. A woman waiting for her on the endless stone stairs had cursed her for taking the bread out of her mouth.

'He always employed me till you came,' she shrieked, shaking her fist at her, 'and now he gives it all to you because you're younger and better looking.'

She gave the woman as much as she dared spare, the calculation did not take long, and went on climbing the stairs.

Something in the poor creature's words, something vague but repulsive in her remembrance of the man who paid her for the work by which she could barely live, fell like lead into Rachel's heart. She looked out dumbly over the wilderness of roofs. The suffering of the world was eating into her soul, the suffering of this vast travailing East London, where people trod each other down to live.

'If any one had told me,' she said to herself, 'when I was rich, that I lived on the flesh and blood of my fellow creatures, that my virtue and ease and pleasure were bought by their degradation, and toil and pain, I should not have believed it, and I should have been angry. If I had been told that the clothes I wore, the food I ate, the pen I wrote with, the ink I used, the paper I wrote on – all these, and everything I touched, from my soap to my matchbox, especially my matchbox, was the result of sweated labour,[33] I should not have believed it, I should have laughed. But yet it is so. If I had not been rich once myself I should think as all these people do, that the rich are devils incarnate to let such things go on. They have the power to help us. We have none to help ourselves. But they never use it. The rich grind the poor for their luxuries with their eyes shut, and we grind each other for our daily bread with our eyes open. I have got that woman's work. I have struggled hard enough to get it, but though I did not realise it, I might have known that I had only got on to the raft by pushing some one else off it.'

Rachel looked out across the miles of roofs which lay below her garret window. The sound was in her ears of that great whirlpool wherein youth and beauty and innocence go down quick day by day. The wilderness of leaden roofs turned suddenly before her eyes into a sullen furrowed sea of shame and crime which, awaiting no future day of judgment, daily gave up its awful dead.[34]

Presently Hester came in, panting a little after the long ascent of worn stairs, and dragging with her a large parcel. It was a fur-lined cloak. Hester spread it mutely before her friend, and looked beseechingly at her. Then she kissed her, and the two girls clung together for a moment in silence.

'Dearest,' said Rachel, 'don't give me new things. It isn't that – you know I did take it when I was in need. But oh, Hester, I know you can't afford it. I should not mind if you were rich, at least, I would try not, but – if you would only give me some of your old clothes instead. I should like them all the better because you had worn them.' And Rachel kissed the lapel of Hester's coat.

'I can't,' whispered Hester into Rachel's hair. 'The best is only just good enough.'

'Wouldn't it be kinder to me?'

Hester trembled, and then burst into tears.

'I will wear it, I will wear it,' said Rachel hurriedly. 'Look, Hester! I have got it on. How deliciously warm, and – do look; it has two little pockets in the fur lining.'

But Hester wept passionately, and Rachel sat down by her on the floor in the new cloak till the paroxysm was over.

How does a subtle affinity find a foothold between natures which present an obvious, a violent contrast to each other? Why do the obvious and the subtle forget their life-long feud at intervals, and suddenly appear for a moment in each other's society?

Rachel was physically strong. Hester was weak. The one was calm, patient, practical, equable, the other imaginative, unbalanced, excitable.

Life had not spoilt Rachel. Lady Susan Gresley had done her best to spoil Hester. The one had lived the unprotected life, and showed it in her bearing. The other had lived the sheltered life, and bore its mark upon her pure forehead and youthful face.

'I cannot bear it,' said Hester at last. 'I think and think, and I can't think of anything. I would give my life for you, and you will hardly let me give you £3 10*s*. 6*d*. That is all it cost. It is only frieze,[35] that common red frieze, and the lining is only rabbit.' A last tear fell at the word rabbit. 'I wanted to get you a velvet one, just the same as my new one, lined with chinchilla, but I knew it would only make you miserable. I wish,' looking vindictively at the cloak, 'I wish rabbits had never been born.'

Rachel laughed. Hester was evidently recovering.

'Mr. Scarlett was saying last night that no one can help any one,' continued Hester, turning her white exhausted face to her friend. 'He said that we are always so placed that we can only look on. And I told him that could not be true, but oh, in my heart, Rachel, I have felt it was true all these long, long five years since you have lived here.'

Rachel came and stood beside her at the little window. There was just room for them between the typewriter and the bed.

Far below, Hester's brougham was pacing up and down.

'Then are love and sympathy nothing?' she said. 'Those are the real gifts. If I were rich to-morrow I should look to you just as I do now for the things which money can't buy. And those are the things' – Rachel's voice shook – 'which you have always given me, and which I can't do without. You feel my poverty more than I do myself. It crushed me at first when I could not support myself. Now that I can – and in everything except money I am very rich – I am comparatively happy.'

There was a long silence.

'Perhaps,' said Rachel at last with difficulty, 'if I had remained an heiress Mr. Tristram might have married me. I feel nearly sure he would have married me. In that case I lost my money only just in time to prevent a much greater misfortune, and I am glad I am as I am.'

Rachel remembered that conversation often in after years with a sense of thankfulness that for once she who was so reticent had let Hester see how dear she was to her.

The two girls stood long together cheek against cheek.

And as Hester leaned against Rachel the yearning of her soul towards her suddenly lit up something which had long lain colossal but inapprehended in the depths of her mind. Her paroxysm of despair at her own powerlessness was followed by a lightning flash of self-revelation. She saw, as in a dream, terrible, beautiful, inaccessible, but distinct, where her power lay, of which restless bewildering hints had so often mocked her. She had but to touch the houses and they would fall down. She held her hands tightly together lest she should do it. The strength as of an infinite ocean swept in beneath her weakness, and bore it upon its surface like a leaf.

'You must go home,' said Rachel gently, remembering Lady Susan's punctual habits.

Hester kissed her absently and went out into the new world which had been pressing upon her all her life, the gate of which Love had opened for her. For Love has many keys besides that of her own dwelling. Some who know her slightly affirm that she can only open her own cheap patent padlock with a secret word on it that everybody knows. But some who know her better hold that hers is the master-key which will one day turn all the locks in all the world.

A year later Hester's first book, 'An Idyll of East London,' was reaping its harvest of astonished indignation and admiration, and her acquaintances – not her friends – were still wondering how she came to know so much of a life of which they decided she could know nothing, when suddenly Lady Susan Gresley died, and Hester went to live in the country with her clergyman brother.

A few months later still, and on a mild April day, when the poor London trees had black buds on them, Rachel brushed and folded away in the little painted chest of drawers her few threadbare clothes, and put the boots – which the cobbler whose wife she had nursed had patched for her – under the shelf which held her few cups and plates and the faithful tin kettle, which had always been a cheerful boiler. And she washed her seven coarse handkerchiefs, and put them in the washhandstand drawer. And then she raked out the fire and cleaned the grate, and set the room in order. It was quickly done. She took up her hat which lay beside a bundle on the bed. Her hands trembled as she put it on. She looked wistfully round her, and her face worked. The little room which had looked so alien when she came to it six years ago had become a home. She went to the window and kissed the pane through which she had learnt to see so much. Then she seized up the bundle, and went quickly out, locking the door behind her, and taking the key with her.

'I am going away for a time, but I shall come back,' she said to the cobbler's wife on the same landing.

'No one comes back as once goes,' said the woman, without raising her eyes from the cheap blouse which she was finishing, which kept so well the grim secret of how it came into being that no one was afraid of buying it.

'I am keeping on the room.'

The woman smiled incredulously, giving one sharp glance at the bundle. She had seen many flittings.[36] She should buy the kettle when Rachel's 'sticks' were sold by the landlord in default of the rent.

'Well, you was a good neighbour,' she said. 'There's a many as 'ull miss you. Good-bye, and good luck to ye. I shan't say as you've left.'

'I shall come back,' said Rachel hoarsely, and she slipped downstairs like a thief. She felt like a thief. For she was rich. The man who had led her father into the speculations which had ruined him had died childless, and had bequeathed to her a colossal fortune.

CHAPTER VII

Cure the drunkard, heal the insane, mollify the homicide, civilise the Pawnee, but what lessons can be devised for the debauchee of sentiment?

EMERSON.[37]

A FORTNIGHT had passed since the drawing of lots, and Lady Newhaven remained in ignorance as to which of the two men had received his death warrant. Few have found suspense easy to bear; but for the self-centred an intolerable element is added to it, which unselfish natures escape. From her early youth Lady Newhaven had been in the habit of viewing life in picturesque *tableaux vivants*[38] of which she invariably formed the central figure. At her confirmation the Bishop, the white-robed clergy, and the other candidates had served but as a nebulous background against which her own white-clad, kneeling figure, bowed in reverent devotion, stood out in high relief.

When she married Lord Newhaven he took so slight a part, though a necessary one, in the wedding groups that their completeness had never been marred by misgivings as to his exact position in them. When, six years later, after one or two mild flirtations which only served as a stimulus to her love of dress, when at last she met, as she would have expressed it, 'the one love of her life,' her first fluctuations and final deviation from the path of honour were the result of new arrangements round the same centre.

The first groups in which Hugh took part had been prodigies of virtue. The young mother with the Madonna face – Lady Newhaven firmly believed that her face, with the crimped fringe drawn down to the eyebrows, resembled that of a Madonna – with her children round her, Lord Newhaven as usual somewhat out of focus in the background; and Hugh, young, handsome, devoted, heartbroken, and ennobled for life by the contemplation of such impregnable virtue.

'You accuse me of coldness,' she had imagined herself saying in a later scene, when the children and the husband would have made too much of a crowd, and were consequently omitted. 'I wish to heaven I were as cold as I appear.'

And she had really said it later on. Hugh never did accuse her of coldness, but that was a detail. Those words, conned over many times, had nevertheless actually proceeded out of her mouth. Few of us have the power of saying anything we intend to say. But Lady Newhaven had that power, and enjoyed also in consequence a profound belief in her prophetic instincts; while others, Hugh not excepted, detected a premeditated tone in her conversation, and a sense of incongruity between her remarks and the occasion which called them forth.

From an early date in their married life Lord Newhaven had been in the habit of discounting these remarks by making them in rapid rotation himself before proceeding to the matter in hand.

'Having noticed that a mother – I mean a young mother – is never really happy in the absence of her children, and that their affection makes up for the carelessness of their father, may I ask, Violet, what day you wish to return to Westhope?' he said one morning at breakfast.

'Any day,' she replied. 'I am as miserable in one place as in another.'

'We will say Friday week, then,' returned Lord Newhaven, ignoring, as he invariably did, any allusions to their relative position, and because he ignored them she made many. 'The country,' he added, hurriedly, 'will be very refreshing after the glare and dust and empty worldly society of London.'

She looked at him in anger. She did not understand the reason, but she had long vaguely felt that all conversation seemed to dry up in his presence. He mopped it all into his own sponge, so to speak, and left every subject exhausted.

She rose in silent dignity, and went to her boudoir and lay down there. The heat was very great, and another fire was burning within her, withering her round cheek, and making her small plump hand look shrunk and thin. A fortnight had passed, and she had not heard from Hugh. She had written to him many times, at first only imploring him to meet her, but afterwards telling him she knew what had happened, and entreating him to put her out of suspense, to send her one line that his life was not endangered. She had received no answer to any of her letters. She came to the conclusion that they had been intercepted by Lord Newhaven, and that no doubt the same fate had befallen Hugh's letters to herself. For some time past, before the drawing of lots, she had noticed that Hugh's letters had become less frequent and shorter in length. She understood the reason now. Half of them had been intercepted. How that fact could account for the shortness of the remainder may not be immediately apparent to the prosaic mind, but it was obvious to Lady Newhaven. That Hugh had begun to weary of her could not force the narrow entrance to her mind. Such a possibility had never been even considered in the pictures of the future with which her imagination busied itself. But what would the future be? The road along which she was walking forked before her eyes, and her usual perspicacity was at fault. She knew not in which of those two diverging paths the future would lie.

Would she in eighteen months' time – she should certainly refuse to marry within the year – be standing at the altar in a 'confection' of lilac and white with Hugh; or would she be a miserable wife, moving ghostlike about her house, in coloured raiment, while a distant grave was always white with flowers sent by a nameless friend of the dead? 'How some one must have loved him,' she imagined Hugh's aged mother saying. And once, as that bereaved mother came in the dusk to weep beside the grave, did she not see a shadowy figure start up black-robed from the flower-laden sod, and hastily drawing a thick veil over a beautiful despairing face, glide away among the trees? At this point Lady Newhaven always began to cry. It was too heart-rending. And her mind in violent recoil was caught once more and broken on the same wheel. 'Which? *Which?*'

A servant entered.

'Would her ladyship see Miss West for a few minutes?'

'Yes,' said Lady Newhaven, glad to be delivered from herself, if only by the presence of an acquaintance.

'It is very charitable of you to see me,' said Rachel. 'Personally, I think morning calls ought to be a penal offence. But I came at the entreaty of a former servant of yours. I feel sure you will let me carry some message of forgiveness to her as she is dying. Her name is Morgan. Do you remember her?'

'I once had a maid called Morgan,' said Lady Newhaven. 'She was drunken, and I had to part with her in the end; but I kept her as long as I could in spite of it. She had a genius for hair-dressing.'

'She took your diamond heart pendant,' continued Rachel. 'She was never found out. She can't return it, for of course she sold it and spent the money. But now at last she feels she did wrong, and she says she will die easier for your forgiveness.'

'Oh! I forgive her,' said Lady Newhaven indifferently. 'I often wondered how I lost it. I never cared about it.' She glanced at Rachel, and added tremulously, 'My husband gave it me.'

A sudden impulse was urging her to confide in this grave, gentle-eyed woman. The temptation was all the stronger because Rachel, who had only lately appeared in society, was not connected with any portion of her previous life. She was as much a chance acquaintance as a fellow passenger in a railway carriage.

Rachel rose and held out her hand.

'Don't go,' whispered Lady Newhaven, taking her out-stretched hand and holding it.

'I think if I stay,' said Rachel, 'that you may say things you will regret later on when you are feeling stronger. You are evidently tired out now. Everything looks exaggerated when we are exhausted, as I see you are.'

'I am worn out with misery,' said Lady Newhaven. 'I have not slept for a fortnight. I feel I must tell some one.' And she burst into violent weeping.

Rachel sat down again, and waited patiently for the hysterical weeping to cease. Those in whom others confide early learn that their own engagements, their own pleasures and troubles are liable to be set aside at any moment. Rachel was a punctual, exact person, but she missed many trains. Those who sought her seldom realised that her day was as full as, possibly fuller, than their own. Perhaps it was only a very small pleasure to which she had been on her way on this particular morning, and for which she had put on that ethereal grey gown for the first time. At any rate, she relinquished it without a second thought.

Presently Lady Newhaven dried her eyes, and turned impulsively towards her.

The strata of impulsiveness and conventional feeling were always so mixed up after one of these emotional upheavals that it was difficult to guess which would come uppermost. Sometimes fragments of both appeared on the surface together.

'I loved you from the first moment I saw you,' she said. 'I don't take fancies to people, you know. I am not that kind of person. I am very difficult to please, and I never speak of what concerns myself. I am *most* reserved. I daresay you have noticed how reserved I am. I live in my shell. But directly I saw you I felt I could talk to you. I said to myself, "I will make a friend of that girl." Although I always feel a married woman is so differently placed from a girl. A girl only thinks of herself. I am not saying this the least unkindly, but of course it is so. Now a married woman has to consider her husband and family in all she says and does. How will it affect *them?* That is what I so often say to myself, and then my lips are sealed. But, of course, being unmarried, you would not understand that feeling.'

Rachel did not answer. She was inured to this time-honoured conversational opening.

'And the temptations of married life,' continued Lady Newhaven, 'a girl cannot enter into them.'

'Then do not tell me about them,' said Rachel smiling, wondering if she might still escape. But Lady Newhaven had no intention of letting her go. She only wished to indicate to her her true position. And gradually, not without renewed outbursts of tears, not without traversing many layers of prepared conventional feelings in which a few thin streaks of genuine emotion were embedded, she told her story – the story of a young, high-minded, and neglected wife, and of a husband callous, indifferent, a scorner of religion, unsoftened even by the advent of the children – 'such sweet children, such little darlings' – and the gradual estrangement. Then came the persistent siege to the lonely heart of one not pretty perhaps, but fatally attractive to men; the lonely heart's unparalleled influence for good over the besieger.

'He would do anything,' said Lady Newhaven, looking earnestly at Rachel. 'My influence over him is simply boundless. If I said, as I sometimes did at balls, how sorry I was to see some plain girl standing out, he would go and dance with her. I have seen him do it.'

'I suppose he did it to please you.'

'That was just it, simply to please me.'

Rachel was not so astonished as Lady Newhaven expected. She certainly was rather wooden, the latter reflected. The story went on. It became difficult to tell, and, according to the teller, more and more liable to misconstruction. Rachel's heart ached as bit by bit the inevitable development was finally reached in floods of tears.

'And you remember that night you were at an evening party here,' sobbed Lady Newhaven, casting away all her mental notes and speaking extempore. 'It is just a fortnight ago, and I have not slept since, and *he* was here, looking so miserable (Rachel started slightly); he sometimes did, if he thought I was hard upon him. And afterwards, when every one had gone, Edward took him to his study and told him he had found us out, and they drew lots which should kill himself within five months – and I listened at the door.'

Lady Newhaven's voice rose half strangled, hardly human in a shrill grotesque whimper above the sobs which were shaking her. There was no affectation about her now.

Rachel's heart went out to her the moment she was natural. She knelt down and put her strong arms round her. The poor thing clung to her, and leaning her elaborate head against her, wept tears of real anguish upon her breast.

'And which drew the short lighter?' said Rachel at last.

'I don't know,' almost shrieked Lady Newhaven. 'It is that which is killing me. Sometimes I think it is Edward, and sometimes I think it is Hugh.'

At the name of Hugh Rachel winced. Lady Newhaven had mentioned no name in the earlier stages of her story while she had some vestige of self-command; but now at last the Christian name slipped out unawares.

Rachel strove to speak calmly. She told herself there were many Hughs in the world.

'Is Mr. Hugh Scarlett the man you mean?' she asked. If she had died for it, she must have asked that question.

'Yes,' said Lady Newhaven.

A shadow fell on Rachel's face, as on the face of one who suddenly discovers, not for the first time, an old enemy advancing upon him under the flag of a new ally.

'I shall always love him,' gasped Lady Newhaven, recovering herself sufficiently to recall a phrase which she had made up the night before. 'I look upon it as a spiritual marriage.'

CHAPTER VIII

A square-set man and honest.
                    TENNYSON.[39]

'DICK,' said Lord Newhaven, laying hold of that gentleman as he was leaving Tattersall's, 'what mischief have you been up to for the last ten days?'

'I lay low till I got my clothes,' said Dick, 'and then I went to the Duke of —. I've just been looking at a hack for him. He says he does not want one that takes a lot of sitting on. I met him the first night I landed. In fact, I stepped out of the train on to his royal toe travelling *incog*.[40] I was just going to advise him to draw in his feelers a bit, and give the Colonies a chance, when he turned round and I saw who it was. I knew him when I was A.D.C.[41] at Melbourne before I took to the drink. He said he thought he'd know my foot anywhere, and asked me down for -- races.'

'And you enjoyed it?'

'Rather. I did not know what to call the family at first, so I asked him if he had any preference and what was the right thing, and he told me how I must hop up whenever he came in, and all that sort of child's play. There was a large party and some uncommonly pretty women. And I won a tenner off his Royal Highness, and here I am.'

'And what are you going to do now?'

'Go down to the city and see what Darnell's cellars are like before I store my wine in them. It won't take long. Er! – I say, Cack – Newhaven?'

'Well?'

'Ought I to – how about my calling on Miss —. I never caught her name?'

'Miss West, the heiress?'

'Yes. Little attention on my part.'

'Did she ask you to call?'

'No, but I think it was an oversight. I expect she would like it.'

'Well, then, go and be – snubbed.'

'I don't want snubbing. A little thing like me wants encouragement.'

'A good many other people are on the look out for encouragement in that quarter.'

'That settles it,' said Dick, 'I'll go at once. I've got to call on Lady Susan Gresley, and I'll take Miss —'

'West. West. West.'

'Miss West on the way.'

'My dear fellow, Miss West does not live on the way to Working. Lady Susan Gresley died six months ago.'

'Great Scot! I never heard of it. And what has become of Hester? She is a kind of cousin of mine.'

'Miss Gresley has gone to live in the country a few miles from us, with her clergyman brother.'

'James Gresley. I remember him. He's a bad egg.'

'Now, Dick, are you in earnest, or are you talking nonsense about Miss West?'

'I'm in earnest.' He looked it.

'Then, for heaven's sake, don't put your foot in it by calling. My wife has taken a violent fancy to Miss West. I don't think it is returned, but that is a detail. If you want to give her a chance leave it to me.'

'I know what that means. You married men are mere sieves. You'll run straight home with your tongue out and tell Lady Newhaven that I want to marry Miss -, I can't clinch her name, and then she'll tell her when they are combing their back hair. And then if I find, later on, I don't like her and step off the grass I shall have behaved like a perfect brute, and all that sort of thing. A man I knew out in Melbourne told me that by the time he'd taken a little notice of a likely girl he'd gone too far to go back and he had to marry her.'

'You need not be so coy. I don't intend to mention the subject to my wife. Besides, I don't suppose Miss West will look at you. You're a wretched match for her. With her money she might marry a brewery or a peerage.'

'I'll put myself in focus anyhow,' said Dick. 'Hang it all. If you could get a woman to marry you, there is hope for everybody. I don't expect it will be as easy as falling off a log. But if she is what I take her to be I shall go for all I'm worth.'

Some one else was going for all he was worth. Lord Newhaven rode early, and he had frequently seen Rachel and Hugh riding together at foot's pace. Possibly his offer to help Dick was partly prompted by an unconscious desire to put a spoke in Hugh's wheel.

Dick, whose worst enemy could not accuse him of diffidence, proved a solid spoke but for a few days only. Rachel suddenly broke all her engagements and left London.

CHAPTER IX

Pour vivre tranquille il faut vivre loin des gens d'église.[42]

THERE is a little stream which flows through Middleshire which seems to reflect the spirit of that quiet county, so slow is its course, so narrow is its width. Even the roads don't take the trouble to bridge it. They merely hump themselves slightly when they feel it tickling underneath them, and go on, vouchsafing no further notice of its existence. Yet the Drone is a local celebrity in Middleshire, and, like most local celebrities, is unknown elsewhere. The squire's sons have lost immense trout in the Drone as it saunters through their lands, and most of them have duly earned thereby the distinction (in Middleshire) of being the best trout rod in England. Middleshire bristles with the 'best shots in England,' and the 'best preachers in England,' and the cleverest men in England. The apathetic Mother country knows, according to Middleshire, 'but little of her greatest men.' At present she associates her loyal county with a breed of small black pigs.

Through this favoured locality the Drone winds, and turns and turns again as if loth to leave the rich low meadow lands and clustering villages upon its way. After skirting the little town of Westhope and the gardens of Westhope Abbey, the Drone lays itself out in comfortable curves and twists innumerable through the length and breadth of the green country till it reaches Warpington, whose church is so near the stream that in time of flood the water hitches all kinds of things it has no further use for among the gravestones of the little churchyard. On one occasion, after repeated prayers for rain, it even overflowed the lower part of the vicar's garden, and vindictively carried away his beehives. But that was before he built the little wall at the bottom of the garden.

Slightly raised above the church, on ground held together by old elms, the white vicarage of Warpington stands, blinking ever through its trees at the church like a fond wife at her husband. Indeed, so like had she become to him that she had even developed a tiny bell-tower near the kitchen chimney, with a single bell in it, feebly rung by a female servant on saints days and G.F.S.[43] gatherings.

About eight o'clock on this particular morning in July the Drone could hear if it wanted to hear, which apparently no one else did, the high unmodulated voice in which Mr. Gresley was reading the morning service[44] to Mrs. Gresley, and to a young thrush which was hurling its person like an inexperienced bicyclist, now against Lazarus and his graveclothes, now against the legs of John the Baptist, with one foot on a river's edge, and the other firmly planted in a distant desert,[45] and against all the other scripture characters in turn which adorned the windows.

The service ended at last, and after releasing his unwilling congregation by catching and carrying it beak agape into the open air, Mr. Gresley and his wife walked through the churchyard – with its one melancholy Scotch fir embarrassed by its trouser of ivy – to the little gate which led into their garden.

They were a pleasing couple, seen at a little distance. He at least evidently belonged to a social status rather above that of the average clergyman, though his wife may not have done so. Mr. Gresley, with his long thin nose and his short upper lip and tall, well-set up figure, bore on his whole personality the stamp of that for which it is difficult to find the right name, so unmeaning has the right name become by dint of putting it to low uses – the maltreated, the travestied name of 'gentleman.'

None of those moral qualities, priggish or otherwise, are assumed for Mr. Gresley which we are told distinguish the true, the perfect gentleman, and some of which, thank heaven! the 'gentleman born' frequently lacks. Whether he had them or not was a matter of opinion, but he had that which some who have it not strenuously affirm to be of no value – the right outside.

To any one who looked beyond the first impression of good breeding and a well-cut coat, a second closer glance was discouraging. Mr. Gresley's suspicious eye and thin compressed lips hinted that both fanatic and saint were fighting for predominance in the kingdom of that pinched brain, the narrowness of which the sloping forehead betokened with such cruel plainness. He looked as if he would fling himself as hard against a truth without perceiving it, as a hunted hare against a stone wall. He was unmistakably of those who only see side issues.

Mrs. Gresley took her husband's arm as he closed the gate. She was still young and still pretty, in spite of the arduous duties of a clergyman's wife, and the depressing fact that she seemed always wearing out old finery. Perhaps her devotion to her husband had served to prolong her youth, for as the ivy is to the oak, and as the moon is to the sun, and as the river is to the sea, so was Mrs. Gresley to Mr. Gresley.

The fortunate couple were advancing through the garden looking fondly at their own vicarage, with their own sponges hanging out of their upper windows, and their offspring waving to them from a third, when a small slight figure appeared on the terrace.

'James!' said Mrs. Gresley with decision. 'It is your duty to speak to Hester about attending early service. If she can go out in the garden she can come to church.'

'I have spoken to her once,' said Mr. Gresley, frowning, 'and though I put it before her very plainly she showed great obstinacy. Fond as I am of Hester, I cannot shut my eyes to the fact that she has an arrogant and callous nature. But we must remember, my love, that Aunt Susan was most lax in all her views, and we must make allowance for Hester, who lived with her till last year. It is only natural that Hester, bred up from childhood in that worldly circle – dinner parties all through Lent, and Sunday luncheons[46] – should have fallen through want of solid church teaching into freethinking,[47] and ideas of her own upon religion.'

Mr. Gresley's voice was of that peculiar metallic note which carries further than the owner is aware. It rose, if contradicted, into a sort of continuous trumpet-blast which drowned all other lesser voices. Hester's little garret was two stories above Mr. Gresley's study on the ground floor, but nevertheless she often heard confused anxious parochial buzzings overwhelmed by that sustained high note which knew no cessation until objection or opposition ceased. As she came towards them, she heard with perfect distinctness what he was saying, but it did not trouble her. Hester was gifted with imagination, and imagination does not find it difficult to read by the short hand of the expressions and habitual opinions and repressions of others what they occasionally say at full length, and to which they fondly believe they are giving utterance for the first time. Mr. Gresley had said all this many times already by his manner, and it had by its vain repetitions lost its novelty. Mr. Gresley was fortunately not aware of this, for unimaginative persons believe themselves to be sealed books, as hermetically sealed as the characters of others are to themselves.

Hester was very like her brother. She had the same nose, slightly too long for her small face, the same short upper lip and light hair, only her brother's was straight and hers was crimped, as wet sand is crimped by a placid outgoing sea. That she had an equally strong will was obvious. But there the likeness ended. Hester's figure was slight, and she stooped a little. Hester's eyes were very gentle, very appealing under their long curled lashes. They were sad, too, as Mr. Gresley's never were, gay as his never were. An infinite patience looked out of them sometimes, that patience of enthusiasm which will cast away its very soul and all its best years for the sake of an ideal. Hester showed her age in her eyes. She was seven and twenty and appeared many years younger, until she looked at you.

Mrs. Gresley looked with veiled irritation at her sister-in-law in her clean holland gown, held in at the waist with a broad lilac ribbon, adroitly drawn in picturesque folds through a little silver buckle.

Mrs. Gresley, who had a waist which the Southminster dressmaker informed her had 'to be kept down,' made a mental note for the hundredth time that Hester 'laced in.'[48]

Hester gave that impression of 'finish' and sharpness of edge so rarely found among the blurred vague outlines of Englishwomen. There was nothing vague about her. Lord Newhaven said she had been cut out body and mind with a sharp pair of scissors. Her irregular profile, her delicate pointed speech and fingers, her manner of picking up her slender feet as she walked, her quick alert movements, everything about her was neat, adjusted, perfect in its way, yet without more apparent effort than the *succés fou*[49] in black and white of the water wagtail, which she so closely resembled.

'Good morning,' she said, turning back with them to the house. 'Abel says it is going to be the hottest day we have had yet. And the letter-bag is so fat that I could hardly refrain from opening it. Really, James, you ought to hide the key, or I shall succumb to temptation.'

Once in the days of her ignorance, when she first came to live at Warpington, Hester had actually turned the key in the lock of the sacred letter-bag when the Gresleys were both late, and had extracted her own letters. She never did it a second time. On the contrary, she begged pardon in real regret at having given such deep offence to her brother and his wife, and in astonishment that so simple an action could offend. She had made an equally distressing blunder in the early days of her life with the Gresleys by taking up the daily paper on its arrival in the afternoon.

'My dear Hester,' Mrs. Gresley said, really scandalised, 'I am sure you won't mind my saying so, but James has not seen his paper yet.'

'I have noticed he never by any chance looks at it till the evening, and you always say you never read it,' said Hester, deep in a political crisis.

'That is his rule, and a very good rule it is, but he naturally likes to be the *first* to look at it,' said Mrs. Gresley with a great exercise of patience. She had heard Hester was clever, but she found her very stupid. Everything had to be explained to her.

Her tone recalled Hester from the Indian tribal rising,[50] and the speech of the Prime Minister, to the realities of life. It was fortunate for her that she was quick-witted. These two flagrant blunders were sufficient for her. She grasped the principle that those who have a great love of power and little scope for it must necessarily exercise it in trivial matters. She extended the principle of the newspaper and the letter-bag over her entire intercourse with the Gresleys, and never offended in that manner again.

On this particular morning she waited decorously beside her brother as he opened the bag, and dealt out the contents into three heaps. Hester pounced on hers, and subsided into her chair at the breakfast-table.

'I wonder,' said Mrs. Gresley, looking at Hester's pile of letters over the top of her share of the morning's correspondence – namely, a list of Pryce Jones, 'that you care to write so many letters, Hester. I am sure I never did such a thing when I was a girl. I should have regarded it as a waste of time.'

'Ha!' said Mr. Gresley, in a gratified tone, opening a little roll. 'What have we here? Proofs! My paper upon 'Modern Dissent.'[51] I told Edwards I would not allow him to put it in his next number of the *Southminster Advertiser* until I had glanced at it in print. I don't know when I shall find time to correct it. I shall be out all the afternoon at the Chapter meeting.'[52]

He looked at Hester. She had laid down her letters and was taking a cup of coffee from Mrs. Gresley. She evidently had not heard her brother's remark.

'You and I must lay our heads together over this, Hester,' he said, holding up with some pride a long slip of proof. 'It will be just in your line. You might run it over after breakfast,' he continued, in high good humour, 'and put in the stops and grammar and spelling – you're more up in that sort of thing than I am – and then we will go through it together.'

Hester was quite accustomed, when her help was asked as to a composition, to receive as a reason for the request the extremely gratifying assurance that she was 'good' at punctuation and spelling. It gave the would-be author a comfortable feeling that after all he was only asking advice on the crudest technical matters on which Hester's superiority could be admitted without a loss of masculine self-respect.

'I would rather not tamper with punctuation and spelling,' said Hester, drily. 'I am so shaky on both myself. You had better ask the schoolmaster. He knows all that sort of A B C better than I do.'

Mr. Gresley frowned and looked suspiciously at her. He wanted Hester's opinion, of which she was perfectly aware. But she intended that he should ask for it.

Mrs. Gresley, behind the coffee-pot, felt that she was overlooked. She had helped Mr. Gresley with his numerous literary efforts until Hester came.

'I saw you correcting some one's manuscript last week,' he said. 'You were at it all day in the hay-field.'

'That was different. I was asked to criticise the style and composition.'

'Oh well!' said Mr. Gresley, 'don't let us split hairs. I don't want an argument about it. If you'll come into my study at ten o'clock I'll get it off my hands at once.'

'With pleasure,' said Hester, looking at him with rueful admiration. She had tried a hundred times to get the better of him in conversation, but she had not yet succeeded.

'I have a message for you,' continued Mr. Gresley, in restored good humour. 'Mrs. Loftus writes that she is returning to Wilderleigh at the end of the week, and that the sale of work[53] may take place in the Wilderleigh gardens at the end of August. And – let me see, I will read what she says:

'"I am not unmindful of our conversation on the duty of those who go annually to London to bring a spiritual influence to bear on society." – (I impressed that upon her before she went up.) – "We had a most interesting dinner-party last week, nearly all celebrated and gifted persons, and the conversation was really beyond anything I can describe to you. I thought my poor brain would turn. I was quite afraid to join in. But Mr. Harvey, the great Mr. Harvey, told me afterwards I was at my best. One lady, Miss Barker, who has done so much for the East End, is coming down to Wilderleigh shortly for a rest. I am anxious you should talk to her. She says she has doubts, and she is tired of the Bible. By the way, please tell Hester, with my love, that she and Mr. Harvey attacked 'The Idyll of East London' and showed it up entirely, and poor little me had to stand up for her against them all."'

'She would never do that,' said Hester, tranquilly. 'She might perhaps have said, "The writer is a friend of mine. I must stand up for her." But she would never have gone beyond saying it to doing it.'

'Hester,' exclaimed Mrs. Gresley, feeling that she might just as well have remained a spinster if she was to be thus ignored in her own house, 'I can't think how you can allow your jealousy of Sybell Loftus, for I can attribute it to nothing else, to carry you so far.'

'Perhaps it had better carry me into the garden,' said Hester, rising with the others. 'You must forgive me if I spoke irritably. I have a racking headache.'

'She looks ill,' said her brother, following Hester's figure with affectionate solicitude as she passed the window a moment later.

'And yet she does next to nothing,' said the hard-worked little wife, intercepting the glance. 'I always thought she wrote her stories in the morning. I know she is never about if the Pratt girls call to see her before luncheon. Yet when I ran up to her room yesterday morning to ask her to take Mary's music, as Fräulein had the headache' – (Mrs. Gresley always spoke of the headache and the toothache) – 'she was lying on her bed doing nothing at all.'

'She is very unaccountable,' said Mr. Gresley. 'Still, I can make allowance for the artistic temperament. I share it to a certain degree. Poor Hester. She is a spoilt child.'

'Indeed, James, she is. And she has an enormous opinion of herself. For my part, I think the Bishop is to blame for making so much of her. Have you never noticed how different she is when he is here, so gay and talkative, and when we are alone she hardly says a word for days together, except to the children.'

'She talked more when she first came,' said Mr. Gresley. 'But when she found I make it a rule to discourage argument' – (by argument Mr. Gresley meant difference of opinion) – 'she seemed gradually to lose interest in conversation. Yet I have heard the Bishop speak of her as a brilliant talker. And Lord Newhaven asked me last spring how I liked having a celebrity for a sister. A celebrity! Why, half the people in Middleshire don't even know of Hester's existence.' And the author of 'Modern Dissent' frowned.

'That was a hit at you, my dear,' said Mrs. Gresley. 'It was just after your pamphlet on 'Schism' appeared. Lord Newhaven always says something disagreeable. Don't you remember when you were thinking of exchanging Warpington for that Scotch living he said he knew you would not do it because with your feeling towards Dissent you would never go to a country where you would be a Dissenter yourself.'

'How about the proofs?' said Hester's voice through the open window. 'I am ready when you are, James.'

CHAPTER X

Wonderful power to benumb possesses this brother.

EMERSON.[54]

'OF course, Hester,' said Mr. Gresley, leading the way to his study and speaking in his lesson-for-the-day voice, 'I don't pretend to write' – ('They always say that,' thought Hester) – 'I have not sufficient leisure to devote to the subject to ensure becoming a successful author. And even if I had I am afraid I should not be willing to sell my soul to obtain popularity, for that is what it comes to in these days. The public must be pandered to. It must be amused. The public likes smooth

things, and the great truths – the only things I should care to write about – are
not smooth, far from it.'

'No, indeed.'

'This little paper on 'Dissent,' which I propose to publish in pamphlet form
after its appearance as a serial – it will run to two numbers in the *Southminster
Advertiser* – was merely thrown off in a few days when I had influenza, and could
not attend to my usual work.'

'It must be very difficult to work in illness,' said Hester, who had evidently
made a vow during her brief sojourn in the garden, and was now obviously going
through that process which the society of some of our fellow creatures makes as
necessary as it is fatiguing – namely, that of thinking before-hand what we are
going to say.

Mr. Gresley liked Hester immensely when she had freshly ironed herself flat
under one of these resolutions. He was wont to say that no one was pleasanter
than Hester when she was reasonable, or made more suitable remarks. He perceived with joy that she was reasonable now, and the brother and sister sat down
close together at the writing-table with the printed sheets between them.

'I will read aloud,' said Mr. Gresley, 'and you can follow me, and stop me if
you think – er – the sense is not quite clear.'

'I see.'

The two long noses, the larger freckled one surmounted by a *pince-nez*, the
other slightly pink as if it had absorbed the tint of the blotting-paper over which
it was so continually poised, both bent over the sheets.

Through the thin wall which separated the schoolroom from the study came
the sound of Mary's scales. Mary was by nature a child of wrath, as far as music
was concerned, and Fraülein – anxious, musical Fraülein – was strenuously
endeavouring to impart to her pupil the rudiments of what was her chief joy in
life.

'Modern Dissent,' read aloud Mr. Gresley, 'by Veritas.'[55]

'*Veritas!*' repeated Hester. Astonishment jerked the word out of her before
she was aware. She pulled herself hastily together.

'Certainly,' said the author, looking at his sister through his glasses, which
made the pupils of his eyes look as large as the striped marbles on which Mary
and Regie spent their pennies. 'Veritas,' he continued, 'is a Latin word signifying
Truth.'

'So I fancied. But is not Truth rather a *large* name to adopt as a *nom de
guerre?*[56] Might it not seem rather – er – in a layman it would appear arrogant.'

'I am not a layman, and I do not pretend to write on subjects of which I am
ignorant,' said Mr. Gresley with dignity. 'This is not a work of fiction. I don't
imagine this, or fancy that, or invent the other. I merely place before the public
forcibly and in a novel manner a few great truths.'

Mary was doing her finger exercises. C C C with the thumb, D D D with the first finger. Fraülein was repeating, 'Won! Two! Free! Won! Two! Free!' with a new intonation of cheerful patience at each repetition.

'Ah!' said Hester. 'A few great truths. Then the name must be Veritas. You would not reconsider it.'

'Certainly not,' said Mr. Gresley, his eye challenging hers. 'It is the name I am known by as the author of "Schism."'

'I had momentarily forgotten "Schism,"' said Hester dropping her glance.

'I went through a good deal of obloquy about "Schism,"' said Mr. Gresley with pride, 'and I should not wonder if "Modern Dissent" caused quite a ferment in Middleshire. If it does I am willing to bear a little spite and ill-will. All history shows that truth is met at first by opposition. Half the country clergy round here are asleep. Good men, but lax. They want waking up. I said as much to the Bishop the other day, and he agreed with me, for he said that if some of his younger clergy could be waked up to a sense of their own arrogance and narrowness he would hold a public thanksgiving in the cathedral. But he added that he thought nothing short of the last trump would do it.'

'I agree with him,' said Hester, having first said the sentence to herself, and having decided it was innocuous.

The climax of the music lesson had arrived. 'The Blue Bells of Scotland'[57] – the sole *Klavier Stück*[58] which Mary's rigidly extended little starfishes of hands could wrench out of the schoolroom piano – was at its third bar.

'Well,' said Mr. Gresley, refreshed by a cheering retrospect. 'Now for "Modern Dissent."'

A strenuous hour ensued.

Hester was torn in different directions, at one moment tempted to allow the most flagrant passages to pass unchallenged rather than attempt the physical impossibility of interrupting the reader only to be drawn into a dispute with him, at another burning to save her brother from the consequences which wait on certain utterances.

Presently Mr. Gresley's eloquence, after various tortuous and unnatural windings, swept in the direction of a pun, as a carriage after following the artificial curves of a deceptive approach nears a villa. Hester had seen the pun coming for half a page, as we see the villa through the trees long before we are allowed to approach it, and she longed to save her brother from what was in her eyes as much a degradation as a *tu quoque*.[59] But she remembered in time that the Gresleys considered she had no sense of humour, and she decided to let it pass. Mr. Gresley enjoyed it so much himself that he hardly noticed her fixed countenance.

Why does so deep a gulf separate those who have a sense of humour and those who, having none, are compensated by the conviction that they possess it more abundantly. The crevasse seems to extend far inland to the very heights and water-sheds of character. Those who differ on humour will differ on principles. The Gresleys and the Pratts belonged to that large class of our fellow creatures, who, conscious of a genius for adding to the hilarity of our sad planet, discover an irresistible piquancy in putting a woman's hat on a man's head, and in that 'verbal romping' which playfully designates a whisky and soda as a gargle, and says 'au reservoir' instead of 'au revoir.'[60]

At last, however, Hester nervously put her hand over the next sheet, as he read the final words of the last.

'Wait a moment,' she said hurriedly. 'This last page, James. Might it not be well to reconsider it? Is it politic to assume such great ignorance on the part of Nonconformists? Many I know are better educated than I am.'

'My dear,' said Mr. Gresley, 'ignorance is at the root of any difference of opinion on such a subject as this. I do not say wilful ignorance, but the want of sound Church teaching. I must cut at the roots of this ignorance.'

'Dear James, it is thrice killing the slain. No one believes these fallacies which you are exposing; the Nonconformists least of all. Those I have talked with don't hold these absurd opinions that you put down to them. You don't even touch their real position. You are elaborately knocking down ninepins that have never stood up because they have nothing to stand on.'

'I am not proposing to play a game of mental skittles,' said the clerical author. 'It is enough for me, as I said before, to cut at the roots of ignorance wherever I see it flourishing, not to pull off the leaves one by one as you would have me to do by dissecting their opinions. This may not be novel, it may not even be amusing, but nevertheless, Hester, a clergyman's duty is to wage unceasing war against spiritual ignorance. And what,' read on Mr. Gresley, after a triumphant moment in which Hester remained silent, 'is the best means of coping against ignorance, against darkness' – ('It was a root a moment ago,' thought Hester) – 'but by the infusion of light? The light shineth in darkness, and the darkness comprehendeth it not.'[61] Half a page more and the darkness was modern Dissent. Hester put her hand over her mouth and kept it there.

The familiar drama of a clerical bull and a red rag[62] was played out before her eyes, and, metaphorically speaking, she followed the example of the majority of laymen, and crept up a tree to be out of the way.

When it was all over she came down trembling.

'Well! what do you think of it?' said Mr. Gresley, rising and pacing up and down the room.

'You hit very hard,' said Hester, after a moment's consideration. She did not say 'You strike home.'

'I have no opinion of being mealy mouthed,' said Mr. Gresley, who was always perfectly satisfied with a vague statement. 'If you have anything worth saying say it plainly. That is my motto. Don't hint this or that, but take your stand upon a truth and strike out.'

'Why not hold out our hands to our fellow creatures instead of striking at them?' said Hester, moving towards the door.

'I have no belief in holding out our hands to the enemies of Christ,' Mr. Gresley began, who in the course of his pamphlet had thus gracefully designated the great religious bodies who did not view Christianity through the convex glasses of his own mental *pince-nez*. 'In these days we see too much of that. I leave that to the Broad Church[63] who want to run with the hare and hunt with the hounds.[64] I, on the contrary –'

But Hester had vanished.

There was a dangerous glint in her grey eyes, as she ran up to her little attic.

'According to him, our Lord must have been the first Nonconformist,' she said to herself. 'If I had stayed a moment longer I should have said so. For once I got out of the room in time.'

Hester's attic was blisteringly hot. It was over the kitchen, and through the open window came the penetrating aroma of roast mutton newly wedded to boiled cabbage. Hester had learned during the last six months all the variations of smells, evil, subtle, nauseous, and overpowering, of which the preparation of food – and still worse the preparation of chicken food – is capable. She seized her white hat and umbrella and fled out of the house.

She moved quickly across a patch of sunlight, looking, with her large white, pink-lined umbrella, like a travelling mushroom on a slender stem, and only drew rein in the shady walk near the beehives, where the old gardener Abel was planting something large in the way of 'runners' or 'suckers,'[65] making a separate hole for each with his thumb.

Abel was a solid, pear-shaped man, who passed through life bent double over the acre of Vicarage garden, to which he committed long lines of seeds, which an attentive Providence brought up in due season as 'curly kebbidge,' or 'salary,' or 'sparrow-grass.'[66]

Abel had his back towards Hester, and only the corduroy half of him was visible as he stooped over his work. Occasionally he could be induced to straighten himself, and – holding himself strongly at the hinge, with earth-ingrained hands – to discourse on politics and religion, and to opine that our policy in China[67] was 'neither my eye nor my elber.' 'The little lady,' as he called Hester, had a knack of drawing out Abel; but to-day, as he did not see her, she slipped past him, and crossing the churchyard sat down for a moment in the porch to regain her breath, under the card of printed texts offered for the consideration of his flock by their young pastor.

'How dreadful is this place. This is none other but the house of God,'[68] was the culling from the Scriptures which headed the selection.* Hester knew that card well, though she never by any chance looked at it. She had offended her brother deeply by remonstrating, or, as he called it, by 'interfering in church matters,' when he nailed it up. After a few minutes she dropped over the low churchyard wall into the meadow below, and flung herself down on the grass in the short shadow of a yew near at hand. What little air there was to be had came to her across the Drone, together with the sound of the water lazily nudging the bank, and whispering to the reeds little jokelets which they had heard a hundred times before.

Hester's irritable nerves relaxed. She stretched out her small neatly shod foot in front of her, leaned her back against the wall, and presently could afford to smile.

'Dear James,' she said, shaking her head gently to and fro, 'I wish we were not both writers, or, as he calls it, 'dabblers with the pen.' One dabbler in a Vicarage is quite enough.'

She took out her letters and read them. Only half of them had been opened.

'I shall stay here till the luncheon bell rings,' she said as she settled herself comfortably.

Rachel's letter was read last, on the principle of keeping the best to the end.

'And so she is leaving London – isn't this rather sudden? – and coming down at once – to-day – no, yesterday, to Southminster, to the Palace. And I am to stay in this afternoon, as she will come over, and probably the Bishop will come too. I should be glad if I were not so tired.'

Hester looked along the white high road which led to Southminster. In the hot haze she could just see the two ears of the cathedral pricking up through the blue. Everything was very silent, so silent that she could hear the church clock of Slumberleigh, two miles away, strike twelve. A whole hour before luncheon!

The miller's old white horse with a dip in his long back and a corresponding curve in his under outline, was standing motionless in the sun, fast asleep, his front legs bent like a sailor's.

A little bunch of red and white cows knee-deep in the water were swishing off the flies with the wet tufts of their tails. Hester watched their every movement. She was no longer afraid of cows. Presently, as if with one consent, they all made up their minds to relieve the tedium of the contemplative life by an exhibition of humour, and scrambling out of the water proceeded to canter along the bank with stiff raised tails, with an artificial noose sustained with difficulty just above the tuft.

---

*   A card, headed by the above text, was seen by the writer in August 1898, in the porch of a country church.

'How like James and the Pratts,' Hester said to herself, watching the grotesque gambols and nudgings of the dwindling humorists. 'It must be very fatiguing to be so comic.'

Hester had been up since five o'clock, utilising the quiet hours before the house was astir. She was tired out. A 'bumble bee' was droning sleepily near at hand. The stream talked and talked and talked about what he was going to do when he was a river. 'How tired the banks must be of listening to him,' thought Hester with closed eyes.

And the world melted slowly away in a delicious sense of well-being, from which the next moment, as it seemed to her, she was suddenly awakened by Mr. Gresley's voice near at hand.

'Hester! *Hester!* HESTER!'

'Here! Here!' gasped Hester with a start, upsetting her lapful of letters, as she scrambled hastily to her feet.

The young Vicar drew near, and looked over the churchyard wall. A large crumb upon his upper lip did not lessen the awful severity of his countenance.

'We have nearly finished luncheon,' he observed. 'The servants could not find you anywhere. I don't want to be always finding fault, Hester, but I wish for your own sake as well as ours you would be more punctual at meals.'

Hester had never been late before, but she felt that this was not the moment to remind her brother of that fact.

'I beg pardon,' she said humbly. 'I feel asleep.'

'You fell asleep!' said Mr. Gresley, who had been wrestling all the morning with platitudes on *Thy will be done.*[69] 'All I can say, Hester, is that it is unfortunate you have no occupation. I cannot believe it is for the good of any of us to lead so absolutely idle a life that we fall asleep in the morning.'

Hester made no reply.

CHAPTER XI

It is as useless to fight against the interpretations of ignorance as to whip the fog.

GEORGE ELIOT.[70]

THE children, who had reached the pear stage, looked with round awed eyes at 'Auntie Hester' as she sat down at the luncheon table, beside the black bottle which marked her place. The Gresleys were ardent total abstainers,[71] and were of opinion that Hester's health would be greatly benefited by following their example. But Hester's doctor differed from them – he was extremely obstinate – with the result that the Gresleys were obliged to tolerate the obnoxious bottle on their very table. It was what Mrs. Gresley called a 'cross,' and Mr. Gresley was always afraid that the fact of its presence might become known and hopelessly misconstrued in Warpington and the world at large.

The children knew that Hester was in disgrace, as she vainly tried to eat the congealed slice of roast mutton with blue slides in it, which had been put before her chair half an hour ago, when the joint was sent out for the servants' dinner. The children liked 'Auntie Hester,' but without enthusiasm, except Regie, the eldest, who loved her as himself. She could tell them stories, and make butter-flies and horses and dogs out of paper, but she could never join in their games, not even in the delightful new ones she invented for them. She was always tired directly. And she would never give them rides on her back, as the large good-natured Pratt girls did. And she was dreadfully shocked if they did not play fair, so much so, that on one occasion Mr. Gresley had to interfere, and to remind her that a game was a game, and that it would be better to let the children play as they liked than to be perpetually finding fault with them.

Perhaps nothing in her life at the Vicarage was a greater trial to Hester than to see the rules of fair play broken by the children with the connivance of their parents. Mr. Gresley had never been to a public school, and had thus missed the A B C of what in its later stages is called 'honour.' He was an admirable hockey player, but he was not in request at the frequent Slumberleigh matches, for he never hit off fair,[72] or minded being told so.

'Auntie Hester is leaving all her fat,' said Mary suddenly in a shrill voice, her portion of pear held in her left cheek as she spoke. She had no idea that she ought not to draw attention to the weakness of others. She was only anxious to be the first to offer interesting information.

'Never mind,' said Mrs. Gresley, admiring her own moderation. 'Finish your pear.'

If there was one thing more than another in Hester's behaviour that annoyed Mrs. Gresley – and there were several others – it was Hester's manner of turning her food over on her plate, and leaving half of it.

Hester did it again now, and Mrs. Gresley, already irritated by her unpunctu-ality, tried to look away so as not to see her and prayed for patience. The hundred a year which Hester contributed to the little establishment had eased the strug-gling household in many ways; but Mrs. Gresley sometimes wondered if the money, greatly needed as it was, counterbalanced the perpetual friction of her sister-in-law's presence.

'Father!'

'Yes, my son.'

'Isn't it wrong to drink wine?'

'Yes, my son.'

'Then why does Auntie Hester drink it?'

Hester fixed her eyes intently on her brother. Would he uphold her before the children?

'Because she thinks it does her good,' said Mr. Gresley.

She withdrew her eyes. Her hand, holding a spoonful of cold rice pudding, shook. A delicate colour flooded her face, and finally settled in the tip of her nose. In her own way she loved the children.

'Ach, mein Herr,' almost screamed Fräulein, who adored Hester, and saw the gravity of the occasion, 'aber Sie vergessen[73] that the Herr Doctor Br-r-r-r-own has so strong – so very strong command –'

'I cannot allow a discussion as to the merits or demerits of alcohol at my table,' said Mr. Gresley. 'I hold one opinion, Dr. Brown holds another. I must beg to be allowed to differ from him. Children, say grace.'[74]

It was Wednesday and a half-holiday, and Mrs. Gresley had arranged to take the children in the pony-carriage to be measured for new boots. These expeditions to Westhope were a great event. At two o'clock exactly the three children rushed downstairs, Regie bearing in his hand his tin moneybox, in which a single coin could be heard to leap. Hester produced a bright threepenny piece for each child, one of which was irretrievably buried in Regie's money-box, and the other two immediately lost in the mat in the pony-carriage. However, Hester found them, and slipped them inside their white gloves, and the expedition started, accompanied by Boulou, a diminutive yellow and white dog of French extraction. Boulou was a well-meaning, kind little soul. There was a certain hurried arrogance about his hind legs, but it was only manner. He was not in reality more conceited than most small dogs who wear their tails high.

Hester saw them drive off, and a few minutes later Mr. Gresley started on his bicycle for a ruri-diaconal Chapter meeting[75] in the opposite direction. She heard the Vicarage gate 'clink' behind him as she crossed the little hall, and then she suddenly stopped short and wrung her hands. She had forgotten to tell either of them that the Bishop of Southminster was going to call that afternoon. She knew he was coming on purpose to see her, but this would have been incredible to the Gresleys. She had not read Rachel's letter announcing his coming till she had taken refuge in the field where she had fallen asleep, and her mental equilibrium had been so shaken by the annoyance she felt she had caused the Gresleys at luncheon that she had entirely forgotten the subject till this moment.

She darted out of the house and flew down the little drive. But Fortune frowned on Hester to-day. She reached the turn of the road only to see the bent figure of Mr. Gresley whisk swiftly out of sight, his clerical coat-tails flowing gracefully out behind like a divided skirt on each side of the back wheel.

Hester toiled back to the house breathless and dusty, and ready to cry with vexation. 'They will never believe I forgot to tell them,' she said to herself. 'Everything I do is wrong in their eyes and stupid in my own.' And she sat down on the lowest step of the stairs, and leaned her head against the banisters.

To her presently came a ministering angel in the shape of Fraülein, who had begged an egg from the cook, had boiled it over her spirit lamp, and now presented it with effusion to her friend on a little tray, with two thin slices of bread and butter.

'You are all goodness, Fraülein,' said Hester, raising her small haggard face out of her hands. 'It is wrong of me to give so much trouble.' She did not want the egg, but she knew its oval was the only shape in which Fraülein could express her silent sympathy. So she accepted it gratefully, and ate it on the stairs, with the tenderly severe Fraülein watching every mouthful.

Life did not seem quite such a hopeless affair when the little meal was finished. There were breaks in the clouds after all. Rachel was coming to see her that afternoon. Hester was, as Fraülein often said, 'easy cast down, and easy cast up.' The mild stimulant of the egg 'cast her up' once more. She kissed Fraülein and ran up to her room, where she divested her small person of every speck of dust contracted on the road, smoothed out an invisible crease in her holland gown, put back the little ring of hair behind her ear which had become loosened in her rush after her brother, and then came down smiling and composed to await her friend in the drawing-room.

Hester seldom sat in the drawing-room, partly because it was her sister-in-law's only sitting-room, and partly because it was the regular haunt of the Pratt girls, who (with what seemed to Hester dreadful familiarity) looked in at the windows when they came to call, and, if they saw any one inside, entered straightway by the same, making retreat impossible.

The Miss Pratts had been willing, when Hester first came into the neighbourhood, to take a good-natured though precarious interest in 'their Vicar's sister.' Indeed, Mrs. Gresley had felt obliged to warn Hester not to count too much on their attentions, 'as they sometimes dropped people as quickly as they took them up.'

Hester was ignorant of country life, of its small society, its inevitable relations with unsympathetic neighbours just because they were neighbours; and she was specially ignorant of the class to which Mrs. Gresley and the Pratts belonged, and from which her aunt had in her lifetime unwisely guarded her niece as from the plague. She was amazed at first at the Pratts calling her by her Christian name without her leave, until she discovered that they spoke of the whole county by their Christian names, even designating Lord Newhaven's two younger brothers – with whom they were not acquainted – as Jack and Harry, though they were invariably called by their own family John and Henry.

When after her aunt's death she had, by the advice of her few remaining relatives, taken up her abode with her brother, as much on his account as her own, for he was poor and with an increasing family, she journeyed to Warpington accompanied by a pleasant feeling that at any rate she was not going among strangers. She had often visited in Middleshire, at Wilderleigh, in the elder Mr. Loftus' time, for whom she had entertained an enthusiastic reverence; at Westhope Abbey, where she had a firm ally in Lord Newhaven, and at several other Middleshire houses. She was silly enough to think she knew Middleshire fairly well, but after she settled at Warpington she gradually discovered the existence of a large under-current of society of which she knew nothing at all, in which, whether she were willing or not, she was plunged by the fact that she was her brother's sister.

Hester perceived clearly enough that her brother did not by birth belong to this set, though his profession brought him in contact with it, but he had evidently though involuntarily adopted it for better for worse;[76] perhaps because a dictatorial habit is generally constrained to find companionship in a social grade lower than its own, where a loud voice and a tendency to monologue chequered by prehistoric jokes and tortured puns may meet with a more patient audience. Hester made many discoveries about herself during the first months of her life at Warpington, and the first of the series amazed her more than any of the later ones.

She discovered that she was proud. Perhaps she had not the enormous opinion of herself which Mrs. Gresley so frequently deplored, for Hester's thoughts seldom dwelt upon herself. But the altered circumstances of her life forced them momentarily upon herself nevertheless, as a burst pipe will spread its waters down a damask curtain.

So far, during the eight years since she had left the schoolroom, she had always been 'Miss Gresley,' a little personage treated with consideration wherever she went, and *choyée*[77] for her delicate humour and talent for conversation. She now experienced the interesting sensation, as novel to her as it is familiar to most of us, of being nobody, and she disliked it. The manners of the set in which she found herself also grated continually on her fastidious taste. She was first amazed and then indignant at hearing her old Middleshire friends, whose simplicity far surpassed that of her new acquaintance, denounced by the latter – without being acquainted with them except officially – as 'fine,' as caring only for 'London people,' and as being 'tuft-hunters,'[78] because they frequently entertained at their houses persons of rank, to half of whom they were related. All this was new to Hester. She discovered that, though she might pay visits at these houses, she must never mention them, as it was considered the height of vulgarity to speak of people of rank.

Mrs. Gresley, who had been quite taken aback when the first of these invitations came, felt it her duty to warn Hester against a love of rank, reminding her that it was a very bad thing to get a name for running after titled people.

'James and I have always kept clear of that,' she remarked with dignity. 'For my part, I daresay you will think me very old-fashioned, but I must own I never can see that people with titles or wealth are one bit nicer or pleasanter than those without them.'

Hester agreed.

'And,' continued Mrs. Gresley, 'it has always been our aim to be independent, not to bow down before any one. If I am unworldly, it is because I had the advantage of parents who impressed on me the hollowness of all social distinctions. If the Pratts were given a title to-morrow I should behave exactly the same to them as I do now.'

If Lady Susan Gresley had passed her acquaintance through a less exclusive sieve, Hester might have had the advantage of hearing all these well-worn sentiments, and of realising the point of view of a large number of her fellow creatures before she became an inconspicuous unit in their midst.

But if Mrs. Gresley was pained by Hester's predilection for the society of what she called 'swells'[79] (the word though quite extinct in civilised parts can occasionally be found in country districts), she was still more pained by the friendships Hester formed with persons whom her sister in-law considered 'not quite.'

Mrs. Gresley was always perfectly civil, and the Pratts imperfectly so to Miss Brown, the doctor's invalid sister. But Hester made friends with her, in spite of the warnings of Mrs. Gresley that kindness was one thing and intimacy another.

'The truth is,' Mrs. Gresley would say, 'Hester loves adulation, and as she can't get it from the Pratts and us, she has to go to those below her in the social scale, like Miss Brown, who will give it to her. Miss Brown may be very cultivated. I dare say she is, but she makes up to Hester.'

Sybell Loftus, who lived close at hand at Wilderleigh, across the Drone, was one of the very few besides Miss Brown among her new acquaintants who hailed Hester at once as a kindred spirit, to the unconcealed surprise of the Pratts and the Gresleys. Sybell adored Hester's book, which the Gresleys and Pratts considered rather peculiar 'as emanating from the pen of a clergyman's sister.' She enthusiastically suggested to Hester several improvements which might easily be made in it, which would have changed its character altogether. She even entrenched on the sacred precinct of a married woman's time to write out the openings of several romances, which she was sure Hester with her wonderful talent could build up into magnificent works of art. She was always running over to the Vicarage to confide to Hester the unique thoughts which had been vouchsafed to her while contemplating a rose, or her child or her husband, or all three together.

Hester was half amused, half fascinated, and ruefully lost many of the mornings still left her by the Pratts and Gresleys, in listening to the outpourings of this butterfly soul which imagined every flower it involuntarily alighted on and drew honey from to be its own special production.

But Hester's greatest friend in Middleshire was the Bishop of Southminster, with whom Rachel was staying, and whom she was expecting this afternoon.

CHAPTER XII

The depth and dream of my desire,
The bitter paths wherein I stray,
Thou knowest Who has made the Fire,
Thou knowest Who has made the Clay!

RUDYARD KIPLING.[80]

THE unbalanced joys and sorrows of emotional natures are apt to arouse the pity of the narrow-hearted, and the mild contempt of the obtuse of their fellow creatures.

But perhaps it is a mistake to feel compassion for persons like Hester, for if they have many evil days and weeks in their usually short lives, they have also moments of sheer bliss, hours of awed contemplation and of exquisite rapture which possibly in the long run equal the more solid joys of a good income and a good digestion, nay, even the perennial glow of that happiest of happy temperaments which limits the nature of others by its own, which sees no uncomfortable difference between a moral and a legal right, and believes it can measure life with the same admirable accuracy with which it measures its drawing-room curtains.

As Hester and Rachel sat together in the Vicarage drawing-room, Rachel's faithful dog-like eyes detected no trace of tears in Hester's dancing, mischievous ones. They were alone, for the Bishop had dropped Rachel on his way to visit a sick clergyman, and had arranged to call at the Vicarage on his way back.

Hester quickly perceived that Rachel did not wish to talk of herself, and drew a quaint picture of her own life at Warpington, which she described 'not wisely but too well.'[81] But she was faithful to her salt. She said nothing of the Gresleys to which those worthies could have objected had they been present. Indeed, she spoke of them in what they would have termed 'a very proper manner,' of their kindness to her when she had been ill, of how Mr. Gresley had himself brought up her breakfast tray every morning, and how in the spring he had taught her to bicycle.

'But oh! Rachel,' added Hester, 'during the last nine months my self-esteem has been perforated with wounds, each large enough to kill the poor creature. My life here has shown me horrible faults in myself of which I never dreamed. I feel as if I had been ironed all over since I came here, and all kinds of ugly words in invisible ink are coming out clear in the process.'

'I am quite alarmed,' said Rachel tranquilly.

'You ought to be. First of all I did think I cared nothing about food. I don't remember ever giving it a thought when I lived with Aunt Susan. But here I – I am difficult about it. I do try to eat it, but often I really can't. And then I leave it on my plate, which is a disgusting habit which always offends me in other people. Now I am as bad as any of them; indeed, it is worse in me because I know poor James is not very rich.'

'I suppose the cooking is vile?'

'I don't know. I never noticed what I ate till I came here, so I can't judge. Perhaps it is not very good. But the dreadful part is that I should mind. I could not have believed it of myself. James and Minna never say anything, but I know it vexes them, as of course it must.'

Rachel looked critically at Hester's innocent, childlike face. When Hester was not a cultivated woman of the world she was a child. There was, alas! no medium in her character. Rachel noticed how thin her face and hands had become, and the strained look in the eyes. The faint colour in her cheek had a violet tinge.

She did not waste words on the cookery question. She saw plainly enough that Hester's weak health was slipping further down the hill.

'And all this time you have been working?'

'If you call it working. I used to call it so once, but I never do now. Yes, I manage about four hours a day. I have made another pleasant discovery about myself, that I have the temper of a fiend if I am interrupted.'

'But surely you told the Gresleys when first you came that you must not be interrupted at certain hours?'

'I did. I did. But of course – it is very natural – they think that rather self-important and silly. I am thought very silly here, Rachel. And James does not mind being interrupted in writing his sermons. And the Pratts have got the habit of running in in the mornings.'

'Who on earth are the Pratts?'

'They are what *they* call 'county people.' Their father made a fortune in oil, and built a house covered with turrets near here a few years ago. I used to know Captain Pratt, the son, very slightly in London. I never would dance with him. He used to come to our 'At Homes,' but he was never asked to dinner.[82] He is a great 'parti'[83] among a certain set down here. His mother and sisters were very kind to me when I came, but I was not so accustomed then as I am now to be treated familiarly and called 'Hessie,' which no one has ever called me before, and I am afraid I was not so responsive as I see now I ought to have been. Down here it seems your friends are the people whom you live near, not the ones you like. It seems a curious arrangement. And as the Pratts are James' and Minna's greatest friends, I did not wish to offend them. And then, of course, I did offend them mortally at last by losing my temper when they came up to my room to what they called 'rout me out,' though I had told them I was busy in the mornings. I was in a very difficult place, and when they came in I did not know who they were, because only the people in the book were real just then. And then when I recognised them, and the scene in my mind which I had been waiting for for weeks was shattered like a pane of glass, I became quite giddy and spoke wildly. And then – I was so ashamed afterwards – I burst into tears of rage and despair.'

Even the remembrance was too much. Hester wiped away two large tears on to a dear little handkerchief just large enough to receive them, and went on with a quaver in her voice.

'I was so shocked at myself that I found it quite easy to tell them next day that I was sorry I had lost my temper, but they have not been the same since. Not that I wanted them to be the same. I would rather they were different. But I was anxious to keep on cordial terms with Minna's friends. She quarrels with them herself, but that is different. I suppose it is inevitable if you are on terms of great intimacy with people you don't really care for.'

'At any rate, *they* have not interrupted you again?'

'N – no. But still, I was often interrupted. Minna has too much to do, and she is not strong just now,[84] and she often sends up one of the children, and I was so nearly fierce with one of them, poor little things, that I felt the risk was becoming too great, so I have left off writing between breakfast and luncheon, and I get up directly it is light instead. It is light very early now. Only the worst part of it is that I am so tired for the rest of the day that I can hardly drag myself about.'

Rachel said nothing. She seldom commented on the confidences that were made to her. She saw that Hester, always delicate, was making an enormous effort under conditions which would be certain to entail disastrous effects on her health. The book was sapping her strength like a vampire, and the Gresleys were evidently exhausting it still further by unconsciously strewing her path with difficulties. Rachel did not know them, but she supposed they belonged to that large class whose eyes are holden.[85]

'And the book itself? Is is nearly finished?.'

Hester's face changed. Eagerly, shyly, enthusiastically, she talked to her friend about the book, as a young girl talks of her lover. Everything else was forgotten. Hester's eyes burned. Her colour came and went. She was transfigured.

The protecting anxious affection died out of Rachel's face as she looked at Hester, and gave place to a certain wistful, half envious admiration. She had *once* been shaken by all these emotions herself, years ago, when she was in love. She had regarded them as a revelation while they lasted; and – afterwards – as a steep step, a very steep step upon the stair of life. But she realised now that such as Hester live constantly in the world which the greater number of us can only enter when human passion lends us the key; the world at which, when the gates are shut against us, the coarser minded among us are not ashamed to level their ridicule and contempt.

Hester spoke brokenly with awe and reverence of her book, as of some mighty presence, some constraining power outside herself. She saw it complete, beautiful, an entrancing vision, inaccessible as a sunset.

'I cannot reach up to it. I cannot get near it,' she said. 'When I try to write it it is like drawing an angel with spread wings with a bit of charcoal. I understate everything. Yet I labour day by day travestying it, caricaturing the beautiful thoughts that come into my mind. I make everything commonplace and vulgar by putting it into words. I go along into the woods and sit for hours quite still with the trees. And gradually I understand and know. And I listen and Nature speaks, really speaks – not a *façon de parler*[86] as some people think who explain to you that you mean this or that by your words which you don't mean – and her spirit becomes one with my spirit. And I feel I can never again misunderstand her, never again fail to interpret her, never again wander so far away from her that every white anemone, and every seedling fern disowns me, and waits in silence till the alien has gone from among them. And I come home, Rachel, and I try, sometimes I try for half the night, to find words to translate it into. But there are no words, or if there are I cannot find them, and at last I fall back on some coarse simile, and in my despair I write it down. And Oh! Rachel, the worst is that presently, when I have forgotten what it ought to have been, when the vision fades, I know I shall *admire* what I have written. It is that that breaks my heart.'

The old, old lament of those who worship art, that sternest mistress in the world, fell into the silence of the little drawing-room. Rachel understood it in part only, for she had always vaguely felt that Hester idealised Nature, as she idealised her fellow-creatures, as she idealised everything, and she did not comprehend why Hester was in despair because she could not speak adequately of life or Nature as she saw them. Rachel thought with bewilderment that that was just what she could do.

At this moment a carriage drew up at the door, and after a long interval, during which the wrathful voice of the cook could be distinctly heard through the kitchen window recalling 'Hemma' to a sense of duty from the backyard, 'Hemma' breathlessly ushered in the Bishop of Southminster.

CHAPTER XIII

Originality irritates the religious classes, who will not be taken out of their indolent ways of thinking; who have a standing grievance against it, and heresy and heterodoxy are bad words ready for it.

W.W. Peyton.[87]

THE Bishop was an undersized, spare man, with a rugged, weather-beaten face and sinewy frame. If you had seen him working a crane in a stonemason's yard, or leading a cut-and-thrust forlorn-hope, or sailing paper-boats with a child, you would have felt he was the right man in the right place. That he was also in his right place as a bishop had never been doubted by any one. Mr. Gresley was the only person who had occasionally had misgivings as to the Bishop's vocation as a true priest, but he had put them aside as disloyal.

Jowett is believed to have said, 'A Bishop without a sense of humour is lost.'[88] Perhaps that may have been one of the reasons why, by Jowett's advice, the See of Southminster was offered to its present occupant. The Bishop's mouth, though it spoke of an indomitable will, had a certain twist of the lip, his deep-set, benevolent eyes had a certain twinkle which made persons like Lord Newhaven and Hester hail him at once as an ally, but which ought to have been a danger-signal to some of his clerical brethren – to Mr. Gresley in particular.

The Bishop respected and upheld Mr. Gresley as a clergyman, but as a conversationalist the young Vicar wearied him. If the truth were known (which it never was) he had arranged to visit Hester when he knew Mr. Gresley would be engaging the reluctant attention of a ruri-diaconal meeting.

He gave a sigh of relief as he became aware that Hester and Rachel were the only occupants of the cool, darkened room. Mrs. Gresley, it seemed, was also out.

Hester made tea, and presently the Bishop, who looked much exhausted, roused himself. He had that afternoon attended two deathbeds, one the deathbed of a friend, and the other that of the last vestige of peace, expiring amid the clamour of a distracted Low Church parish and High Church parson,[89] who could only meet each other after the fashion of cymbals. For the moment even his courageous spirit had been disheartened.

'I met a son of Anak[90] the other night at the Newhavens,' he said to Hester, 'who claimed you as a cousin – a Mr. Richard Vernon. He broke the ice by informing me that I had confirmed him, and that perhaps I should like to know that he had turned out better than I expected.'

'How like Dick,' said Hester.

'I remembered him at last. His father was the squire of Farlow, where I was rector before I came to Southminster. Dick was not a source of unmixed pleasure to his parents. As a boy of eight he sowed the parental billiard-table with mustard and cress in his father's absence, and raised a very good crop, and performed other excruciating experiments. I believe he beat all previous records of birch rods at Eton.[91] I remember while he was there he won a bet from another boy who could not pay, and he foreclosed on the loser's cricketing trousers. His parents were distressed about it when he brought them home, and I tried to make him see that he ought not to have taken them. But Dick held firm. He said it was like tithe, and if he could not get his own in money as I did he must collect it in trousers. I must own he had me there. I noticed that he wore the garments daily as long as any question remained in his parents' minds as to whether they ought to be returned. After that I felt sure he would succeed in life.'

'I believe he is succeeding in Australia.'

'I advised his father to send him abroad. There really was not room for him in England, and unfortunately for the army, the examiners jibbed at his strictly phonetic spelling.[92] He tells me he has given up being an A.D.C. and has taken to vine-growing, because if people are up in the world they always drink freely, and if they are 'down on their luck' they drink all the more to drown care. The reasoning appeared to me sound.'

'He and James used to quarrel frightfully in the holidays,' said Hester. 'It was always the same reason, about playing fair. Poor James did not know that games were matters of deadly importance, and that a rule was a sacred thing. I wonder why it is that clergymen so often have the same code of honour as women; quite a different code from that of the average man.'

'I think,' said the Bishop, 'it is owing to that difference of code that women clash so hopelessly with men when they attempt to compete or work with them. Women have not to begin with the *esprit de corps*[93] which the most ordinary men possess. With what difficulty can one squeeze out of a man any fact that is detrimental to his friend, or even to his acquaintance, however obviously necessary it may be that the information should be asked for and given. Yet I have known many good and earnest and affectionate women who lead unselfish lives, who will 'give away' their best woman friend at the smallest provocation, or without any provocation at all; will inform you *à propos* of nothing[94] that she was jilted years ago, or that her husband married her for her money. The causes of humiliation and disaster in a woman's life seem to have no sacredness for her women friends. Yet if that same friend whom she has run down is ill, the runner down will nurse her day and night with absolutely selfless devotion.'

'I have often been puzzled by that,' said Rachel. 'I seem to be always making mistakes about women, and perhaps that is the reason. They show themselves capable of some deep affection or some great self-sacrifice, and I respect and admire them, and think they are like that all through. And the day comes when they are not quite straightforward, or are guilty of some petty meanness, which a man who is not fit to black their boots would never stoop to.'

Hester's eyes fixed on her friend.

'Do you tell them? Do you show them up to themselves?' she asked; 'or do you leave them?'

'I do neither,' said Rachel. 'I treat them just the same as before.'

'Then aren't you a hypocrite, too?'

Hester's small face was set like a flint.

'I think not,' said Rachel tranquilly, 'any more than they are. The good is there for certain, and the evil is there for certain. Why should I take most notice of the evil which is just the part which will be rubbed out of them presently while the good will remain.'

'I think Rachel is right,' said the Bishop.

'I don't think she is, at all,' said Hester, her plumage ruffled, administering her contradiction right and left to her two best friends like a sharp peck from a wren. 'I think we ought to believe the best of people until they prove themselves unworthy, and then –'

'Then what?' said the Bishop, settling himself in his chair.

'Then leave them in silence.'

'I only know of a woman's silence by hearsay. I have never met it. Do you mean bitterly reproach the thistle for not bearing grapes?'

'I do not. It is my own fault if I idealise a thistle until the thistle and I both think it is a vine. But if people appear to love and honour certain truths which they know are everything to me, and claim kinship with me on that common ground, and then desert when the pinch comes, as it always does come, and act from worldly motives, then I know that they have never really cared for what they professed to love, that what I imagined to be a principle was only a subject of conversation – and – I withdraw.'

'You withdraw!' echoed the Bishop. 'This is terrible.'

'Just as I should,' continued Hester, 'if I were in political life. If a man threw in his lot with me, and then, when some means of worldly advancement seemed probable from the other side, deserted to it, I should not in consequence think him incapable of being a good husband and father and landlord. But I should never again believe that he cared for what I had staked my all on. And when he began to talk as if he cared (as they always do, as if nothing had happened) I should not show him up to himself. I have tried that and it is no use. I should –'

'Denounce him as an apostate?'[95] suggested the Bishop.

'No. He should be to me thenceforward as a heathen.'

'Thrice miserable man!'

'You would not have me treat him as a brother after that?'

'Of course not, because he would probably dislike that still more.'

At this moment a hurricane seemed to pass through the little house, and the three children rushed into the drawing-room, accompanied by Boulou, in a frantic state of excitement. Boulou, like Hester, had no happy medium in his character. He was what Mrs. Gresley called 'very Frenchy,' and he now showed his 'Frenchyness' by a foolish exhibition of himself in coursing round and round the room with his silly foreign tail crooked the wrong way.

'Mother got out at Mrs. Brown's,' shrieked Regie, in his highest voice, 'and I drove up.'

'Oh, Regie,' expostulated Mary the virtuous, the invariable corrector of the statements of others. 'You held the reins, but William walked beside.'

Hester made the children shake hands with her guests, and then they clustered round her to show what they had bought.

Though the Bishop was fond of children, he became suddenly restive. He took out his watch, and was nervously surprised at the lapse of time. The carriage was sent for, and in a few minutes that dignified vehicle was bowling back to Southminster.

'I am not satisfied about Hester,' said the Bishop. 'She looks ill and irritable, and she has the tense expression of a person who is making a colossal effort to be patient, and whose patience, after successfully meeting twenty calls upon it in the course of the day, collapses entirely at the twenty-first. That is a humiliating experience.'

'She spoke as if she were a trial to her brother and his wife.'

'I think she is. I have a sort of sympathy with Gresley as regards his sister. He has been kind to her according to his lights, and if she could write little goody-goody books[96] he would admire her immensely, and so would half the neighbourhood. It would be felt to be suitable. But Hester jars against the preconceived ideas which depute that clergymen's sisters and daughters should, as a matter of course, offer up their youth and hair and teeth and eyesight on the altar of parochial work. She does and is nothing that long custom expects her to do and be. Originality is out of place in a clergyman's family, just because it is so urgently needed. It is a constant source of friction. But, on the other hand, the best thing that could happen to Hester is to be thrown for a time among people who regard her as a nonentity, who have no sense of humour, and to whom she cannot speak of any of the subjects she has at heart. If Hester had remained in London after the success of her 'Idyll' she would have met with so much sympathy and admiration that her next book would probably have suffered in consequence. She is so susceptible, so expansive, that repression is positively necessary to her to enable her, so to speak, to get up steam. There is no place for getting up steam like a country vicarage with an inner *cordon*[97] of cows round it, and an outer one of amiable country neighbours, mildly contemptuous of originality in any form. She cannot be in sympathy with them in her present stage. It is her loss, not theirs. At forty she will be in sympathy with them, and appreciate them as I do; but that is another story. She has been working at this new book all winter with a fervour and concentration which her isolation has helped to bring about. She owes a debt of gratitude to her surroundings, and some day I shall tell her so.'

'She says her temper has become that of a fiend.'

'She is passionate, there is no doubt. She nearly fell on us both this afternoon. She is too much swayed by every little incident. Everything makes a vivid impression on her and shakes her to pieces. It is rather absurd and disproportionate now, like the long legs of a foal, but it is a sign of growth. My experience is that people without that fire of enthusiasm on the one side and righteous indignation on the other never achieve anything except in domestic life. If Hester lives she will outgrow her passionate nature, or at least she will grow up to it and become passive, contemplative. Then instead of unbalanced anger and excitement, the same nature which is now continually upset by them will have learnt to receive impressions calmly, and, by reason of that receptiveness and insight, she will go far.'

CHAPTER XIV

Only those who know the supremacy of the intellectual life – the life which has a seed of ennobling thought and purpose within it – can understand the grief of one who falls from that serene activity into the absorbing soul-wasting struggle with worldly annoyances.
GEORGE ELIOT.[98]

HESTER in the meanwhile was expressing wonder and astonishment at the purchases of the children, who, with the exception of Mary, had spent their little all on presents for Fraülein, whose birthday was on the morrow. After Mary's tiny white bone umbrella had been discovered to be a needle-case, and most of the needles had been recovered from the floor, Regie extracted from its paper a little china cow. But, alas! the cow's ears and horns remained in the bag, owing possibly to the incessant passage of the parcel from one pocket to another on the way home. Regie looked at the remnants in the bag and his lip quivered, while Mary, her own umbrella safely warehoused, exclaimed, 'Oh! Regie' in tones of piercing reproach.

But Hester quickly suggested that she could put them on again quite easily, and Fraülein would like it just as much. Still it was a blow. Regie leaned his head against Hester's shoulder.

Hester pressed her cheek against his little dark head. Sybell Loftus had often told Hester that she could have no idea of the happiness of a child's touch till she was a mother: that she herself had not an inkling till then. But perhaps some poor substitute for that exquisite feeling was vouchsafed to Hester.

'The tail is still on,' she whispered, not too cheerfully, but as one who in darkness sees light beyond.

The cow's tail was painted in blue upon its side.

'When I bought it,' said Regie, in a strangled voice, 'and it was a great deal of money cow, I did wish its tail had been out behind; but I think now it is safer like that.'

'All the best cows have their tails on the side,' said Hester. 'And to-morrow morning, when you are dressed, run up to my room, and you will find it just like it was before.' And she carefully put aside the bits with the injured animal.

'And now what has Stella got?'

Stella produced a bag of 'bull's-eyes'[99] which, in striking contrast with the cow, had, in the course of the drive home, cohered so tightly together that it was doubtful if they would ever be separated again.

'Fraülein never eats bull's-eyes,' said Mary, who was what her parents called 'a very truthful child.'

'I eats them,' said Stella, reversing her small cauliflower-like person on the sofa, till only a circle of white rims with a nucleus of coventry frilling, with two pink legs kicking gently upwards, were visible.

Stella always turned upside down if the conversation took a personal turn. In later and more conventional years we find a poor equivalent for marking our disapproval by changing the subject.

Hester had hardly set Stella right side upwards when the door opened once more and Mrs. Gresley entered, hot and exhausted.

'Run upstairs, my pets,' she said. 'Hester, you should not keep them down here now. It is past their tea-time.'

'We came ourselves, mother,' said Regie. 'Fraülein said we might, to show Auntie Hester our secrets.'

'Well, never mind; run away now,' said the poor mother, sitting down heavily in a low chair, 'and take Boulou.'

'You are tired out,' said Hester, slipping on to her knees and unlacing her sister-in-law's brown boots.

Mrs. Gresley looked with a shade of compunction at the fragile kneeling figure, with its face crimsoned by the act of stooping, and by the obduracy of the dust-ingrained bootlaces. But as she looked she noticed the flushed cheeks, and being a diviner of spirits, wondered what Hester was ashamed of now.

As Hester rose her sister-in-law held out, with momentary hesitation, a thin paper bag, in which an oval form allowed its moist presence to be discerned by partial adhesion to its envelope.

'I saw you ate no luncheon, Hester, so I have brought you a little sole for supper.'

Some of us poor Marthas spend all our existence, so to speak, in the kitchens of life. We never get so far as the drawing-room. Our conquests, our self-denials are achieved through the medium of suet and lard and necks of mutton. We wrestle with the dripping, and rise on stepping-stones – not of our dead selves,[100] but of sheep and oxen – to higher things.

The sole was a direct answer to prayer. Mrs. Gresley had been enabled to stifle her irritation against this delicate, whimsical, fine lady of a sister-in-law – laced

in, too, we must not forget that – who, in Mrs. Gresley's ideas, knew none of
the real difficulties of life, its butcher's bills, its monthly nurses,[101] its constant
watchfulness over delicate children, its long, long strain at two ends which won't
meet. We must know but little of our fellow creatures if the damp sole in the bag
appears to us other than the outward and homely sign of an inward and spiritual
conquest.

As such Hester saw it, and she kissed Mrs. Gresley and thanked her, and then
ran herself to the kitchen with the peace offering, and came back with her sister-
in-law's down-at-heel indoor shoes.

Mr. Gresley was stabling his bicycle in the hall as she crossed it. He was generally excessively jocose with his bicycle. He frequently said, 'Woah, Emma!' to
it. But to-day he, too, was tired, and put Emma away in silence.

When Hester returned to the drawing-room Mrs. Gresley had recovered sufficiently to notice her surroundings. She was sitting with her tan-stockinged feet
firmly planted on the carpet instead of listlessly outstretched, her eyes ominously
fixed on the tea-table and seed cake.

Hester's silly heart nudged her side like an accomplice.

'Who has been here to tea?' said Mrs. Gresley. 'I met the Pratts and the
Thursbys in Westhope.'

Hester was frightened. We need to be, in the presence of those who judge
others by themselves.

'The Bishop was here and Rachel West,' she said colouring. 'They left a few
minutes ago.'

'Well, of all unlucky things that James and I should have been out. James, do
you hear that? The Bishop's been while we were away. And I do declare, Hester,'
looking again at the table, 'you never so much as asked for the silver teapot.'

'I never thought of it,' said Hester ruefully. It was almost impossible to her to
alter the habit of a lifetime, and to remember to dash out and hurriedly change
the daily routine if visitors were present. Lady Susan had always used her battered
old silver teapot every day, and for the life of her Hester could not understand
why there should be one kind one day and one kind another. She glanced resentfully at the little brown earthenware vessel which she had wielded so cheerfully
half an hour ago. Why did she never remember the Gresleys' wishes?

'Hester,' said Mrs. Gresley suddenly, taking new note of Hester's immaculate
brown holland gown,[102] which contrasted painfully with her own dilapidated
pink shirt with hard collars and cuffs and imitation tie,[103] tied for life in the shop
where it was born. 'You are so smart;[104] I do believe you knew they were coming.'

If there was one thing more than another which offended Hester, it was
being told that she was *smart*.

'I trust I am never smart,' she replied; not with any touch of the haughtiness
that some ignorant persons believe to be the grand manner, but with a subtle

change of tone and carriage which seemed instantly to remove her to an enormous distance from the other woman with her insinuation and tan stockings. Mrs. Gresley unconsciously drew in her feet. 'I did not know when I dressed this morning that the Bishop was coming to-day.'

'Then you *did* know later that he was coming?'

'Yes, Rachel West wrote to tell me so this morning, but I did not open her letter at breakfast, and I was so vexed at being late for luncheon that I forgot to mention it then. I remembered as soon as James had started and ran after him, but he was too far off to hear me call to him.'

It cost Hester a good deal to give this explanation, as she was aware that the Bishop's visit had been to her and to her alone.

'Come, come,' said Mr. Gresley, judicially, with the natural masculine abhorrence of a feminine skirmish. 'Don't go on making foolish excuses, Hester, which deceive no one; and you, Minna, don't criticise Hester's clothes. It is the Bishop's own fault for not writing his notes himself. He might have known that Miss West would have written to Hester instead of to me. I can't say I think Hester behaved kindly towards us in acting as she did, but I won't hear any more argument about it. I desire the subject should now DROP.'

The last words were uttered in the same tone in which Mr. Gresley closed morning service,[105] and were felt to be final. He was not in reality greatly chagrined at missing the Bishop, whom he regarded with some of the suspicious distrust with which a certain class of mind ever regards that which is superior to it. Hester left the room, closing the door gently behind her.

'James,' said Mrs. Gresley, looking at her priest with tears of admiration in her eyes, 'I shall never be good like you, so you need not expect it. How you can be so generous and patient with her I don't know. It passes me.'

'We must learn to make allowances for each other,' said Mr. Gresley, in his most affectionate cornet, drawing his tired, tearful little wife down beside him on the sofa. And he made some fresh tea for her, and waited on her, and she told him about the children's boots and the sole, and he told her about a remarkable speech he had made at the chapter meeting, and a feeling that had been borne in on him on the way home that he should shortly write something striking about Apostolic Succession.[106] And they were happy together; for though he sometimes reproved her as a priest if she allowed herself to dwell on the probability of his being made a Bishop, he was very kind to her as a husband.

CHAPTER XV

Beware of a silent dog and of still water.[107]

IF you are travelling across Middleshire on the local line between Southminster and Westhope, after you have passed Wilderleigh with its grey gables and park wall, close at hand you will perceive to nestle (at least Mr. Gresley said it nestled) Warpington Vicarage; and perhaps, if you know where to look, you will catch a glimpse of Hester's narrow bedroom window under the roof. Half a mile further on Warpington Towers, the gorgeous residence of the Pratts, bursts into view, with flag on turret flying, and two tightly-bitted rustic bridges leaping high over the Drone. You cannot see all the lodges of Warpington Towers from the line, which is a source of some regret to Mr. Pratt; but if he happens to be travelling with you he will point out two of them, chaste stucco Gothic erections with church windows,[108] and inform you that the three others are on the northern and eastern sides, vaguely indicating the directions of Scotland and Ireland.

And the Drone kept in order on your left by the low line of the Slumberleigh hills will follow you and leave you, leave you and return all the way to Westhope. You are getting out at Westhope, of course, if you are a Middleshire man. For Westhope is on the verge of Middleshire, and the train does not go any further; at least, it only goes into one of the insignificant counties which jostle each other to hold on to Middleshire, unknown Saharas,[109] where passengers who oversleep themselves wake to find themselves cast away.

Westhope Abbey stands in its long low meadows and level gardens, close to the little town, straggling red roof above red roof, up its steep cobbled streets.

Down the great central aisle you may walk on mossy stones between the high shafts of broken pillars under the sky. God's stars look down once more where the piety of man had for a time shut them out. Through the slender tracery of what was once the east window, instead of glazed saint and crucifix, you may see the little town clasping its hill.

The purple clematis and the small lizard-like leaf of the ivy have laid tender hands on all that is left of that stately house of prayer. The pigeons wheel round it, and nest in its niches. The soft contented murmur of bird praise has replaced the noise of bitter human prayer. A thin wind-shipped grass holds the summit of the broken walls against all comers. The fallen stones, quaintly carved with angel and griffin, are going slowly back year by year, helped by the rain and hindered by the frost, slowly back through the sod to the generations of human hands that held and hewed them, and fell to dust below them hundreds of years ago. The spirit returns to the God who gave it, and the stone to the hand that fashioned it.

The adjoining monastery had been turned into a dwelling house, without altering it externally, and it was here that Lord Newhaven loved to pass the summer months. Into its one long upper passage all the many rooms opened, up

white stone steps through arched doors, rooms which had once been monks'
dormitories, abbots' cells, where Lady Newhaven and her guests now crimped
their hair, and slept under down quilts till noon.

It was this long passage with its interminable row of low latticed windows
that Lord Newhaven was turning into a depository for the old English weapons
which he was slowly collecting. He was standing now gazing lovingly at them,
drawing one finger slowly along an inlaid arquebus, when a yell from the garden
made him turn and look out.

It was not a yell of anguish, and Lord Newhaven remained at the window
leaning on his elbows, and watching at his ease the little scene which was taking
place below him.

On his bicycle on the smooth shaven lawn was Dick wheeling slowly in and
out among the stone-edged flower-beds, an apricot in each broad palm, while
he discoursed in a dispassionate manner to the two excited little boys who were
making futile rushes for the apricots. The governess and Rachel were looking
on. Rachel had arrived at Westhope the day before from Southminster. 'Take
your time, my son,' said Dick, just eluding by a hairsbreadth a charge through a
geranium bed on the part of the eldest boy. 'If you are such jolly little fools as to
crack your little skulls on the sun-dial I shall eat them both myself. Miss Turner
says you may have them, so you've only got to take them. I can't keep on offering
them all day long. My time' (Dick ran his bicycle up a terrace, and as soon as the
boys were up, glided down again) 'my time is valuable. You don't want them?' A
shrill disclaimer and a fresh onslaught. 'Miss Turner, they thank you very much;
but they don't care for apricots.'

Half a second more and Dick skilfully parted from his bicycle and was
charged by his two admirers and severely pummelled as high as they could reach.
When they had been led away by Miss Turner, each biting an apricot and casting
longing backward looks at their friend, Rachel and Dick wandered to the north
side of the abbey and sat down there in the shade.

Lord Newhaven could still see them, could still note her amused face under
her wide white hat. He was doing his best for Dick, and Dick was certainly having his chance, and making the most of it according to his lights.

'But all the same I don't think he has a chance,' said Lord Newhaven to himself. 'That woman, in spite of her frank manner and her self-possession, is afraid
of men; not of being married for her money, but of man himself. And whatever
else he may not be, Dick is a man, It's the best chance she will ever get, so it is
probable she won't take it.'

Lord Newhaven sauntered back down the narrow black oak staircase to his
own room on the ground-floor. He sat down at his writing-table and took out
of his pocket a letter which he had evidently read before. He now read it slowly
once more.

'Your last letter to me had been opened,' wrote his brother from India, 'or else it had not been properly closed. As you wrote on business, I wish you would be more careful.'

'I will,' said Lord Newhaven, and he wrote a short letter in his small upright hand, closed the envelope, addressed and stamped it, and sauntered out through the low-arched door into the garden.

Dick was sitting alone on the high-carved stone edge of the round pool where the monks used to wash, and where gold-fish now lived cloistered lives. A moment of depression seemed to have overtaken that cheerful personage.

'Come as far as the post-office,' said Lord Newhaven.

Dick gathered himself together, and rose slowly to his large feet.

'You millionaires are all the same,' he said. 'Because you have a house crawling with servants till they stick to the ceiling you have to go to the post-office to buy a penny stamp. It's like keeping a dog and barking yourself.'[110]

'I don't fancy I bark much,' said Lord Newhaven.

'No, and you don't bite *often*, but when you do you take out the piece. Do you remember that coloured chap at Broken Hill?'

'He deserved it,' said Lord Newhaven.

'He richly deserved it. But you took him in, poor devil, all the same. You were so uncommonly mild and limp beforehand, and letting pass things you ought not to have let pass, that, like the low beast he was, he thought he could play you any dog's trick, and that you would never turn on him.'

'It's a way worms have.'[111]

'Oh, hang worms; it does not matter whether they turn or not. But cobras have no business to imitate them till poor rookies think they have no poison in them, and that they can tickle them with a switch. What a great hulking brute that man was! You ricked him when you threw him! I saw him just before I left Adelaide. He's been lame ever since.'

'He'd have done for me if he could.'

'Of course he would. His blood was up. He meant to break your back. I saw him break a chap's back once, and it did not take so very long either. I heard it snap. But why did you let him go so far to start with before you pulled him up? That's what I've never been able to understand about you. If you behaved different to start with they would behave different to you. They would know they'd have to.'

'I have not your art,' said Lord Newhaven tranquilly, 'of letting a man know when he's getting out of hand that unless he goes steady there will be a row and he'll be in it. I'm not made like that.'

'It works well,' said Dick. 'It's a sort of peaceful way of rubbing along and keeping friends. If you let those poor bullies know what to expect they aren't as a rule over anxious to toe the mark. But you never *do* let them know.'

'No,' said Lord Newhaven, as he shot his letter into the brass mouth in the cottage wall, just below a window of 'bulls'-eyes' and peppermints, 'I never do. I don't defend it. But –'

'But what?'

Lord Newhaven's face underwent some subtle change. His eyes fixed themselves on a bottle of heart-shaped peppermints, and then met Dick's suddenly, with the clear frank glance of a schoolboy.

'But somehow, for the life of me, until things get serious – *I can't.*'

Dick, whose perceptions were rather of a colossal than an acute order, nevertheless perceived that he had received a confidence, and changed the subject.

'Aren't you going to buy some stamps?' he asked, perfectly aware that Lord Newhaven had had his reasons for walking to the post-office.

Lord Newhaven, who was being watched with affectionate interest from behind the counter by the grocer postmaster, went in, hit his head against a pendant ham, and presently emerged with brine in his hair, and a shilling's worth of stamps in his hand.

Later in the day, when he and Dick were riding up the little street with a view to having a look at the moor – for Middleshire actually has a grouse moor, although it is in the Midlands – the grocer in his white apron rushed out and waylaid them.

'Very sorry about the letter, my lord,' he repeated volubly, touching his forelock. 'Hope her la-ship told you as I could not get it out again, or I'm sure I would have done to oblige your lordship, and her la-ship calling on purpose. But the post-office is that mean and distrustful as it don't leave me the key, and once anything is it, in it is.'[112]

'Ah!' said Lord Newhaven slowly. 'Well, Jones, it's not your fault. I ought not to have changed my mind. I suppose her ladyship gave you my message that I wanted it back?'

'Yes, my lord, and her la-ship come herself, not ten minutes after you was gone. But I've no more power over that there recepticle than a hunlaid hegg, and that's the long and short of it. I've allus said, and I say it again, "Them as have charge of the post-office should have the key."'

'When I am made postmaster-general you *shall* have it,' said Lord Newhaven, smiling. 'It is the first reform that I shall bring about.' And he nodded to the smiling apologetic man and trotted on, Dick beside him, who was apparently absorbed in the action of his roan cob.

But Dick's mind had sustained a severe shock. That Lady Newhaven, 'that jolly little woman,' the fond mother of those two 'jolly little chaps,' should have been guilty of an underhand trick, was astonishing to him.

Poor Dick had started life with a religious reverence for woman; had carried out his brittle possession to bush life in Australia, from thence through two A.D.C.-ships, and, after many vicissitudes, had brought it safely back with a large consignment of his own Burgundy to his native land. It was still sufficiently intact – save for a chip or two – to make a pretty wedding present to his future wife. But it had had a knock since he mounted the roan cob. For unfortunately the kind of man who has what are called 'illusions' about women, is too often the man whose discrimination lies in other directions, in fields where little high-heeled shoes are not admitted.

Rachel had the doubtful advantage of knowing that in spite of Dick's shrewdness respecting shades of difference in muscatels, she and Lady Newhaven were nevertheless ranged on the same pedestal in Dick's mind, as flawless twins of equal moral beauty. But after this particular day she observed that Lady Newhaven had somehow slipped off the pedestal, and that she, Rachel, had the honour of occupying it alone.

CHAPTER XVI

Une grande passion malheureuse est un grand moyen de sagesse.[113]

RACHEL had left London precipitately after she had been the unwilling confidant of Lady Newhaven's secret, and had taken refuge with that friend of all perplexed souls the Bishop of Southminster. She felt unable to meet Hugh again without an interval of breathing time. She knew that if she saw much more of him he would confide in her, and she shrank from receiving a confidence the ugliest fact of which she already knew. Perhaps she involuntarily shrank also from fear lest he should lower himself in her eyes by only telling her half the truth. Sad confessions were often poured into Rachel's ears which she had known for years. She never alluded to that knowledge, never corrected the half-lie which accompanies so many whispered self-accusations. Confidences and confessions are too often a means of evasion of justice, a laying of the case for the plaintiff before a judge without allowing the defendant to be present or to call a witness. Rachel, by dint of long experience, which did slowly for her the work of imagination, had ceased to wonder at the faithfully chronicled harsh words and deeds of generous souls. She knew or guessed at the unchronicled treachery or deceit which had brought about that seemingly harsh word or deed.

She had not the exalted ideas about her fellow creatures which Hester had, but she possessed the rare gift of reticence. She exemplified the text – 'Whether it be to friend or foe, talk not of other men's lives.'[114] And in Rachel's quiet soul a vast love and pity dwelt for these same fellow creatures. She had lived and worked for years among those whose bodies were half starved, half clothed, degraded. When she found money at her command she had spent sums (as her lawyer told her) out of all proportion on that poor human body, stumbling between vice and starvation. But now, during the last year, when her great wealth had thrown her violently into society, she had met, until her strong heart flinched before it, the other side of life: the starved soul in the delicately nurtured, richly clad body, the atrophied spiritual life in hideous contrast with the physical ease and luxury which were choking it. The second experience was harder to bear than the first. And just as in the old days she had shared her bread and cheese with those hungrier than herself, and had taken but little thought for those who had bread and to spare, so now she felt but transient interest in those among her new associates who were successfully struggling against the blackmail of luxury, the leprosy of worldliness, the selfishness that at last coffins the soul it clothes. Her heart yearned instead towards the spiritually starving, the tempted, the fallen in that great little world, whose names are written in the book, not of life, but of Burke[115] – the little world which is called 'Society.'

She longed to comfort them, to raise them up, to wipe from their hands and garments the muddy gold stains of the gutter into which they had fallen, to smoothe away the lines of mean care from their faces. But it had been far simpler in her previous life to share her hard-earned bread with those who needed it than it was now to share her equally hard-earned thoughts and slow gleanings of spiritual knowledge, to share the things which belonged to her peace.

Rachel had not yet wholly recovered from the overwhelming passion of love which, admitted without fear a few years ago, had devastated the little city of her heart, as by fire and sword, involving its hospitable dwellings, its temples and its palaces in one common ruin. Out of that desolation she was unconsciously rebuilding her city, but it was still rather gaunt and bare, the trees had not had time to grow in the streets, and there was an ugly fortification round it of defaced, fire-seared stones which had once stood aloft in minaret and tower, and which now served only as a defence against all comers.

If Dick had been in trouble, or rather if she had known the troubles he had been through, and which had made his crooked mouth shut so firmly, Rachel might possibly have been able to give him something more valuable than the paper money of her friendship. But Dick was obviously independent. He could do without her, while Hugh had a claim upon her. Rachel's thoughts turned to Hugh again and ever again. Did he see his conduct as she saw it? A haunting fear was upon her that he did not. And she longed with an intensity that outbalanced for the time every other feeling that he should confess his sin fully, entirely – see it in all its ugliness and gather himself together into a deep repentance before he went down into silence, or before he made a fresh start in life. She would have given her right hand to achieve that.

And in a lesser degree she was drawn towards Lady Newhaven. Lady Newhaven was conscious of the tender compassion which Rachel felt for her, and used it to the uttermost, but unfortunately she mistook it for admiration of her character, mixed with sympathetic sorrow for her broken heart. If she had seen herself as Rachel saw her she would have conceived, not for herself but for Rachel, some of the aversion which was gradually distilling bitter drop by drop into her mind for her husband. She would not have killed him. She would have thought herself incapable of an action so criminal, so monstrous. But if part of the ruin in the garden were visibly trembling to its fall, she would not have warned him if he had been sitting beneath it, nor would her conscience have ever reproached her afterwards.

'I wish Miss Gresley would come and stay here instead of taking you away from me,' she said plaintively to Rachel one morning, when she made the disagreeable discovery that Rachel and Hester were friends. 'I don't care much about her myself, she is so profane, and so dreadfully irreligious. But Edward likes to talk to her. He prefers artificial people. I wonder he did not marry her. That old cat, Lady Susan Gresley, was always throwing her at his head. I wish she was not always persuading you to leave me for hours together. I get so frightened when I am left alone with Edward. I live in perpetual dread that he will say something before the children or the servants. He is quite cruel enough.'

'He will never say anything.'

'You are always so decided, Rachel. You don't see possibilities, and you don't know him as I do. He is capable of anything. I will write a note now, and you can take it to Miss Gresley if you *must* go there to-day.'

'I wish to go very much.'

'And you will stay another week whether she comes or not?'

There was a momentary pause before Rachel said cheerfully, 'I will stay another week, with pleasure. But I am afraid Lord Newhaven will turn restive at taking me in to dinner.'

'Oh! he likes you. He always prefers people who are not of his own family.'

Rachel laughed. 'You flatter me.'

'I never flatter any one. He does like you, and, besides, there are people coming next week for the grouse shooting. I suppose that heavy young Vernon is going to lumber over with you. It's not my fault if he is always running after you. Edward insisted on having him. I don't want him to dance attendance on *me*.'

'He and I are going to bicycle to Warpington together. The Gresleys are cousins of his. If it turns very hot we will wait till after sunset to return, if we may.'

'Just as you like,' said Lady Newhaven with asperity. 'But I advise you to be careful, my dear Rachel. It never seems to occur to you what onlookers see at a glance, namely, that Mr. Vernon is in love with your fortune.'

'According to public opinion that is a very praiseworthy attachment,' said Rachel, who had had about enough. 'I often hear it commended.'

Lady Newhaven stared. That her conversation could have the effect of a mustard leaf did not strike her. She saw that Rachel was becoming restive, and, of course, the reason was obvious. She was thinking of marrying Dick.

'Well, my dear,' she said, lying down on a low couch near the latticed window, and opening a novel. 'You need not be vexed with me for trying to save you from a mercenary marriage. I only speak because I am fond of you. But one marriage is as good as another. I was married for love myself; I had not a farthing. And yet you see my marriage has turned out a tragedy – a bitter, bitter tragedy.'

Tableau.[116] – A beautiful, sad-faced young married woman in white, reclining among pale-green cushions near a bowl of pink carnations, endeavouring to rouse the higher feelings of an inexperienced though not youthful spinster in a short bicycling skirt. Decidedly, the picture was not flattering to Rachel.

CHAPTER XVII

On s'ennuie presque toujours avec ceux qu'on ennuie.[117]

HESTER did not fail a second time to warn the Gresleys of the arrival of guests. She mentioned it in time to allow of the making of cakes, and Mr. Gresley graciously signified his intention of returning early from his parochial rounds[118] on the afternoon when Dick and Rachel were expected, while Mrs. Gresley announced that the occasion was a propitious one for inviting the Pratts to tea.

'Miss West will like to meet them,' she remarked to Hester, whose jaw dropped at the name of Pratt. 'And it is very likely if they take a fancy to her they will ask her to stay at the Towers while she is in the neighbourhood. If the captain is at home I will ask him to come too. The Pratts are always so pleasant and hospitable.'

Hester was momentarily disconcerted at the magnitude of the social effort which Rachel's coming seemed to entail. But for once she had the presence of mind not to show her dismay, and she helped Mrs. Gresley to change the crewel-work antimacassars with their washed-out kittens swinging and playing leap-frog for the best tussore silk ones.[119] The afternoon was still young when all the preparations had been completed, and Mrs. Gresley went upstairs to change her gown, while Hester took charge of the children, as Fraülein had many days previously arranged to make music with Dr. and Miss Brown on this particular afternoon. And very good music it was which proceeded out of the open windows of the doctor's red brick house opposite Abel's cottage. Hester could just hear it from the bottom of the garden near the churchyard wall, and there she took the children, and under the sycamore, with a bench round it, the dolls had a tea-party. Hester had provided herself with a lump of sugar and a biscuit, and out of these many dishes were made, and were arranged on a clean pocket-handkerchief spread on the grass. Regie carried out his directions as butler with solemn exactitude, and though Mary, who had inherited the paternal sense of humour, thought fit to tweak the handkerchief and upset everything, she found the witticism so coldly received by 'Auntie Hester,' although she explained that father always did it, that she at once suited herself to her company and helped to repair the disaster.

It was very hot. The dolls, from the featureless midshipman to the colossal professional beauty sitting in her own costly perambulator (a present from Mrs. Pratt), felt the heat, and showed it by their moist countenances. The only person who was cool was a small nude china infant in its zinc bath, the property of Stella, whose determination to reach central facts and to penetrate to the root of the matter, at present took the form of tearing or licking off all that could be torn or licked from objects of interest. Hester, who had presented her with the floating baby in the bath, sometimes wondered as she watched Stella conscientiously work through a well-dressed doll down to its stitched sawdust compartments, what Mr. Gresley would make of his daughter when she turned her attention to theology.

They were all sitting in a tight circle round the handkerchief, Regie watching Hester cutting a new supply of plates out of smooth leaves with her little gilt scissors, while Mary and Stella tried alternately to suck an inaccessible grain of sugar out of the bottom of an acorn cup.

Rachel and Dick had come up on their silent wheels, and were looking at them over the wall before Hester was aware of their presence.

'May we join the tea-party?' asked Rachel, and Hester started violently.

'I am afraid the gate is locked,' she said. 'But perhaps you can climb it.'

'We can't leave the bicycles outside though,' said Dick, and he took a good look at the heavy padlocked gate. Then he slowly lifted it off its hinges, wheeled in the bicycles, and replaced the gate in position.

Rachel looked at him.

'Do you always do what you want to do?' she said involuntarily.

'It saves trouble,' he said, 'especially as no one can be such a first-class fool as to think a padlock will keep a gate shut. He would expect it to be opened.'

'But father said no one could come in there now,' explained Regie, who had watched open-mouthed the upheaval of the gate. 'Father said it could not be opened any more. He told mother.'

'Did he, my son?' said Dick, and he kissed every one, beginning with Hester, and finishing with the dolls. Then they all sat down to the tea-party, and partook largely of the delicacies, and after tea Dick solemnly asked the children if they had seen the flying halfpenny he had brought back with him from Australia. The children crowded round him, and the halfpenny was produced and handed round. Each child touched it and found it real. Auntie Hester and Auntie Rachel examined it. Boulou was requested to smell it. And then it was laid on the grass, and the pocket-handkerchief which had done duty as a tablecloth was spread over it.

The migrations of the halfpenny were so extraordinary that even Rachel and Hester professed amazement. Once it was found in Rachel's hand, into which another large hand had gently shut it. But it was never discovered twice in the same place, though all the children rushed religiously to look for it where it was last discovered.

Another time, after a long search, the doll in the bath was discovered to be sitting upon it, and once it actually flew down Regie's back, and amid the wild excitement of the children its cold descent was described by Regie in piercing minuteness until the moment when it rolled out over his stocking at his knee.

'Make it fly down my back too, Uncle Dick,' shrieked Mary. 'Regie, give it to me.'

But Regie danced in a circle round Dick, holding aloft the wonderful halfpenny.

'Make it fly down my throat,' he cried, too excited to know what he was doing, and he put the halfpenny in his mouth.

'Put it out this instant,' said Dick, without moving.

A moment's pause followed, in which the blood ebbed away from the hearts of the two women.

'I can't,' said Regie, 'I've swallowed it.' And he began to whimper, and then suddenly rolled on the grass screaming.

Dick pounced upon him like a panther, and held him by the feet head downwards, shaking him violently.

The child's face was terrible to see.

Hester hid her face in her hands. Rachel rose and stood close to Dick.

'I think the shaking is rather too much for him,' she said, watching the poor little purple face intently.

'I'm bound to go on,' said Dick, fiercely. 'Is it moving, Regie?'

'It's going down,' screamed Regie, suddenly.

'That it's not,' said Dick, and he shook the child again, and the halfpenny flew out upon the grass.

'Thank God,' said Dick, and he laid the gasping child on Hester's lap and turned away.

A few minutes later Regie was laughing and talking and feeling himself a hero. Presently he slipped off Hester's knee, and ran to Dick, who was lying on the grass a few paces off, his face hidden in his hands.

'Make the halfpenny fly again, Uncle Dick,' cried all the children, pulling at him.

Dick raised an ashen face for a moment and said hoarsely, 'Take them away.'

Hester gathered up the children and took them back to the house through the kitchen garden.

'Don't say we have arrived,' whispered Rachel to her. 'I will come on with him presently.' And she sat down near the prostrate vinegrower. The president of the South Australian Vinegrowers' Association looked very large when he was down.

Presently he sat up. His face was drawn and haggard, but he met Rachel's dog-like glance of silent sympathy with a difficult crooked smile.

'He is such a jolly little chap,' he said, winking his hawk eyes.

'It was not your fault.'

'That would not have made it any better for the parents,' said Dick. 'I had time to think of that while I was shaking that little money-box. Besides, it was my fault in a way. I'll never play with other people's children again. They are too brittle. I've had shaves up the Fly River and in the South Sea Islands, but never anything as bad as this, in this blooming little Vicarage garden with a church looking over the wall.'

Hester was skimming back towards them.

'Don't mention it to James and his wife,' she said to Dick, 'He has to speak at a temperance meeting to-night. I will tell them when the meeting is over.'

'That's just as well,' said Dick, 'for I know if James jawed much at me I should act on the text that it is more blessed to give than to receive.[120]

'In what way?'

'Either way,' said Dick. 'Tongue or fist. It does not matter which so long as you give more than you get. And the text is quite right. It *is* blessed for I've tried it over and over again, and found it true every time. But I don't want to try it on James if he's anything like what he was as a curate.'[121]

'He is not much altered,' said Hester.

'He is the kind of man that would not alter much,' said Dick. 'I expect God Almighty likes him as he is.'

Mr. and Mrs. Gresley meanwhile were receiving Mrs. Pratt and the two Miss Pratts in the drawing-room. Selina and Ada Pratt were fine handsome young women with long upper lips, who wore their smart sailor hats tilted backwards to show their bushy fringes, and whose muff-chains[122] with swinging pendant hearts, silk blouses and sequin belts and brown boots represented to Mrs. Gresley the highest pinnacle of the world of fashion.

Selina was the most popular, being liable to shrieks of laughter at the smallest witticisms, and always ready for that species of amusement termed 'bally-ragging' or 'hay-making.' But Ada was the most admired. She belonged to that type which in hotel society and country towns is always termed 'queenly.' She 'kept the men at a distance.' She 'never allowed them to take liberties,' &c, &c. She held her chin up and her elbows out, and was considered by the section of Middleshire society in which she shone to be very distinguished. Mrs. Pratt was often told that her daughter looked like a duchess; and this facsimile of the aristocracy, or rather of the most distressing traits of its latest recruits,[123] had a manner of lolling with crossed legs in the parental carriage and pair, which was greatly admired. 'Looks as if she was born to it all,' Mr. Pratt would say to his wife.

Mrs. Gresley was just beginning to fear her other guests were not coming when two tall figures were seen walking across the lawn, with Hester between them.

Mr. Gresley sallied forth to meet them, and blasts of surprised welcome were borne into the drawing-room by the summer air.

'But it was locked. I locked it myself.'

Inaudible reply.

'Padlocked, Only opens to the word Moon. Key on my own watch chain.'

Inaudible reply.

'Hinges!! Ha! Ha! Ha! very good, Dick. Likely story that. I see you're the same as ever. Travellers' tales. But we are not so easily taken in, are we, Hester?'

Mrs. Gresley certainly had the gift of prophecy as far as the Pratts were concerned. Mrs. Pratt duly took the expected 'fancy' to Rachel, and pressed her to stay at 'The Towers,' while she was in the neighbourhood, and make further acquaintance with her 'young ladies.'

'Ada is very pernickety,' she said, smiling towards that individual conversing with Dick. 'She won't make friends with everybody, and she gives it me (with maternal pride) when I ask people to stay whom she does not take to. She says there's a very poor lot round here, and most of the young ladies so ill-bred and empty she does not care to make friends with them. I don't know where she gets all her knowledge from. I'm sure it's not from her mother. Ada, now you come and talk a little to Miss West.'

Ada rose with the air of one who confers a favour, and Rachel made room for her on the sofa while Mrs. Pratt squeezed herself behind the tea-table with Mrs. Gresley.

The conversation turned on bicycling.

'I bike now and then in the country,' said Ada, 'but I have not done much lately. We have only just come down from town, and *of course* I never bike in London.'[124]

Rachel had just said that she did.

'Perhaps you are nervous about the traffic,' said Rachel.

'Oh! I'm not the least afraid of the traffic, but it's such bad form to bike in London.'

'That of course depends on how it's done,' said Rachel; 'but I am sure in your case you need not be afraid.'

Ada glared at Rachel, and did not answer.

When the Pratts had taken leave she said to her mother. 'Well, you can have Rachel West if you want to, but if you do I shall go away. She is only Birmingham, and yet she's just as stuck up as she can be.'

The Pratts were 'Liverpool.'[125]

'Well, my dear,' said Mrs. Pratt with natural pride. 'It's well known no one is good enough for you. But I took to Miss West, and an orphan and all, with all that money, poor thing.'

'She has no style,' said Selina, 'but she has a nice face, and she's coming to stay with Sibbie Loftus next week, when she leaves Vi Newhaven. She may be Birmingham, Ada, but she's just as thick with county people as we are.'

'I did not rightly make out,' said Mrs. Pratt reflectively, 'whether that tall gentleman, Mr. Vernon, was after Miss West or Hessie Gresley.'

'Oh! Ma! You always think some one's after somebody else,' said Ada impatiently, whose high breeding obliged her to be rather peremptory with her simple parent. 'Mr. Vernon is a pauper, and so is Hessie. And besides Hessie is not the kind of girl that anybody would want to marry.'

'Well, I'm not so sure of that,' said Selina. 'But if she had had any chances I know she would have told me because I told her all about Captain Cobbett and Mr. Baxter.'

CHAPTER XVIII

Le monde est plein de gens qui ne sont pas plus sages.
La Fontaine[126]

IF, after the departure of the Pratts, Rachel had hoped for a word with Hester she was doomed to disappointment. Mr. Gresley took the seat on the sofa beside Rachel which Ada Pratt had vacated, and after a few kindly eulogistic remarks on the Bishop of Southminster and the responsibilities of wealth, he turned the conversation into the well-worn groove of Warpington.

Rachel proved an attentive listener, and after Mr. Gresley had furnished her at length with nutritious details respecting parochial work, he went on:

'I am holding this evening a temperance meeting[127] in the Parish Room.[128] I wish, Miss West, that I could persuade you to stay for it, and thus enlist your sympathies in a matter of vital importance.'

'They have been enlisted in it for the last ten years,' said Rachel, who was not yet accustomed to the invariable assumption on the part of Mr. Gresley that no one took an interest in the most obvious good work until he had introduced and championed it. 'But,' she added, 'I will stay with pleasure.'

Dick, who was becoming somewhat restive under Mrs. Gresley's inquiries about the Newhavens, became suddenly interested in the temperance meeting.

'I've seen many a good fellow go to the dogs through drink in the Colonies, more's the pity,' Dick remarked. 'I think I'll come, too, James. And if you want a few plain words you call on me.'

'I will,' said Mr. Gresley, much gratified. 'I always make a point of encouraging the laity, at least those among them who are thoroughly grounded in Church teaching, to express themselves. Hear both sides, that is what I always say. The Bishop constantly enjoins on his clergy to endeavour to elicit the lay opinion. The chair this evening will be taken by Mr. Pratt, a layman.'

The temperance meeting was to take place at seven o'clock, and possibly Rachel may have been biased in favour of that entertainment by the hope of a quiet half-hour with Hester in her own room. At any rate, she secured it.

When they were alone Rachel produced Lady Newhaven's note.

'Do come to Westhope,' she said. 'While you are under this roof it seems almost impossible to see you, unless we are close to it,' and she touched the sloping ceiling with her hand. 'And yet I came to Westhope, and I am going on to Wilderleigh partly in order to be near you.'

Hester shook her head.

'The book is nearly finished,' she said, the low light from the attic window striking sideways on the small face with its tightly compressed lips.

A spirit indomitable, immortal, looked for a moment out of Hester's grey eyes. The spirit was indeed willing, but the flesh was becoming weaker day by day.

'When it is finished,' she went on, 'I will go anywhere and do anything, but stay here I must till it is done. Besides, I am not fit for society at present. I am covered with blue mould. Do you remember how that horrid Lady Carbury used to laugh at the country squires' daughters for being provincial? I have gone a peg lower than being provincial, I have become parochial.'

A knock came at the door, and Fraülein's mild, musical face appeared in the aperture.

'I fear to disturb you,' she said, 'but Regie say he cannot go to sleep till he see you.'

Hester introduced Fraülein to Rachel, and slipped downstairs to the night nursery.

Mary and Stella were already asleep in their high-barred cribs. The blind was down, and Hester could only just see the white figure of Regie sitting up in his nightgown. She sat down on the edge of the bed and took him in her arms.

'What is it, my treasure?'

'Auntie Hester, was I naughty about the flying half-penny?'

'No, darling. Why?'

'Because mother always says not to put pennies in my mouth, and I never did till to-day. And now Mary says I have been very naughty.'

'It does not matter what Mary says,' said Hester, with a withering glance towards the sleeping angel in the next crib, who was only Mary by day. 'But you must never do it again, and you will tell mother all about it to-morrow.'

'Yes,' said Regie; 'but, but –'

'But what?'

'Uncle Dick did say it was a flying halfpenny, and you said so, too, and that other auntie. And I thought it did not matter putting in flying halfpennies, only common ones.'

Hester saw the difficulty in Regie's mind.

'It felt common when it was inside,' said Regie doubtfully, 'and yet you and Uncle Dick *did* say it was a flying one.'

Regie's large eyes were turned upon her with solemn inquiry in them. It is in crises like this that our first ideals are laid low.

Regie had always considered Hester as the very soul of honour, that mysterious honour which he was beginning to dimly apprehend through her allegiance to it, and which, in his mind, belonged as exclusively to her as the little bedroom under the roof.

'Regie,' said Hester, tremulously, seeing that she had unwittingly put a stumbling-block before the little white feet she loved, 'when we played at the doll's tea-party, and you were the butler, I did not mean you were *really* a butler, did I? I knew, and you knew, and we all knew, that you were Regie all the time.'

'Ye-es.'

'It was a game. And so when Uncle Dick found us playing the tea-party game he played another game about the flying halfpenny.'

'Then it was a common halfpenny after all,' said Regie with a deep sigh.

'Yes, it was a common halfpenny, only the game was that it could fly, like the other game was that the acorn-cups were real tea-cups. So Uncle Dick and all of us were not saying what was not true. We were all playing at a game. Do you understand, my little mouse?'

'Yes,' said Regie, with another voluminous sigh, and Hester realized with thankfulness that the halfpenny and not herself had fallen from its pedestal. 'I see now, but when he said, Hi! Presto! and it flew away, I thought I saw it flying. Mary said she did. And I suppose the gate was only a game too.'

Hester felt that the subject would be quite beyond her powers of explanation if once the gate were introduced into it.

She laid Regie down and covered him.

'And you will go to sleep now. And I will ask Uncle Dick when next he comes to show us how he did the game with the halfpenny.'

'Yes,' said Regie dejectedly. 'I'd rather know what there is to be known. Only I *thought* it was a flying one. Good night, Auntie Hester.'

She stayed beside him a few minutes until his even breathing showed her he was asleep, and then slipped back to her own room. The front door bell was ringing as she came out of the nursery. The temperance deputation from Liverpool had arrived. Mr. Gresley's voice of welcome could be heard saying that it was only ten minutes to seven.

Accordingly a few minutes before that hour, Mr. Gresley and his party entered the parish room. It was crammed. The back benches were filled with a large contingent of young men, whose half-sheepish, half-sullen expression showed that their presence was due to pressure. Why the parishioners had come in such numbers it would be hard to say. Perhaps even a temperance meeting was a change in the dreary monotony of rural life at Warpington. Many of the faces bore the imprint of this monotony, Rachel thought, as she refused the conspicuous front seat pointed out to her by Mrs. Gresley, and sat down near the door with Hester.

Dick, who had been finishing his cigarette outside, entered a moment later, and stood in the gangway, entirely filling it up, his eye travelling over the assembly, and as Rachel well knew, looking for her. Presently he caught sight of her, wedged in four or five deep by the last arrivals. There was a vacant space between her and the wall, but it was apparently inaccessible. Entirely disregarding the anxious churchwardens who were waving him forward Dick disappeared among the young men at the back, and Rachel thought no more of him until a large Oxford shoe[129] descended quietly out of space upon the empty seat near her, and Dick, who had persuaded the young men to give him foot room on their seats, and had stepped over the high backs of several 'school forms,'[130] sat down beside her.

It was neatly done, and Rachel could not help smiling. But the thought darted through her mind that Dick was the kind of man who somehow or other would succeed where he meant to succeed, and would marry the woman he intended to marry. There was no doubt that she was that woman, and as he sat tranquilly beside her she wished with a nervous tremor that his choice had fallen on some one else.

The meeting opened with nasal and fervent prayer on the part of a neighbouring Archdeacon.[131] No one could kneel down except the dignitaries on the platform, but every one pretended to do so. Mr. Pratt, who was in the chair, then introduced the principal speaker. Mr. Pratt's face, very narrow at the forehead, became slightly wider at the eyes, widest when it reached round the corners of the mouth, and finally split into two long parti-coloured whiskers. He assumed on these occasions a manner of pontifical solemnity towards his 'humble brethren,' admirably suited to one, who after wrestling for many years with a patent oil, is conscious that he has blossomed out into a 'county family.'

The Warpington parishioners listened to him unmoved.

The deputation from Liverpool followed, a thin ascetic looking man of many bones and little linen, who spoke with the concentrated fury of a fanatic against alcohol in all its varieties. Dick who had so far taken more interest in Rachel's gloves, which she had dropped, and with which he was kindly burdening himself, than in the proceedings, drew himself up and fixed his steel eyes on the speaker.

A restive movement in the audience followed the speech, which was loudly clapped by Mr. Gresley and the Pratts.

Mr. Gresley then mounted the platform.

Mr. Gresley had an enormous advantage as a platform speaker, and as a preacher in the twin pulpits of church and home, owing to the conviction that he had penetrated to the core of any subject under discussion, and could pronounce judgment upon it in a conclusive manner. He was wont to approach every subject by the preliminary statement that he had 'threshed it out.' This threshing out had been so thorough that there was hardly a subject even of the knottiest description which he was unable to dismiss with a few pregnant words. 'Evolution! Ha! ha!! Descended from an ape. I don't believe that for one.' While women's rights received their death-blow from a jocose allusion to the woman following the plough, while the man sat at home and rocked the cradle.[132]

With the same noble simplicity he grappled with the difficult and complex subject of temperance, by which he meant total abstinence.[133] He informed his hearers, 'in the bigoted tones of a married teetotaler,' that he had gone to the root of the matter – the roots were apparently on the surface – and that it was no use calling black white and white black. He for one did not believe in muddling up black and white as some lukewarm people advocated till they were only a dirty grey. No; either drink was right or it was wrong. If it was not wrong to get drunk, he did not know what was wrong. He was not a man of compromise. Alcohol was a servant of the devil, and to tamper with it was to tamper with the evil one[134] himself; touch not; taste not; handle not. He for his part should never side with the devil.

This lofty utterance having been given time to sink in, Mr. Gresley looked round at the sea of stolid, sullen faces, and concluded with saying that the chairman would now call upon his cousin, Mr. Vernon, to speak to them on the shocking evils he himself had witnessed in Australia as the results of drink.

Dick was not troubled by shyness. He extricated himself from his seat with the help of the young men, and slowly ascended the platform. He looked a size too large for it, and for the other speakers, and his loose tweed suit and heather stockings were as great a contrast to the tightly buttoned up black of the other occupants as were his strong keen face and muscular hands to those of the previous speakers.

'That's a man,' said a masculine voice behind Rachel. 'He worn't reared on ditch water, you bet.'

'Mr. Chairman, and ladies and gentlemen,' said Dick, 'You've only got to listen to me for half a minute, and you'll find out without my telling you that Nature did not cut me out for a speaker. I'm no talker. I'm a working man' – an admission which Mr. Pratt would rather have been boiled in his own oil than have made – 'for the last seven years I've done my twelve hours a day, and I've come to think more of what a man gets through with his hands than the sentiments which he can wheeze out after a heavy meal. But Mr. Gresley has asked me to tell you what I know about drink, as I have seen a good many samples of it in Australia.'

Dick then proceeded, with a sublime disregard of grammar, and an earnestness that increased as he went on, to dilate on the evil effects of drink as he himself had witnessed them. He described how he had seen men who could not get spirits make themselves drunk on 'Pain-killer'; how he had seen strong young station hands, who had not tasted spirits for months, come down from the hills with a hundred pounds in their pockets, and drink themselves into 'doddery' old men in a fortnight in the nearest township, where they were kept drunk on drugged liquor till all their hard-earned wages were gone.

The whole room listened in dead silence. No feet shuffled. Mr. Gresley looked patronisingly at Dick's splendid figure and larged outstretched hand, with the crooked middle finger which he had cut off by mistake in the Bush, and had stuck on again himself. Then the young Vicar glanced smiling at the audience, feeling that he had indeed elicited a 'lay opinion' of the best kind.

'Now what are the causes of all these dreadful things?' continued Dick. 'I'm speaking to the men here, not the women. What are the causes of all this poverty and vice and scamped workmanship, and weak eyes and shaky hands on the top of high wages? I tell you they come from two things, and one is as bad as the other. One is drinking too much, and the other is drinking bad liquor. Every man who's worth his salt,' said Dick, balancing his long bent finger on the middle of his other palm, 'should know when he has had enough. Some can carry more, some less.' Mr. Gresley started and signed to Dick, but Dick did not notice. 'Bad liquor is at the root of half the drunkenness I know. I don't suppose there are many publicans here to-night, for this meeting isn't quite in their line, and if there are, they can't have come expecting compliments. But if you fellows think you get good liquor at the publics round here, I tell you, you are jolly well mistaken.'

'Hear! Hear!' shouted several voices.

'I've been in the course of the last week to most of the public-houses in Southminster and Westhope and Warpington to see what sort of stuff they sold, and upon my soul, gentlemen, if I settled in Warpington I'd, I'd' – Dick hesitated for a simile strong enough – 'I'd turn teetotaler until I left it again, rather than swallow the snake poison they serve out to you.'

There was a general laugh, in the midst of which Mr. Gresley, whose complexion had deepened, sprang to his feet and endeavoured to attract Dick's attention, but Dick saw nothing but his audience. Mr. Gresley began to speak in his high sing-song voice.

'My young friend,' he said, 'has mistaken the object of this meeting. In short I must –'

'Not a bit,' said Dick, 'not a bit; but if the people have had enough of me I'll take your chair while you have another innings.'

In a moment the room was in an uproar.

Shouts of 'No, no,' 'Go on,' 'Let him speak.'

In the tumult Mr. Gresley's voice instead of being the solo became but as one instrument – albeit a trombone – in an orchestra.

'But I thoroughly agree with the gentlemen who spoke before me,' said Dick, when peace was restored. 'Total abstinence is a long chalk below temperance, but it's better than drunkenness any day. And if a man can't get on without three finger-nips let him take the pledge.[135] There are one or two here to-night who would be the better for it. But to my thinking total abstinence is like a water mattress. It is good for a sick man, and it's good for a man with a weak will, which is another kind of illness. But temperance is for those who are in health. There is a text in the Bible about wine making glad the heart of man.[136] That's a good text and one to go on. As often as not texts are like bags, and a man crams all his own rubbish into them, and expects you to take them together. There are some men who ought to know better who actually get out of that text by saying the Bible means unfermented liquor' – Mr. Gresley became purple. 'Does it? Then how about the other place where we hear of new wine bursting old bottles.[137] What makes them burst? Fermentation, of course, as every village idiot knows. No, I take it when the Bible says wine it means wine. Wine's fermented liquor, and what's unfermented liquor? Nothing but 'pop'.[138]

Dick pronounced the last word with profound contempt, which was met with enthusiastic applause.

'My last word to you, gentleman,' continued Dick, 'is keep in mind two points: first, look out for an honest publican, if there is such an article, who will buy only the best liquor from the best sources, and is not bound by the breweries to sell any stuff they send along. Join together, and make it hot for a bound publican. Kick him out, even if he is the Squire's butler.' Mr. Pratt's complexion became apoplectic. 'And the second point is, remember some men have heads and some haven't. It is no use for a lame man entering for a hurdle race. A strong man can take his whack – if it's with his food – and it will do him good, while a weak man can't hang up his hat after the first smile.'

A storm of applause followed, which was perhaps all the heartier by reason of the furious face of Mr. Gresley. Dick was clapped continuously as he descended the platform, and slowly left the room feeling in his pockets for his tobacco pouch. A squad of young men creaked out after him, and others followed by twos and threes, so that the mellifluous voice of Mr. Pratt was comparatively lost, who, disregarding his position as chairman, now rose to pour oil – of which in manner alone he had always a large supply – on the troubled waters.[139] Mr. Pratt had felt a difficulty in interrupting a member of a county family, which with the eye of faith he plainly perceived Dick to be, and at the same time a guest of 'Newhaven's.' The Pratts experienced in the rare moments of their intercourse with the Newhavens some of that sublime awe, that subdued rapture, which others experience in cathedrals. Mr. Pratt had also taken a momentary pleasure in the defeat of Mr. Gresley, who did not pay him the deference which he considered due to him and his 'seat.'[140] Mr. Pratt always expected that the Vicar should, by reason of his small income, take the position of a sort of upper servant of the Squire; and he had seen so many instances of this happy state of things that he was perpetually nettled by Mr. Gresley's 'independent' attitude; while Mr. Gresley was equally irritated by 'the impatience of clerical control' and shepherding which Mr. Pratt, his largest and woolliest sheep, too frequently evinced.

As the chairman benignly expressed his approval of both views, and toned down each to meet the other, the attention of the audience wandered to the occasional laughs and cheers which came from the school playground. And when a few minutes later Rachel emerged with the stream she saw Dick standing under the solitary lamp-post speaking earnestly to a little crowd of youths and men. The laughter had ceased. Their crestfallen appearance spoke for itself.

'Well, good-night, lads,' said Dick cordially, raising his cap to them, and he rejoined Rachel and Hester at the gate.

When Dick and Rachel had departed on their bicycles, and when the deputation after a frugal supper had retired to rest, and when the drawing-room door was shut, then, and not till then, did Mr. Gresley give vent to his feelings.

'And he would not stop,' he repeated over and over again almost in hysterics, when the total abstinence hose of his wrath had been turned on Dick until every reservoir of abuse was exhausted. 'I signed to him; I spoke to him. You saw me speak to him, Minna, and he would not stop.'

Hester experienced that sudden emotion which may result either in tears or laughter at the cruel anguish brought upon her brother by the momentary experience of what he so ruthlessly inflicted.

'He talked me down,' said Mr. Gresley, his voice shaking. 'He opposed me in my own school-room. Of course, I blame myself for asking him to speak. I ought to have inquired into his principles more thoroughly, but he took me in entirely by saying one thing in this room and the exact opposite on the platform.'

'I thought his views were the same in both places,' said Hester, 'and at the time I admired you for asking him to speak, considering he is a vine-grower.'

'A what?' almost shrieked Mr. Gresley.

'A vine-grower. Surely you know he has one of the largest vineyards in South Australia?'

For a moment Mr. Gresley was bereft of speech.

'And you knew this and kept silence,' he said at last, while Mrs. Gresley looked reproachfully, but without surprise, at her sister-in-law.

'Certainly. What was there to speak about? I thought you knew.'

'I never heard it till this instant. That quite accounts for his views. He wants to push his own wines. Of course, drunkenness is working for his interests. I understand it all now. He has undone the work of years by that speech for the sake of booking a few orders. It is contemptible. I trust, Hester, he is not a particular friend of yours, for I shall feel it my duty to speak very strongly to him if he comes again.'

But Dick did not appear again. He was off and away before the terrors of the Church could be brought to bear on him.

But his memory remained green at Warpington.

'They do say,' said Abel to Hester a few days later, planting his spade on the ground, and slowly scraping off upon it the clay from his nailed boots, 'as that Muster Vernon gave 'em a dusting in the school-yard as they won't forget in a hurry. He said he could not speak out before the women folk, but he was noways nesh[141] to pick his words onst he was outside. Barnes said as his tongue 'ud 'ave raised blisters on a hedge stake. But he had a way with him for all that. There was a deal of talk about him at market last Wednesday, and Jones and Peg is just silly to go back to Australy with 'im.[142] I ain't sure,' continued Abel, closing the conversation by a vigorous thrust of his spade into the earth, 'as one of the things that fetched 'em all most[143] wasn't his saying that since he's been in a hot climate he knowed what it was to be tempted himself when he was a bit down on his luck or a bit up. Pratts would never have owned to that.' The village always spoke of Mr. Pratt in the plural without a prefix. 'I've been to a sight of temperance meetings because,' with indulgence, 'master likes it, tho' I always has my glass, as is natural. But I never heard one of the speakers kind of settle to it like that. That's what the folks say; that for all he was a born gentleman he spoke to 'em as man to man, not as if we was servants or childer.'

CHAPTER XIX

Le bruit est pour le fat.
La plainte est pour le sot.
L' honnête homme trompé
S'en va et ne dit mot.

M. DELANONI.[144]

'AND so you cannot persuade Miss Gresley to come to us next week?' said Lord Newhaven, strolling into the dining-room at Westhope Abbey, where Rachel and Dick were sitting at a little supper-table laid for two in front of the high altar. The dining-room had formerly been the chapel, and the carved stone altar still remained under the east window.

Lord Newhaven drew up a chair, and Rachel felt vaguely relieved at his presence. He had a knack of knowing when to appear, and when to efface himself.

'She can't leave her book,' said Rachel.

'Her first book was very clever,' said Lord Newhaven, 'and what was more, it was true. I hope for her own sake she will outgrow her love of truth, or it will make deadly enemies for her.'

'And good friends,' said Rachel.

'Possibly,' said Lord Newhaven, looking narrowly at her, and almost obliged to believe that she had spoken without self-consciousness. 'But if she outgrows all her principles, I hope at any rate she won't outgrow her sharp tongue. I liked her ever since she first came to this house, ten years ago, with Lady Susan Gresley. I remember saying that Captain Pratt, who called while she was here, was a 'bounder.' And Miss Gresley said she did not think he was quite a bounder, only on the boundary line. If you knew Captain Pratt, that describes him exactly.'

'I wish she had not said it,' said Rachel with a sigh. 'She makes trouble for herself by saying things like that. Is Lady Newhaven in the drawing-room?'

'Yes, I heard her singing 'The Lost Chord' not ten minutes ago.'

'I will go up to her,' said Rachel.

'I do believe,' said Lord Newhaven, when Rachel had departed, 'that she has an affection for Miss Gresley.'

'It is not necessary to be a detective in plain clothes[145] to see that,' said Dick.

'No, It generally needs to be a magnifying glass to see a woman's friendship, and then they are only expedients till we arrive, Dick. You need not be jealous of Miss Gresley. Miss West will forget all about her when she is Mrs. Vernon.'

'She does not seem very keen about that,' said Dick grimly. 'I'm only marking time. I'm no forwarder than I was.'[146]

'Well, it's your own fault for fixing your affections on a woman who is not anxious to marry. She has no objection to you. It is marriage she does not like.'

'Oh! That's bosh,' said Dick. 'All women wish to be married, and if they don't they ought to.'

He felt that an invidious reflection had been cast on Rachel.

'All the same, a man with one eye can see that women with money or anything that makes them independent of us don't flatter us by their alacrity to marry us. They will make fools of themselves for love, none greater, and they will marry for love. But their different attitude towards us, their natural lords and masters, directly we are no longer necessary to them as stepping-stones to a home and a recognised position revolts me. If you had taken my advice at the start, you would have made up to one among the mob of women who are dependent on marriage for their very existence.[147] If a man goes into that herd he will not be refused. And if he is it does not matter. It is the blessed custom of piling everything on to the eldest son, and leaving the women of the family almost penniless,[148] which provides half of us with wives without any trouble to ourselves. Whatever we are, they have got to take us. The average dancing young woman living in luxury in her father's house is between the devil and the deep sea. We are frequently the devil, but it is not surprising that she can't face the alternative, a poverty to which she was not brought up, and in which she has seen her old spinster aunts. But I suppose in your case you really want the money?'

Dick looked rather hard at Lord Newhaven.

'I should not have said that unless I had known it to be a lie,' continued the latter, 'because I dislike being kicked. But, Dick, listen to me. You have not,' with sudden misgiving, 'laid any little matrimonial project before her this evening, have you?'

'No, I was not quite such a fool as that.'

'Well! Such things do occur. Moonlight, you know, &c. &c. I was possessed by a devil once, and proposed by moonlight, as all my wife's friends know, and probably her maid. But seriously, Dick, you are not making progress, as you say yourself.'

'Well!' rather sullenly.

'Well, onlookers see most of the game. Miss West may – I don't say she is – but if things go on as they are for another week she may become slightly bored. That was why I joined you at supper. She had had, for the time, enough.'

'Of me?' said Dick, reddening under his tan.

'Just so. It is a matter of no importance after marriage, but it should be avoided beforehand. Are you really in earnest about this?'

Dick delivered himself slowly and deliberately of certain platitudes.

'Well, I hope I shall hear you say all that again some day in a condensed form before a clergyman. In the meanwhile –'

'In the meanwhile I had better clear out.'

'Yes; I don't enjoy saying so in the presence of my own galantine[149] and mayonnaise, but that is it. Go, and – come back.'

'If you have a Bradshaw,'[150] said Dick, 'I'll look out my train now. I think there is an express to London[151] about seven in the morning, if you can send me to the station.'

'But the post only comes in at eight.'

'Well, you can send my letters after me.'

'I daresay I can, my diplomatist. But you are not going to leave till the post has arrived, when you will receive business letters, requiring your immediate presence in London. You are not going to let a woman know that you leave on her account.'

'You are very sharp, Cackles,' said Dick, drearily. 'And I'll take a leaf out of your book and lie, if you think it is the right thing. But I expect she will know very well that the same business which took me to that infernal temperance meeting has taken me to London.'

Rachel was vaguely relieved when Dick went off next morning. She was not, as a rule, oppressed by the attentions she received from young men, which in due season became 'marked,' and then resulted in proposals neatly or clumsily expressed. But she was disturbed when she thought of Dick, and his departure was like the removal of a weight, not a heavy, but still a perceptible one. For Rachel was aware that Dick was in deadly earnest, and that his love was growing steadily, almost unconsciously, was accumulating like snow, flake by flake, upon a mountain-side. Some day, perhaps not for a long time, but some day, there would be an avalanche, and, in his own language, she 'would be in it.'

CHAPTER XX

Si l'on vous a trahi, ce n'est pas la trahison qui importe; c'est le pardon qu'elle a fait naitre dans votre âme ... Mais si la trahison n'a pas accru la simplicité, la confiance plus haute, l'étendue de l'amour, on vous aura trahi bien inutilement, et vous pouvez vous dire qu'il n'est rien arrivé.
MAETERLINCK.[152]

RACHEL and Hester were sitting in the shadow of the churchyard wall where Hester had so unfortunately fallen asleep on a previous occasion. It was the first of many clandestine meetings. Mr. and Mrs. Gresley did not realise that Hester and Rachel wished to 'talk secrets,' as they would have expressed it, and Rachel's arrival was felt by the Gresleys to be the appropriate moment to momentarily lay aside their daily avocations, and to join Hester and Rachel in the garden for social intercourse. The Gresleys liked Rachel. Listeners are generally liked. Perhaps also her gentle, unassuming manner was not an unpleasant change after the familiar nonchalance of the Pratts.

The two friends bore their fate for a time in inward impatience, and then, not without compunction, 'practised to deceive.'[153] Certain obtuse persons push others, naturally upright, into eluding and outwitting them, just as the really wicked people, who give *vivâ voce* invitations,[154] goad us into crevasses of lies, for which, if there is any justice anywhere, they will have to answer at the last day. Mr. Gresley gave the last shove to Hester and Rachel by an exhaustive harangue on what he called socialism.[155] Finding they were discussing some phase of it, he drew up a chair and informed them that he had 'threshed out' the whole subject.

'Socialism,' he began, delighted with the polite resignation of his hearers, which throughout life he mistook for earnest attention. 'Community of goods. People don't see that if everything were divided up to-day, and everybody was given a shilling, by next week the thrifty man would have a sovereign, and the spendthrift would be penniless. Community of goods is impossible as long as human nature remains what it is. But I can't knock that into people's heads. I spoke of it once to Lord Newhaven, after his speech in the House of Lords. I thought he was more educated and a shade less thoughtless than the idle rich usually are, and that he would see it if it was put plainly before him. But he only said my arguments were incontrovertible, and slipped away.'

It was after this conversation, or rather, monologue, that Hester and Rachel arranged to meet by stealth.

They were sitting luxuriously in the short grass, with their backs against the churchyard wall, and their hats tilted over their eyes.

'I wish I had met this Mr. Dick five or six years ago,' said Rachel with a sigh.

Hester was the only person who knew about Rachel's previous love disaster.

'Dick always gets what he wants in the long run,' said Hester. 'I should offer to marry him at once if I were you. It will save a lot of trouble, and it will come to just the same in the end.'

Rachel laughed, but not light-heartedly. Hester had only put into words a latent conviction of her own which troubled her.

'Dick is the right kind of man to marry,' continued Hester, dispassionately. 'What lights he has he lives up to. If that is not high praise I don't know what is. He is good, but somehow his goodness does not offend one. One can condone it. And if you care for such things, he has a thorough-going respect for women, which he carries about with him in a little patent safe[156] of his own.'

'I don't want to marry a man for his qualities and mental furniture,' said Rachel, wearily. 'If I did I would take Mr. Dick.'

There was a short silence.

'I am sure,' said Rachel at last, 'that you do not realise how commonplace I am. You know those conventional heroines of second-rate novels who love tremendously once, and then, when things go wrong, promptly turn into marble statues, and go through life with hearts of stone. Well, my dear, I am just like that. I know it's despicable. I have struggled against it. It is idiotic to generalise from one personal experience. I keep before my mind that other men are *not* like *him*. I know they aren't, but yet – somehow I think they are. I am frightened.'

Hester turned her wide eyes towards her friend.

'Do you still consider after these four years that *he* did you an injury?'

Rachel looked out upon the mournful landscape. The weariness of midsummer was upon it. A heavy hand seemed laid upon the brow of the distant hills.

'I gave him everything I had,' she said slowly, 'and he threw it away. I have nothing left for any one else. Perhaps it is because I am naturally economical,' she added, smiling faintly, 'that it seems now, looking back, such a dreadful waste.'

'Only in appearance, not in reality,' said Hester. 'It looks like a waste of life, that mowing down of our best years by a relentless passion which itself falls dead on the top of them. But it is not so. Every year I live I am more convinced that the waste of life lies in the love we have not given, the powers we have not used, the selfish prudence which will risk nothing, and which, shirking pain, misses happiness as well. No one ever yet was the poorer in the long run for having once in a lifetime "let out all the length of all the reins."'[157]

'You mean it did me good,' said Rachel, 'and that *he* was a kind of benefactor in disguise. I dare say you are right, but you see I don't take a burning interest in my own character. I don't find my mental standpoint – isn't that what Mrs. Loftus calls it? – very engrossing.'

'He was a benefactor all the same,' said Hester with decision. 'I did not think so at the time, and if I could have driven over him in an omnibus I would have done so with pleasure. But I believe that the day will come when you will cover that grave with a handsome monument, erected out of gratitude to him for not marrying you. And now, Rachel, will you forgive me beforehand for what I am going to say?'

'Oh!' said Rachel ruefully. 'When you say that I know it is the prelude to something frightful. You are getting out a dagger, and I shall be its sheath directly.'

'You are a true prophet, Rachel.'

'Yes, executioner.'

'My dear, dear friend, whom I love best in the world, when that happened my heart was wrung for you. I would have given everything I had, life itself – not that that is saying much – to have saved you from that hour.'

'I know it.'

'But I should have been the real enemy if I had had power to save you, which, thank God, I had not. That hour had to be. It was necessary. You may not care about your own character, but I do. There is something stubborn and inflexible in you – the seamy side of your courage and stead-fastness – which cannot readily enter into the feelings of others or put itself in their place. I think it is want of imagination – I mean the power of seeing things as they are. You are the kind of woman who, if you had married comfortably some one you rather liked, might have become like Sybell Loftus, who never understands any feeling beyond her own microscopic ones, and who measures love by her own small preference for Doll. You would have had no more sympathy than she has. People, like Sybell, believe one can only sympathise with what one has experienced. That is why they are always saying 'as a mother,' or 'as a wife.' If that were true the world would have to get on without sympathy, for no two people have the same experience. Only a shallow nature believes that a resemblance in two cups means that they both contain the same wine. Sybell believes it, and you would have been very much the same, not from lack of perception, as in her case, but for want of using your powers of perception. If you had not undergone an agonised awakening all the great realities of life – love, hatred, temptation, enthusiasm – would have remained for you as they have remained for Sybell, merely pretty words to string on light conversation. That is why I can't bear to hear her speak of them because every word she says proves she has not known them. But the sword that pierced your heart forced an entrance for angels, who had been knocking where there was no door – until then.'

Silence.

'Since when is it that people have turned to you for comfort and sympathy?'

No answer.

'Rachel, on your oath, did you ever really care for the London poor until you became poor yourself, and lived among them?'

'No.'

'But they were there all the time. You saw them in the streets. It was not as if you only heard of them. You saw them. Their agony, their vice, was written large on their faces. There was a slum almost at the back of that great house in Portman Square where you lived many years in luxury with your parents.'

'Don't,' said Rachel, her lip trembling.

'I must. You did not care then. If a flagrant case came before you you gave something like other uncharitable people who hate feeling uncomfortable. But you care *now*. You seek out those who need you. Answer me. Were they cheaply bought or not, that compassion and love for the degraded and the suffering, which were the outcome of your years of poverty in Museum Buildings?'

'They were cheaply bought,' said Rachel with conviction, speaking with difficulty.

'Would you have learnt them if you had gone on living in Portman Square?'

'Oh, Hester! would anybody?'

'Yes, they would. But that is not the question. Would *you?*'

'N – no,' said Rachel.

There was a long silence.

Rachel's mind took its staff and travelled slowly, humbly, a few more diffi-cult steps up that steep path where 'Experience is converted into thought as a mulberry-leaf is converted into satin.'[158]

At last she turned her grave eyes upon her friend.

'I see what you mean,' she said, 'I have not reached the place yet, but I can believe that I shall come to it some day when I shall feel as thankful for that trou-ble as I do feel now for having known poverty. Yes, Hester, you are right. I was a hard woman without imagination. I have been taught in the only way I could learn – by experience. I have been very fortunate.'

Hester did not answer, but bent down and kissed Rachel's hands. It was as if she had said, 'Forgive me for finding fault with one so far above me.' And the action was so understood.

Rachel coloured, and they sat for a moment hand close in hand, heart very near to heart.

'How is it you are so sure of these things, Hester?' said Rachel in a whisper. 'When you say them I see they are true, and I believe them, but how do you *know* them?'

A shadow, a very slight one, fell across Hester's face. '"Love knows the secret of grief."[159] But can Love claim that knowledge if he is asked how he came by it by one who should have known?' The question crept in between the friends and moved them apart. Hester's voice altered.

'Minna would say that I picked them up from the conversation of James. You know the Pratts are perfectly aware of what I have, of course, tried to conceal, namely, that the love scenes in the 'Idyll' were put together from scraps I had col-lected of James' engagement to Minna. And all the humorous bits are claimed by a colony of cousins in Devonshire who say that any one 'who had heard them talk' could have written the 'Idyll.' And any one who had not heard them appar-ently. The so-called profane passages are all that are left to me as my own.'

'You are profane now,' said Rachel smiling, but secretly wounded by the flip-pancy which she had brought upon herself.

A distant whoop distracted their attention, and they saw Regie galloping towards them imitating a charger, while Fraülein and the two little girls followed.

Regie stopped short before Rachel, and looked suspiciously at her.

'Where is Uncle Dick?' he said.

'I don't know,' said Rachel, reddening in spite of herself, and her eyes falling guiltily before her questioner.

'Then he has not come with you?'

Regie's mind was what his father called 'sure and steady.' Mr. Gresley often said he preferred a child of that kind to one that was quick-witted and flashy.

'No, he has not come with me.'

'Mary,' shrieked Regie, 'he has not come.'

'I knew he had not,' said Mary. 'When I saw he was not there I knew he was somewhere else.'

Dear little Mary was naturally the Gresleys' favourite child. However thoroughly they might divest themselves of parental partiality, they could not but observe that she was as sensible as a grown-up person.

'I thought he might be somewhere near,' explained Regie, 'in a tree or something,' looking up into the little yew. 'You can't tell with a conjurer like Uncle Dick, can you Auntie Hester, whatever Mary may say?'

'Mary is generally wrong,' said Hester, 'but she is right for once.'

Mary, who was early acquiring the comfortable habit of hearing only the remarks that found an echo in her own breast, heard she was right, and said shrilly:

'I told Regie when we was still on the road that Uncle Dick wasn't there. Mother doesn't always go with father, but he said he'd run and see.'

'We shall be ver'r late for luncheon,' said Fräulein hastily, blushing down to the onyx brooch at her turn-down collar, and drawing Mary away.

'Perhaps he left the halfpenny with you,' said Regie. 'Fräulein would like to see it.'

'No, no,' said Fräulein, the tears in her eyes. 'I do not vish at all. I cry half the night when I hear of it.'

'I only cry when baby beats me,' said Mary, balancing on one leg.

'I have not got the halfpenny,' said Rachel, the three elders studiously ignoring Mary's personal reminiscences.

The children were borne away by Fräulein, and the friends kissed and parted.

'I am coming to Wilderleigh to-morrow,' said Rachel. 'I shall be much nearer to you then.'

'It is no good contending against Dick and fate,' said Hester, shaking her finger at her. 'You see it is all decided for you. Even the children have settled it.'

CHAPTER XXI

If a fool be associated with a wise man all his life, he will perceive the truth as little as a spoon perceives the taste of soup.
Buddhist Dhammopada.

I CAN'T think what takes you to Wilderleigh,' said Lady Newhaven to Rachel. 'I am always bored to death when I go there. Sybell is so self-centred.'

Perhaps one of the reasons why Lady Newhaven and Sybell Loftus did not 'get on,' was owing to a certain superficial resemblance between them.

Both exacted attention, and if they were in the same room together it seldom contained enough attention to supply the needs of both. Both were conscious, like 'Celia Chettam,'[160] that since the birth of their first child their opinions respecting literature, politics, and art had acquired additional weight and solidity, and that a wife and mother could pronounce with decision on important subjects where a spinster would do well to hold her peace. Each was fond of saying, 'As a married woman I think this or that'; yet each was conscious of dislike and irritation when she heard the other say it. And there is no doubt that Sybell had been too unwell to appear at Lady Newhaven's garden party the previous summer, because Lady Newhaven had the week before advanced her cherished theory of 'one life one love,' to the delight of Lord Newhaven, and the natural annoyance of Sybell, whose second husband was at that moment handing tea, and answering, 'That depends,' when appealed to.

'As if,' as Sybell said afterwards to Hester, 'a woman can help being the ideal of two men.'

'Sybell is such a bore now,' continued Lady Newhaven, 'that I don't know what she will be when she is older. I don't know why you go to Wilderleigh of all places.'

'I go because I am asked,' said Rachel, 'and partly because I shall be near Hester Gresley.'

'I don't think Miss Gresley can be very anxious to see you, or she would have come here when I invited her. I told several people she was coming, and that Mr. Carstairs, who thinks so much of himself, came on purpose to meet her. It is very tiresome of her to behave like that, especially as she did not say she had any engagement. You make a mistake Rachel, in running after people who won't take any trouble to come and see you. It is a thing I never do myself.'

'She is buried in her book at present.'

'I can't think what she has to write about. But I suppose she picks up things from other people.'

'I think so. She is a close observer.'

'I think you are wrong, there, Rachel, for when she was here some years ago, she never looked about her at all. And I asked her how she judged of people, and she said, 'By appearances.' Now that was very silly, because as I explained to her, appearances were most deceptive, and I had often thought a person with a cold manner was cold-hearted, and afterwards found I was quite mistaken.'

Rachel did not answer. She wondered in what the gift consisted, which Lady Newhaven and Sybell both possessed, of bringing all conversation to a standstill.

'It seems curious, ' said Lady Newhaven after a pause, 'how the books are mostly written by the people who know least of life. Now the 'Sonnets from the Portuguese.' People think so much of them. I was looking at them the other day. Why, they are nothing to what I have felt. I sometimes think if *I* wrote a book – I don't mean that I have any special talent – but if I really sat down and wrote a book with all the deep side of life in it, and one's own religious feelings, and described love and love's tragedy as they really are, what a sensation it would make. It would take the world by storm.'

'Any book dealing sincerely with one of those subjects could not fail to be a great success.'

'Oh, yes. I am not afraid I should fail. I do wish you were not going, Rachel. We have so much in common. And it is such a comfort to be with some one who knows what one is going through. I believe you feel the suspense, too, for my sake.'

'I do feel it – deeply.'

'I sometimes think,' said Lady Newhaven, her face ageing suddenly under an emotion so disfiguring that Rachel's eyes fell before it. 'I am sometimes almost certain that Edward drew the short lighter. Oh! do you think if he did he will really *act up to it* when the time comes?'

'If he drew it he will certainly take the consequences.'

'Will he, do you think? I am almost sure he drew it. He is doing so many little things that look as if he knew he were not going to live. I heard Mr. Carstairs ask him to go to Norway with him next spring, and Edward laughed, and said he never looked more than a few months ahead.'

'I am afraid he may have said that intending you to hear it.'

'But he did not intend me to hear it. I overheard it.'

Rachel's face fell.

'You did promise after you told me about the letter that you would never do that kind of thing again.'

'Well, Rachel, I have not. I have not even looked at his letters since. I could not help it that once, because I thought he might have told his brother in India. But don't you think his saying that to Mr. Carstairs looks –'

Rachel shook her head.

'He is beyond me,' she said. 'There may be something more behind which we don't know about.'

'I have a feeling, it has come over me again and again lately, that I shall be released, and that Hugh and I shall be happy together yet.'

And Lady Newhaven turned her face against the high back of her carved oak chair, and sobbed hysterically.

'Could you be happy if you had brought about Lord Newhaven's death?' said Rachel.

Her voice was full of tender pity, not for the crouching unhappiness before her, but for the poor atrophied soul. Could she reach it? She would have given everything she possessed at that moment for one second of Christ's power to touch those blind eyes to sight.[161]

'How can you say such things. I should *not* have brought it about. I did not even know of that dreadful drawing of lots till the thing was done. That was all his own doing.'

Rachel sighed. The passionate yearning towards her companion shrank back upon herself.

'The fault is in me,' she said to herself. 'If I were purer, humbler, more loving, I might have been allowed to help her.'

Lady Newhaven rose, and held Rachel tightly in her arms.

'I count the days,' she said hoarsely, shaking from head to foot. 'It is two months and three weeks to-day. November the twenty-ninth. You will promise faithfully to come to me and be with me then? You will not desert me? Whatever happens you will be sure – to come?'

'I will come. I promise,' said Rachel. And she stooped and kissed the closed eyes. She could at least do that.

CHAPTER XXII

Brother, thy tail hangs down behind.
Song of the Bandar-log.[162]

RACHEL arrived after tea at Wilderleigh, and went straight to her room on a plea of fatigue. It was a momentary cowardice that tempted her to yield to her fatigue. She felt convinced that she should meet Hugh Scarlett at Wilderleigh. She had no reason for the conviction beyond the very inadequate one that she had met him at Sybell's London house. Nevertheless she felt sure that he would be among the guests, and she longed for a little breathing space after parting with Lady Newhaven before she met him. Presently Sybell flew in and embraced her with effusion.

'Oh! what you have missed!' she said breathlessly. 'But you do look tired. You were quite right to lie down before dinner, only you aren't lying down. We have had such a conversation downstairs. The others are all out boating with Doll but Mr. Harvey, the great Mr. Harvey, you know.'

'I am afraid I don't know.'

'Oh yes, you do. The author of "Unashamed".'

'I remember now.'

'Well, he is here, resting after his new book, "Rahab." And he has been reading us the opening chapters, just to Miss Barker and me. It is quite wonderful. So painful, you know. He does not spare the reader anything, he thinks it wrong to leave out anything, but so powerful.'

'Is it the same Miss Barker whom I met at your house in the season who denounced "The Idyll"?'

'Yes. How she did cut it up. You see she knows all about East London, and that sort of thing. I knew you would like to meet her again because you are philanthropic, too. She hardly thought she could spare the time to come, but she thought she would go back fresher if the wail were out of her ears for a week. The wail! Isn't it dreadful. I feel we ought to do more than we do, don't you?'

'We ought, indeed.'

'But, then, you see as a married woman – I can't leave my husband and child, and bury myself in the East End, can I?'

'Of course not. But surely it is an understood thing that marriage exempts women from all impersonal duties.'

'Yes, that is just it. How well you put it. But others could. I often wonder why after writing 'The Idyll' Hester never goes near East London. I should have gone straight off, and have cast in my lot with them if I had been in her place.'

'Do you ever find people do what you would have done if you had been in their place?'

'No, never. They don't seem to see it. It's a thing I can't understand, the way people don't act up to their convictions. And I do know, though I would not tell Hester so for worlds, that the fact that she goes on living comfortably in the country after bringing out that book makes thoughtful people, not me, of course, but other earnest-minded people, think she is a humbug.'

'It would – naturally,' said Rachel.

'Well, now I am glad you agree with me, for I said something of the same kind to Mr. Scarlett last night, and he could not see it. He's rather obtuse. I daresay you remember him?'

'Perfectly.'

'I don't care about him, he is so superficial, and Miss Barker says he is very lethargic in conversation. I asked him because – don't breathe a word of it – but because as a married woman one ought to help others, and – do you remember how he stood up for Hester that night in London?'

'For her book, you mean.'

'Well, it's all one. Men are men, my dear. Let me tell you he would never have done that if he had not been in love with her.'

'Do you mean that men never defend obvious truths unless they are in love!'

'Now you are pretending to misunderstand me,' said Sybell joyously, making her little squirrel face into a becoming pout. 'But it's no use trying to take me in. And it's coming right. He's there at this moment!'

'At the Vicarage?'

'Where else! I asked him to go. I urged him. I said I felt sure she expected him. One must help on these things.'

'But if he is obtuse and lethargic and superficial, is he likely to suit Hester?'

'My dear, the happiest lot for a woman is marriage. And you and I are Hester's friends. So we ought to do all we can for her happiness. That is why I just mentioned this.'

The dressing-gong began to boom.

'I must fly,' said Sybell, depositing a butterfly kiss on Rachel's forehead. And she flew.

'I wish I knew what I felt about him,' said Rachel to herself. 'I don't much like hearing him called obtuse and superficial, but I suppose I should like still less to hear Sybell praise him. I have never heard her praise anything but mediocrity yet.'

If Rachel had been at all introspective she might have found a clue as to her feeling for Hugh in the unusual care with which she arranged her hair, and her decision at the last moment to discard the pale-green gown lying in state on the bed for a white satin one embroidered at long intervals with rose-coloured carnations. The gown was a masterpiece, designed especially for her by a great French milliner. Rachel often wondered whose eyesight had been strained over those marvellous carnations,[163] but to-night she did not give them a thought. She looked with grave dissatisfaction at her pale nondescript face and nondescript hair and eyes. She did not know that only women with marriageable daughters saw her as she saw herself in the glass.

As she left her room a door opened at the further end of the same wing, and a tall man came out. The middle-class element in her said, 'Superfine.'[164] His fastidious taste said, 'A plain woman.'

In another instant they recognised each other.

'Superfine! What nonsense,' she thought, as she met his eager tremulous glance.

'A plain woman. Rachel plain!' He had met the welcome in her eyes, and there was beauty in every movement, grace in every fold of her white gown.

As they met the gong suddenly boomed out close beneath them, and they could only smile at each other as they shook hands. The butler, who was evidently an artist in his way, proved the gong[165] to the uttermost; and they had descended the staircase together, and had crossed the hall before its dying tremors allowed them to speak.

As he was about to do so he saw her wince suddenly. She was looking straight in front of her at the little crowd in the drawing-room. For an instant her face turned from white to grey, and she involuntarily put out her hand as if to ward off something. Then a lovely colour mounted to her cheek; she drew herself up and entered the room, while Hugh, behind her, looked fiercely at each man in succession.

It is always the unexpected that happens. As Rachel's half-absent eyes passed over the group in the brilliantly lighted drawing-room her heart reared without warning and fell back upon her. She had only just sufficient presence of mind to prevent her hand pressing itself against her heart. He was there, he was before her – the man whom she had loved with passion for four years, and who had tortured her.

Mr. Harvey (the great Mr. Harvey) strode forward, and Rachel found her hand engulfed in a large soft hand which seemed to have a poached egg in the palm.

'This is a pleasure to which I have long looked forward,' murmured the great man, all cuff and solitaire, bending in what he would have termed a 'chivalrous manner' over Rachel's hand; while Doll, standing near, wondered drearily 'why these writing chaps were always such bounders.'

Rachel passed on to greet Miss Barker, standing on the hearthrug, this time in magenta velveteen, but presumably still tired of the Bible, conversing with Rachel's former lover, whose eyes were on the floor, and whose hand gripped the mantelpiece. He had seen her – recognised her.

'May I introduce Mr. Tristram?' said Sybell to Rachel.

'We have met before,' said Rachel gently, as he bowed without looking at her, and she put out her hand.

He was obliged to touch it, obliged to meet for one moment the clear calm eyes that had once held boundless love for him, boundless trust in him; that had, as he well knew, wept themselves half blind for him.

Mr. Tristram was one of the many who judge their actions in the light of after circumstances, and who towards middle age discover that the world is a treacherous world. He had not been 'in a position to marry' when he had fallen in love with Rachel. But he had been as much in love with her as was consistent with a permanent prudential passion for himself and his future, that future which the true artist must ever preserve untrammelled. 'High hopes faint on a warm hearth-stone,'[166] &c. He had felt keenly breaking with Rachel. Later on, when a tide of wealth flowed up to the fifth floor of Museum Buildings, he had recognised for the first time that he had made a great mistake in life. To the smart of baffled love had been added acute remorse, not so much for wealth missed as for having inflicted upon himself and upon her a frightful and unnecessary pain. But how could he have foreseen such a thing? How could he tell? he had asked himself in mute stupefaction when the news reached him. What a cheat life was! What a fickle jade was Fortune!

Since the memorable day when Rachel had found means to lay the ghost that haunted her he had made no sign.

'I hardly expected you would remember me,' he said, catching at his self-possession.

'I have a good memory,' she said, aware that Miss Barker was listening, and that Hugh was bristling at her elbow. 'And the little Spanish boy whom you were so kind to, and who lodged just below me in Museum Buildings, has not forgotten either. He still asks after the "Cavaliere."'

'Mr. Tristram is positively blushing at being confronted with his good deeds,' said Sybell, intervening on discovering that the attention of some of her guests had been distracted from herself. 'Yes, darling' – to her husband – 'you take in Lady Jane. Mr. Scarlett, will you take in Miss West?'

'I have been calling on your friend, Miss Gresley,' said Hugh, after he had overcome his momentary irritation at finding Mr. Harvey was on Rachel's other side. 'I did not know until her brother dined here last night that she lived so near.'

'Did not Mrs. Loftus tell you?' said Rachel, with a remembrance of Sybell's remarks before dinner.

'She told me after I had mentioned my wish to go and see her. She even implored me so repeatedly to go that I –'

'Nearly did not go at all.'

'Exactly. But in this case I preserved because I am, or hope I am, a friend of hers. But I was not rewarded.'

'I thought you said you had seen her.'

'Oh, yes, I saw her, and I saw that she looked very ill. But I found it impossible to have any conversation with her in the presence of Mr. and Mrs. Gresley. Whenever I spoke to her Mr. Gresley answered, and sometimes Mrs. Gresley also. In fact, Mr. Gresley considered the call as paid to himself. Mrs. Loftus tells me he is much cleverer than his sister, but I did not gain that impression. And after I had given tongue to every platitude I could think of I had to take my leave.'

'Hester ought to have come to the rescue.'

'She did try. She offered to show me the short cut to Wilderleigh across the fields. But unluckily –'

'I can guess what you are going to say.'

'I am sure you can. Mr. Gresley accompanied us, and Miss Gresley turned back at the first gate.'

'You have my sympathy.'

'I hope I have, for I have had a severe time of it. Mr. Gresley was most cordial,' continued Hugh ruefully, 'and said what a pleasure it was to him to meet any one who was interested in intellectual subjects. I suppose he was referring to my platitudes. He said living in the country cut him off almost entirely from the society of his mental equals, so much so that at times he had thoughts of moving to London, and making a little centre for intellectual society. According to him the whole neighbourhood was sunk in a state of hopeless apathy, with the exception of Mrs. Loftus. He said she was the only really clever cultivated person in Middleshire.'

'Did he? How about the Bishop of Southminster?'

'He did not mention him. My acquaintance with Mrs. Loftus is of the slightest,' added Hugh, interrogatively, looking at his graceful, animated hostess.

'I imagined you knew her fairly well, as you are staying here.'

'No. She asked me rather late in the day. I fancy I was a "fill up."[167] I accepted in the hope, rather a vague one, that I might meet you here.'

To Rachel's surprise her heart actually paid Hugh the compliment of beating a shade faster than its wont. She looked straight in front of her, and her absent eyes fell on Mr. Tristram sitting opposite, talking somewhat sulkily to Miss Barker. Rachel looked steadily at him.

Mr. Tristram had been handsome once, and four years had altered him but little in that respect. He had not yet grown stout, but it was evident that Nature had that injury in reserve for him. To grow stout is not necessarily to look common, but if there is an element of inherent commonness in man or woman, a very little additional surface will make it manifest, as an enlarged photograph magnifies its own defects. The 'little more and how much it is'[168] had come upon the unhappy Tristram, once the slimmest of the slim. Life had evidently not gone too well with him. Self-pity and the harassed look which comes of annoyance with trifles had set their mark upon him. His art had not taken possession of him. 'High hopes faint on a warm hearth-stone.' But they sometimes faint also in bachelor lodgings. The whole effect of the man was second rate, mentally, morally, socially. He seemed exactly on a par with the second-rate friends with whom Sybell loved to surround herself. Hugh and Dick were taking their revenge on the rival who blocked their way. Whatever their faults might be, they were gentlemen, and Mr. Tristram was only 'a perfect gentleman.'[169] Rachel had not known the difference when she was young. She saw it now.

'I trust, Miss West,' said the deep voice of the Harvey, revolving himself and his solitaire slowly towards her, 'that I have your sympathy in the great cause to which I have dedicated myself, the emancipation of woman.'

'I thought the new woman had effected her own emancipation,' said Rachel.

Mr. Harvey paid no more attention to her remark than any one with a theory to propound which must be delivered to the world as a whole.

'I venture to think,' he continued, his heavy, lustreless eyes coming to a standstill upon her, 'that though I accept in all reverence the position of woman as the equal of man, as promulgated in "The Princess," by our lion-hearted Laureate,[170] nevertheless I advance beyond him in that respect. I hold,' in a voice calculated to impress the whole table, 'that woman is man's superior, and that she degrades herself when she endeavours to place herself on an equality with him.'

There was a momentary silence, like that which travellers tell us succeeds the roar of the lion in his primeval forest, silencing even the twitter of the birds.

'How true that is,' said Sybell, awed by the lurid splendour of Mr. Harvey's genius. 'Woman is man's superior, not his equal. I have felt that all my life, but I never quite saw how until this moment. Don't you think so, too, Miss Barker?'

'I have never lost an opportunity of asserting it,' said the Apostle, her elbow on Mr. Tristram's bread, looking at Mr. Harvey with some asperity, for poaching on her manor. 'All sensible women have been agreed for years on that point.'

CHAPTER XXIII

With aching hands and bleeding feet
We dig and heap, lay stone on stone;
We bear the burden and the heat
Of the long day, and wish 'twere done!
Not till the hours of light return,
All we have built do we discern.
MATTHEW ARNOLD.[171]

IT was Sunday morning. The night was sinking out of the sky to lean faint unto death upon the bosom of the earth. The great forms of the trees, felt rather than seen, were darkness made visible. Among the night of high elms round Warpington a single yellow light burned in an upper window. It had been burning all night. And now, as the night waned, the little light waned with it. At last, it was suddenly blown out.

Hester came to the window and looked out. There was light, but there was no dawn as yet. In the grey sky over the grey land the morning star, alone and splendid, kept watch in the east.

She sat down and leaned her brow against the pane. She did not know that it was aching. She did not know that she was cold, exhausted, so exhausted that the morning star in the outer heaven and the morning star in her soul were to her the same. They stooped together, they merged into one great light, heralding a perfect day presently to be.

The night was over, and that other long night of travail and patience and faith, and strong rowing in darkness against the stream, was over, too, at last – at last. *The book was finished.*

The tears fell slowly from Hester's eyes on to her clasped hands, those blessed tears which no human hand shall ever intervene to wipe away.

To some of us Christ comes in the dawn of the spiritual life walking upon the troubled waves of art.[172] And we recognise Him, and would fain go to meet Him. But our companions and our own fears dissuade us. They say it is only a spirit, and that Christ does not walk on water, that the land whither we are rowing is the place He has Himself appointed for us to meet Him. So our little faith keeps us in the boat, or fails us in the waves of that wind-swept sea.

It seemed to Hester as if once, long ago, shrinking and shivering, she had stood in despair upon the shore of a great sea, and had heard a voice from the other side say, 'Come over.' She had stopped her ears, she had tried not to go. She had shrunk back a hundred times from the cold touch of the water that each time she essayed let her trembling foot through it. And now, after an interminable interval, after she had trusted and doubted, had fallen and been sustained, had met the wind and the rain, after she had sunk in despair, and risen again, she knew not how, now at length a great wave – the last – had cast her up half-drowned upon the shore. A miracle had happened. She had reached the other side, and was lying in a great peace after the storm upon the solemn shore under a great white star.

Hester sat motionless. The star paled and paled before the coming of a greater than he. Across the pause which God has set 'twixt night and day came the first word of the robin. It reached Hester's ear as from another world, a world that had been left behind. The fragmentary notes floated up to her from an immeasurable distance like scattered bubbles through deep water.

The day was coming. God's creatures of tree and field and hill took form. Man's creature, the little stout church in their midst, thrust once more its plebeian outline against God's sky. Dim shapes moved athwart the vacancy of the meadows. Voices called through the grey. Close against the eaves a secret was twittered, was passed from beak to beak. In the nursery below a little twitter of waking children broke the stillness of the house.

But Hester did not hear it. She had fallen into a deep sleep in the low window-seat, with her pale forehead against the pane; a sleep so deep that even the alarum of the baby did not rouse her, nor the entrance of Emma with the hot water.

'James,' said Mrs. Gresley, an hour later, as she and her husband returned through the white mist from early celebration, 'Hester was not there. I thought she had promised to come.'

'She had.'

There was a moment's silence.

'Perhaps she is not well,' said Mr. Gresley, closing the churchyard gate into the garden.

Mrs. Gresley's heart swelled with a sense of injustice. She had often been unwell, often in feeble health before the birth of her children, but had she ever pleaded ill-health as an excuse for absenting herself from one of the many services which her husband held to be the mainspring of the religious life?

'I do not think she can be very unwell. She is standing by the magnolia now,' she said, her lip quivering, and withdrawing her hand from her husband's arm. She almost hated the slight graceful figure, which was not of her world, which was, as she thought, coming between her and her husband.

'I will speak seriously to her,' said Mr. Gresley, dejectedly, who recollected that he had 'spoken seriously' to Hester many times at his wife's instigation without visible result. And as he went alone to meet his sister he prayed earnestly that he might be given the right word to say to her.

A ray of sunlight, faint as an echo, stole through the lingering mist, parting it on either hand, and fell on Hester.

Hester, standing in a white gown under the veiled trees in a glade of silver and trembling opal, which surely mortal foot had never trod, seemed infinitely removed from him. Dimly he felt that she was at one with this mysterious morning world, and that he, the owner, was an alien and a trespasser in his own garden.

But a glimpse of his cucumber frames in the background reassured him. He advanced with a firmer step, as one among allies.

Hester did not hear him.

She was gazing with an absorption that shut out all other sights and sounds at the solitary blossom on the magnolia tree. Yesterday it had been a bud. But to-day the great almond white petals which guarded it, overlapping each other so jealously, had opened wide, and the perfect flower, keeping nothing back, had laid bare all its pure white soul before its God.

As Mr. Gresley stopped beside her, Hester turned her little pinched ravaged face towards him and smiled. Something of the passionate self-surrender of the flower was reflected in her eyes.

'Dear Hester,' he said, seeing only the wan drawn face. 'Are you ill?'

'Yes. No. I don't think so,' said Hester tremulously, recalled suddenly to herself. She looked hastily about her. The world of dew and silver had deserted her, had broken like an iridescent bubble at a touch. The magnolia withdrew itself. Hester found herself suddenly transplanted into the prose of life, emphasised by a long clerical coat, and a bed of Brussels sprouts.

'I missed you,' said Mr. Gresley with emphasis.

'Where? When?' Hester's eyes had lost their fixed look, and stared vacantly at him.

Mr. Gresley tried to subdue his rising annoyance.

Hester was acting, pretending not to understand, and he saw through it.

'At God's altar,' he said gravely, the priest getting the upper hand of the man.

'Have you not found me, there?' said Hester below her breath, but so low that fortunately her brother did not catch the words, and was spared their profanity.

'I will appeal to her better feelings,' he said to himself. 'They must be there if I can only touch them.'

He did not know that in order to touch the better feelings of our fellow natures we must be able to reach up to them, or by reason of our low stature we may succeed only in appealing to the lowest in them in spite of our tip-toe good intentions. Is that why such appeals too often meet with bitter sarcasm and indignation?

But fortunately a robust belief in the assiduities of the devil as the cause of all failures, and a conviction that whose opposed Mr. Gresley opposed the Diety, supported and blindfolded the young Vicar in emergencies of this kind.

He spoke earnestly and at length to his sister. He waved aside her timid excuse that she had overslept herself after a sleepless night, and had finished dressing but the moment before he found her in the garden. He entreated her to put aside such insincerity as unworthy of her. He reminded her of the long months she had spent at Warpington with its peculiar spiritual opportunities; that he should be to blame if he did not press upon her the first importance of the religious life, the ever-present love of God, and the means of approaching Him through the sacraments.[173] He entreated her to join her prayers with his that she might be saved from the worship of her own talent which had shut out the worship of God, from this dreadful indifference to holy things, and the impatience of all religious teaching which he grieved to see in her.

He spoke well, the earnest blind would be leader endeavouring to guide her to the ditch from which he knew not how she had emerged, passionately distressed at the opposition he met with as he would have drawn her lovingly towards it.

The tears were in Hester's eyes, but the eyes themselves were as flint seen through water. She stifled many fierce and cruel impulses to speak as plainly as he did, to tell him that it was not religion that was abhorrent to her, but the form in which he presented it to her, and that the sin against the Holy Ghost was disbelief, like his in the religion of others. But when have such words availed anything? When have they been believed? Hester had a sharp tongue, and she was slowly learning to beware of it as her worst enemy. She laid down many weapons before she trusted herself to speak.

'It is good of you to care what becomes of me,' she said gently, but her voice was cold. 'I am sorry you regard me as you do. But from your point of view you were right to speak – as – as you have done. I value the affection that prompted it.'

'She can't meet me fairly,' said Mr. Gresley to himself, with sudden anger at the meanness of such tactics. 'They say she is so clever, and she can't refute a word I say. She appears to yield and then defies me. She always puts me off like that.'

The sun had vanquished the mist, and in the brilliant light the two figures moved silently side by side back to the house, one with something very like rage in his heart, the rage that in bygone days found expression in stake and faggot.[174]

Perhaps the heaviest trouble which Hester was ever called upon to bear had its mysterious beginnings on that morning of opal and gossamer when the magnolia opened.

CHAPTER XXIV

Il le fit avec des arguments inconsistants et irréfutables, de ces arguments qui fondent devant la raison comme la neige au feu, et qu'on ne peut saisir, des arguments absurdes et triomphants de cure de campagne qui demontre Dieu.

GUY DE MAUPASSANT.[175]

SYBELL'S party broke up on Saturday, with the exception of Rachel and Mr. Tristram, who had been unable to finish by that date a sketch he was making of Sybell. When Doll discovered that his wife had asked that gentleman to stay over Sunday he entreated Hugh in moving terms to do the same.

'I am not literary,' said Doll, who always thought it necessary to explain that he was not what no one thought he was. 'I hate all that sort of thing. Utter rot I call it. For goodness' sake, Scarlett, sit tight. I must be decent to the beast in my own house, and if you go I shall have to have him alone jawing at me till all hours of the night in the smoking-room.'

Hugh was easily persuaded, and so it came about that the morning congregation at Warpington had the advantage of furtively watching Hugh and Mr. Tristram as they sat together in the carved Wilderleigh pew, with Sybell and Rachel at one end of it and Doll at the other. No one looked at Rachel. Her hat attracted a momentary attention, but her face none.

The Miss Pratts, on the contrary, well caparisoned by their man milliner, well groomed, well curled, were a marked feature of the sparse congregation. The spectator of so many points, all made the most of, unconsciously felt with a sense of oppression that everything that could be done had been done. No stone had been left unturned.

Their brother, Captain Algernon Pratt, sitting behind them, looked critically at them, and owned that they were smart women. But he was not entirely satisfied with them as he had been in the old days, before he went into the Guards and began the real work of his life, raising himself in society.

Captain Pratt was a tall, pale young man – *assez beau garçon*[176] – faultlessly dressed, with a quiet acquired manner. He was not ill-looking, the long upper lip concealed by a perfectly kept moustache, but the haggard eye and the thin line in the cheek, which did not suggest thought and over-work as their cause, made his appearance vaguely repellant.

Jesu, lover of my soul,[177]

sang the shrill voices of the choir boys, echoed by Regie and Mary, standing together, holding their joint hymn-book exactly equally between them, their two small thumbs touching.

Fraülein, on Hester's other side, was singing with her whole soul, accompanied by a pendulous movement of the body:

Cover my defenceless 'ead,
Wiz ze sadow of zy wing.

Mr. Gresley, after baying like a bloodhound through the opening verses, ascended the pulpit and engaged in prayer. The congregation amen-ed and settled itself. Mary leaned her blonde head against her mother, Regie against Hester.

The supreme moment of the week had come for Mr. Gresley.

He gave out the text:

'Can the blind lead the blind? Shall they not both fall into the ditch?'[178]

All of us who are Churchmen are aware that the sermon is a period admirably suited for quiet reflection.

'A good woman loves but once,' said Mr. Tristram to himself in an attitude of attention, his fine eyes fixed decorously on a pillar in front of him. Some of us would be as helpless without a Bowdlerised[179] generality or a platitude to sustain our minds as the invalid would be without his peptonised beef-tea.[180]

'Rachel is a good woman, a saint. Such a woman does not love in a hurry, but when she does she loves for ever.' What was that poem he and she had so often read together? Tennyson, wasn't it? about love not altering 'when it alteration finds,'[181] but bears it out even to the crack of doom. Fine poet, Tennyson, he knew the human heart. She had certainly adored him four years ago, just in the devoted way in which he needed to be loved. And how he had worshipped her! Of course he had behaved badly. He saw that now. But if he had it was not from want of love. She had been unable to see that at the time. Good women were narrow, and they were hard, and they did not understand men. Those were their faults. Had she learnt better by now? Did she realise that she had far better marry a man who had loved her for herself, and who still loved her, rather than some fortune-hunter like that weedy fellow Scarlett. (Mr. Tristram called all slender men weedy.) He would frankly own his fault and ask for forgiveness. He glanced for a moment at the gentle familiar face beside him.

'She will forgive me,' he said, reassuring himself in spite of an inward qualm of misgiving. 'I am glad I arranged to stay on. I will speak to her this afternoon. She has become much softened, and we will bury the past, and make a fresh start together.'

'I will walk up to Beaumere this afternoon,' said Doll, stretching a leg outside the open end of the pew. 'I wish Gresley would not call the Dissenters worms. They are some of my best tenants, and they won't like it when they hear of it. And I'll go round the young pheasants. (Doll did this or something similar every Sunday afternoon of his life, but he always rehearsed it comfortably in thought on Sunday mornings.) And if Withers is about I'll go out in the boat, the big one, the little one leaks, and set a trimmer or two for to-morrow. I'm not sure I'll set one under the south bank, for there was the devil to pay last time when that beast of an eel got among the roots. I'll ask Withers what he thinks. I wish Gresley would not call the Dissenters blind leaders of the blind. It's such bad form, and I don't suppose the text meant that to start with, and what's the use of ill-feeling in a parish. And I'll take Scarlett with me. We'll slip off after luncheon, and leave that bounder to bound by himself. And poor old Crack shall come too. Uncle George always took him.'

'James is simply surpassing himself,' said Mrs. Gresley to herself, her arm round her little daughter. 'Worms! what a splendid comparison. The Churchman the full-grown man after the stature of Christ, and the Dissenter invertebrate (I think dear James means inebriate) like a worm cleaving to the earth. But possibly God in his mercy may let them slip in by a back door to heaven! How like him to say that, so generous, so wide-minded, taking the hopeful view of everything. How noble he looks. These are days in which we should stick to our colours.[182] I wonder how he can think of such beautiful things. For my part I think the duty of the true priest is not to grovel to the crowd and call wrong right and right wrong for the sake of a fleeting popularity. How striking! What a lesson to the Bishop if he were only here. He is so lax about Dissent, as if right and wrong were mere matters of opinion. What a gift he has. I know he will eat nothing for luncheon. If only we were somewhere else where the best joints were a little cheaper, and his talents more appreciated.' And Mrs. Gresley closed her eyes and prayed earnestly, a tear sliding down her cheek on to Mary's floss-silk mane, that she might become less unworthy to be the wife of one so far above her, that the children might all grow up like him, and that she might be given patience to bear with Hester even when she vexed him.

Captain Pratt's critical eye travelled over the congregation. It absolutely ignored Mrs. Gresley and Fraülein. It lingered momentarily on Hester. He knew what he called 'breeding' when he saw it, and he was aware that Hester possessed it, though his sisters would have laughed at the idea. He had seen many well-bred women on social pinnacles look like that, whose houses were at present barred against him. The Pratt sisters were fixed into their smartness as some faces are fixed into a grin. It was not spontaneous, fugitive, evanescent as a smile, grace-fully worn, or lightly laid aside as in Hester's case. He had known Hester slightly in London for several years. He had seen her on terms of intimacy, such as she never showed to his sisters, with inaccessible men and women with whom he had achieved a bare acquaintance, but whom, in spite of many carefully concealed advances, he had found it impossible to know better. Captain Pratt had reached that stage in his profession of raising himself when he had become a social barometer. He was excessively careful whom he knew, what women he danced with, what houses he visited, and any of his acquaintances who cared to ascertain their own social status to a hairsbreadth had only to apply to it the touchstone of Captain Pratt's manner towards them.

Hester, who grasped many facts of that kind, was always amused by the cold consideration with which he treated her on his rare visits to the parental Towers; and which his sisters could only construe as a sign that 'Algy was gone on Hessie.'

'But he will never marry her,' they told each other. 'Algy looks higher.'

It was true. If Hester had been Lady Hester, it is possible that the surname of Pratt, if frequently refused by stouter women, might eventually have been offered to her. But Captain Pratt was determined to marry rank, and nothing short of a Lady Something was of any use to him. An Honourable was better than nothing, but it did not count for much with him. It had a way of absenting itself when wanted. No one was announced as an Honourable. It did not even appear on cards.[183] It might be overlooked. Rank, to be of any practical value, must be apparent, obvious. Lady Georgiana Pratt, Lady Evelina Pratt! Any name would do with that prefix. His eye travelled as far as Sybell and stopped again. She was 'the right sort' herself, and she dressed in the right way. Why could not Ada and Selina imitate her? But he had never forgiven her the fact that he had met 'a crew of cads' at her house, whom he had been obliged to cut afterwards in the Row. No, Sybell would not have done for him. She surrounded herself with vulgar people.

Captain Pratt was far too well-mannered to be guilty of staring, except at pretty maidservants or shop girls, and his eye was moved on by the rigid police of etiquette which ruled his every movement. It paused momentarily on Rachel. He knew about her, as did every bachelor in London. A colossal heiress. She was neither plain nor handsome. She had a good figure, but not good enough to counterbalance her nondescript face. She had not the air of distinction which he was so quick to detect and appraise. She was a social nonentity. He did not care to look at her a second time. 'I would not marry her with twice her fortune,' he said to himself.

Regie's hand had stolen into Hester's. His even breathing, felt rather than heard, as he dropped asleep against her shoulder, surrounded Hester with the atmosphere of peace and comfort which his father had broken earlier in the day. Regie often brought back to her what his father wrested from her.

She listened to the sermon as from a warm nest safely raised above the quaggy ground of personal feeling.

'Dear James! How good he is; how much in earnest. But worms don't go in at back doors. Why are not clergymen taught a few elementary rules of composition before they are ordained? But perhaps no one will notice it except myself. James is certainly a saint. He has the courage of his opinions. I believe he loves God and the Church with his whole heart, and would go to the stake for them, or send me there if he thought it was for the good of my soul. Why has he no power? Why is he so much disliked in the parish and neighbourhood? I am sure it is not because he has small abilities and makes puns, and says cut-and-dried things. How many excellent clergymen who do the same are beloved? Is it because he deals with every one as he deals with me? What dreadful things he thinks of me. I don't wonder he is anxious about me. What unworthy motives of wilful blindness and arrogance he is attributing to the Nonconformists! Oh, James! James! will you never see that it is disbelief in the sincerity of the religion of others, because it is not in the same narrow form as your own, which makes all your zeal and earnestness of none effect! You think the opposition you meet with everywhere is the opposition of evil to good, of indifference to piety. When will you learn that it is the good in your hearers which opposes you, the love of God in them which is offended by your representation of Him!'

Hugh's eyes were fixed on the same pillar as Mr. Tristram's, but if he had been aware of that fact he would have chosen another pillar. His thin handsome face was beginning to show the marks of mental strain. His eyes had the set impassive look of one who, hedged in on both sides, sees a sharp turn head of him on an unknown road.

'Rachel! Rachel! Rachel! Don't you hear me calling to you? Don't you hear me telling you that I can't live without you? The hymn was right. "Other refuge have I none, Hangs my helpless soul on Thee,"[184] only it was written of you, not of that far, far away God who does not care. Only care for me. Only love me. Only give me those cool hands that I may lean my forehead against them. No help can come to me except through you. Stoop down to me and raise me up, for I love you.'

The sun went in suddenly, and a cold shadow fell on the pillar and on Hugh's heart.

Love and marriage were not for him. That far-away God, that Judge in the black cap,[185] had pronounced sentence against him, had doomed that he should die in his sins. When he had sat in his own village church only last Sunday between his mother and sister, he had seen the empty place on his chancel wall[186] where the tablet to his memory would be put up. When he walked through the churchyard, his mother leaning on his arm, his step regulated by her feeble one, he had seen the vacant space by his father's grave already filled by the mound of raw earth which would shortly cover him. His heart had ached for his mother, for the gentle feeble-minded sister who had transferred the interest in life, which keeps body and soul together, from her colourless existence to that of her brother. Hughie was the romance of her grey life: what Hughie said, what Hughie thought, Hughie's wife – oh, jealous thought only to be met by prayer! But later on, joy of joys – Hughie's children! He realised it, now and then, vaguely, momentarily, but never as fully as last Sunday. He shrank from the remembrance, and his mind wandered anew in the labyrinth of broken twisted thought, from which he could find no way out.

There must be some way out. He had stumbled callously through one day after another of these weeks in which he had not seen Rachel, towards his next meeting with her, as a half blind man stumbles towards the light. But the presence of Rachel afforded no clue to the labyrinth. What vain hope was this that he had cherished unconsciously that she could help him. There was no help for him. There was no way out. He was in a trap. He must die, and soon, by his own hand. Incredible, preposterous fate! He shuddered, and looked around him involuntarily.

His glance, reverent, full of timid longing fell on Rachel, and his heart cried aloud suddenly, 'If she loves me, I shall not be able to leave her.'

CHAPTER XXV

Look in my face! my name is Might-have-been;
I am also called No-more, Too-late, Farewell.
DANTE GABRIEL ROSSETTI.[187]

IT was Sunday afternoon. Mr. Tristram leaned on the stone balustrade that bounded the long terrace at Wilderleigh. He was watching two distant figures, followed by a black dot, stroll away across the park. One of them seemed to drag himself unwillingly. Mr. Tristram congratulated himself on the acumen which had led him to keep himself concealed until Doll and Hugh had started for Beaumere.

Sybell had announced at luncheon, in the tone of one who observes a religious rite, that she should rest till four o'clock, and would be ready to sit for the portrait of her upper lip at that hour.

It was only half-past two now. Mr. Tristram had planted himself exactly in front of Rachel's windows, with his back to the house. 'She will keep me waiting, but she will come out in time,' he said to himself, nervous and self-confident by turns, resting his head rather gracefully on his hand. His knowledge of womankind supported him like a life-belt,[188] but it has been said that life-belts occasionally support their wearers upside down. Theories have been known to exhibit the same spiteful tendency towards those who place their trust in them.

'Of course, she has got to show me that she is offended with me,' he reflected, gazing steadily at the Welsh hills. 'She would not have come out if I had asked her, but she will certainly come as I did not. I will give her half an hour.'

Rachel, meanwhile, was looking fixedly at Mr. Tristram from her bedroom window with that dispassionate scrutiny to avoid which the vainest would do well to take refuge in noisome caves.

'I wonder,' she said to herself, 'whether Hester always saw him as I see him now. I believe she did.'

Rachel put on her hat and took up her gloves. 'If this is really I, and that is really he, I had better go down and get it over,' she said to herself.

Mr. Tristram had given her half an hour. She appeared in the low stone doorway before the first five minutes of the allotted time had elapsed, and he gave a genuine start of surprise as he heard her step on the gravel. His respect for her fell somewhat at this alacrity.

'I have been waiting in the hope of seeing you,' he said, after a moment's hesitation. 'I am anxious to have a serious conversation with you.'

'Certainly,' she said.

They walked along the terrace, and presently found themselves in the little coppice adjoining it. They sat down together on a wooden seat round an old cedar, in the heart of the golden afternoon.

It was an afternoon the secret of which autumn and spring will never tell to winter and summer, when the wildest dreams of love might come true, when even the dead might come down and put warm lips to ours, and we should feel no surprise.

A kingfisher flashed across the open on his way back to the brook near at hand, fleeing from the still splendour of the sun-fired woods where he was but a courtier, to the little winding world of grey stones and water, where he was a jewelled king.

When the kingfisher had left them *tête-à-tête*[189] Mr. Tristram found himself extremely awkwardly placed on the green bench. He felt that he had not sufficiently considered before-hand the peculiar difficulties which, in the language of the law, 'had been imported into his case.'[190]

Rachel sat beside him in silence. If it could be chronicled that sympathetic sorrow for her companion's predicament was the principal feeling in her mind, she would have been an angel.

Mr. Tristram halted long between two opinions. At last he said brokenly:

'Can you forgive me?'

What woman, even in her white hair, even after a lifetime spent out of ear-shot, ever forgets the tone her lover's voice takes when he is in trouble? Rachel softened instantly.

'I forgave you long ago,' she said gently.

Something indefinable in the clear full gaze that met his daunted him. He stared apprehensively at her. It seemed to him as if he were standing in cold and darkness, looking in through the windows of her untroubled eyes at the warm sunlit home which had once been his, when it had been exceeding well with him, but of which he had lost the key.

A single yellow leaf, crisped and hollowed to a fairy boat, came sailing on an imperceptible current of air to rest on Rachel's knee.

'I was angry at first,' she said, her voice falling across the silence like another leaf. 'And then after a time I forgave you. And later still, much later, I found out that you had never injured me – that I had nothing to forgive.'

He did not understand, and as he did not understand he explained volubly – for here he felt he was on sure ground – that, on the contrary, she had much to forgive, that he had acted like an infernal blackguard, that men were coarse brutes, not fit to kiss a good woman's shoe latchet, &c. &c. He identified his conduct with that of the whole sex, without alluding to it as that of the individual Tristram. He made it clear that he did not claim to have behaved better than 'most men.'

Rachel listened attentively. 'And I actually loved him,' she said to herself.

'But the divine quality of woman is her power of forgiving. Her love raises a man, transfigures him, ennobles his whole life,' &c. &c.

'My love did not appear to have quite that effect upon you at the time,' said Rachel, regretting the words the moment they were spoken.

Mr. Tristram felt relieved. Here at last was the reproach he had been expecting.

He assured her she did well to be angry. He accused himself once more. He denounced the accursed morals of the day above which he ought to have risen, the morals, if she did but know it, of all unmarried men.

'That is a hit at Mr. Scarlett,' she said scornfully to herself, and then her cheek blanched as she remembered that Hugh was not exempt after all. She became suddenly tired, impatient, but she waited quietly for the inevitable proposal.

Mr. Tristram, who had the gift of emphatic and facile utterance, which the conventional consider to be the sign-manual of genius, had become so entangled in the morals of the age, that it took him some time to extricate himself from the subject before he could pass on to plead in an impassioned manner the cause of the man, unworthy though he might be, who had long loved her, loved her now, and would always love her, in this world and the next.

It was the longest proposal Rachel had ever had, and she had had many. But if the proposal was long the refusal was longer. Rachel, who had a good memory, led up to it by opining that the artistic life made great demands, that the true artist must live entirely for his art, that domestic life might prove a hindrance. She had read somewhere that high hopes fainted on warm hearthstones.[191] Mr. Tristram demolished these objections as ruthlessly as ducks peck their own ducklings if they have not seen them for a day or two.

Even when she was forced to become more explicit it was at first impossible to Mr. Tristram to believe she would finally reject him. But the knowledge, deep-rooted as a forest oak, that she had loved him devotedly could not at last prevail against the odious conviction that she was determined not to marry him.

'Then, in that case you never loved me?'

'I do not love you now.'

'You are determined not to marry?'

'On the contrary, I hope to do so.'

Rachel's words took her by surprise. She had no idea till that moment that she hoped anything of the kind.

'You prefer some one else. That is the real truth.'

'I prefer several others.'

Mr. Tristram looked suspiciously at her. Her answers did not tally with his previous knowledge of her. Perhaps he forgot that he had set his docile pupil rather a long holiday task to learn in his absence and she had learnt it.

'You think you would be happier with some fortune-hunter of an aristocrat than with a plain man of your own class, who, whatever his faults may be, loves you for yourself.'

Why is it that the word aristocrat as applied to a gentleman is as offensive as that of flunkey[192] applied to a footman?

Rachel drew herself up imperceptibly.

'That depends upon the fortune-hunter,' she said with that touch of *hauteur*[193] which, when the vulgar have at last drawn it upon themselves by the insolence which is the underside of their courtesy, always has the same effect on them as a red rag on a bull.[194]

In their own language they invariably 'stand up to it.' Mr. Tristram stood up physically and mentally. He also raised his voice, causing two rabbits to hurry back into their holes.

Women, he said, were incalculable. He would never believe in one again. His disbelief in woman rose even to the rookery in the high elms close at hand. That she, Rachel, whom he had always regarded as the first among women, should be dazzled by the empty glamour of rank, now that her fortune put such marriages within her reach, was incredible. He should have repudiated such an idea with scorn if he had not heard it from her own lips. Well, he would leave her to the life she had chosen. It only remained for him to thank her for stripping his last illusions from him, and to bid her good-bye.

'We shall never meet again,' he said, holding her hand, and looking very much the same without his illusions as he did when he had them on. He had read somewhere a little poem about 'A Woman's No,' which at the last moment meant 'Yes.' And then there was another which chronicled how after several stanzas of upbraiding 'we rushed into each other's arms.'[195] Both recurred to him now. He had often thought how true they were.

'I do not think we shall meet again,' said Rachel, who apparently had an unpoetic nature; 'but I am glad for my own sake that we have met this once, and have had this conversation. I think we owed it to each other and to our – former attachment.'

'Well, good-bye.' He still held her hand. If she was not careful she would lose him.

'Good-bye.'

'You understand it is for always?'

'I do.'

He became suddenly livid. He loved her more than ever. Would she really let him go?

'I am not the kind of man to be whistled back,' he said fiercely. It was an appeal and a defiance, for he was just the kind of man, and they both knew it.

'Of course not.'

'That is your last word?'

'My last word.'

He dropped her hand, and half turned to go.

She made no sign.

Then he strode violently out of the wood without looking behind him. At the little gate he stopped a moment listening intently. No recalling voice reached him. Poets did not know what they were talking about. With a trembling hand he slammed the gate and departed.

Rachel remained a long time sitting on the wooden bench, so long that the stooping sun found out the solemn outstretched arms of the cedar, and touched them till they gleamed green as a beetle's wing. Each little twig and twiglet was made manifest, raw gold against the twilight that lurked beneath the heavy boughs.

She sat so still that a squirrel came tip-toeing across the moss, and struck tail momentarily to observe her. He looked critically at her, first with one round eye, and then, turning his sleek head, with the other, and decided that she was harmless.

Presently a robin dropped down close to her, flashing up his grey underwing as he alighted, and then flew up into the cedar, and from its sun-stirred depths said his say.

The robin never forgets. In the autumn afternoons when the shadows are lengthening he sings sadness into your heart. If you are joyful shut your ears against him, for you may keep peace but never joy while he is singing. He knows all about it, 'love's labour lost,'[196] the grey face of young Love dead, the hard-wrought grave in the live rock where he is buried. And he tells of it again, and again and again, as if Love's sharp sword had indeed reddened his little breast, until the heart aches to hear him. But he tells also that consolation is folded not in forgetfulness, but in remembrance. That is why he sings in the silence of the autumn dawn, before memory closes her eyes, and again near sunset, when memory wakes.

Still Rachel sat motionless.

She had laboured with dumb unreasoning passion to forget, as a man works his hand to the bone night after night, week after week, month after month, to file through the bars of his prison. She found at last that forgetfulness came not of prayer and fasting; that it was not in her to forget. The past had seemed to stretch its cruel desecrating hand over all the future, cutting her off from the possibility of love and marriage, and from the children who in dreams she held in her arms. As she had said to Hester, she thought she 'had nothing left to give.'

But now the dead past had risen from its grave in her meeting with her former lover, and in a moment, in two short days and wakeful nights, the past relinquished its false claim upon her life. She saw that it was false, that she had been frightened where no fear was, that her deliverance lay in remembrance itself, not in the handcuffs with which until now she had bound her deliverer.

Mr. Tristram had come back into her life, and with his own hands had destroyed the overthrown image of himself, which lay like a barrier across her heart. He had replaced it by an accurate presentment of himself as he really was.

'Only that which is replaced is destroyed,'[197] and it is often our real self in its native rags, and not as we jealously imagine another king in richer purple[198] who has replaced us in the throne-room of the heart that loved us. To the end of life Rachel never forgot Mr. Tristram, any more than the amber forgets its fly. But she was vaguely conscious as he left her that he had set her free. She listened to his retreating step hardly daring to breathe. It was too good to be true. At last there was dead silence. No echo of a footfall. Quite gone. He had departed not only out of her presence but out of her life.

She breathed again. A tremor like that which shakes the first green leaf against the March sky stole across her crushed heart, empty at last, empty at last. She raised her hand timidly in the sunshine. She was free. She looked round dazzled, bewildered. The little world of sunshine and the turquoises of sky strewn among the golden network of the trees smiled at her, as one who brings good tidings.

A certain familiar hold on life and nature, so old that it was almost new, which she had forgotten, but which her former self used to feel, came back suddenly upon her like a lost friend from over seas. Scales seemed to fall from her eyes.[199] The light was too much for her. She had forgotten how beautiful the world was. Everything was possible.

Some in the night of their desolation can take comfort when they see the morning star shuddering white in the east, and can say 'Courage, the day is at hand.'

But others never realise that their night is over till the sun is up. Rachel had sat in a long stupor. The message writ large for her comfort in the stars that the night was surely waning had not reached her, bowed as she thought beneath God's hand. And the sure return of the sun at last came upon her like a miracle.

CHAPTER XXVI

'Tis not for every one to catch a salmon.[200]

EVERY one who knows Middleshire knows that the little lake of Beaumere is bounded on the one side by the Westhope and on the other by the Wilderleigh property, the boundary being the ubiquitous Drone which traverses the mere in a desultory fashion, and with the assistance of several springs makes Beaumere what it is, namely (to quote from the local guide-book), 'the noblest expanse of water surrounded by some of the most picturesque scenery in Middleshire.'

Thither Doll and Hugh took their way in the leisurely manner of men whose orthodoxy obliges them to regard Sunday as a day of rest.

Doll pointed out to Hugh the coppice which his predecessor Mr. George Loftus had planted. Hugh regarded it without excitement. Both agreed that it was coming on nicely. Hugh thought he ought to do a little planting at his own place. Doll said you could not do everything at once. A large new farm was the next object of interest. 'Uncle George rebuilt Greenfields from the ground,' remarked Doll, as they crossed the high road and took to the harvesting fields where 'the ricks stood grey to the sun.'[201]

Hugh nodded. Doll thought he was a very decent chap, though rather low spirited. Hugh thought that if Mr. George Loftus had been alive he might have consulted him. In an amicable silence, broken occasionally by whistling for Crack, who hurried blear-eyed and asthmatic out of rabbit holes, the pair reached Beaumere; and, after following the path through the wood, came suddenly upon the little lake locked in the heart of the steeply climbing forest.

Doll stood still and pointed with his stick for fear Hugh might overlook it. 'I come here every Sunday,' he remarked.

A sense of unreality and foreboding seized on Hugh, as the still face of the water looked up at him. Where had he seen it before, this sea of glass reflecting the yellow woods that stooped to its very edge? What had it to do with him?

'I've been here before,' he said, involuntarily.

'I daresay,' said Doll. 'Newhaven marches with me here. The boundary is by that clump of silver birch. The Drone comes in there, but you can't see it. The Newhavens are friends of yours, aren't they?'

'Acquaintances,' said Hugh absently, looking hard at the water. He had never been here before. Memory groped blindly for a lost link, as one who momentarily recognises a face in a crowd, and tries to put a name to it and fails. As the face disappears, so the sudden impression passed from Hugh's mind.

'I expect you have been here with them,' said Doll. 'Good man, Newhaven.'

'I used to see a good deal of them at one time,' said Hugh, 'but they seem to have forgotten me of late.'

'Oh! that's her,' said Doll. 'She is always off and on with people. Takes a fancy one day and a dislike the next. But he's not like that. You always know where to find him. Solid man, Newhaven. He doesn't say much, but what he says he sticks to.'

'He gives one that impression,' said Hugh.

'I rather think he is there now,' said Doll, pointing to the further shore. 'I see a figure moving, and two little specks. I should not wonder if it were him and the boys. They often come here on Sunday afternoons.'

'You have long sight,' said Hugh. He had met Lord Newhaven several times since the drawing of lots, and they had always greeted each other with cold civility. But Hugh avoided him when he could without drawing attention to the fact that he did so.

'Are you going over to his side?' he asked.

'Rather not,' said Doll. 'I have never set a single trimmer or fired a shot beyond that clump of birch, or Uncle George before me.'

The two men picked their way down the hillside among the tall thin tree trunks. There was no one except the dogs at the keeper's cottage in a clearing half-way down. Doll took the key of the boathouse from a little hole under the eaves.

'I think Withers must be out,' he remarked at last, after knocking and calling at the locked door and peering through the closed window. Hugh had been of that opinion for some time. 'Gone out with his wife, I expect. Never mind, we can do without him.'

They went slipping over the dry beech-mast to the boat-house. Doll unlocked the door and climbed into one of the boats, Hugh and Crack followed. They got a perch rod off a long shelf, and half a dozen trimmers. Then they pulled out a little way and stopped near an archipelago of water-lily leaves.

Doll got out the perch rod and float and made a cast.

'It's not fishing,' he said apologetically, half to his guest and half to his Maker. 'But we are bound to get some baits.'

Hugh nodded and gazed down at the thin forest below. He could see the perch moving in little companies in the still water beyond the water trees. Presently a perch, a very small one, out alone for the first time, came up, all stiff head and shoulders and wagging tail, to the carelessly covered hook.

'Don't, don't, you young idiot,' said Hugh below his breath. But the perch knew that the time had come when a perch must judge for himself.

The float curtsied and went under, and in another second the little independent was in the boat.

'There are other fools in the world besides me, it seems,' said Hugh to himself.

'He'll do, but I wish he was a dace,' said Doll, slipping the victim into a tin with holes in the top. 'Half a dozen will be enough.'

They got half a dozen, baited and set the trimmers white side up, and were turning to row back, when Doll's eye became suddenly fixed.

'By Jove, there's something at it,' he said, pointing to a trimmer at some distance.

Both men looked intently at it. Crack felt that something was happening, and left off smelling the empty fish-can.

The trimmer began to nod, to tilt, and then turned suddenly upside down, and remained motionless.

'He's running the line off it,' said Doll.

As he spoke the trimmer gave one jerk and went under. Then it reappeared, awkwardly bustling out into the open.

'Oh! hang it all, it's Sunday,' said Doll with a groan. 'We can't be catching pike on a Sunday.'[202] And he caught up the oars and rowed swiftly towards the trimmer.

As soon as they were within a boat's length it disappeared again, came up again, and went pecking along the top of the water. Doll pursued warily and got hold of it.

'Gently now,' he said, as he shipped the oars. 'He'll go under the boat and break us if we don't look out. I'll play him, and you shove the net under him. Damn! – God forgive me! – We have come out without a landing-net.[203] Good Lord, Scarlett, you can't gaff him with a champagne-opener. There, you pull him in, and I'll grab him somehow. I've done it before. Crack, lie down, you infernal fool. Scarlett, if you pull him like that you'll lose him to a certainty. By George, he's a big one.' Doll tore off his coat and pulled up his shirt-sleeves. 'He's going under the boat. If you let him go under the boat, I tell you he'll break us. I'm quite ready.' Doll was rubbing his waistcoat-buttons against the gunwale. 'Bring him in gradually. For goodness' sake, keep your feet off the line, or, if he makes a dash, he'll break you. Give him line. Keep your elbows out. Keep your hands free. Don't let him jerk you. If you don't give him more line when he runs, you'll lose him. He's not half done yet. Confound you, Scarlett, hold on for all you're worth. All right, old chap, all right. Don't mind me. You're doing it first-class. Right as rain. Now, now. By George, did you see him that time? He's a nailer. Steady on him. Bring him in gently. Keep an even pull on him. Keep steady.'

Doll craned over the gunwale,[204] his arms in the water. There was a swirl, a momentary glimpse of a stolid fish face, and heavy shoulders, and the boat righted itself.

'Missed him as I live!' gasped Doll. 'Bring him in again.'

Hugh let out the slippery line and drew it in again slowly, hand over hand. Doll's round head was over the side, his long legs spread adhesively in the bottom of the boat. Crack, beyond himself with excitement, got on the seat and barked without ceasing.

'He's coming up again,' said Doll gutturally, sliding forward his left hand. 'I must get him by the eyes, and then I doubt if I can lift him. He's a big brute. He's dragging the whole boat and everything. He's about done now. Steady! Now!'

The great side of the pike lay heaving on the surface for a second, and Doll's left forefinger and thumb were groping for its eyes. But the agonised pike made a last effort. Doll had him with his left hand, but could not raise him. 'Pull him in now for all you're worth,' he roared to Hugh, as he made a grab with his right hand. His legs began to lose their grip under the violent contortions of the pike. The boat tilted madly. Hugh reached forward to help him. There was a frantic effort, and it capsized.

'Bad luck,' said Doll, coming up spluttering, shaking his head like a spaniel. 'But we shall get him yet. He's bleeding like a pig. He'll come up directly. Good Lord, the water's like ice. We must be over one of the springs. I suppose you are all right, Scarlett.'

Hugh had come up, but in very different fashion.

'Yes,' he said faintly, clutching the upturned boat.

'I'm not sure,' said Doll, keeping going with one hand, 'that we had not better get ashore, and fetch the other boat. The water's enough to freeze one.'

'I can't swim,' said Hugh, his teeth chattering.

He was a delicate man at the best of times, and the cold was laying hold of him.

Doll looked at his blue lips and shaking hands, and his face became grave. He measured the distance to the shore with his eye. It had receded in a treacherous manner.

'I'm not much of a performer myself,' he said, 'since I broke my arm last winter, but I can get to the shore. The question is, can you hold on while I go back and bring the other boat, or shall we have a try at getting back together?'

'I can hold on all right,' said Hugh, instantly aware that Doll did not think he could tow him to land, but was politely ready to risk his existence in the attempt.

'Back directly,' said Doll, and without a second's delay he was gone. Hugh put out his whole strength in the endeavour to raise himself somewhat out of the ice-cold water. But the upturned boat sidled away from him like a skittish horse, and after grappling with it he only slipped back again exhausted, and had to clutch it as best he could.

As he clung to the gunwale he heard a faint coughing and gasping close to his ear. Some one was drowning. Hugh realised that it must be Crack, under the boat. He called to him, he chirruped as if all were well. He stretched one hand as far as he could under the boat feeling for him. But he could not reach him. Presently the faint difficult sound ceased, began again, stopped, and was heard no more.

A great silence seemed to rush in on the extinction of that small sound. It stooped down and enveloped Hugh in it. Everything was very calm, very still. The boat kept turning slowly round and round, the only thing that moved. The sunlight quivered on the wet upturned keel. Already it was drying in patches. Hugh watched it. The cold was sapping his powers as if he were bleeding.

'I could have built a boat in the time Loftus takes to fetch one,' he said to himself, and he looked round him. No sign of Doll. He was alone in the world. The cold was gaining on him slowly, surely. Why had he on such heavy gloves which made him fumble so clumsily. He looked at his bare cut hands, and realised that their grip was leaving them. He felt that he was in measurable distance of losing his hold.

Suddenly a remembrance flashed across him of the sinister face of the water as it had first looked up at him through the trees. Now he understood. This was the appointed place for him to die. Hugh tightened his hold with his right hand, for his left was paralysed.

'I will not,' he said. 'Nothing shall induce me. I will live and marry Rachel.'

The cold advanced suddenly on him as at the point of the bayonet.

'Why not die?' said another voice. 'Will it be easier in three months' time than it is now? Will it ever be so easy again? See how near death is to life, a wheel within a wheel, two rings linked together. A touch, and you pass from one to the other.'

Hugh looked wildly round him. The sun lay warm upon the tree tops. It could not be that he was going to die *here* and *now;* here in the living sunshine, with the quiet friendly faces of the hills all round him.

He strengthened his numb hold fiercely, all but lost it, regained it. Cramp long held at bay overcame him.

And the boat kept turning in the twilight. He reached the end of his strength and held on beyond it. He heard some one near at hand suffocating in long-drawn gasps. Not Crack this time, but himself.

The boat was always turning in the darkness.

The struggle was over. 'It is better so,' said the other voice, through the roaring of a cataract near at hand, 'Your mother will bear it better so. And all the long difficulties are over, and pain is past, and life is past, and sleep is best.'

'But Rachel?'

She was here in the warm swaying darkness. She was with him. She was Death. Death was only her arms round him in a great peace. Death was better than life. He let go the silly boat that kept him from her, and turned wholly to her, his closed eyes against her breast.

CHAPTER XXVII

The main difference between people seems to be that one man can come under obligations on which you can rely – is obligable; and another is not. As he has not a law within him, there's nothing to tie him to.

EMERSON.[205]

'FATHER,' said Teddy to Lord Newhaven, 'Do, do be a horse, and I will ride you in the water.'

'Me, too,' said Pauly.

'I am not anxious to be a horse, Teddy. I'm quite content as I am.'

Lord Newhaven was stretched in an easy but undefensive attitude on the heathery bank, with his hands behind his head. His two sons rushed simultaneously at him and knelt on his chest.

'Promise,' they cried, punching him. 'Two turns each.' There was a free fight, and Lord Newhaven promised.

'Honour bright. Two turns each, and really deep.'

'Honour bright,' said Lord Newhaven.

His two sons got off his chest, and Teddy climbed on his back in readiness as his father sat up and began to unlace his boots.

'Higher,' said Teddy over his shoulder, his arms tightly clasped round his father's neck, as Lord Newhaven rolled up his trousers.

'You young slave-driver, they won't go up any higher.'

'You did say "Honour Bright."'

'Well, Shylock, I *am* "honour bright."'

'You had them over your knees last time.'

'I had knickerbockers[206] on, then.'

'Won't these do the same?'

'They won't come up another inch.'

'Then one, two, three – off!' shrieked Teddy, digging his heels into the parental back.

The horse displayed surprising agility. It curveted, it kicked, it jumped a little drain, it careered into the water, making a tremendous splashing.

The two boys screamed with delight.

But at last the horse sat down on the bank gasping, wiped its forehead, and, in spite of frenzied entreaties, proceeded to put on its socks and boots.

Lord Newhaven was not to be moved a second time. He lit a cigarette, and observed that the moment for sailing boats had arrived.

The boats were accordingly sailed. Lord Newhaven tilted his hat over his eyes and acted umpire.

'It is not usual to sail boats upside down,' he said, seeing Teddy deliberately upset his.

'They are doing it out there,' said Teddy, who had a reason for most things. And he continued to sail his boat upside down.

Lord Newhaven got up, and swept the water with his eye. His face became keen. Then his glance fell anxiously on the children.

'Teddy and Pauly,' he said, 'promise me that you will both play on this one bit of sand, and not go in the water till I come back.'

They promised, staring bewildered at their father.

In another moment Lord Newhaven was tearing through the brushwood that fringed the water's edge.

As he neared the boathouse he saw another figure trying to shove out the remaining boat.

It was Doll. Lord Newhaven pushed her off and jumped in.

Doll was almost speechless. His breath came in long gasps. The sweat hung on his forehead. He pointed to the black upturned boat.

'This one leaks,' said Lord Newhaven sharply.

'It's got to go all the same, and sharp,' said Doll, hoarsely.

Lord Newhaven seized up a fishing-tin, and thrust it into Doll's hands.

'You bale while I row,' he said, and he rowed as he had never rowed before.

'Who is it?' he said, as the boat shot out into the open.

Doll was baleing like a madman.

'Scarlett,' he said. 'And he's over one of the springs. He'll get cramp.'

Lord Newhaven strained at his oars.

Consciousness was coming back, was slowly climbing upwards, upwards through immense intervals of time and space, to where at last with a wrench pain met it half-way. Hugh stirred feebly in the dark of a great forlornness and loneliness.

'Rachel,' he said, 'Rachel.'

His head was gently raised, and a cup pressed to his lips. He swallowed something.

He groped in the darkness for a window, and then opened his eyes. Lord Newhaven withdrew a pace or two, and stood looking at him.

Their eyes met.

Neither spoke, but Hugh's eyes, dark with the shadow of death, said plainly, 'Hast thou found me, oh mine enemy?'

Then he turned them slowly, as an infant turns them, to the sky, the climbing woods, leaning over each other's shoulders to look at him, to the warm earth on which he lay. At a little distance was stretched a small rough-haired form. Hugh's eyes fixed on it. It lay very still.

'Crack,' he said suddenly, raising himself on his elbow.

There was neither speech nor language. Crack's tail, that courteous member, made no sign.

'He was under the boat,' said Lord Newhaven, looking narrowly at the exhausted face of the man he had saved, and unable for the life of him to help a momentary fellow-feeling about the little dog.

Hugh remembered. It all came back, the boat, Crack's dying gasps, the agonised struggle, the strait gate of death, the difficult passage through it, the calm beyond. He had almost got through, and had been dragged back.

'Why did you interfere?' he said, in sudden passion, his eyes flaming in his white face.

A dull colour rose to Lord Newhaven's cheek.

'I thought it was an accident,' he said. 'If it was not I beg your pardon.'

There was a moment's silence.

'It *was* an accident,' said Hugh hoarsely, and he turned on his elbow and looked fixedly at the water, so that his companion might not see the working of his face.

Lord Newhaven walked slowly away in the direction of Doll, whose distant figure followed by another was hurrying towards them.

'And so there is a Rachel as well, is there?' he said to himself, vainly trying to steel himself against his adversary.

'How is he now?' said Doll, coming within earshot.

'He's all right, but you'd better get him into dry clothes and yourself too.'

'Change on the bank,' said Doll, seizing a bundle from the keeper. 'It's as hot as an oven in the sun. Why Scarlett's sitting up! I thought when we laid into him on the bank that he was too far gone, didn't you? I suppose' – hesitating – Crack?'

Lord Newhaven shook his head.

'I must go back to my boys now,' he said, 'or they will be getting into mischief.'

Doll nodded. He and Lord Newhaven had had a hard fight to get the leaking boat to land with Hugh at the bottom of it. It had filled ominously when Doll ceased baleing to help to drag in the heavy unconscious body.

There had been a moment when, inapprehensive as he was, Doll had remembered with a qualm that Lord Newhaven could not swim.

'Every fellow ought to swim,' was the moral he drew from the incident and repeated to his wife, who, struck by the soundness of the remark, repeated it to the Gresleys.

Lord Newhaven retraced his steps slowly along the bank in his water-logged boots. He was tired and he did not hurry, for he could see in the distance two small figures sitting faithfully on a log where he had left them.

'Good little chaps,' he said half aloud.

In spite of himself his thoughts went back to Hugh. His feelings towards him had not changed, but they had been forced during the last half-hour out of their original intrenchments into the open, and were liable to attack from new directions.

It was not that he had virtually saved Hugh's life, for Doll would never have got him into the leaking boat and kept it afloat single-handed. That first moment of enthusiasm when he had rubbed the senseless limbs and breathed into the cold lips, and had felt his heart leap when the life came halting back into them, that moment had passed and left him cold.

But Hugh's melancholy eyes, as they opened once more on this world and met his unflinching, haunted him, and the sudden anger at his interference. It was the intrenchment of his contempt that Lord Newhaven missed.

A meaner nature would not have let him off so easily as Hugh had done.

'It *was* an accident,' he said to himself unwillingly. 'He need not have admitted that, but I should have been on a gridiron if he had not. In different circumstances that man and I might have been friends. And if he had got into a scrape of this kind a little further afield I might have helped to get him out of it. He feels it. He has aged during the last two months. But as it is – Upon my word, if he were a boy I should have had to let him off. It would have been too blood-thirsty. But he is seven and twenty. He is old enough to know better. She made a fool of him, of course. She made a greater one of me once, for I – married her.'

Lord Newhaven reviewed with a dispassionate eye his courtship and marriage.

'A wood anemone,' he said to himself; 'I likened her to a wood anemone. Good Lord! And I was thirty years of age, while this poor devil is twenty-seven.'

Lord Newhaven stopped short with fixed eyes.

'I believe I should have to let him off,' he said half-aloud.

'I believe I would let him off if I was not as certain as I stand here that he will never do it.'

CHAPTER XXVIII

The less wit a man has, the less he knows that he wants it.[207]

HESTER always took charge of the three elder children and Fraülein of the baby during the six o'clock service,[208] so that the nurse might go to church. On this particular Sunday afternoon Hester and the children were waiting in the little hall till the bell stopped, before which moment they were forbidden to leave the house. Mr. and Mrs. Gresley had just started for the church, Mr. Gresley looking worn and harassed, for since luncheon he had received what he called 'a perfectly unaccountable letter' from one of his principal parishioners, a Dissenter, who had been present at the morning service,[209] and who Mr. Gresley had confidently hoped might have been struck by the sermon. This hope had been justified, but not in the manner Mr. Gresley had expected. Mr. Walsh opined in a large round hand that as worms (twice underdashed) did not usually pay voluntary church and school rates[210] he no longer felt himself under an obligation to do so, &c. &c. The letter was a great, an unexpected blow. Who could have foreseen such a result of the morning's eloquence.

'The truth is,' said Mr. Gresley tremulously, 'that they can't and won't hear reason. They can't controvert what I say, so they take refuge in petty spite like this. I must own I am disappointed in Walsh. He is a man of some education, and liberal as regards money. I had thought he was better than most of them, and now he turns on me like this.'

'It's a way worms have,' said Hester.

'Oh, don't run a simile to death, Hester,' said Mr. Gresley impatiently. 'If you had listened to what I tried to say this morning, you would have seen I only used the word *worm* figuratively. I never meant it literally, as any one could see who was not determined to misunderstand me. Worms pay school rates! Such folly is positively sickening if it were not malicious.'

Hester had remained silent. She had been deeply vexed for her brother at the incident.

As the church bell stopped the swing door opened and Boulou hurried in like a great personage, conscious that others have waited, and bearing with him an aroma of Irish stew[211] and onions, which showed that he had been exchanging affabilities with the cook. For the truth must be owned. No spinster over forty could look unmoved on Boulou. Alas! for the Vicarage cook, who 'had kept herself *to* herself' for nearly fifty years, only to fall the victim of a 'grande passion'[212] for Boulou.

The little Lovelace bounded in, and the expedition started. It was Regie's turn to choose where they should go, and he decided on the 'shrubbery,' a little wood through which ran the private path to Wilderleigh. Doll Loftus had given the Gresleys leave to take the children there.

'Oh, Regie, we always go there,' said Mary plaintively, who invariably chose the Pratts' park, with its rustic bridges and *châlets*, which Mr. Pratt in a gracious moment had 'thrown open' to the Gresleys on Sundays, because, as he expressed it, 'they must feel so cramped in their little garden.'

But Regie adhered to his determination, and to the 'shrubberies' they went. Hester was too tired to play with them, too tired even to tell them a story; so she sat under a tree while they circled in the coppice near at hand.

As we grow older we realise that in the new gardens where life leads us we never learn the shrubs and trees by heart as we did as children in our old garden of Eden,[213] round the little gabled house where we were born. We were so thorough as children. We knew the underneath of every laurel bush, the shape of its bunches of darkling branches, the green dust that our small restless bodies rubbed off from its under twigs. We see now as strangers those little hanging horsetails of pink which sad-faced elders call *ribes*,[214] but once long ago when the world was young we knew them eye to eye, and the compact little black insects on them, and the quaint taste of them, and the clean clean smell of them. Everything had a taste in those days and was submitted to that test, just as until it had been licked the real colour of any object of interest was not ascertained. There was a certain scarlet berry, very red without and very white within, which we were warned was deadly poison.[215] How well, after a quarter of a century, we remember the bitter taste of it, how much better than many other forbidden fruits duly essayed in later years. We ate those scarlet berries and lived though warned to the contrary.

Presently Boulou, who could do nothing simply, found a dead mouse, where any one else could have found it, in the middle of the path, and made it an occasion for a theatrical display of growlings and shakings. The children decided to bury it, and after a becoming silence their voices could be heard singing 'Home, Sweet Home'[216] as the body was being lowered into the grave previously dug by Boulou, who had to be forcibly restrained from going on digging it after the obsequies were over.

'He never knows when to stop,' said Regie, wearily, as Boulou, with a little plaister of earth on his nose, was carried coughing back to Hester.

As she took him Rachel and Sybell came slowly down the path towards them, and the latter greeted Hester with an effusion which suggested that when two is not company three may be.

'A most vexing thing has happened,' said Sybell in a gratified tone, sitting down under Hester's tree. 'I really don't think I am to blame. You know Mr. Tristram, the charming artist who has been staying with us?'

'I know him,' said Hester.

'Well, he was set on making a sketch of me for one of his large pictures, and it was to have been finished to-day. I don't see any harm myself in drawing on Sunday.[217] I know the Gresleys do, and I love the Gresleys, he has such a powerful mind; but one must think for oneself, and it was only the upper lip, so I consented to sit to him at four o'clock. I noticed he seemed a little – well rather –'

'Just so,' said Hester.

'The last few days. But, of course, I took no notice of it. A married woman often has to deal with such things without making a fuss about them. Well, I overslept myself, and it was nearly half-past four before I awoke. And when I went into my sitting-room a servant brought me a note. It was from him, saying he had been obliged to leave Wilderleigh suddenly on urgent business, and asking that his baggage might be sent after him.'

Hester raised her eyes slightly as if words failed her. Sybell's conversation always interested her.

'Perhaps the reason she is never told anything,' she said to herself, 'is because the ground the confidence would cover is invariably built over already by a fiction of her own which it would not please her to see destroyed.'

'Who would have thought,' continued Sybell, 'that he would have behaved in that way because I was one little half-hour late. And of course the pretext of urgent business is too transparent, because there is no Sunday post, and the telegraph boy had not been up. I asked that. And he was so anxious to finish the sketch. He almost asked to stay over Sunday on purpose.'

Rachel and Hester looked on the ground.

'Rachel said he was all right in the garden just before, didn't you, Rachel?'

'I said I thought he was a little nervous.'

'And what did he talk to you about?'

'He spoke about the low tone of the morals of the day, and about marriage.'

'Ah! I don't wonder he talked to you, Rachel, you are so sympathetic. I expect lots of people confide in you about their troubles and love affairs. Morals of the day! Marriage! Poor, poor Mr. Tristram! I shall tell Doll quietly this evening. On the whole, it is just as well he is gone.'

'Just as well,' said Rachel and Hester with surprising unanimity.

CHAPTER XXIX

So fast does a little leaven spread within us – so incalculable is the effect of one personality on another. – GEORGE ELIOT.[218]

HUGH was not ill after what Mr. Gresley called 'his immersion,' but for some days he remained feeble and exhausted. Sybell quite forgot she had not liked him, insisted on his staying on indefinitely at Wilderleigh, and, undaunted by her distressing experience with Mr. Tristram, read poetry to Hugh in the afternoons and surrounded him with genuine warm-hearted care. Doll was steadily, quietly kind.

It was during these days that Hugh and Rachel saw much of each other, during these days that Rachel passed in spite of herself beyond the anxious impersonal interest which Hugh had awakened in her, on to that slippery much trodden ground of uncomfortable possibilities where the unmarried meet.

Hugh attracted and repelled her.

It was, alas! easy to say why she was repelled. But who shall say why she was attracted? Has the secret law ever been discovered which draws one man and woman together amid the crowd? Hugh was not among the best men who had wished to marry her, but nevertheless he was the only man since Mr. Tristram who had succeeded in making her think continually of him. And perhaps she half knew that though she had been loved by better men, Hugh loved her better than they had.

Which would prove the stronger, the attraction or the repulsion?

'How can I?' she said to herself over and over again. 'When I remember Lady Newhaven, how can I? When I think of what his conduct was for a whole year, how can I? Can he have any sense of honour to have acted like that? Is he even really sorry? He is very charming, very refined, and he loves me. He looks good, but what do I know of him except evil. He looks as if he could be faithful, but how can I trust him?'

Hugh fell into a deep dejection after his narrow escape. Dr. Brown said it was nervous prostration, and Doll rode into Southminster and returned laden with comic papers. Who shall say whether the cause was physical or mental. Hugh had seen death very near for the first time, and the thought of death haunted him. He had not realised when he drew lots that he was risking the possibility of anything like *that*, such an entire going away, such an awful rending of his being as the short word *death* now conveyed to him. He had had no idea it would be like *that*. And he had got to do it again. There was the crux. He had got to do it again.

He leant back faint and shuddering in the deck chair in the rose garden where he was lying.

Presently Rachel appeared, coming towards him down the narrow grass walk between two high walls of hollyhocks. She had a cup of tea in her hand.

'I have brought you this,' she said, 'with a warning that you had better not come in to tea. Mr. Gresley has been sighted walking up the drive. Mrs. Loftus thought you would like to see him, but I reminded her that Dr. Brown said you were to be kept very quiet.'

Mr. Gresley had called every day since the accident in order to cheer the sufferer to whom he had been greatly attracted. Hugh had seen him once, and afterwards had never felt strong enough to repeat the process.

'Must you go back?' he asked.

'No,' she said. 'Mrs. Loftus and he are great friends. I should be rather in the way.'

And she sat down by him.

'Are you feeling ill?' she said gently, noticing his careworn face.

'No,' he replied. 'I was only thinking. I was thinking,' he went on after a pause, 'that I would give everything I possess not to have done something which I have done.'

Rachel looked straight in front of her. The confession was coming at last. Her heart beat.

'I have done wrong,' he said slowly, 'and I am suffering for it, and I shall suffer more before I've finished. But the worst is –'

She looked at him.

'The worst is that I can't bear all the consequences myself. An innocent person will pay the penalty of my sin.'

Hugh's voice faltered. He was thinking of his mother.

Rachel's mind instantly flew to Lord Newhaven.

'Then Lord Newhaven drew the short lighter,' she thought, and she coloured deeply.

There was a long silence.

'Do you think,' said Hugh, smiling faintly, 'that people are ever given a second chance?'

'Always,' said Rachel. 'If not here – afterwards.'

'If I were given another,' said Hugh. 'If I might only be given another now in this life I should take it.'

He was thinking if only he might be let off this dreadful, self-inflicted death. She thought he meant that he repented of his sin, and would fain do better.

There was a sound of voices near at hand. Sybell and Mr. Gresley came down the grass walk towards them.

'London society,' Mr. Gresley was saying, 'to live in a stuffy street away from the beauties of Nature, its birds and flowers, to spend half my days laying traps for invitations, and half my nights grinning like a fool in stifling drawing-rooms, listening to vapid talk. No, thanks! I know better than to care for London society. Hester does, I know, but then Hester does not mind making up to big people, and I do. In fact –'

'I have brought Mr. Gresley after all, in spite of Dr. Brown,' said Sybell, 'because we were in the middle of such an interesting conversation on the snares of society that I knew you would like to hear it. You have had such a dull day with Doll away at his County Council.'[219]

That night as Rachel sat in her room she went over that half-made, ruthlessly interrupted confidence.

'He does repent,' she said to herself, recalling the careworn face. 'If he does, can I overlook the past? Can I help him to make a fresh start? If he had not done this one dishonourable action, I could have cared for him. Can I now?'

CHAPTER XXX

A fool's mouth is his destruction.[220]

THE superficial reader of these pages may possibly have forgotten, but the earnest one will undoubtedly remember that in an earlier chapter a sale of work was mentioned which was to take place in the Wilderleigh gardens at the end of August.

The end of August had now arrived, and with it two white tents, which sprang up suddenly one morning like giant mushrooms on one of Doll's smooth-shaven lawns. He groaned in spirit as he watched their erection. They would ruin the turf.

'Might as well iron it with a hot iron,' he said disconsolately to Hugh. 'But, of course, this sort of thing – Diocesan Fund, eh? In these days we must stand by our colours.' He repeated Mr. Gresley's phrase. Doll seldom ventured on an opinion not sanctioned by the ages, or that he had not heard repeated till its novelty had been comfortably rubbed off by his wife or the Gresleys.

The two men watched the proceedings mournfully. They could not help, at least they were told they could not help the women busily engaged in draping and arranging the stalls. They were still at large, but Doll knew as well as a dog who is going to be washed, what was in store for him in the afternoon, and he was depressed beforehand.

'Don't let yourself be run in,' he said generously to Hugh. 'You're not up to it. It takes a strong man to grapple with this sort of thing. Kills off the weakly ones like flies. You lie low in the smoking-room till it's all over.'

'All I can say is,' remarked Mrs. Gresley, as she and Hester led the Vicarage donkey and cart up the drive, heavily laden with the work of many months, 'that the Pratts have behaved exceedingly badly. Here they are, the richest people by far in the parish, and they would not even take a stall, they would not even furnish half of one, and they said they would be away, and they are at the Towers after all. No one likes the Pratts more than I do, or sees their good points as I do, but I can't shut my eyes to the fact that they are the meanest of the mean.'

The Pratts had only contributed two 'bed-spreads,'[221] and a 'sheet-sham,'[222] and a set of antimacassars. If the reader wishes to know what 'bed-spreads' and 'sheet-shams' are, let him ask his intended, and let him see to it that he marries a woman who cannot tell him.

Mrs. Pratt had bought the antimacassars for the Towers, and secretly adored them until Ada pronounced them to be vulgar. The number of things which Ada discovered to be vulgar increased every day, and included the greater part of her mother's wardrobe, much to the distress of that poor lady. Mrs. Pratt had reached the size when it is prudent to concentrate a love of bright colours in one's parasol. On this particular afternoon she shed tears over the fact that Ada refused to accompany her if her mother wore a unique garment of orange satin covered with what appeared to be a plague of black worms.

Of course, the sale of work was combined with a garden party, and a little after three o'clock carriage after carriage began to arrive, and Sybell, with a mournful, handsome, irreproachably dressed husband, took up her position on the south front to receive her guests.

The whole neighbourhood had been invited, and it can generally be gauged with tolerable accuracy by a hostess of some experience who will respond to the call and who will stay away. Sybell and her husband were among those who were not to be found at these festivities, neither were the Newhavens, save at their own, nor the Pontisburys, nor the Bishop of Southminster. Cards had, of course, been sent to each, but no one expected them to appear.

Presently, among the stream of arrivals, Sybell noticed the slender figure of Lady Newhaven, and – astonishing vision – Lord Newhaven beside her.

'Wonders will never cease,' said Doll, shaken for a moment out of the apathy of endurance.

Sybell raised her eyebrows, and advanced with the prettiest air of *empressement*[223] to meet her unexpected guests. No, clearly it was impossible that the two women should like each other. They were the same age, about the same height and colouring, their social position was too similar, their historic houses too near each other. Lady Newhaven was by far the best looking, but that was not a difference which attracted Sybell towards her. On this occassion Sybell's face assumed its most squirrel-like expression, for as ill-luck would have it they were dressed alike.

Lady Newhaven looked very ethereal as she came slowly across the grass in her diaphanous gown of rich white, covered with a flowing veil of thinnest transparent black. Her blue eyes looked restlessly bright, her lips wore a mechanical smile. Rachel watching her, experienced a sudden pang at her undeniable loveliness. It wounded her suddenly as it never had done before. 'I am a common-looking square-built woman compared to her,' she said to herself. 'No wonder he –'

She instinctively drew back as Lady Newhaven turned quickly towards her.

'You dear person,' said Lady Newhaven, her eyes moving restlessly over the crowd, 'are you still here? Let us go and buy something together. How nice you look,' without looking at her. She drew Rachel apart in the direction of the tents.

'Where is he?' she said sharply. 'I know he is here. I heard all about the accident, though Edward never told me. I don't see him.'

'He is not in the gardens. He is not coming out. He is still rather knocked up.'

'I thought I should have died when I heard it Ah, Rachel, never love any one. You don't know what it's like. But I must see him. I have come here on purpose.'

'So I supposed.'

'Edward would come, too. He appeared at the last moment when the carriage came round, though I have never known him to go to a garden-party in his life.[224] But where is he, Rachel?'

'Somewhere in the house, I suppose.'

'I shan't know where to find him. I can't be wandering about that woman's house by myself. We must slip away together, Rachel, and you must take me to him. I must see him alone for five minutes.'

Rachel shook her head.

Captain Pratt, tall, pale, cautious, immaculate, his cane held along his spinal column, appeared suddenly close at hand.

'Mrs. Loftus is fortunate in her day,' he remarked, addressing himself to Lady Newhaven, and observing her fixedly with cold admiration. 'I seldom come to this sort of thing, but neighbours in the country must support each other. I see you are on your way to the tents. Pray allow me to carry your purchases for you.'

'Oh! don't let me trouble you,' said Lady Newhaven, shrinking imperceptibly. But it was no trouble to Captain Pratt, and they walked on together.

Lord Newhaven, who could not have been far off, joined Rachel.

'Well, my dear,' said Mrs. Pratt to Ada, 'you might have let me wear my black and orange, after all, for you see Lady Newhaven has something very much the same, only hers is white underneath. And do you see she has got two diamond butterflies on, the little one at her throat and the big one holding her white carnations. And you would not let me put on a single thing. There now, Algy has joined her,' continued Mrs. Pratt, her attention quickly diverted from her own wrongs. 'Now they are walking on together. How nice he looks in those beautiful clothes. Algy and Lord Newhaven and Mr. Loftus all have the same look, haven't they? All friends together, as I often say, such a mercy among county people. You might walk a little with Lord Newhaven, Ada. It's unaccountable how seldom we see him, but always so pleasant when we do. Ah! he's speaking to Rachel West. They are going to the tents, after all. Well, whatever you may say, I do think we ought to go and buy something, too. Papa says he won't put his hand in his pocket if the Loftuses are to get all the credit, and we ought to have had the choice of having the sale at the Towers, so he shan't do anything; but I think it would be nice if we went and bought a little something. Just a five-pound note. You shall spend it, my dear, if you like.'

'This is sheer recklessness,' said Lord Newhaven, as Rachel bought an expensive tea-cosy[225] from Fraülein. 'In these days of death-duties[226] you cannot possess four teapots, and you have already bought three teapot costumes.'

'That is what I am here for,' said Rachel, producing a cheque-book. 'How much did you say, Fraülein?'

'Twenty-seven and seex,' said Fraülein.

'Now I see it in the full light, I have taken a fancy to it myself,' said Lord Newhaven. 'I never saw anything the least like it. I don't think I can allow you to appropriate it, Miss West. You are sweeping up all the best things.'

'I have a verr' pretty thing for gentlemen,' said Fraülein. 'Herr B-r-r-rown has just bought one.'

'Very elaborate indeed. Bible-markers,[227] I presume? Oh! Braces! Never mind, they will be equally useful to me. I'll have them. Now for the tea-cosy. It is under-priced. I consider that, with the chenille swallow, it is worth thirty shillings. I will give thirty for it.'

'Thirty-two and six,' said Rachel.

'The landed interest is not going to be brow-beaten by coal-mines.[228] Thirty-three and twopence.'

'Forty shillings,' said Rachel.

'Forty-two,' said Lord Newhaven.

Every one in the tent had turned to watch the bidding.

'Forty-two and six,' said Rachel.

Fraülein blushed. She had worked the tea-cosy. It was to her a sonata in red plush.

'Three guineas,' said Captain Pratt, by an infallible instinct perceiving and placing himself within the focus of general interest.

The bidding ceased instantly. Lord Newhaven shrugged his shoulders and turned away. Fraülein, still shaking with conflicting emotions, handed the tea-cosy to Captain Pratt. He took it with an acid smile, secretly disgusted at the sudden cessation of interest, for which he had paid rather highly, and looked round for Lady Newhaven.

But she had disappeared.

'Fancy you and Algy bidding against each other like that,' said Ada Pratt archly to Lord Newhaven, for though Ada was haughty in general society she could be sportive, and even friskily ingratiating, towards those of her fellow creatures whom she termed 'swells.' 'Why half Middleshire will be saying that you have quarrelled next.'

'Only those who do not know how intimate Captain Pratt and I really are could think we have quarrelled,' said Lord Newhaven, his eye wandering over the crowd. 'But I am blocking your way and Mrs. Pratt's. How do you do, Mrs. Pratt. Miss West, your burden is greater than you can bear.[229] You are dropping part of it. I don't know what it is, but I can shut my eyes as I pick it up. I insist on carrying half back to the house. It will give a pleasing impression that I have bought largely. Weren't you pleased at the money we wrung out of Captain Pratt? He never thought we should stop bidding. It's about all the family will contribute, unless that good old Mama Pratt buys something. She is the only one of the family I can tolerate. Is Scarlett still here? I ought to have asked after him before.'

'He's here, but he's not well. He's in hiding in the smoking-room.'

'He is lucky he is no worse. I should have had rheumatic fever if I had been in his place. How cool it is in here after the glare outside. Must you go out again? Well, I consider I have done my duty, and that I may fairly allow myself a cigarette in peace.'

'Really, Mr. Loftus, I'm quite shocked. This absurd faintness! The tent was very crowded, and there is not much air to-day, is there? I shall be all right if I may sit quietly in the hall a little. How deliciously cool in here after the glare outside. A glass of water? Thanks. Yes, only I hate to be so troublesome. And how are you after that dreadful accident in the boat?'

'Oh! I am all right,' said Doll, who by this time hated the subject. 'It was Scarlett who was nearly frozen like New Zealand lamb.'

Doll had heard Mr. Gresley fire off the simile of the lamb, and considered it sound.

'How absurd you are. You always make me laugh. I suppose he has left now that he is unfrozen.'

'Oh! no. He is still here. We would not let him go till he was better. He is not up to much. Weak chap at the best of times I should think. He's lying low in the smoking-room till the people are gone.'

'Mr. Scarlett is an old friend of ours,' said Lady Newhaven, sipping her glass of water, and spilling a little, 'but I can't quite forgive him, no, I really can't, for the danger he caused to Edward. You know, or perhaps you don't know, that Edward can't swim, either. Even now I can't bear to think what might have happened.'

She closed her eyes with evident emotion.

Doll's stolid garden party face relaxed. 'Good little woman,' he thought. 'As fond of him as she can be.'

'All's well that ends well,'[230] he remarked aloud.

Doll did not know that he was quoting Shakespeare, but he did know by long experience that this sentence could be relied on as suitable to the occasion, or to any occasion that looked a little 'doddery,' and finished up all right.

'And now, Mr. Loftus, positively I must insist on your leaving me quietly here. I am quite sure you are wanted outside, and I should blame myself if you wasted another minute on me. It was only the sun which affected me. Don't mention it to Edward. He is always so fussy about me. I will rest quietly here for a quarter of an hour, and then rejoin you all again in the garden.'

'I hope I am not disturbing any one,' said Lord Newhaven, quietly entering the smoking-room. 'Well, Scarlett, how are you getting on?'

Hugh, who was lying on a sofa with his arms raised and his hands behind his head, looked up and his expression changed.

'He was thinking of something uncommonly pleasant,' thought Lord Newhaven, 'not of me or mine, I fancy. I have come to smoke a cigarette in peace,' he added aloud, 'if you don't object.'

'Of course not.'

Lord Newhaven lit his cigarette and puffed a moment in silence.

'Hot outside,' he said.

Hugh nodded. He wondered how soon he could make a pretext for getting up and leaving the room.

There was a faint silken rustle, and Lady Newhaven, pale, breathless, came swiftly in and closed the door. The instant afterwards she saw her husband and shrank back with a little cry. Lord Newhaven did not look at her. His eyes were fixed on Hugh.

Hugh's face became suddenly ugly, livid. He rose slowly to his feet, and stood motionless.

'He hates her,' said Lord Newhaven to himself. And he removed his glance and came forward.

'You were looking for me, Violet?' he remarked. 'I have no doubt you are wishing to return home. We will go at once.' He threw away his cigarette. 'Well, good-bye, Scarlett, in case we don't meet again. I daresay you will pay Westhope a visit later on. Ah, Captain Pratt! so you have fled, like us, from the madding crowd.[231] I can recommend Loftus's cigarettes. I have just had one myself. Good-bye. Did you leave your purchases in the hall, Violet? Yes? Then we will collect them on our way.'

The husband and wife were half-way down the grand staircase before Lord Newhaven said in his usual even voice:

'I must ask you once more to remember that I will not have any scandal attaching to your name. Did not you see that that white mongrel Pratt was on your track? If I had not been there when he came in he would have drawn his own vile conclusions, and for once they would have been correct.'

'He could not think worse of me than you do,' said the wife, half cowed, half defiant.

'No, but he could say so, which I don't, or, what is more probable, he could use his knowledge to obtain a hold over you. He is a dangerous man. Don't put yourself in his power.'

'I don't want to, or in anybody's.'

'Then avoid scandal instead of courting it, and don't repeat the folly of this afternoon.'

Captain Pratt did not remain long in the smoking-room. He had only a slight acquaintance with Hugh, which did not appear capable of expansion. Captain Pratt made a few efforts, proved its inelastic properties, and presently lounged out again.

Hugh moved slowly to the window, and leaned his throbbing forehead against the stone mullion. He was still weak, and the encounter with Lady Newhaven had shaken him.

'What did he mean?' he said to himself, bewildered and suspicious. 'Perhaps I should be staying at Westhope later on!' But of course I shall never go there again. He knows that as well as I do. What did he mean?'

CHAPTER XXXI

The Bird of Time has but a little way
To flutter – and the Bird is on the wing.

Omar Khayyim.[232]

It was the third week of November. Winter, the destroyer, was late, but he had come at last. There was death in the air. A whisper of death stole across the empty fields and bare hill-side. The birds heard it and were silent. The November wind was hurrying round Westhope Abbey, shaking its bare trees.

Lord Newhaven stood looking fixedly out eastward across the level land to the low hills beyond. He stood so long that the day died, and twilight began to rub out first the hills and then the long white lines of flooded meadow and blurred pollard willows. Presently the river mist rose up to meet the coming darkness. In the east, low and lurid, a tawny moon crept up the livid sky. She made no moonlight on the grey earth.

Lord Newhaven moved away from the window, where he had become a shadow among the shadows, and sat down in the dark at his writing-table.

Presently he turned on the electric lamp at his elbow and took a letter out of his pocket. The circle of shaded light fell on his face as he read – the thin grave face, with the steady, inscrutable eyes.

He read the letter slowly, evidently not for the first time.

'If I had not been taken by surprise at the moment I should not have con-sented to the manner in which our differences were settled. Personally, I consider the old arrangement to which you regretfully alluded at the time' – ('pistols for two and coffee for four,' I remember perfectly) – 'as preferable, and as you appeared to think so yourself, would it not be advisable to resort to it? Believing that the old arrangement will meet your wishes as fully as it does mine, I trust that you will entertain this suggestion, and that you will agree to a meeting with your own choice of weapons on any pretext you may choose to name within the next week.'

The letter ended there. It was unsigned.

'The time is certainly becoming short,' said Lord Newhaven. 'He is right in saying there is only a week left. If it were not for the scandal for the boys, and if I thought he would really hold to the compact, I would meet him, but *he won't*. He flinched when he drew lots. He won't. He has courage enough to stand up in front of me for two minutes, and take his chance, but not to blow his own brains out. No. And if he knew what is in store for him if he does not, he would not have courage to face that either. Nor should I, if I were in his shoes, poor devil. The first six foot of earth would be good enough for me.'

He threw the letter with its envelope into the fire and watched it burn.

Then he took up the gold pen which his wife had given him, examined the
nib, dipped it very slowly in the ink, and wrote with sudden swiftness.

'Allow me to remind you that you made no objection at the time to the manner of our encounter and my choice of weapons, by means of which publicity was
avoided. The risk was equal. You now, at the last moment, propose that I should
run it a second time, and in a manner to cause instant scandal. I must decline
to do so, or to reopen the subject, which had received my careful consideration
before I decided upon it. I have burnt your letter, and desire you will burn mine.'

'Poor devil!' said Lord Newhaven, putting the letter, not in the post-box at
his elbow, but in his pocket. 'Loftus and I did him an ill turn when we pulled
him out of the water.'

The letter took its own time, for it had to avoid possible pitfalls. It shunned
the company of the other Westhope letters, it avoided the village post-office, but
after a day's delay it was launched, and lay among a hundred others in a station
pillar-box.[233] And then it hurried, hurried, as fast as express train could take it,
till it reached its London address, and went softly upstairs, and laid itself with a
few others on Hugh's breakfast table.

For many weeks since his visit at Wilderleigh, Hugh had been like a man
in a boat without oars, drifting slowly, imperceptibly on the placid current of a
mighty river, who far away hears the fall of Niagara droning like a bumble bee
in a lily cup.

Long ago, in the summer, he had recognised the sound, had realised the steep
agony towards which the current was bearing him, and had struggled horribly,
impotently, against the inevitable. But of late, though the sound was ever in his
ears, welling up out of the blue distance, he had given up the useless struggle, and
lay still in the sunshine watching the summer woods slide past, and the clouds
sail away, always away and away, to the birthplace of the river, to that little flutter-
ing pulse in the heart of the hills which a woman's hand might cover, the infant
pulse of the great river to be.

Hugh's thoughts went back like the clouds towards that tiny spring of passion in his own life. He felt that he could have forgiven it – and himself – if he
had been swept into the vortex of a headlong mountain torrent leaping down
its own wild water-way, carrying all before it. Other men he had seen who had
been wrested off their feet, swept out of their own keeping by such a torrent
on the steep hillside of their youth. But it had not been so with him. He had
walked more cautiously than they. As he walked he had stopped to look at the
little thread of water which came bubbling up out of its white pebbles. It was so
pretty, it was so feeble, it was so clear. Involuntarily he followed it, watched it
grow, amused himself half contemptuously with it, helped its course by turning
obstacles from its path. It never rushed. It never leaped. It was a toy. The day
came when it spread itself safe and shallow on level land and he embarked upon

it. But he was quickly tired of it. It was beginning to run muddily through a commonplace country, past squalid polluting towns and villages. The hills were long since gone. He turned to row to the shore. And behold his oars were gone! He had been trapped to his destruction.

Hugh had never regarded seriously his intrigue with Lady Newhaven. He had been attracted, excited, partially, half-willingly enslaved. He had thought at the time that he loved her, and that supposition had confirmed him in his cheap cynicism about woman. This, then, was her paltry little court, where man offered mock homage, and where she played at being queen. Hugh had made the discovery that love was a much overrated passion. He had always supposed so, but when he tired of Lady Newhaven he was sure of it. His experience was, after all, only the same as that which many men acquire by marriage, and hold unshaken through long and useful lives. But Hugh had not been able to keep the treasures of this early experience. It had been rendered worthless, perhaps rather contemptible by a later one, that of falling in love with Rachel, and the astonishing discovery that he was in love for the first time. He had sold his birthright for a mess of red pottage,[234] as surely as any man or woman who marries for money or liking. He had not believed in his birthright, and holding it to be worthless, had given it to the first person who had offered him anything in exchange.

His whole soul had gradually hardened itself against Lady Newhaven. If he had loved her, he said to himself, he could have borne his fate. But the play had not been worth the candle. His position was damnable, but that he could have borne – at least so he thought if he had had his day. But he had not had it. That thought rankled. To be hounded out of life because he had mistaken paper-money for real was not only unfair, it was grotesque.

Gradually, however, Hugh forgot his smouldering hate of Lady Newhaven, his sense of injustice and anger against fate, he forgot everything in his love for Rachel. It became the only reality of his life.

He had remained in London throughout October and November, cancelling all his engagements because she was there. What her work was he vaguely apprehended: that she was spending herself and part of her colossal fortune in the East End, but he took no interest in it. He was incapable of taking more interests into his life at this time. He passed many quiet evenings with her in the house in Park Lane which she had lately bought. The little secretary who lived with her had always a faint smile and more writing to do than usual on the evenings when he dined with them.

A great peace was over all their intercourse. Perhaps it was the hush before the storm, the shadow of which was falling, falling, with each succeeding day across the minds of both. Once only a sudden gust of emotion stirred the quiet air, but it dropped again immediately. It came with the hour when Hugh confessed to her the blot upon his past. The past was taking upon itself ever an uglier and more repulsive aspect as he saw more of Rachel. It was hard to put into words, but he spoke of it. The spectre of love rose like a ghost between them as they looked earnestly at each other, each pale even in the ruddy firelight.

Hugh was truthful in intention. He was determined he would never lie to Rachel. He implied an intrigue with a married woman, a deviation not only from morality but from honour. More he did not say. But as he looked at her strained face it seemed to him that she expected something more. A dreadful silence fell between them when he had finished. Had she then no word for him. Her eyes, mute, imploring, dark with an agony of suspense, met his for a second and fell instantly. She did not speak. Her silence filled him with despair. He got up. 'It's getting late. I must go,' he stammered.

She rose mechanically and put out her hand.

'May I come again?' he said, holding it more tightly than he knew and looking intently at her. Was he going to be dismissed?

The pain he caused her hand recalled her to herself. A look of bewilderment crossed her face, and then she realised his suspense and said gravely, 'You may come again.'

He kissed the hand he held, and as he did so he knew for the first time that she loved him. But he could not speak of love after what he had just told her. He looked back when he reached the door and saw her standing where he had left her. She had raised the hand he had kissed to her lips.

That was three days ago. Since then he had not dared to go and see her. He could not ask her to marry him when he was within a few days of the time when he was bound in so-called honour to give Lord Newhaven satisfaction. He certainly could not be in her presence again without asking her. The shadows of the last weeks had suddenly become ghastly realities once more. The roar of Niagara drowned all other sounds. What was he going to do? What was he going to do in the predicament towards which he had been drifting so long, which was now actually upon him? Who shall say what horror, what agony of mind, what frenzied searching for a way of escape, what anguish of baffled love crowded in on Hugh's mind during those last days? At the last moment he caught at a straw, and wrote to Lord Newhaven offering to fight him. He did not ask himself what he should do if Lord Newhaven refused. But when Lord Newhaven did refuse, his determination, long unconsciously fostered, sprang full-grown into existence in a sudden access of passionate anger and blind rage.

'He won't fight, won't he! He thinks I will die like a rat in a trap with all my life before me. I will not. I offered him a fair chance of revenging himself – I would have fired into the air – and if he won't take it it is his own look out, damn him. He can shoot me at sight if he likes. Let him.'

CHAPTER XXXII

On ne peut jamais dire.
'Fontaine je ne boirai jamais de ton eau.'[235]

IF we could choose our ills we should not choose suspense. Rachel aged perceptibly during these last weeks. Her strong white hands became thinner, her lustreless eyes and haggard face betrayed her. In years gone by she had said to herself, when a human love had failed her, 'I will never put myself through this torture a second time. Whatever happens I will not endure it again.'

And now she was enduring it again, though in a different form. There is an element of mother love in the devotion which some women give to men. In the first instance it had opened the door of Rachel's heart to Hugh, and had gradually merged with other feelings and deepened into the painful love of a woman not in her first youth for a man of whom she is not sure.

Rachel was not sure of Hugh. Of his love for her she was sure, but not of the man himself, the gentle, refined, lovable nature that mutely worshipped and clung to her. She could not repulse him any more than she could repulse a child. But through all her knowledge of him, the knowledge of love – the only true knowledge of our fellow creatures – a thread of doubtful anxiety was interwoven. She could form some idea how men like Dick, Lord Newhaven, or the Bishop would act in given circumstances, but she could form no definite idea how Hugh would act in the same circumstances. Yet she knew Hugh a thousand times better than any of the others. Why was this? Many women before Rachel have sought diligently to find, and have shut their eyes diligently, lest they should discover what it is that is dark to them in the character of the man they love.

Perhaps Rachel half knew all the time the subtle inequality in Hugh's character. Perhaps she loved him all the better for it. Perhaps she knew that if he had been without a certain undefinable weakness he would not have been drawn towards her strength. She was stronger than he, and perhaps she loved him more than she could have loved an equal.

'*Les esprits faibles ne sont jamais sincères.*'[236] She had come across that sentence one day in a book she was reading, and had turned suddenly blind and cold with anger. 'He is sincere,' she said fiercely, as if repelling an accusation. 'He would never deceive me.' But no one had accused Hugh.

The same evening he made the confession for which she had waited so long. As he began to speak an intolerable suspense, like a new and acute form of a familiar disease, lay hold on her. Was he going to live or die? She should know at last. Was she to part with him, to bury love for the second time, or was she to keep him, to be his wife, the mother of his children?

As he went on, his language becoming more confused, she hardly listened to him. She had known all that too long. She had forgiven it, not without tears; but still, she had forgiven it long ago. Then he stopped, It seemed to Rachel as if she had reached a moment in life which she could not bear. She waited, but still he did not speak. Then she was not to know. She was to be ground between the millstones of four more dreadful days and nights. She suddenly became aware, as she stared at Hugh's blanching face, that he believed she was about to dismiss him. The thought had never entered her mind.

'Do you not know that I love you?' she said silently to him as he kissed her hand.

When he had left her a gleam of comfort came to her, the only gleam that lightened the days and nights that followed. It was not his fault if he had made a half confession. If he had gone on, and had told her of the drawing of lots, and which had drawn the fatal lot, he would have been wanting in sense of honour. He owed it to the man he had injured to preserve entire secrecy.

'He told me of the sin which might affect my marrying him,' said Rachel, 'but the rest had nothing to do with me. He was right not to speak of it. If he had told me, and then a few days afterwards Lord Newhaven had committed suicide, he would know I should put two and two together, and who the woman was, and the secret would not have died with Lord Newhaven as it ought to do. But if Hugh were the man who had to kill himself, he might have told me so without a breach of confidence, because then I should never have guessed who the others were. If he were the man he could have told me, he certainly *would* have told me, for it could have done no harm to any one. Surely Lady Newhaven must be right when she was so certain that her husband had drawn the short lighter. And she herself had gained the same impression from what Hugh had vaguely said at Wilderleigh. But what are impressions, suppositions, except the food of suspense. Rachel sighed and took up her burden as best she could. Hugh's confession had at least one source of comfort in it, deadly cold comfort if he were about to leave her. She knew that night as she lay awake that she had not quite trusted him up till now, by the sense of entire trust and faith in him which rose up to meet his self-accusation. What might have turned away Rachel's heart from him had had the opposite effect. 'He told me the worst of himself, though he risked losing me by doing it. He wished me to know before he asked me to marry him. Though he acted dishonourably once he is an honourable man. He has shown himself upright in his dealing with me.'

Hugh came back no more after that evening. Rachel told herself she knew why, she understood. He could not speak of love and marriage when the man he had injured was on the brink of death. Her heart stood still when she thought of Lord Newhaven, the gentle, kindly man who was almost her friend, and who was playing with such quiet dignity a losing game. Hugh had taken from him his wife, and by that act was now taking from him his life too.

'It was an even chance,' she groaned. 'Hugh is not responsible for his death. Oh, my God! At least he is not responsible for that. It might have been he who had to die instead of Lord Newhaven. But if it is he, surely he could not leave me without a word. If it is he, he would have come to bid me good-bye. He cannot go down into silence without a word. If it is he, he will come yet.'

She endured through the two remaining days, turning faint with terror each time the door-bell rang, lest it might be Hugh.

But Hugh did not come.

Then, after repeated frantic telegrams from Lady Newhaven, she left London precipitately to go to her, as she had promised, on the twenty-eighth of November, the evening of the last day of the five months.

CHAPTER XXXIII

And he went out immediately, and it was night.[237]

It was nearly dark when Rachel reached Westhope Abbey. A great peace seemed to pervade the long dim lines of the gardens, and to be gathered into the solemn arches of the ruins against the darkening sky. Through the low doorway a faint light of welcome peered. As she drove up she was aware of two tall figures pacing amicably together in the dusk. As she passed them she heard Lord Newhaven's low laugh at something his companion said.

A sense of unreality seized her. It was not the world which was out of joint, which was rushing to its destruction. It must be she who was mad, stark mad to have believed these chimeras.

As she got out of the carriage a step came lightly along the gravel, and Lord Newhaven emerged into the little ring of light by the archway.

'It is very good of you to come,' he said cordially, with extended hand. 'My poor wife is very unwell, and expecting you anxiously. She told me she had sent for you.'

All was unreal – the familiar rooms and passages, the flickering light of the wood fire in the drawing-room, the darkened room, into which Rachel stole softly and knelt down beside a trembling white figure, which held her with a drowning clutch.

'I will be in the drawing-room after dinner,' Lady Newhaven whispered hoarsely. 'I won't dine down. I can't bear to see him.'

It was all unreal except the jealousy which suddenly took Rachel by the throat and nearly choked her.

'I have undertaken what is beyond my strength,' she said to herself, as she hastily dressed for dinner. 'How shall I bear it when she speaks of him? How shall I go through with it?'

Presently she was dining alone with Lord Newhaven. He mentioned that it was Dick Vernon with whom he had been walking when she arrived. Dick was staying in Southminster for business combined with hunting, and had ridden over. Lord Newhaven looked furtively at Rachel as he mentioned Dick. Her indifference was evidently genuine.

'She has not grown thin and parted with what little looks she possessed on Dick's account,' he said to himself; and the remembrance slipped across his mind of Hugh's first word when he recovered consciousness after drowning – 'Rachel.'

'I would have asked Dick to dine,' continued Lord Newhaven, when the servants had gone, 'but I thought two was company and three none, and that it was not fair on you and Violet to have him on your hands, as I am obliged to go to London on business by the night express.'

He was amazed at the instantaneous effect of his words.

Rachel's face became suddenly livid, and she sank back in her chair. He saw that it was only by a supreme effort that she prevented herself from fainting. The truth flashed into his mind.

'She knows,' he said to himself. 'That imbecile, that brainless viper to whom I am tied, has actually confided in her. And she and Scarlett are in love with each other, and the suspense is wearing her out.'

He looked studiously away from her, and continued a desultory conversation, but his face darkened.

The little boys came in, and pressed themselves one on each side of their father, their eyes glued on the crystallised cherries. Rachel had recovered herself, and she watched the children and their father with a pain at her heart which was worse than the faintness.

She had been unable to believe that if Lord Newhaven had drawn the short lighter he would remain quietly here over the dreadful morrow, under the same roof as Teddy and Pauly. Oh! surely nothing horrible could happen so near them. Yet he seemed to have no intention of leaving Westhope. Then perhaps he had not drawn the short lighter after all. At the moment when suspense, momentarily lulled, was once more rising hideous, colossal, he casually mentioned that he was leaving by the night train. The reason was obvious. The shock of relief almost stunned her.

'He will do it quietly to-morrow away from home,' she said to herself, watching him with miserable eyes as he divided the cherries equally between the boys. She had dreaded going upstairs to Lady Newhaven, but anything was better than remaining in the dining-room. She rose hurriedly, and the boys raced to the door and struggled which should open it for her.

Lady Newhaven was lying on a sofa by the wood fire in the drawing-room.

Rachel went straight up to her, and said hoarsely:

'Lord Newhaven tells me he is going to London this evening by the night express.'

Lady Newhaven threw up her arms.

'Then it is he,' she said. 'When he stayed on and on up to to-day I began to be afraid that it was not he, after all; and yet little things made me feel sure it was, and that he was only waiting to do it before me and the children. I have been so horribly frightened. Oh! if he might only go away, and that I might never, never look upon his face again.'

Rachel sat down by the latticed window and looked out into the darkness. She could not bear to look at Lady Newhaven. Was there any help anywhere from this horror of death without, from this demon of jealousy within?

'I am her only friend,' she said to herself over and over again. 'I cannot bear it, and I must bear it. I cannot desert her now. She has no one to turn to but me.'

'Rachel, where are you?' said the feeble, plaintive voice.

Rachel rose and went unsteadily towards her. It was fortunate the room was lit only by the firelight.

'Sit down by me here on the sofa, and let me lean against you. You do comfort me, Rachel, though you say nothing. You are the only true friend I have in the world, the only woman who really loves me. Your cheek is quite wet, and you are actually trembling. You always feel for me. I can bear it now you are here, and he is going away.'

When the boys had been reluctantly coerced to bed, Lord Newhaven rang for his valet, told him what to pack, that he should not want him to accompany him, and then went to his sitting-room on the ground floor.

'Scarlett seems a fortunate person,' he said, pacing up and down. 'That woman loves him, and if she marries him she will reform him. Is he going to escape altogether in this world and the next, if there is a next? Is there no justice anywhere? Perhaps at this moment he is thinking that he has salved his conscience by offering to fight, and that, after all, I can't do anything to prevent his living and marrying her if he chooses. He knows well enough I shall not touch him, or sue for a divorce, for fear of the scandal. He thinks he has me there. And he is right. But he is mistaken if he thinks I can do nothing. I may as well go up to London and see for myself whether he is still on his feet to-morrow night. It is a mere formality, but I will do it. I might have guessed that she would try to smirch her own name, and the boys through her, if she had the chance. She will defeat me yet, unless I am careful. Oh! ye gods! why did I marry a fool who does not even know her own interests. If I had life over again I would marry a Becky Sharp,[238] any she-devil incarnate, if only she had brains. One cannot circumvent a fool because one can't foresee their line of action. But Miss West, for a miracle, is safe. She has a lock-and-key face. But she is not for Scarlett. Did Scarlett tell her himself in an access of moral spring cleaning[239] preparatory to matrimony? No. He may have told her that he had got into trouble with some woman, but not about the drawing of lots. Whatever his faults are, he has the instincts of a gentleman, and his mouth is shut. I can trust him like myself there. But she is not for him. He may think he will marry her, but I draw the line there. Violet and I have other views for him. He can live if he wants to, and apparently he does want to, though whether he will continue to want to is another question. But he shall not have Rachel. She must marry Dick.'

A distant rumbling was heard of the carriage driving under the stable archway on its way to the front door.

Lord Newhaven picked up a novel with a mark in it, and left the room. In the passage he stopped a moment at the foot of the narrow black oak staircase to the nurseries, which had once been his own nurseries. All was very silent. He listened, hesitated, his foot on the lowest stair. The butler came round the corner to announce the carriage.

'I shall be back in four days at furthest,' Lord Newhaven said to him, and turning, went on quickly to the hall, where the piercing night air came in with the stamping of the impatient horses' hoofs.

A minute later the two listening women upstairs heard the carriage drive away into the darkness, and a great silence settled down upon the house.

CHAPTER XXXIV

The fool saith, Who would have thought it?[240]

WINTER had brought trouble with it to Warpington Vicarage. A new baby had arrived, and the old baby was learning, not in silence, what kings and ministers undergo when they are deposed. Hester had never greatly cared for the old baby. She was secretly afraid of it. But in its hour of adversity she took to it, and she and Regie spent many hours consoling it for the arrival of the little chrysalis upstairs.

Mrs. Gresley recovered slowly, and before she was downstairs again Regie sickened with one of those swift sudden illnesses of childhood which make childless women thank God for denying them their prayers.

Mrs. Gresley was not well enough to be told, and for many days Mr. Gresley and Hester and Doctor Brown held Regie forcibly back from the valley of the shadow[241] where, since the first cradle was rocked, the soft feet of children have cleft so sharp an entrance over the mother hearts that vainly barred the way.

Mr. Gresley's face grew as thin as Hester's as the days went by. On his rounds, for he let nothing interfere with his work, heavy farmers in dog carts, who opposed him at vestry meetings, stopped to ask after Regie. The most sullen of his parishioners touched their hats to him as he passed, and mothers of families who never could be induced to leave their cooking to attend morning service, and were deeply offended at being called 'after-dinner Christians'[242] in consequence, forgot the opprobrious term, and brought little offerings of new-laid eggs and rosy apples to tempt 'the little master.'

Mr. Gresley was touched, grateful.

'I don't think I have always done them justice,' he actually said to Hester one day. 'They do seem to understand me a little better at last. Walsh has never spoken to me since my sermon on Dissent, though I always make a point of being friendly to him, but to-day he stopped and said he knew what trouble was, and how he had lost' – Mr. Gresley's voice faltered. 'It is a long time ago – but how, when he was about my age, he lost his eldest boy, and how he always remembered Regie in his prayers, and I must keep up a good heart. We shook hands,' said Mr. Gresley. 'I sometimes think Walsh means well, and that he may be a good-hearted man after all.'

Beneath the arrogance which a belief in Apostolic succession seems to induce in natures like Mr. Gresley's, as mountain air induces asthma in certain lungs, the shaft of agonised anxiety had pierced to a thin layer of humility. Hester knew that that layer was only momentarily disturbed, and that the old self would infallibly reassert itself, but the momentary glimpse drew her heart towards her brother. He was conscious of it, and love almost grew between them as they watched by Regie's bed.

At last, after an endless night, the little faltering feet came to the dividing of the ways, and hesitated. The dawn fell grey on the watchful faces of the doctor and Hester, and on the dumb suspense of the poor father. And with a sigh, as one who half knows he is making a life-long mistake, Regie settled himself against Hester's shoulder and fell asleep.

The hours passed. The light grew strong, and still Regie slept. Doctor Brown put cushions behind Hester, and gave her food. He looked anxiously at her. 'Can you manage?' he whispered later, when the sun was streaming in at the nursery window. And she smiled back in scorn. Could she manage? What did he take her for?

At last Regie stretched himself and opened his eyes. The doctor took him gently from Hester, gave him food, and laid him down.

'He is all right,' he said. 'He will sleep all day.'

Mr. Gresley, who had hardly stirred, hid his face in his hands.

'Don't try to move, Miss Hester,' said Doctor Brown gently.

Hester did not try. She could not. Her hands and face were rigid. She looked at him in terror. 'I shall have to scream in another moment,' she whispered.

The old doctor picked her up, and carried her swiftly to her room, where Fraülein ministered to her.

At last he came down and found Mr. Gresley waiting for him at the foot of the stair.

'You are sure he is all right?' he asked.

'Sure! Fraülein is with him. He got the turn at dawn.'

'Thank God!'

'Well, I should say thank your sister too. She saved him. I tell you, Gresley, neither you nor I could have sat all those hours without stirring as she did. She had cramp after the first hour. She has a will of iron in that weak body of hers.'

'I had no idea she was uncomfortable,' said Mr. Gresley, half incredulous.

'That is one of the reasons why I always say you ought not to be a clergyman,' snapped the little doctor, and was gone.

Mr. Gresley was not offended. He was too overwhelmed with thankfulness to be piqued.

'Good old Brown,' he said indulgently. 'He has been up all night, and he is so tired he does not know he is talking nonsense. As if a man who did not understand cramp was not qualified to be a priest. Ha! Ha! He always likes to have a little hit at me, and he is welcome to it. I must just creep up and kiss dear Hester. I never should have thought she had it in her to care for any one as she has shown she cares for Regie. I shall tell her so, and how surprised I am, and how I love her for it. She has always seemed so insensible, so callous. But, please God, this is the beginning of a new life for her. If it is she shall never hear one word of reproach about the past from me.'

A day or two later the Bishop of Southminster had a touch of rheumatism, and Doctor Brown attended him. This momentary malady may possibly account to the reader for an incident which remained to the end of life inexplicable to Mr. Gresley.

Two days after Regie had taken the turn towards health, and on the afternoon of the very same day when Doctor Brown had interviewed the Bishop's rheumatism, the episcopal carriage might have been seen squeezing its august proportions into the narrow drive of Warpington Vicarage; at least, it was always called the drive, though the horses' noses were reflected in the glass of the front door while the hind-wheels still jarred the gate-posts.

Out of the carriage stepped, not the Bishop, but the tall figure of Dick Vernon, who rang the bell, and then examined a crack in the portico.

He had plenty of time to do so.

'Lord! what fools!' he said half aloud. 'The crazy thing is shouting out that it is going to drop on their heads, and they put a clamp across the crack. Might as well put a respirator on a South Sea Islander.[243] Is Mr. Gresley in? Well then, just ask him to step this way, will you? Look here, James, if you want to be had up for manslaughter, you leave this porch as it is. No, I did not drive over from Southminster on purpose to tell you, but I mention it now I am here.'

'I added the portico myself when I came here,' said Mr. Gresley stiffly, who had not forgotten or forgiven the enormity of Dick's behaviour at the temperance meeting.

'So I should have thought,' said Dick, warming to the subject, and mounting on a small garden-chair. 'And some escaped lunatic has put a clamp on the stucco.'

'I placed the clamp myself,' replied Mr. Gresley. 'There really is no necessity for you to waste your time and mine here. I understand the portico perfectly. The crack is merely superficial.'

'Is it?' said Dick; 'then why does it run round those two consumptive little pillars? I tell you it's tired of standing up. It's going to sit down. Look here' – Dick tore at the stucco with his knife, and caught the clamp as it fell – 'that clamp was only put in the stucco. It never reached the stone or the wood, whichever the little kennel is made of. You ought to be thankful it did not drop on one of the children, or on your own head. It would have knocked all the texts out of it for some time to come.'

Mr. Gresley did not look very grateful as he led the way to his study.

'I was lunching with the Bishop to-day,' said Dick, 'and Doctor Brown was there. He told us about the trouble here. He said the little chap Regie was going on like a house on fire. The Bishop told me to ask after him particularly.'

'He is wonderfully better every day,' said Mr. Gresley softening. 'How kind of the Bishop to send you to inquire. Not having children himself, I should never have thought –'

'No,' said Dick, 'you wouldn't. Do you remember when we were at Cheam, and Ogilvy's marked sovereign was found in the pocket of my flannel trousers. You were the only one of the boys, you and that sneak Field, who was not sure I might not have taken it. You said it looked awfully bad, and so it did.'

'No one was gladder than I was when it was cleared up,' said Mr. Gresley.

'No,' said Dick; 'but we don't care much what any one thinks when it's cleared up. It's before that matters. Is Hester in? I've two notes for her. One from Brown, and one from the Bishop, and my orders are to take her back with me. That is why the Bishop sent the carriage.'

'I am afraid Hester will hardly care to leave us at present,' said Mr. Gresley. 'My wife is on her sofa, and Regie is still very weak. He has taken one of those unaccountable fancies of children for her, and can hardly bear her out of his sight.'

'The Bishop has taken another of those unaccountable fancies for her,' said Dick, looking full at Mr. Gresley in an unpleasant manner. 'I'm not one that holds that parsons should have their own way in everything. I've seen too much of missionaries. I just shove out curates[244] and vicars and all that small fry if they get in my way. But when they break out in buttons and gaiters,[245] by Jove, I knock under to them, at least, I do to men like the Bishop. He knows a thing or two. He has told me not to come back without Hester, and I'm not going to. Ah! There she is in the garden.' Dick's large back had been turned towards the window, but he had seen the reflection of a passing figure in the glass of a framed testimonial[246] which occupied a prominent place on the study wall, and he at once marched out into the garden and presented the letters to Hester.

Hester was bewildered at the thought of leaving Warpington, into which she seemed to have grown like a Buddhist into his tree.[247] She was reluctant, would think it over, &c. But Dick, after one glance at her strained face, was obdurate. He would hear no reason. He would not go away. She and Fräulein nervously cast a few clothes into a box, Fräulein so excited by the apparition of a young man and a possible love affair, that she could hardly fold Hester's tea-gowns.[248]

When Hester came down with her hat on she found Dick untying Mr. Gresley's bicycle in the most friendly manner while the outraged owner stood by remonstrating.

'I assure you, Dick, I don't wish it to be touched. I know my own machine. If it were a common puncture I could mend it myself, but I don't want the whole thing ruined by an ignorant person. I shall take it in to Southminster on the first opportunity.'

'No need to do that,' said Dick cheerfully. 'Might as well go to a doctor to have your nails cut. Do it at home. You don't believe in the water test? Oh! that's rot. You'll believe in it when you see it. You're learning it now. There! Now I've got it in the pail; see all these blooming little bubbles jostling up in a row. There's a leak at the valve. No, there isn't. It's only unscrewed. Good Lord, James, it's only unscrewed, and you thought the whole machine was out of order. There, now, I've screwed it up. Devil a bubble! What's that you're saying about swearing in your presence? Oh! don't apologise! You can't help being a clergyman. Look for yourself. You will never learn if you look the other way just when a good-natured chap is showing you. I would have put the tyre on again, but as you say you can do it better yourself, I won't. Sorry to keep you waiting, Hester. And look here, James, you ought to bicycle more. Strengthen your legs for playing the harmonium on Sundays. Well, I could not tell you had an organ in that little one-horse church.[249] Good-bye, Fräulein, good-bye, James. Home, Coleman. And look here,' said Dick, putting his mischievous face out of the window as the carriage turned, 'if you are getting up steam for another temperance meeting I'm your man.'

'Good-bye, dear James,' interrupted Hester hastily, and the carriage drove away.

'He looks pasty,' said Dick, after an interval. 'A chap like James has no power in his arms and legs. He can kneel down in church, and put his arm round Mrs. Gresley's waist, but that's about all he's up to. He doesn't take enough exercise.'

'He is not well. I don't think I ought to have left them.'

'You had no choice. Brown said, unless you could be got away at once you would be laid up. I was at luncheon at the Palace when he said it. The Bishop's sister was too busy with her good works to come herself so I came instead. I said I should not come back alive without you. They seemed to think I should all the same, but of course that was absurd. I wanted the Bishop to bet upon it, but he wouldn't.'

'Do you always get what you want?' said Hester.

'Generally, if it depends on myself. But sometimes things depend on others besides me. Then I may be beaten.'

They were passing Westhope Abbey wrapped in a glory of sunset and mist.

'Did you know Miss West was there?' Dick said suddenly.

'No,' said Hester surprised. 'I thought she was in London.'

'She came down last night to be with Lady Newhaven who is not well. Miss West is a great friend of yours, isn't she?'

'Yes.'

'Well, she has one fault, and it is one I can't put up with. She won't look at me.'

'Don't put up with it,' said Hester softly. 'We women all have our faults, dear Dick. But if men point them out to us in a nice way we can sometimes cure them.'

CHAPTER XXXV

When the sun sets, who doth not look for night?
SHAKESPEARE.[250]

Two nights had passed since Lord Newhaven had left the Abbey. And now the second day, the first day of December, was waning to its close. How Rachel had lived through them she knew not. The twenty-ninth had been the appointed day. Both women had endured till then, feeling that that day would make an end. Neither had contemplated the possibility of hearing nothing for two days more. Long afterwards in quiet years Rachel tried to recall those two days and nights. But memory only gave lurid glimpses as of lightning across darkness. In one of those glimpses she recalled that Lady Newhaven had become ill, that the doctor had been sent for, that she had been stupefied with narcotics. In another she was walking in the desolate frost-nipped gardens, and the two boys were running towards her across the grass.

As the sun sank on the afternoon of the second day it peered in at her sitting alone by her window. Lady Newhaven after making the whole day frightful was mercifully asleep. Rachel sat looking out into the distance beyond the narrow confines of her agony. Has not every man and woman who has suffered sat thus by the window, looking out, seeing nothing, but still gazing blindly out hour after hour?

Perhaps the quiet mother earth watches us, and whispers to our deaf ears –

Warte nur, balde
Ruhest du auch.[251]

Little pulse of life writhing in your shirt of fire,[252] the shirt is but of clay of your mother's weaving, and she will take it from you presently when you lay back your head on her breast.

There had been wind all day, a high, dreadful wind, which had accompanied all the nightmare of the day as a wail accompanies pain. But now it had dropped with the sun, who was setting with little pageant across the level land. The whole sky, from north to south, from east to west, was covered with a wind-threshed floor of thin wan clouds, and shreds of clouds, through which, as through a veil, the steadfast face of the heaven beyond looked down.

And suddenly, from east to west, from north to south, as far as the trees and wolds in the dim, forgotten east, the exhausted livid clouds blushed wave on wave, league on league, red as the heart of a rose. The wind-whipped earth was still. The trees held their breath. Very black against the glow the carved cross on the adjoining gable stood out. And in another moment the mighty tide of colour went as it had come, swiftly ebbing across its infinite shores of sky. And the waiting night came down suddenly.

'Oh! my God,' said Rachel, stretching out her hands to ward off the darkness. 'Not another night. I cannot bear another night.'

A slow step came along the gravel; it passed below the window and stopped at the door. Some one knocked. Rachel tore open the throat of her gown. She was suffocating. Her long-drawn breathing seemed to deaden all other sounds. Nevertheless she heard it – the faint footfall of some one in the hall, a distant opening and shutting of doors. A vague, indescribable tremor seemed to run through the house.

She stole out of her room and down the passage. At Lady Newhaven's door her French maid[253] was hesitating, her hand on the handle.

Below, on the stairs, stood a clergyman and the butler.

'I am the bearer of sad tidings,' said the clergyman. Rachel recognised him as the Archdeacon[254] at whom Lord Newhaven had so often laughed. 'Perhaps you would prepare Lady Newhaven before I break them to her.'

The door was suddenly opened, and Lady Newhaven stood in the doorway. One small clenched hand held together the long white dressing-gown which she had hastily flung round her, while the other was outstretched against the doorpost. She swayed as she stood. Morphia and terror burned in her glassy eyes fixed in agony upon the clergyman. The light in the hall below struck upwards at her colourless face. In later days this was the picture which Lady Newhaven recalled to mind as the most striking of the whole series.

'Tell her,' said Rachel, sharply.

The Archdeacon advanced.

'Prepare yourself, dear Lady Newhaven,' he said sonorously. 'Our dear friend, Lord Newhaven, has met with a serious accident. Er – the Lord gave, and the Lord hath taken away. Blessed be the name of the Lord.'[255]

'Is he dead?' whispered Lady Newhaven.

The Archdeacon bowed his head.

Every one except the children heard the scream which rang through the house.

Rachel put her arms round the tottering, distraught figure, drew it gently back into the room, and closed the door behind her.

CHAPTER XXXVI

And Nicanor lay dead in his harness.
1 MACCABEES, xv. 28.[256]

RACHEL laid down the papers which were full of Lord Newhaven's death.

'He has managed it well,' she said to herself. 'No one could suspect that it was not an accident. He has played his losing game to the bitter end, weighing each move. None of the papers even hint that his death was not an accident. He has provided against that.'

The butler received a note from Lord Newhaven the morning after his death, mentioning the train by which he should return to Westhope that day, and ordering a carriage to meet him. A great doctor made public the fact that Lord Newhaven had consulted him the day before about the attacks of vertigo from which it appeared he had suffered of late. A similar attack seemed to have seized upon him while waiting at Clapham Junction when the down express thundered past. The few who saw him said that, as he was pacing the empty platform, he staggered suddenly as the train was sweeping up behind him, put his hand to his head, and stumbled over the edge on to the line. Death was instantaneous. Only his wife and one other woman knew that it was premeditated.

'The only thing I cannot understand about it,' said Rachel to herself, 'is why a man, who from first to last could act with such caution, and with such deliberate determination, should have been two days late. The twenty-ninth of November was the last day of the five months, and he died on the afternoon of December the first. Why did he wait two days after he left Westhope? I should have thought he would have been the last man in the world to overstep the allotted time by so much as an hour. Yet nevertheless he waited two whole days. I don't understand it.'

After an interminable interval Lord Newhaven's luggage returned, the familiar portmanteaux and dressing-bag,[257] and even the novel which he was reading when he left Westhope, with the mark still in it. All came back. And a coffin came back, too, and was laid before the little altar in the disused chapel.

'I will go and pray for him in the chapel as soon as the lid is fastened down,' said Lady Newhaven to Rachel, 'but I dare not before. I can't believe he is really dead. And they say somebody ought to look, just to verify. I know it is always done. Dear Rachel, would you mind?'

So Rachel, familiar with death as all are who have known poverty, or who have loved their fellows, went alone into the chapel, and stood a long time looking down upon the muffled figure, the garment of flesh which the soul had so deliberately rent and flung aside.

The face was fixed in a grave attention, as of one who sees that which he awaits. The sarcasm, the weariness, the indifference, the impatient patience, these were gone, these were indeed dead. The sharp thin face knew them no more. It looked intently, unflinchingly through its half-closed eyes into the beyond which some call death, which some call life.

'Forgive him,' said Rachel, kneeling beside the coffin. 'My friend, forgive him. He has injured you, I know. And your just revenge, for you thought it just, has failed to reach him. But the time for vengeance has passed. The time for forgiveness has come. Forgive my poor Hugh, who will never forgive himself. Do you not see now, you who see so much, that it was harder for him than for you; that it would have been the easier part for him if he had been the one to draw death, to have atoned to you for his sin against you by his death, instead of feeling, as he always must, that your stroke failed, and that he has taken your life from you as well as your honour. Forgive him,' said Rachel, over and over again.

But the unheeding face looked earnestly into the future. It had done with the past.

'Ah!' said Rachel, 'if I who love him can forgive him, cannot you, who only hated him, forgive him, too? For love is greater than hate.'

She covered the face and went out.

CHAPTER XXXVII

Le nombre des êtres qui veulent voir vrai est extraordinairement petit. Ce qui domine les hommes, c'est la peur de la vérité, à moins que la vérité ne leur soit utile.

AMIEL.[258]

LADY NEWHAVEN insisted on attending the funeral, a little boy in either hand. Rachel had implored that she would spare the children, knowing how annoyed their father would have been, but Lady Newhaven was obdurate.

'No,' she said. 'He may not have cared much about them, but that is no reason why they should forget he is their father.'

So Teddy and Pauly stared with round eyes at the crowd, and at the coffin, and the wealth of flowers, and the deep grave in which their old friend and play-fellow was laid. Perhaps they did not understand. They did not cry.

'They are like their father. They have not much heart,' Lady Newhaven said to Rachel.

Dick, who was at the funeral, looked at them, winking his hawk eyes a little, and afterwards he came back boldly to the silent house, and obtained leave to take them away for the afternoon. He brought them back towards bedtime, with a dancing doll he had made for them, and a man's face cut out of cork. They met Rachel and the governess in the garden on their return, and flew to them with their trophies.

Dick waited a moment after the others had gone in.

'It seems hard on him to have left it all,' he said. 'His wife and the little chaps, and his nice home and everything.'

Rachel could say nothing.

'He was very fond of the boys,' he went on. 'He would have done anything for them.'

'He did what he could,' said Rachel almost inaudibly, and then added. 'He was very fond of you.'

'He was a good friend,' said Dick, his crooked mouth twitching a little, 'and a good enemy. That was why I liked him. He was hard to make a friend of or an enemy, but when he once did either he never let go.'

Rachel shivered. The frost was settling white upon the grass.

'I must go in,' she said, holding out her hand.

'Are you staying much longer?' said Dick, keeping it in his.

'I leave to-morrow morning very early.'

'You will be in London perhaps.'

'I think so for the present.'

'May I come and see you?'

The expression of Dick's eyes was unmistakable. In the dusk he seemed all eyes and hand.

'Dear Mr. Dick, it's no use.'

'I like plain speaking,' said Dick. 'I can't think why it's considered such a luxury. You are quite right to say that, and I should be quite wrong if I did not say that I mean to keep on till you are actually married.'

He released her hand with difficulty. It was too dark to see his face. She hesitated a moment, and then fled into the house.

It is a well-known fact that after the funeral the strictest etiquette permits, nay, encourages, certain slight relaxations on the part of the bereaved.[259]

Lady Newhaven lay on the sofa in her morning-room in her long black draperies, her small hands folded. They were exquisite, little blue-veined hands. There were no rings on them except a wedding-ring. Her maid, who had been living in an atmosphere of pleasurable excitement since Lord Newhaven's death, glanced with enthusiastic admiration at her mistress. Lady Newhaven was a fickle, inconsiderate mistress, but at this moment her behaviour was perfect. She, Angélique, knew what her own part should be, and played it with effusion. She suffered no one to come into the room. She, who would never do a hand's turn for the English servants, put on coal with her own hands. She took the lamps from the footman at the door. Presently she brought in a little tray with food and wine, and softly besought 'Miladi' to eat. Perhaps the mistress and maid understood each other. Lady Newhaven impatiently shook her head, and Angélique wrung her hands. In the end Angélique prevailed.

'Have they all gone?' Lady Newhaven asked after the little meal was finished and, with much coaxing, she had drunk a glass of champagne.

Angélique assured her they were all gone, the relations who had come to the funeral – 'Milor Windham and l'Honorable Carson' were the last. They were dining with Miss West, and they were leaving immediately after dinner by the evening express.

'Ask Miss West to come to me as soon as they have gone,' she said.

Angélique hung about the room, and was finally dismissed.

Lady Newhaven lay quite still, watching the fire. A great peace had descended upon that much tossed soul. The dreadful restlessness of the last weeks was gone. The long suspense, prolonged beyond its time, was over. The shock of its ending, which shattered her at first, was over too. She was beginning to breathe again, to take comfort once more: not the comfort that Rachel had tried so hard to give her, but the comfort of feeling that happiness and ease were in store for her once more; that these five hideous months were to be wiped out, and not her own past, to which she still secretly clung, out of which she was already building her future.

'It is December now. Hugh and I shall be married next December, D.V.,[260] not before. We will be married quietly in London and go abroad. I shall have a few tailor-made gowns from Vernon, but I shall wait for my other things till I am in Paris on my way back. The boys will be at school by then. Pauly is rather young, but they had better go together, and they need not come home for the holidays just at first. I don't think Hugh would care to have the boys always about. I won't keep my title. I hate everything to do with *him*' – (Lord Newhaven was still *him*) – 'and I know the Queen does not like it. I will be presented as Mrs. Scarlett, and we will live at his place in Shropshire, and at last we shall be happy. Hugh will never turn against me as *he* did.'

Lady Newhaven's thoughts travelled back in spite of herself to her marriage with Lord Newhaven, and the humble, boundless admiration which she had accepted as a matter of course, which had been extinguished so entirely, so inexplicably, soon after marriage, which had been succeeded by still more inexplicable paroxysms of bitterness and contempt. Other men, Lady Newhaven reflected, respected and loved their wives even after they lost their complexions, and – she had kept hers. Why had he been different from others? It was impossible to account for men and their ways. And how he had sneered at her when she talked gravely to him, especially on religious subjects. Decidedly, Edward had been very difficult, until he settled down into the sarcastic indifference that had marked all his intercourse with her after the first year.

'Hugh will never be like that,' she said to herself, 'and he will never laugh at me for being religious. He understands me as Edward never did. And I will be married in a pale shade of violet velvet trimmed with ermine, as it will be a winter wedding. And my bouquet shall be of Neapolitan violets to match my name.'

'May I come in?' said Rachel's voice.

'Do,' said Lady Newhaven, but without enthusiasm.

She no longer needed Rachel. The crisis during which she had clung to her was past. What shipwrecked seaman casts a second thought after his rescue to the log which supported him upon a mountainous sea. Rachel interrupted pleasant thoughts. Lady Newhaven observed that her friend's face had grown unbecomingly thin, and that what little colour there was in it was faded. 'She is the same age as I am, but she looks much older,' said Lady Newhaven to herself, adding aloud:

'Dear Rachel!'

'Every one has gone,' said Rachel,' and I have had a telegram from Lady Trentham. She has reached Paris, and will be here to-morrow afternoon.'

'Dearest mamma,' said Lady Newhaven.

'So now,' said Rachel, sitting down near the sofa with a set countenance, 'I shall feel quite happy about leaving you.'

'Must you go?'

'I must. I have arranged to leave by the seven-thirty to-morrow morning. I think it will be better if we say good-bye over night.'

'I shall miss you dreadfully.' Lady Newhaven perceived suddenly, and with resentment, that Rachel was anxious to go.

'I do not think you will miss me.'

'I don't know why you say that. You have been so dear and sympathetic. You understand me much better than mamma. And then mamma was always so fond of Edward. She cried for joy when I was engaged to him. She said her only fear was that I should not appreciate him. She never could see that he was in fault. I must say he was kind to her. I do wish I was not obliged to have her now. I know she will do nothing but talk of him. Now I come to think of it, do stay, Rachel.'

'There is a reason why I can't stay, and why you won't wish me to stay when I tell it you.'

'Oh, Mr. Vernon! I saw you and him holding hands in the dusk. But I don't mind if you marry him, Rachel. I believe he is a good sort of young man – not the kind I could ever have looked at, but what does that matter? I am afraid it has rankled in your mind that I once warned you against him. But, after all, it is your affair, not mine.'

'I was not going to speak of Mr. Vernon.'

Lady Newhaven sighed impatiently. She did not want to talk of Rachel's affairs. She wanted, now the funeral was over, to talk of her own. She often said there were few people with less curiosity about others than herself.

Rachel pulled herself together.

'Violet,' she said, 'we have known each other five months, haven't we?'

'Yes, exactly. The first time you came to my house was that dreadful night of the drawing of lots. I always thought Edward drew the short lighter. It was so like him to turn it off with a laugh.'

'I want you to remember, if ever you think hardly of me, that during those five months I did try to be a friend. I may have failed, but – I did my best.'

'But you did not fail. You have been a real friend, and you will always be so, dear Rachel. And when Hugh and I are married you will often come and stay with us.'

A great compassion flooded Rachel's heart for this poor creature, with its house of cards. Then her face became fixed as a surgeon's who gets out his knife.

'I think I ought to tell you – you ought to know – that I care for Mr. Scarlett.'

'He is mine,' said Lady Newhaven instantly, her blue eyes dilating.

'He is unmarried and I am unmarried,' said Rachel hoarsely. 'I don't know how it came about, but I have gradually become attached to him.'

'He is not unmarried. It is false. He is my husband in the sight of heaven. I have always through everything looked upon him as such.'

This seemed more probable than that heaven had so regarded him. Rachel did not answer. She had confided her love to no one, not even to Hester; and to speak of it to Lady Newhaven had been like tearing the words out of herself with hot pincers.

'I knew he was poor, but I did not know he was as poor as that,' said Lady Newhaven after a pause.

Rachel got up suddenly, and moved away to the fireplace. She felt it would be horribly easy to strangle that voice.

'And you came down here pretending to be my friend while all the time you were stealing his heart from me.'

Still Rachel did not answer. Her forehead was pressed against the man-telshelf.[261] She prayed urgently that she might stay upon the hearthrug, that whatever happened she might not go near the sofa.

'And you think he is in love with you?'

'I do.'

'Are you not rather credulous? But I suppose he has told you over and over again that he cares for you yourself alone. Is the wedding-day fixed?'

'No, he has not asked me to marry him yet. I wanted to tell you before it happened.'

Lady Newhaven threw herself back on the sofa. She laughed softly. A little mirror hung tilted at an angle which allowed her to see herself as she lay. She saw a very beautiful woman, and then she turned and looked at Rachel, who had no beauty as she understood it, and laughed again.

'My poor dear,' she said, in a voice that made Rachel wince, 'Hugh is no bet-ter than the worst. He has made love to you *pour passer le temps*,[262] and you have taken him seriously, like the dear simple woman you are. But he will never marry you. You own he has not proposed. Of course not. Men are like that. It is hateful of them, but they will do it. They are the vainest creatures in the world. Don't you see that the reason he has not asked you is because he knew that Edward had to – and that I should soon be free to marry him. And Rachel, you need not feel the least little bit humiliated, for I shan't tell a soul, and, after all, he loved me first.'

Lady Newhaven was quite reassured. It had been a horrible moment, but it was past.

'Why do I always make trouble?' she said, with plaintive self-complacency. 'Rachel, you must not be jealous of me. I can't help it.'

Rachel tried to say 'I am not,' but the words would not come. She *was* jealous, jealous of the past, cut to the heart every time she noticed that Lady Newhaven's hair waved over her ears, and that she had taper fingers.

'I think it is no use talking of this any more,' Rachel said. 'Perhaps I was wrong to speak of it at all. I did as I would be done by. As I am starting early I think I will say goodnight and good-bye.'

'Good-night, dear Rachel, and perhaps, as you say, it had better be good-bye. You may remain quite easy in your mind that I shall never breathe a word of what you have said to any living soul – except Hugh,' she added to herself as Rachel left the room.

CHAPTER XXXVIII

To every coward safety, and afterwards his evil hour.[263]

SLEEP, that fickle courtier of our hours of ease, had deserted Hugh. When the last hour of the last day was over, and the dawn which he had bound himself in honour not to see found him sitting alone in his room, where he had sat all night, horror fell upon him at what he had done. Now that its mire was upon him he saw by how foul, by how dastardly a path he had escaped.

'To every coward safety, and afterwards his evil hour.' Hugh's evil hour had come. But was he a coward? Men not braver than he have earned the Victoria Cross,[264] have given up their lives freely for others. Hugh had it in him to do as well as any man in hot blood, but not in cold. That was where Lord Newhaven had the advantage of him. He had been overmatched from the first. The strain without had been greater than the power of resistance within. As the light grew, Hugh tasted of that cup which God holds to no man's lips – *remorse*. Would the cup of death which he had pushed aside have been more bitter?

He took up his life like a thief. Was it not stolen? He could not bear his rooms. He could not bear the crowded streets. He could not bear the parks. He wandered aimlessly from one to the other, driven out of each in turn, consumed by the smouldering flame of his self-contempt. Scorn seemed written on the faces of the passers-by. As the day waned he found himself once again for the twentieth time in the park, pacing in 'the dim persistent rain,'[265] which had been falling all day.

But he could not get away from the distant roar of the traffic. He heard it everywhere, like the Niagara which he had indeed escaped, but the sound of which would be in his ears till he died. He drew nearer and nearer to the traffic, and stood still in the rain listening to it intently. Might one of those thousand wheels be even now bringing his enemy towards him, to force him to keep his unspoken word. Hugh had not realised that his worst enemy was he who stood with him in the rain.

The forlorn London trees, black and bare, seemed to listen too, and to cling closer to their parks and grass, as if they dimly foresaw the inevitable time coming when they too should toil, and hate, and suffer, as they saw on all sides those stunted uprooted figures toil and suffer, which had once been trees like themselves. 'We shall come to it,' they seemed to say, shivering in all their branches, as they peered through the iron rails at the stream of human life, much as man peers at a passing funeral.

The early night drove Hugh back to the house. He found a note from a man who had rooms above him enclosing a theatre ticket, which at the last moment he had been prevented using. He instantly clutched at the idea of escaping from himself for a few hours at least. He hastily changed his wet clothes, ate the food that had been prepared for him, and hurried out once more.

The play was 'Julius Cæsar,'[266] at Her Majesty's. He had seen it several times, but to-night it appealed to him as it had never done before. He hardly noticed the other actors. His whole interest centred in the awful figure of Cassius, splendid in its unswerving deathless passion of a great hate and a great love. His eyes never left the ruthless figure as it stood in silence with its unflinching eyes upon its victim. Had not Lord Newhaven thus watched him, Hugh, ready to strike when the hour came.

The moment of the murder was approaching. Hugh held his breath. Cassius knelt with the rest before Cæsar. Hugh saw his hand seek the handle of his sword, saw the end of the sheath tilt upwards under his robe as the blade slipped out of it. Then came the sudden outburst of animal ferocity long held in leash, of stab on stab, the self-recovery, the cold stare at the dead figure with Cassius' foot upon its breast.

For a moment the scene vanished. Hugh saw again the quiet study with its electric reading-lamp, the pistols over the mantelpiece, the tiger glint in Lord Newhaven's eyes. He was like Cassius. He, too, had been ready to risk life, everything in the prosecution of his hate.

'He shall never stand looking down on my body,' said Hugh to himself, 'with his cursed foot upon me.' And he realised that if he had been a worthier antagonist, that also might have been. The play dealt with men. Cassius and Lord Newhaven were men. But what was he?

The fear of death leading the love of life by the hand took with shame a lower seat. Hugh saw them at last in their proper places. If he could have died then he would have died cheerfully, gladly, as he saw Cassius die by his own hand, counting death the little thing it is. Afterwards, as he stood in the crowd near the door, where the rain was delaying the egress, he saw suddenly Lord Newhaven's face watching him. His heart leapt. 'He has come to make me keep my word,' he said to himself, the exaltation of the play still upon him. 'I will not avoid him. Let him do it,' and he pressed forward towards him.

Lord Newhaven looked fixedly at him for a moment, and then disappeared.

'He will follow me and stab me in the back,' said Hugh. 'I will walk home by the street where the pavement is up, and let him do it.'

He walked slowly, steadily on, looking neither to right nor left. Presently he came to a barrier across a long deserted street, with a red lamp keeping guard over it. He walked deliberately up it. He had no fear. In the middle he stopped, and fumbled in his pocket for a cigarette.

A soft step was coming up behind him.

'It will be quickly over,' he said to himself. 'Wait. Don't look round.'

He stood motionless. His silver cigarette case dropped from his hand. He looked at it for a second, forgetting to pick it up. A dirty hand suddenly pounced upon it, and a miserable ragged figure flew past him up the street. Hugh stared after it bewildered, and then looked round. The street was quite empty. He drew a long breath, and something between relief and despair took hold of him.

'Then he does not want to after all. He has not even followed me. Why was he there? He was waiting for me. What horrible revenge is he planning against me. Is he laying a second trap for me?'

The following night Hugh read in the evening papers that Lord Newhaven had been accidentally killed on the line. The revulsion of feeling was too sudden, too overwhelming. He could not bear it. He could not live through it. He flung himself on his face upon the floor, and sobbed as if his heart would break.

The cyclone of passion which had swept Hugh into its vortex spent itself and him, and flung him down at last. How long a time elapsed he never knew between the moment when he read the news of the accident and the moment when shattered, exhausted, disfigured by emotion, he raised himself to his feet. He opened the window, and the night air laid its cool mother touch upon his face and hands. The streets were silent. The house was silent. He leaned with closed eyes against the window post. Time passed by on the other side.

And after a while angels came and ministered to him. Thankfulness came softly, gently, to take his shaking hand in hers. The awful past was over. A false step, a momentary giddiness on the part of his enemy, and the hideous strangling meshes of the past had fallen from him at a touch, as if they had never wrapped him round. Lord Newhaven was gone to return no more. The past went with him. Dead men tell no tales. No one knew of the godless compact between them, and of how he, Hugh, had failed to keep to it, save they two alone. He and one other. And that other was dead, was dead.

Hope came next, shyly, silently, still pale from the embrace of her sister Despair, trimming anew her little lamp, which the labouring breath of Despair had well-nigh blown out. She held the light before Hugh, shading it with her veil, for his eyes were dazed with long gazing into darkness. She turned it faintly upon the future, and he looked where the light fell. And the light grew.

He had a future once more. He had been given that second chance for which he had so yearned. His life was his own once more: not the shamed life in death, worse than death of the last two days, but his own to take up again, to keep, to enjoy, best of all to use worthily. No horrible constraint was upon him to lay it down, or to live in torment because he still held it. He was free, free to marry

Rachel whom he loved, and who loved him. He saw his life with her. Hope smiled, and turned up her light. It was too bright. Hugh hid his face in his hands.

And last of all, dwarfing Hope, came a divine constraining presence who ever stretches out strong hands to them that fall, who alone sets the stumbling feet upon the upward path. Repentance came to Hugh at last. In all this long time she had not come while he was suffering, while smouldering Remorse had darkened his soul with smoke. But in this quiet hour she came and stood beside him.

Hugh had in the past leaned heavily on extenuating circumstances. He had made many excuses for himself. But now he made none. Perhaps for the first time in his life, under the pressure of that merciful, that benign hand, he was sincere with himself. He saw his conduct – that easily condoned conduct – as it was. Love and Repentance, are not these the great teachers? Some of us so frame our lives that we never come face to face with either, or with ourselves. Hugh came to himself at last. He saw how, whether detected or not, his sin had sapped his manhood, spread like a leaven of evil through his whole life, laid its hideous touch of desecration and disillusion even on his love for Rachel. It had tarnished his mind, his belief in others, his belief in good. These ideals, these beliefs had been his possession once, his birthright. He had sold his birthright for red pottage. Until now he had scorned the red pottage. Now he saw that his sin lay deeper, even in his original scorn of his birthright, his disbelief in the Divine Spirit Who dwells with man.

Nevertheless his just punishment had been remitted. Hitherto he had looked solely at that punishment, feeling that it was too great. He had prayed many times that he might escape it. Now for the first time he prayed that he might be forgiven.

Repentance took his hands and locked them together.

'God helping me,' he said, 'I will lead a new life.'

CHAPTER XXXIX

Les sots sont plus à craindre que les méchans.[267]

MR. GRESLEY had often remarked to persons in affliction that when things are at their worst they generally take a turn for the better. This profound truth was proving itself equal to the occasion at Warpington Vicarage.

Mrs. Gresley was well again, after a fortnight at the seaside with Regie. The sea air had blown back a faint colour into Regie's cheeks. The new baby's vaccination was ceasing to cast a vocal gloom over the thin-walled house. The old baby's whole attention was mercifully diverted from his wrongs to the investigation of that connection between a chair and himself, which he perceived the other children could assume at pleasure. He stood for hours looking at his own little chair, solemnly seating himself at long intervals where no chair was. But his mind was working, and work, as we know, is the panacea for mental anguish.

Mr. Gresley had recovered that buoyancy of spirits which was the theme of Mrs. Gresley's unceasing admiration.

On this particular evening, when his wife had asked him if the beef were tender, he had replied, as he always did if in a humorous vein: 'Douglas, Douglas, tender and true.'[268] The arrival of the pot of marmalade (that integral part of the mysterious meal which begins with meat and is crowned with buns) had been hailed by the exclamation, 'What! More family jars.' In short, Mr. Gresley was himself again.

The jocund Vicar, with his arm round Mrs. Gresley, proceeded to the drawing-room.

On the hall table was a large parcel insured for two hundred pounds. It had evidently just arrived by rail.

'Ah! Ha!' said Mr. Gresley, 'my pamphlets at last. Very methodical of Smithers insuring them for such a large sum,' and without looking at the address he cut the string.

'Well packed,' he remarked. 'Waterproof sheeting, I do declare. Smithers is certainly a cautious man. Ha! at last!'

The inmost wrapping shelled off, and Mr. Gresley's jaw dropped. Where were the little green and gold pamphlets entitled 'Modern Dissent,' for which his parental soul was yearning? He gazed down frowning at a solid mass of manuscript, written in a small, clear hand.

'This is Hester's writing,' he said. 'There is some mistake.'

He turned to the direction on the outer cover.

'Miss Hester Gresley, care of Rev. James Gresley.' He had only seen his own name.

'I do believe,' he said, 'that this is Hester's book, refused by the publisher. Poor Hester! I am afraid she will feel that.'

His turning over of the parcel dislodged an unfolded sheet of notepaper, which made a parachute expedition to the floor. Mr. Gresley picked it up, and laid it on the parcel.

'Oh! it's not refused after all,' he said, his eye catching the sense of the few words before him. 'Hester seems to have sent for it back to make some alterations, and Mr. Bentham,[269] I suppose that is the publisher, asks for it back with as little delay as possible. Then she has sold it to him. I wonder what she got for it. She got a hundred for 'The Idyll.' It is wonderful to think of, when Bishop Heavysides got nothing at all for his Diocesan sermons, and had to make up thirty pounds out of his own pocket as well. But as long as the public is willing to pay through the nose for trashy fiction to amuse its idleness, so long will novelists reap in these large harvests.[270] If I had Hester's talent –'

'You have. Mrs. Loftus was saying so only yesterday.'

'If I had time to work it out I should not pander to the depraved public taste as Hester does. I should use my talent, as I have often told her, for the highest ends, not for the lowest. It would be my aim,' Mr. Gresley's voice rose sonorously, 'to raise my readers, to educate them, to place a high ideal before them, to ennoble them.'

'You could do it,' said Mrs. Gresley with conviction. And it is probable that the conviction both felt was a true one, that Mr. Gresley could write a book which would, from their point of view, fulfil these vast requirements.

Mr. Gresley shook his head, and put the parcel on a table in his study.

'Hester will be back the day after to-morrow,' he said, 'and then she can take charge of it herself.' And he filled in the railway form of its receipt.

Mrs. Gresley, who had been to tea with the Pratts for the first time since her convalescence, was tired, and went early to bed, or, as Mr. Gresley termed it, 'Bedfordshire;'[271] and Mr. Gresley retired to his study to put a few finishing touches to a paper he was writing on St. Augustine[272] – not by request – for that receptacle of clerical genius, the parish magazine.[273]

Will the contents of parish magazines always be written by the clergy? Is it Utopian to hope that a day will dawn when it will be perceived even by clerical editors that Apostolic Succession[274] does not invariably confer literary talent? What can an intelligent artisan think when he reads – what he reads – in his parish magazine. A serial story by a Rector unknown to fame, who, if he possesses talent, conceals it in some other napkin than the parish magazine; a short paper on 'Bees,' by an Archdeacon; 'An Easter Hymn,' by a Bishop, and such a good Bishop, too – but what a hymn! 'Poultry Keeping,' by Alice Brown. We draw breath, but the relief is only momentary; 'Side Lights on the Reformation,' by a Canon. 'Half-hours with the Young,' by a Rural Dean.

But as an invalid will rebel against a long course of milk puddings, and will crave for the jam roll which is for others, so Mr. Gresley's mind revolted from St. Augustine, and craved for something different.

His wandering eye fell on Hester's book.

'I can't attend to graver things to-night,' he said, 'I will take a look at Hester's story. I showed her my paper on "Dissent," so of course I can dip into her book. I hate lop-sided confidences, and I daresay I could give her a few hints, as she did me. Two heads are better than one. The Pratts and Thursbys all think that bit in "The Idyll" where the two men quarrelled was dictated by me. Strictly speaking, it wasn't, but no doubt she picked up her knowledge of men which surprises people so much from things she has heard me say. She certainly did not want me to read her book. She said I should not like it. But I shall have to read it some time, so I may as well skim it before it goes to the printers. I have always told her I did not feel free from responsibility in the matter after "The Idyll" appeared with things in it which I should have made a point of cutting out if she had only consulted me before she rushed into print.'

Mr. Gresley lifted the heavy mass of manuscript to his writing-table, turned up his reading-lamp and sat down before it.

The church clock struck nine. It was always wrong, but it set the time at Warpington.

There were two hours before bedtime – I mean 'Bedfordshire.'

He turned over the first blank sheet and came to the next, which had one word only written on it.

'*Husks!*' said Mr. Gresley. 'That must be the title. Husks that the swine did eat.[275] Ha! I see. A very good sound story might be written on that theme of a young man who left the Church, and how inadequate he found the teaching – the spiritual food – of other denominations compared to what he had partaken freely of in his Father's house.[276] Husks! It is not a bad name, but it is too short. "The Consequences of Sin" would be better, more striking, and convey the idea in a more impressive manner.' Mr. Gresley took up his pen, and then laid it down.' I will run through the story before I alter the name. It may not take the line I expect.'

It did not.

The next page had two words on it:

'To Rachel.'

What an extraordinary thing! Any one, be they who they might, would naturally have thought that if the book were dedicated to any one it would be to her only brother. But Hester, it seemed, thought nothing of blood relations. She disregarded them entirely.

The blood relation began to read. He seemed to forget to skip. Page after page was slowly turned. Sometimes he hesitated a moment to change a word. He had always been conscious of a gift for finding the right word. This gift Hester did not share with him. She often got hold of the wrong end of the stick. He could hardly refrain from a smile when he came across the sentence, 'He was young enough to know better,' as he substituted in a large illegible hand the word *old* for *young*. There were many obvious little mistakes of this kind that he corrected as he read, but now and then he stopped short.

One of the characters, an odious person, was continually saying things she had no business to say. Mr. Gresley wondered how Hester had come across such doubtful women – not under his roof. Lady Susan must have associated with thoroughly unsuitable people.

'I keep a smaller spiritual establishment than I did,' said the odious person. 'I have dismissed that old friend of my childhood, the devil. I really had no further use for him.'[277]

Mr. Gresley crossed through the passage at once. How could Hester write so disrespectfully of the devil?

'This is positive nonsense,' said Mr. Gresley irritably; coming as it does just after the sensible chapter about the new vicar who made a clean sweep of all the old dead regulations in his parish because he felt he must introduce spiritual life into the place. Now that is really good. I don't quite know what Hester means by saying he took exercise in his clerical *cul-de-sac*. I think she means *surtout*, but she is a good French scholar, so she probably knows what she is talking about.'

Whatever the book lacked it did not lack interest. Still it bristled with blemishes.

And then what could the Pratts, or indeed any one, make of such a sentence as this:

'When we look back at what we were seven years ago, five years ago, and perceive the difference in ourselves, a difference amounting almost to change of identity; when we look back and see in how many characters we have lived and loved and suffered and died before we reached the character that momentarily clothes us, and from which our soul is struggling out to clothe itself anew; when we feel how the sympathy even of those who love us best is always with our last expression, never with our present feeling, always with the last dead self[278] on which our climbing feet are set –'

'She is hopelessly confused,' said Mr. Gresley without reading to the end of the sentence, and substituting the word *ladder*, for *dead self*. 'Of course, I see what she means, the different stages of life, the infant, the boy, the man, but hardly any one else will so understand it.'

The clock struck ten. Mr. Gresley was amazed. The hour had seemed like ten minutes.

'I will just see what happens in the next chapter,' he said. And he did not hear the clock when it struck again. The story was absorbing. It was as if through that narrow shut-up chamber a gust of mountain air were sweeping like a breath of fresh life. Mr. Gresley was vaguely stirred in spite of himself, until he remembered that it was all fantastic, visionary. He had never felt like that, and his own experience was his measure of the utmost that is possible in human nature. He would have called a kettle visionary if he had never seen one himself. It was only saved from that reproach by the fact that it hung on his kitchen hob. What was so unfair about him was that he took gorillas and alligators, and the 'wart pig' and all its warts on trust, though he had never seen them. But the emotions which have shaken the human soul since the world began, long before the first 'wart pig' was thought of – these he disbelieved.

All the love which could not be covered by his own mild courtship of the obviously grateful Mrs. Gresley, Mr. Gresley put down as exaggerated. There was a good deal of such exaggeration in Hester's book, which could only be attributed to the French novels of which he had frequently expressed his disapproval when he saw Hester reading them. It was given to Mr. Gresley to perceive that the French classics are only read for the sake of the hideous improprieties contained in them.[279] He had explained this to Hester, and was indignant that she had continued to read them just as frequently as before, even translating parts of some of them into English, and back again into the original. She would have lowered the Bishop for ever in his Vicar's eyes, if she had mentioned by whose advice and selection she read, so she refrained.

Suddenly as he read, Mr. Gresley's face softened. He came to the illness and death of a child. It had been written long before Regie fell ill, but Mr. Gresley supposed it could only have been the result of what had happened a few weeks ago since the book was sent up to the publisher.

Two large tears fell on to the sheet. Hester's had been there before them. It was all true every word. Here was no exaggeration, no fantastic over-colouring for the sake of effect.

'Ah! Hester,' he said, wiping his eyes. 'If only the rest were like that. If you would only write like that.'

A few pages more, and his eyes were like flint. The admirable clergyman who had attracted him from the first reappeared. His opinions were uncommonly well put. But gradually it dawned upon Mr. Gresley that the clergyman was toiling in very uncomfortable situations, in which he did not appear to advantage. Mr. Gresley did not see that the uncomfortable situations were the inevitable result of holding certain opinions, but he did see that 'Hester was running down the clergy.' Any fault found with the clergy was in Mr. Gresley's eyes an attack upon the Church, nay, upon religion itself. That a protest against a certain class of the clergy might be the result of a close observation of the causes that bring ecclesiastical Christianity into disrepute could find no admission to Mr. Gresley's mind. Yet a protest against the ignorance or inefficiency of some of our soldiers he would have seen without difficulty might be the outcome, not of hatred of the army, but of a realisation of its vast national importance, and of a desire of its well-being.

Mr. Gresley was outraged. 'She holds nothing sacred,' he said striking the book. 'I told her after the "Idyll," that I desired she would not mention the subject of religion in her next book, and this is worse than ever. She has entirely disregarded my expressed wishes. Everything she says has a sting in it. Look at this. It begins well, but it ends with a sneer.'

'Christ lives. He wanders still in secret over the hills and the valleys of the soul, that little kingdom which should not be of this world, which knows not the things that belong unto its peace. And earlier or later there comes an hour when Christ is arraigned before the judgment bar in each individual soul. Once again the Church and the world combine to crush Him Who stands silent in their midst, to condemn Him who has already condemned them. Together they raise their fierce cry "Crucify Him. Crucify Him."'

Mr. Gresley tore the leaf out of the manuscript, and threw it in the fire.

But worse remained behind. To add to its other sins, the book, now drawing to its close, took a turn which had been led up to inevitably step by step from the first chapter, but which, in its reader's eyes, who perceived none of the steps, was a deliberate gratuitous intermeddling with vice. Mr. Gresley could not help reading, but as he laid down the manuscript for a moment to rest his eyes he felt that he had reached the limit of Hester's powers, and that he could only attribute the last volume to the Evil One[280] himself.

He had hardly paid this high tribute to his sister's talent when the door opened, and Mrs. Gresley came in in a wrapper that had once been white.

'Dear James,' she said, 'is anything wrong? It is past one o'clock. Are you never coming to bed?'

'Minna,' said her pastor and master, 'I have been reading the worst book I have come across yet, and it was written by my own sister under my own roof.'

He might have added 'close under the roof,' if he had remembered the little attic chamber where the cold of winter and the heat of summer had each struck in turn and in vain at the indomitable perseverance of the writer of those many pages.

CHAPTER XL

The only sin which we never forgive in each other is difference of opinion.

EMERSON.[281]

MR. GRESLEY was troubled, more troubled than he had ever been since a never-to-be-forgotten period before his ordination, when he had come in contact with worldly minds, and had had doubts as to the justice of eternal punishment.[282] He was apt to speak in after years of the furnace through which he had passed, and from which nothing short of a conversation with a bishop had had power to save him, as a great experience which he could not regret, because it had brought him into sympathy with so many minds. As he often said in his favourite language of metaphor, he 'had threshed out the whole subject of agnosticism,[283] and could consequently meet other minds still struggling in its turbid waves.'

But now again he was deeply perturbed, and it was difficult to see in what blessing to his fellow creatures this particular agitation would result. He walked with bent head for hours in the garden. He could not attend to his sermon, though it was Friday. He entirely forgot his Bible-class at the almshouses[284] in the afternoon.

Mrs. Gresley watched him from her bedroom window, where she was mending the children's stockings. At last she laid aside her work and went out.

She might not be his mental equal. She might be unable, with her small feminine mind, to fathom the depths and heights of that great intelligence, but still she was his wife. Perhaps, though she did not know it, it troubled her to see him so absorbed in his sister, for she was sure it was of Hester and her book that he was thinking. 'I am his wife,' she said to herself, as she joined him in silence and passed her arm through his. He needed to be reminded of her existence. Mr. Gresley pressed it, and they took a turn in silence.

He had not a high opinion of the feminine intellect. He was wont to say that he was tired of most women in ten minutes. But he had learnt to make an exception of his wife. What mind does not feel confidence in the sentiments of its echo?

'I am greatly troubled about Hester,' he said at last.

'It is not a new trouble,' said Mrs. Gresley. 'I sometimes think, dearest, it is we who are to blame in having her to live with us. She is worldly – I suppose she can't help it – and we are unworldly. She is irreligious, and you are deeply religious. I wish I could say I was too, but I lag far behind you. And though I am sure she does her best – and so do we – her presence is a continual friction. I feel she always drags us down.'

Mr. Gresley was too much absorbed in his own thoughts to notice the diffident plea which his wife was putting forward that Hester might cease to live with them.

'I was not thinking of that,' he said, 'so much as of this novel which she has written. It is a profane, immoral book, and will do incalculable harm if it is published.'

'I feel sure it will,' said Mrs. Gresley, who had not read it.

'It is dreadfully coarse in places,' continued Mr. Gresley, who had the same opinion of George Eliot's works. 'And I warned Hester most solemnly on that point when I found she had begun another book. I told her that I well knew that to meet the public taste it was necessary to interlard fiction with *risqué*[285] things in order to make it sell, but that it was my earnest hope she would in future resist this temptation. She only said that if she introduced improprieties into her book in order to make money, in her opinion she deserved to be whipped in the public streets. She was very angry, I remember, and became as white as a sheet, and I dropped the subject.'

'She can't bear even the most loving word of advice,' said Mrs. Gresley.

'She holds nothing sacred,' went on Mr. Gresley, remembering an unfortunate incident in the clergyman's career. 'Her life here seems to have had no softening effect upon her. She sneers openly at religion. I never thought, I never allowed myself to think, that she was so dead to spiritual things as her book forces me to believe. Even her good people, her heroine, have not a vestige of religion, only a sort of vague morality, right for the sake of right, and love teaching people things; nothing real.'

There was a moment's silence.

'Hester is my sister,' said Mr. Gresley, 'and I am fond of her in spite of all, and she has no one to look to for help and guidance but me. I am her only near relation. That is why I feel so much the way she disregards all I say. She does not realise that it is for her sake I speak.'

Mr. Gresley thought he was sincere, because he was touched.

Mrs. Gresley's cheek burned. That faithful devoted little heart, which lived only for her husband and children, could not brook – *what*? That her priest should be grieved and disregarded? Or was it any affection for and interest in another woman that it could not brook?

'I have made up my mind,' said Mr. Gresley, 'to forbid her most solemnly when she comes back to-morrow to publish that book.'

'She does not come back to-morrow, but this evening,' said the young wife, and pushed by some violent nameless feeling which was too strong for her, she added, 'She will not obey you. When has she ever listened to what you say? She will laugh at you, James. She always laughs at you. And the book will be published all the same.'

'It shall not,' said Mr. Gresley, colouring darkly. 'I shall not allow it.'

'You can't prevent it,' said Mrs. Gresley, her breath coming quickly. She was not thinking of the book at all, but of the writer. What was a book, one more or one less? It was her duty to speak the truth to her husband. His sister, whom he thought so much of, had no respect for his opinion, and he ought to know it. Mr. Gresley did know it, but he felt no particular satisfaction in his wife's presentment of the fact.

'It is no use saying I can't prevent it,' he said coldly, letting his arm fall by his side. He was no longer thinking of the book either, but of the disregard of his opinion, nay, of his authority which had long gravelled him in his sister's attitude towards him. 'I shall use my authority when I see fit, and if I have so far used persuasion rather than authority, it was only because in my humble opinion it was the wisest course.'

'It has always failed,' said Mrs. Gresley, stung by the slackening of his arm. Yes. In spite of the new baby, she would rather have a hundred a year less than have this woman in the house. The wife ought to come first. By first, Mrs. Gresley meant without a second. She had this morning seen Emma laying Hester's clean clothes on her bed, just returned from a distant washerwoman whom the Gresleys did not employ, and whom they had not wished Hester to employ. The sight of those two white dressing gowns beautifully 'got up' with goffered frills,[286] had aroused afresh in Mrs. Gresley, what she believed to be indignation at Hester's extravagance, an indignation which had been increased when she caught sight of her own untidy wrapper over her chair. She always appeared to disadvantage in Hester's presence. The old smouldering grievance about the washing set alight to other feelings. They caught. They burned. They had been drying in the oven a long time.

'It has always failed,' said Mrs. Gresley, with subdued passion, 'and it will fail again. I heard you tell Mrs. Loftus that you would never let Hester publish another book like the 'Idyll.' But though you say this one is worse, you won't be able to stop her. You will see when she comes back that she will pack up the parcel and send it back to the publishers, whatever you may say.'

The young couple were so absorbed in their conversation that they had not observed the approach of a tall clerical figure whom the parlour-maid was escorting towards them.

'I saw you through the window, and I said I would join you in the garden,' said Archdeacon Thursby majestically. 'I have been lunching with the Pratts. They naturally wished to hear the details of the lamented death of our mutual friend, Lord Newhaven.'

Archdeacon Thursby was the clergyman who had been selected as a friend of Lady Newhaven's to break to her her husband's death.

'It seems,' he added, 'that a Miss West, who was at the Abbey at the time, is an intimate friend of the Pratts.'

Mrs. Gresley slipped away to order tea, the silver tea-pot, &c.

The Archdeacon was a friend of Mr. Gresley's. Mr. Gresley had not many friends among the clergy, possibly because he always attributed the popularity of any of his brethren to a laxity of principle on their part, or their success if they did succeed to the peculiarly easy circumstances in which they were placed. But he greatly admired the Archdeacon, and made no secret of the fact, that in his opinion, he ought to have been the Bishop of the diocese.

A long conversation now ensued on clerical matters, and Mr. Gresley's drooping spirits revived under a refreshing *douche*[287] of compliments on 'Modern Dissent.'

The idea flashed across his mind of asking the Archdeacon's advice regarding Hester's book. His opinion carried weight. His remarks on 'Modern Dissent' showed how clear, how statesmanlike his judgment was. Mr. Gresley decided to lay the matter before him, and to consult him as to his responsibility in the matter. The Archdeacon did not know Hester. He did not know – for he lived at a distance of several miles – that Mr. Gresley had a sister who had written a book.

Mr. Gresley did not wish him to become aware of this last fact, for we all keep our domestic skeletons in their cupboards, so he placed a hypothetical case before his friend.

Supposing some one he knew, a person for whose actions he felt himself partly responsible, had written a most unwise letter, and this letter, by no fault of Mr. Gresley's, had fallen into his hands and been read by him. What was he, Mr. Gresley, to do? The letter, if posted, would certainly get the writer into trouble, and would cause acute humiliation to the writer's family. What would the Archdeacon do, in his place?

Mr. Gresley did not perceive that the hypothetical case was not 'on all fours' with the real one.[288] His first impulse had been to gain the opinion of an expert without disclosing family dissensions. Did some unconscious secondary motive impel him to shape the case so that only one verdict was probable?

The good Archdeacon ruminated, asked a few questions, and then said without hesitation:

'I cannot see your difficulty. Your course is clear. You are responsible –'

'To a certain degree.'

'To a certain degree for the action of an extremely injudicious friend or relation who writes a letter which will get him and others into trouble. It providentially falls into your hands. If I were in your place I should destroy it, inform your friend that I had done so principally for his own sake, and endeavour to bring him to a better mind on the subject.'

'Supposing the burning of the letter entailed a money loss?'

'I judge from what you say of this particular letter that any money that accrued from it would be ill-gotten gains.'

'Oh! decidedly.'

'Then burn it; and if your friend remains obstinate he can always write it again; but we must hope that by gaining time you will be able to arouse his better feelings, and at least induce him to moderate its tone.'

'Of course he could write it again if he remains obstinate. I never thought of that,' said Mr. Gresley in a low voice. 'So he would not eventually lose the money if he were still decided to gain it in an unscrupulous manner. Or I could help him to re-write it. I never thought of that before.'

'Your course is perfectly clear, my dear Gresley,' said the Archdeacon, not impatiently, but as one who is ready to open up a new subject. 'Your tender conscience alone makes the difficulty. Is not Mrs. Gresley endeavouring to attract our attention?'

Mrs. Gresley was beckoning them in to tea.

When the Archdeacon had departed Mr. Gresley said to his wife: 'I have talked over the matter with him, not mentioning names, of course. He is a man of great judgment. He advises me to burn it.'

'Hester's book?'

'Yes.'

'He is quite right, I think,' said Mrs. Gresley, her hands trembling as she took up her work. Hester would never forgive her brother if he did that. It would certainly cause a quarrel between them. Young married people did best without a third person in the house.

'Will you follow his advice?' she asked.

'I don't know. I – you see – poor Hester! It has taken her a long time to write. I wish to goodness she would leave writing alone.'

'She is coming home this evening,' said his wife significantly.

Mr. Gresley abruptly left the room, and went back to his study. He was irritated, distressed.

Providence seemed to have sent the Archdeacon to advise him. And the Archdeacon had spoken with decision. 'Burn it.' That was what he had said, 'and tell your friend that you have done so.'

It did not strike Mr. Gresley that the advice might have been somewhat different if the question had been respecting the burning of a book instead of a letter. Such subtleties had never been allowed to occupy Mr. Gresley's mind. He was, as he often said, no splitter of hairs.

He told himself that from the very first moment of consulting him he had dreaded that the Archdeacon would counsel exactly as he had done. Mr. Gresley stood a long time in silent prayer by his study window. If his prayers took the same bias as his recent statements to his friend, was that his fault? If he silenced as a sign of cowardice a voice within him which entreated for delay, was that his fault? If he had never educated himself to see any connection between a seed and a plant, a cause and a result, was that his fault? The first seedling impulse to destroy the book was buried and forgotten. If he mistook this towering, full-grown determination which had sprung from it for the will of God, the direct answer to prayer, was that his fault?

As his painful duty became clear to him, a thin veil of smoke drifted across the little lawn.

Regie came dancing and caracoling round the corner.

'Father,' he cried, rushing to the window, 'Abel has made such a bonfire in the backyard, and he is burning weeds and all kinds of things, and he has given us each a "'tato" to bake, and Fraülein has given us a bandbox[289] she did not want, and we've filled it quite full of dry leaves. And do you think if we wait a little Auntie Hester will be back in time to see it burn?'

It was a splendid bonfire. It leaped. It rose and fell. It was replenished. Something alive in the heart of it died hard. The children danced round it.

'Oh, if only Auntie Hester was here!' said Regie, clapping his hands as the flame soared.

But 'Auntie Hester' was too late to see it.

CHAPTER XLI

And we are punished for our purest deeds,
And chasten'd for our holiest thoughts; alas!
There is no reason found in all the creeds,
Why these things are, nor whence they come to pass.

OWEN MEREDITH.[290]

IT was while Hester was at the Palace that Lord Newhaven died. She had perhaps hardly realised till he was gone how much his loyal friendship had been to her. Yet she had hardly seen him for the last year, partly because she was absorbed in her book, and partly because, to her astonishment, she found that her brother and his wife looked coldly upon 'an unmarried woman receiving calls from a married man.'

For in the country individuality has not yet emerged. People are married or they are unmarried – that is all. Just as in London they are agreeable or dull – that is all.

'Since I have been at Warpington,' Hester said to Lord Newhaven one day, the last time he found her in, 'I have realised that I am unmarried. I never thought of it all the years I lived in London, but when I visit among the country people here, as I drive through the park, I remember with a qualm that I am a spinster, no doubt because I can't help it. As I enter the hall I recall with a pang that I am eight and twenty. By the time I am in the drawing-room I am an old maid.'

She had always imagined she would take up her friendship with him again, and when he died she reproached herself for having temporarily laid it aside. Perhaps no one, except Lord Newhaven's brothers, felt his death more than Dick and Hester and the Bishop. The Bishop had sincerely liked Lord Newhaven. A certain degree of friendship had existed between the two men, which had often trembled on the verge of intimacy. But the verge had never been crossed. It was the younger man who always drew back. The Bishop, with the instinct of the true priest, had an unshaken belief in his cynical neighbour. Lord Newhaven, who trusted no one, trusted the Bishop. They might have been friends. But there was a deeper reason for grief at his death than any sense of personal loss. The Bishop was secretly convinced that he had died by his own hand.

Lord Newhaven had come to see him, the night he left Westhope, on his way to the station. He had only stayed a few minutes, and had asked him to do him a trifling service. The older man had agreed, had seen a momentary hesitation as Lord Newhaven turned to leave the room, and had forgotten the incident immediately in the press of continuous business. But with the news of his death the remembrance of that momentary interview returned, and with it the instant conviction that that accidental death had been carefully planned.

And now Hester's visit at the Palace had come to an end, and the Bishop's carriage was taking her back to Warpington.

The ten days at Southminster had brought a little colour back to her thin cheeks, a little calmness to her glance. She had experienced the rest – better than sleep – of being understood, of being able to say what she thought without fear of giving offence. The Bishop's hospitality had been extended to her mind, instead of stopping short at the *menu*.[291]

Her hands were full of chrysanthemums which the Bishop had picked for her himself, her small head full of his parting words and counsel.

Yes, she would do as he so urgently advised, give up the attempt to live at Warpington. She had been there a whole year. If the project had failed, as he seemed to think it had, at any rate it had been given a fair trial. Both sides had done their best. She might ease money matters later for her brother by laying by part of the proceeds of this book for Regie's schooling. She could see that the Bishop thought highly of the book. He had read it before it was sent to the publisher. While she was at the Palace he had asked her to reconsider one or two passages in it which he thought might give needless offence to her brother and others of his mental calibre, and she had complied at once, and had sent for the book. No doubt she should find it at Warpington on her return.

When it was published she should give Minna a new sofa for the drawing-room, and Fräulein a fur boa and muff, and Miss Brown a typewriter for her G.F.S.[292] work, and Abel a barometer, and each of the servants a new gown, and James those four enormous volumes of Pusey[293] for which his soul yearned. And what should she give Rachel, dear Rachel? Ah! What need to give her anything? The book itself was hers. Was it not dedicated to her? And she would make her home with Rachel for the present, as the Bishop advised, as Rachel had so urgently begged her to do.

'And we will go abroad together after Christmas as she suggests,' said Hester to herself. 'We will go to Madeira or one of those warm places where one can sit like a cat in the sun, and do nothing, nothing, nothing, from morning till night. I used to be so afraid of going back to Warpington, but now that the time is coming to an end I am sure I shall not irritate them so much. And Minna will be glad. One can always manage if it is only for a fixed time. And they shall not be the losers by my leaving them. I will put by the money for my little Regie. I shall feel parting with him.'

The sun was setting as she reached Warpington. All was grey, the church tower, the trees, the pointed gables of the Vicarage, set small together as in a Christmas card, against the still red sky. It only needed 'Peace and Good Will' and a robin in the foreground to be complete. The stream was the only thing that moved, with its shimmering mesh of fire-tipt ripples fleeing into the darkness of the reeds. The little bridge, so vulgar in everyday life, leaned a mystery of darkness over a mystery of light. The white frost held the meadows, and binding them to the grey house and church and bare trees was a thin floating ribbon of – was it mist or smoke? In her own window a faint light wavered. They had lit a fire in her room. Hester's heart warmed to her sister-in-law at that little token of care and welcome. Minna should have all her flowers, except one small bunch for Fraülein. In another moment she was ringing the bell, and Emma's smiling red face appeared behind the glass door.

Hester ran past her into the drawing-room. Mrs. Gresley was sitting near the fire with the old baby beside her. She returned Hester's kiss somewhat nervously. She looked a little frightened.

The old baby, luxuriously seated in his own little armchair, rose, and holding it firmly against his small person to prevent any disconnection with it, solemnly crossed the hearthrug, and placed the chair with himself in it by Hester.

'You would like some tea,' said Mrs. Gresley. 'It is choir practice this evening, and we don't have supper till nine.'

But Hester had had tea before she started.

'And you are not cold?'

Hester was quite warm. The Bishop had ordered a foot-warmer[294] in the carriage for her.

'You are looking much better.'

Hester felt much better, thanks.

'And what lovely flowers!'

Hester suggested with diffidence that they would look pretty in the drawing-room.

'I think,' said Mrs. Gresley, who had thought the same till that instant, 'that they would look best in the hall.'

'And the rest of the family,' said Hester, whose face had fallen a little. 'Where are they?'

'The children have just come in. They will be down directly. Come back to me, Toddy; you are boring your aunt. And James is in his study.'

'Is he busy, or may I go in and speak to him?'

'He is not busy. He is expecting you.'

Hester gathered up her rejected flowers and rose. She felt as if she had been back at Warpington a year – as if she had never been away.

She stopped a moment in the hall to look at her letters, and laid down her flowers beside them. Then she went on quickly to the study, and tapped at the door.

'Come in,' said the well-known voice.

Mr. Gresley was found writing. Hester instantly perceived that it was a pose, and that he had taken up the pen when he heard her tap.

Her spirits sank a peg lower.

'He is going to lecture me about something,' she said to herself as he kissed her.

'Have you had tea? It is choir practice this evening, and we don't have supper till nine.'

Hester had had tea before she started.

'And you are not cold?'

On the contrary, Hester was quite warm, thanks. Bishop, foot-warmer, &c.

'You are looking much stronger.'

Hester felt much stronger. Certainly married people grew very much alike by living together.

Mr. Gresley hesitated. He never saw the difficulties entailed by any action until they were actually upon him. He had had no idea he would find it well-nigh impossible to open a certain subject.

Hester involuntarily came to his assistance.

'Well, perhaps I ought to look at my letters. By the way, there ought to be a large package for me from Bentham. It was not with my letters. Perhaps you sent it to my room.'

'It did arrive,' said Mr. Gresley, 'and perhaps I ought to apologise, for I saw my name on it and I opened it by mistake. I was expecting some more copies of my "Modern Dissent."'

'It does not matter. I have no doubt you put it away safely. Where is it?'

'Having opened it, I glanced at it.'

'I am surprised to hear that,' said Hester, a pink spot appearing on each cheek, and her eyes darkening. 'When did I give you leave to read it?'

Mr. Gresley looked dully at his sister, and went on without noticing her question.

'I glanced at it. I do not see any difference between reading a book in manuscript or in print. I don't pretend to quibble on a point like that. After looking at it, I felt that it was desirable I should read the whole. You may remember, Hester, that I showed you my "Modern Dissent." If I did not make restrictions, why should you?'

'The thing is done,' said Hester. 'I did not wish you to read it, and you have read it. It can't be helped. We won't speak of it again.'

'It is my duty to speak of it.'

Hester made an impatient movement.

'But it is not mine to listen,' she said. 'Besides, I know all you are going to say – the same as about "The Idyll," only worse. That it is coarse and profane and exaggerated, and that I have put in improprieties in order to make it sell, and that I run down the clergy, and that the book ought never to be published. Dear James, spare me. You and I shall never agree on certain subjects. Let us be content to differ.'

Mr. Gresley was disconcerted. Your antagonist has no business to discount all you were going to remark by saying it first.

His colour was gradually leaving him. This was worse than an Easter vestry meeting, and that was saying a good deal.

'I cannot stand by calmly and see you walk over a precipice if I can forcibly hold you back,' he said. 'I think, Hester, you forget that it is my affection for you that makes me try to restrain you. It is for your own sake that – that –'

'That what?'

'That I cannot allow this book to be published,' said Mr. Gresley in a low voice. He hardly ever lowered his voice.

There was a moment's pause. Hester felt the situation was serious. How not to wound him, yet not to yield?

'I am eight and twenty,' she said. 'I am afraid I must follow my own judgment. You have no responsibility in the matter. If I am blamed,' she smiled proudly – at that instant she knew all that her book was worth – 'the blame will not attach to you. And, after all, Minna and the Pratts and the Thursbys need not read it.'

'No one will read it,' said Mr. Gresley. 'It was a profane, wicked book. No one will read it.'

'I am not so sure of that,' said Hester.

The brother and sister looked at each other with eyes of flint.

'No one will read it,' repeated Mr. Gresley – he was courageous, but all his courage was only just enough – 'because, for your own sake, and for the sake of the innocent minds which might be perverted by it, I have – I have – burnt it.'

Hester stood motionless, like one struck by lightning, livid, dead already – all but the eyes.

'You dared not,' said the dead lips. The terrible eyes were fixed on him. They burnt into him.

He was frightened.

'Dear Hester,' he said, 'I will help you to re-write it. I will give up an hour every morning till –' Would she never fall? Would she always stand up like that? 'Some day you will know I was right to do it. You are angry now, but some day –' If she would only faint, or cry, or look away.

'When Regie was ill,' said the slow difficult voice, 'I did what I could. I did not let your child die. Why have you killed mine?'

There was a little patter of feet in the passage. The door was slowly opened by Mary, and Regie walked solemnly in, holding with extreme care a small tin plate, on which reposed a large potato.

'I baked it for you, Auntie Hester,' he said in his shrill voice, his eyes on the offering. 'It was my very own 'tato Abel gave me. And I baked it in the bonfire and kept it for you.'

Hester turned upon the child like some blinded infuriated animal at bay, and thrust him violently from her. He fell shrieking. She rushed past him out of the room, and out of the house, his screams following her. 'I've killed him,' she said.

The side gate was locked. Abel had just left for the night. She tore it off its hinges and ran into the backyard.

The bonfire was out. A thread of smoke twisted up from the crater of grey ashes. She fell on her knees beside the dead fire, and thrust apart the hot ashes with her bare hands.

A mass of thin black films that had once been paper met her eyes. The small writing on them was plainly visible as they fell to dust at the touch of her hands.

'It is dead,' she said in a loud voice, getting up. Her gown was burnt through where she had knelt down.

In the still air a few flakes of snow were falling in a great compassion.

'Quite dead,' said Hester. 'Regie and the book.'

And she set off running blindly across the darkening fields.

It was close on eleven o'clock. The Bishop was sitting alone in his study writing. The night was very still. The pen travelled, travelled. The fire had burnt down to a red glow. Presently he got up, walked to the window, and drew aside the curtain.

'The first snow,' he said, half aloud.

It was coming down gently through the darkness. He could just see the white rim on the stone sill outside.

'I can do no more to-night,' he said, and he bent to lock his despatch box with the key on his watch chain.[295]

The door suddenly opened. He turned to see a little figure rush towards him and fall at his feet, holding him convulsively by the knees.

'Hester!' he said in amazement. 'Hester!'

She was bareheaded. The snow was upon her hair and shoulders. She brought in the smell of fire with her.

He tried to raise her, but she held him tightly with her bleeding hands, looking up at him with a convulsed face. His own hands were red as he vainly tried to loosen hers.

'They have killed my book,' she said. 'They have killed my book. They burnt it alive when I was away. And my head went. I don't know what I did, but I think I killed Regie. I know I meant to.'

CHAPTER XLII

Is it well with the child?[296]

'I AM not really anxious,' said Mr. Gresley, looking out across the Vicarage laurels
to the white fields and hedges. All was blurred and vague and very still. The only
thing that had a distinct outline was the garden railing, with a solitary rook on it.

'I am not really anxious,' he said again, sitting down at the breakfast table.
But his face contradicted him. It was blue and pinched, for he had just returned
from reading the morning service[297] to himself in an ice-cold church, but there
was a pucker in the brow that was not the result of cold. The Vicarage porch had
fallen down in the night, but he was evidently not thinking of that. He drank a
little coffee and then got up and walked to the window again.

'She is with the Pratts,' he said with decision. 'I am glad I sent a note over
early, if it will relieve your mind, but I am convinced she is with the Pratts.'

Mrs. Gresley murmured something. She looked scared. She made an attempt
to eat something, but it was a mere pretence.

The swing door near the back staircase creaked. In the Vicarage you could
hear everything.

Mr. and Mrs. Gresley looked eagerly at the door. The parlourmaid[298] came in
with a note between her finger and thumb.

'She is not there,' said Mr. Gresley in a shaking voice. 'I wrote Mr. Pratt such
a guarded letter saying Hester had imprudently run across to see them on her
return home, and how grateful I was to Mrs. Pratt for not allowing her to return,
as it had begun to snow. He says he and Mrs. Pratt have not seen her.'

'James,' said Mrs. Gresley, 'where *is* she?'

A second step shuffled across the hall, and Fraülein stood in the doorway.
Her pale face was drawn with anxiety. In both hands she clutched a trailing skirt
plaistered with snow, hitched above a pair of large goloshed feet, into which the
legs were grafted without ankles.

'She has not return?'

'No,' said Mr. Gresley, 'and she is not with the Pratts.'

'I know always she is not wiz ze Pratts,' said Fraülein scornfully. 'She never go
to Pratt if she is in grief. I go out at half seven this morning to ze Br-r-rowns, but
Miss Br-r-rown know nozing. I go to Wilderleigh, I see Mrs. Loftus still in bed,
but she is not there. I go to Evannses, I go to Smeeth, I go last to Mistair Valsh,
but she is not there.'

Mr. Gresley began to experience something of what Fraülein had been enduring all night.

'She would certainly not go from my house to a Dissenter's,' he said stiffly.
'You might have saved yourself the trouble of calling there, Fraülein.'

'She like Mr. and Mrs. Valsh. She give them her book,'

Fräulein's voice drowned the muffled rumbling of a carriage, and a ring at the bell, the handle of which, uninjured amid the chaos, kept watch above the remains of the late porch,

The Bishop stood a moment in the little hall while the maid went into the dining-room to tell the Gresleys of his arrival. His eyes rested on the pile of letters on the table, on the dead flowers beside them. They had been so beautiful yesterday when he gave them to Hester. Hester herself had been so pretty yesterday.

The maid came back and asked him to 'step' into the dining-room.

Mr. and Mrs. Gresley had risen from their chairs. Their eyes were fixed anxiously upon him. Fräulein gave a little shriek and rushed at him.

'She is viz you?' she gasped, shaking him by the arm.

'She is with me,' said the Bishop, looking only at Fräulein and taking her shaking hands in his.

'Thank God,' said Mr. Gresley, and Mrs. Gresley sat down and began to cry.

Some of the sternness melted out of the Bishop's face as he looked at the young couple.

'I came as soon as I could,' he said. 'I started soon after seven, but the roads are heavy.'

'This is a great relief,' said Mr. Gresley. He began on his deepest organ note, but it quavered quite away on the word relief for want of wind.

'How is Regie?' said the Bishop. It was his turn to be anxious.

'Regie is verr vell,' said Fräulein with decision. 'Tell her he is so vell as he vas.'

'He is very much shaken,' said Mrs. Gresley, indignant mother-love flashing in her wet eyes. 'He is a delicate child, and she, Hester – may God forgive her – struck him in one of her passions. She might have killed him. And the poor child fell and bruised his arm and shoulder. And he was bringing her a little present when she did it. The child had done nothing whatever to annoy her, had he, James?'

'Nothing,' said Mr. Gresley, and his conscience pricking him, he added, 'I must own Hester had always seemed fond of Regie till last night.'

He felt that it would not be entirely fair to allow the Bishop to think that Hester was in the habit of maltreating the children.

'I have told him that his own mother will take care of him,' said Mrs. Gresley, 'and that he need not be afraid, his aunt shall never come back again. When I saw his little arm I felt I could never trust Hester in the house again.' As Mrs. Gresley spoke she felt she was making certainty doubly sure that the woman of whom she was jealous would return no more.

'Regie cry till his 'ead ache because you say Miss Gresley no come back,' said Fräulein, looking at Mrs Gresley as if she would have bitten a piece out of her.

'I think, Fraülein, it is the children's lesson-time,' said Mr. Gresley majestically.

Who could have imagined that unobtrusive, submissive Fraülein, gentlest and shyest of women, would put herself forward in this aggressive manner. The truth is, it is all very well to talk, you never can tell what people will do. They suddenly turn round and act exactly opposite to their whole previous character. Look at Fraülein!

That poor lady, recalled thus to a sense of duty, hurried from the room, and the Bishop, who had opened the door for her, closed it gently behind her.

'You must excuse her, my lord,' said Mr. Gresley; 'the truth is, we are all somewhat upset this morning. Hester would have saved us much uneasiness, I may say anxiety, if she had mentioned to us yesterday evening that she was going back to you. No doubt she overtook your carriage, which put up at the inn for half an hour.'

'No,' said the Bishop, 'she came on foot. She – walked all the way.'

Mr. Gresley smiled. 'I am afraid, my lord, Hester has given you an inaccurate account. I assure you, she is incapable of walking five miles, much less ten.'

'She took about five hours to do it,' said the Bishop, who had hesitated an instant, as if swallowing something unpalatable. 'In moments of great excitement nervous persons like your sister are capable of almost anything. The question is, whether she will survive the shock that drove her out of your house last night. Her hands are severely burnt. Dr. Brown, whom I left with her, fears brain fever.'

The Bishop paused, giving his words time to sink in. Then he went on slowly in a level voice, looking into the fire.

'She still thinks that she has killed Regie. She won't believe the doctor and me when we assure her she has not. She turns against us for deceiving her.'

Mr. Gresley wrestled with a very bitter feeling towards his sister, overcame it, and said hoarsely:

'Tell her from me that Regie is not much the worse, and tell her that I – that his mother and I – forgive her.'

'Not me, James,' sobbed Mrs. Gresley. 'It is too soon. I don't. I can't. If I said I did I should not feel it.'

'Hester is not in a condition to receive messages,' said the Bishop. 'She would not believe them. Dr. Brown says the only thing we can do for her is to show Regie to her. If she sees him she may believe her own eyes, and this frightful excitement may be got under. I came to take him back with me now in the carriage.'

'I will not let him go,' said Mrs. Gresley, the mother in her overriding her awe of the Bishop. 'I am sorry if Hester is ill. I will,' and Mrs. Gresley made a superhuman effort, 'I will come and nurse her myself, but I won't have Regie frightened a second time.'

'He shall not be frightened a second time. But it is very urgent. While we are wasting time talking, Hester's life is ebbing away as surely as if she were bleeding to death. If she were actually bleeding in this room how quickly you two would run to her and bind up the wound. There would be nothing you would not do to relieve her suffering.'

'If I would let Regie go,' said Mrs. Gresley, 'he would not be willing, and we could not have him taken away by force, could we, James?'

The door opened, and Regie appeared, gently pushed from behind by Fraülein's thin hand. Boulou followed. The door was closed again immediately, almost on Boulou's tail.

The Bishop and Regie looked hard at each other.

'I send my love to Auntie Hester,' said Regie in his catechism voice, 'and I am quite well.'

'I should like to have some conversation with Regie alone,' said the Bishop.

Mrs. Gresley wavered, but the Bishop's eye remained fixed on Mr. Gresley, and the latter led his wife away. The door was left ajar, but the Bishop closed it. Then he sat down by the fire and held out his hand.

Regie went up to him fearlessly, and stood between his knees. The two faces were exactly on the same level. Boulou sat down before the fire, his tail uncurling in the heat.

'Auntie Hester is very sorry,' said the Bishop. 'She is so sorry that she can't even cry.'

'Tell her not to mind,' said Regie.

'It's no good telling her. Does your arm hurt much?'

'I don't know. Mother says it does, and Fraülein says it doesn't. But it isn't that.'

'What is it, then?'

'It isn't that, or the 'tato being lost, it was only crumbs afterwards; but, Mr. Bishop, *I hadn't done nothing.*'

Regie looked into the kind keen eyes, and his own little red ones filled again with tears.

'I had not done nothing,' he repeated. 'And I'd kept my 'tato for her. It's that – that – I don't mind about my arm. I'm Christian soldiers about my arm; but it's that – that –'

'That hurts you in your heart,' said the Bishop, putting his arm round him.

'Yes,' said Regie, producing a tight little ball that had once been a handkerchief. 'Auntie Hester and I were such friends. I told her all my secrets, and she told me hers. I knew long before, when she gave father the silver cream-jug, and about Fraülein's muff. If it was a mistake, like father treading on my foot at the school feast, I should not mind, but she did it on purpose.'

The Bishop's brow contracted. Time was ebbing away, ebbing away like a life. Yet Dr. Brown's warning remained in his ears. 'If the child is frightened of her, and screams when he sees her, I won't answer for the consequences.'

'Is that your little dog?' he said, after a moment's thought.

'Yes, that is Boulou.'

'Was he ever in a trap?' asked the Bishop with a vague recollection of the ways of clergymen's dogs, those 'little rifts within the lute'[299] which so often break the harmony between a sporting squire and his clergyman.

'He was once. Mr. Pratt says he hunts, but father says not, that he could not catch anything if he tried.'

'I had a dog once,' said the Bishop, 'called Jock. And he got in a trap like Boulou did. Now, Jock loved me. He cared for me more than anybody in the world. Yet, as I was letting him out of the trap, he bit me. Do you know why he did that?'

'Why?'

'Because the trap hurt him so dreadfully that he could not help biting something. He did not really mean it. He licked me afterwards. Now, Auntie Hester was like Jock. She was in dreadful, dreadful pain like a trap, and she hit you like Jock bit me. But Jock loved me best in the world all the time. And Auntie Hester loves you, and is your friend she tells secrets to, all the time.'

'Mother says she does not love me really. It was only pretence.' Regie's voice shook. 'Mother says she must never come back because it might be baby next. She said so to father.'

'Mother has made a mistake. I'm so old that I know better even than mother. Auntie Hester loves you, and can't eat any breakfast till you tell her you don't mind. Will you come with me and kiss her, and tell her so? And we'll make up a new secret on the way.'

'Yes,' said Regie eagerly, his wan little face turning pink. 'But mother?' he said, stopping short.

'Run and get your coat on. I will speak to mother. Quick, Regie.'

Regie rushed curveting out of the room. The Bishop followed more slowly, and went into the drawing-room where Mr. and Mrs. Gresley were sitting by the fireless hearth. The drawing-room fire was never lit till two o'clock.

'Regie goes with me of his own free will,' he said, 'so that is settled. He will be quite safe with me, Mrs. Gresley.'

'My wife demurs at sending him,' said Mr. Gresley.

'No, no, she does not,' said the Bishop gently. 'Hester saved Regie's life, and it is only right that Regie should save hers. You will come over this afternoon to take him back,' he continued to Mr. Gresley. 'I wish to have some conversation with you.'

Fraülein appeared breathless, dragging Regie with her.

'He has not got on his new overcoat,' said Mrs. Gresley. 'Regie, run up and change at once.'

Fräulein actually said, 'Bozzer ze new coat,' and she swept Regie into the carriage, the Bishop following, stumbling over the ruins of the porch.

'Have they had their hot mash?' he said to the coachman, who was tearing off the horses' clothing.

'Yes, my lord.'

'Then drive all you know. Put them at the hills at a gallop.'

Fräulein pressed a packet of biscuits into the Bishop's hand, 'He eat no breakfast,' she said.

'Uncle Dick said the porch would sit down, and it has,' said Regie in an awe-struck voice, as the carriage swayed from side to side of the road. 'Father knows a great deal, but sometimes I think Uncle Dick knows most of all. First gates and flying half pennies, and now porches.'

'Uncle Dick is staying in Southminster. Perhaps we shall see him.'

'I should like to ask him about his finger, if it isn't a secret.'

'I don't think it is. Now, what secret shall we make up on the way?' The Bishop put his head out of the window, 'Drive faster,' he said.

It was decided that the secret should be a Christmas present for 'Auntie Hester,' to be bought in Southminster. The Bishop found that Regie's entire capital was sixpence. But Regie explained that he could spend a shilling, because he was always given sixpence by his father when he pulled a tooth out. 'And I've one loose now,' he said. 'When I suck it it moves. It will be ready by Christmas.'

There was a short silence. The horses' hoofs beat the muffled ground all together.

'Don't you find, Mr. Bishop,' said Regie tentatively, 'that this riding so quick in carriages, and talking secrets, does make people very hungry?'

The Bishop blushed. 'It is quite true, my boy. I ought to have thought of that before. I am uncommonly hungry myself,' he said, looking in every pocket for the biscuits Fräulein had forced into his hand. When they were at last discovered in a somewhat dilapidated condition in the rug, the Bishop found they were a kind of biscuit that always made him cough, so he begged Regie, who was dividing them equally, as a personal favour to eat them all.

It was a crumb be-sprinkled Bishop who, half an hour later, hurried up the stairs of the Palace.

'What an age you have been,' snapped Dr. Brown from the landing.

'How is she?'

'The same, but weaker. Have you got Regie?'

'Yes, but it took time.'

'Is he frightened?'

'Not a bit.'

'Then bring him up.'

The doctor went back into the bedroom, leaving the door ajar,

A small shrunken figure with bandaged head and hands was sitting in an armchair. The eyes of the rigid, discoloured face were fixed.

Dr. Brown took the bandage off Hester's head, and smoothed her hair.

'He is coming upstairs now,' he said, shaking her gently by the shoulders. 'Regie is coming upstairs now to see you. Regie is quite well, and he is coming in now to see you.'

'Regie is dead, you old grey wolf,' said Hester in a monotonous voice. 'I killed him in the backyard. The place is quite black and it smokes.'

'Look at the door,' repeated Dr. Brown, over and over again. 'He is coming in at the door now.'

Hester trembled and looked at the door. The doctor noticed with a frown that she could hardly move her eyes.

Regie stood in the doorway, holding the Bishop's hand. The cold snow light fell upon the gallant little figure and white face.

The doctor moved between Hester and the window. His shadow was upon her.

The hearts of the two men beat like hammers.

A change came over Hester's face.

'My little Reg,' she said, holding out her bandaged hands.

Regie ran to her, and put his arms round her neck. They clasped each other tightly. The doctor winced to watch her hands.

'It's all right, Auntie Hester,' said Regie. 'I love you just the same, and you must not cry any more.'

For Hester's tears were falling at last, quenching the wild fire in her eyes.

'My little treasure, my little mouse,' she said over and over again, kissing his face and hands and little brown overcoat.

Then all in a moment her face altered. Her agonised eyes turned to the doctor.

In an instant Dr. Brown's hand was over Regie's eyes, and he hurried him out of the room.

'Take him out of hearing,' he whispered to the Bishop, and darted back.

Hester was tearing the bandages off her hands.

'I don't know what has happened,' she wailed, 'but my hands hurt me so that I can't bear it.'

'Thank God,' said the old doctor, blowing his nose.

CHAPTER XLIII

The Devil has no stauncher ally than *want of perception*.
PHILIP H. WICKSTEED.[300]

It takes two to speak truth – one to speak and another to hear.
THOREAU.[301]

MRS. GRESLEY had passed an uncomfortable day. In the afternoon all the Pratts had called, and Mr. Gresley, who departed early in the afternoon for Southminster, had left his wife no directions as to how to act in this unforeseen occurrence, or how to parry the questions with which she was overwhelmed.

After long hesitation she at last owned that Hester had returned to Southminster in the Bishop's carriage not more than half an hour after it had brought her back.

'I can't explain Hester's actions,' she would only repeat over and over again. 'I don't pretend to understand clever people. I'm not clever myself. I can only say Hester went back to Southminster directly she arrived here.'

Hardly had the Pratts taken their departure when Doll Loftus was ushered in. His wife had sent him to ask where Hester was, as Fraülein had alarmed her earlier in the day. Doll at least asked no questions. He had never asked but one in his life, and that had been of his wife, five seconds before he had become engaged to her.

He accepted with equanimity the information that Hester had returned to Southminster, and departed to impart the same to his exasperated wife.

'But why did she go back? She had only that moment arrived,' inquired Sybell. How should Doll know. She, Sybell, had said she could not rest till she knew where Hester was, and he, Doll, had walked to Warpington through the snow-drifts to find out for her. And he had found out, and now she wanted to know something else. There was no satisfying some women. And the injured husband retired to unlace his boots.

Yes, Mrs. Gresley had passed an uncomfortable day. She had ventured out for a few minutes, and had found Abel, with his arms akimbo, contemplating the little gate which led to the stables. It was lying on the ground. He had swept the snow off it.

'I locked it up the same as usual last night,' he said to Mrs. Gresley. 'There's been somebody about as has tampered it off its hinges. Yet nothing hasn't been touched, the coal nor the stack. It don't seem natural, twisting the gate off for nothing.'

Mrs. Gresley did not answer. She did not associate Hester with the gate. But she was too much perturbed to care about such small matters at the moment.

'His lordship's coachman tell me as Miss Gresley was at the Palace,' continued Abel, 'while I was a hotting up his mash for him, for William had gone in with a note, and onst he's in the kitchen the hanimals might be stocks and stones for what he cares. He said his nevvy, the footman, heard the front door-bell ring just as he was getting into bed last night, and Miss Gresley come in without her hat, with the snow upon her. The coachman said as she must ha' run afoot all the way.'

Abel looked anxiously at Mrs. Gresley.

'I was just thinking,' he said, 'as perhaps the little lady wasn't quite right in her 'ead. They do say as too much learning flies to the 'ead,[302] the same as spirits to them as ain't manured to 'em. And the little lady does work desperate hard.'

'Not as hard as Mr. Gresley,' said Mrs. Gresley.

'Maybe not, Mem, maybe not. But when I come up when red cow was sick at four in the morning, or may be earlier, there was always a light in her winder, and the shadder of her face agin the blind. Yes, she do work precious hard.'

Mrs. Gresley retreated into the house, picking her way over the *débris*[303] of the porch. At any other time its demise would have occupied the minds of the Vicarage household for days. But until this moment it had hardly claimed the tribute of a sigh. Mrs. Gresley did sigh as she crossed the threshold. That prostrate porch meant expense. She had understood from her husband that Dick had wantonly torn out the clamp that supported it, and that the whole thing had in consequence given way under the first snowfall. 'He meant no harm,' Mr. Gresley had added, 'But I suppose in the Colonies they mistake horseplay for wit.'

Mrs. Gresley went back to the drawing-room, and sat down to her needlework. She was an exquisite needlewoman, but all the activity of her untiring hands was hardly able to stem the tide of mending that was for ever flowing in upon her. When was she to find time to finish the darling little garments which the new baby required? Fräulein had been kind in helping, but Fräulein's eyes were not very strong, or her stitches in consequence very small. Mrs. Gresley would have liked to sit in the schoolroom when lessons were over, but Fräulein had been so distant at luncheon about a rissole that she had not the courage to go in.

So she sat and stitched with a heavy heart awaiting her husband's return. The fly[304] was another expense. Southminster was ten miles from Warpington, eleven according to the Loftus Arms, from which it issued, the owner of which was not on happy terms with his 'teetotal' vicar. Yet it had been absolutely necessary to have the fly, in order that Regie, who so easily caught cold, might return in safety.

The dusk was already falling, and more snow with it.

It was quite dark when Mrs. Gresley at last caught the sound of wheels and hurried to the door.

Mr. Gresley came in, bearing Regie, fast asleep in a fur rug, and laid him carefully on the sofa, and then went out to have an altercation with the driver, who demurred in forcible language to the arrangement, adhered to by Mr. Gresley, that the cost of the fly should be considered as part payment of certain arrears of tithe which in those days it was the unhappy duty of the clergyman to collect himself. Mr. Gresley's methods of dealing with money matters generally brought in a high rate of interest in the way of friction, and it was a long time before the driver drove away, turning his horse deliberately on the little patch of lawn under the dining-room windows.

Regie in the meanwhile had waked up, and was having tea in the drawing-room as a great treat.

He had much to tell about his expedition; how the Bishop had given him half a crown, and Uncle Dick had taken him into the town to spend it, and how after dinner he had ridden on Uncle Dick's back.

'And Auntie Hester. How was she?'

'She was very well, only she cried a little. I did not stay long because Mr. Bishop was wanting to give me the half-crown, and he kept it downstairs. And when I went in again she was in bed, and she was so sleepy she hardly said anything at all.'

Mr. Gresley came in wearily, and dropped into a chair.

Mrs. Gresley gave him his tea, and presently took Regie upstairs. Then she came back and sat down in a low chair close to her husband. It was the first drop of comfort in Mr. Gresley's cup to-day.

'How is Hester?'

'According to Dr. Brown she is very ill,' said Mr. Gresley in an extinguished voice. 'But they would not let me see her.'

'Not see her own brother! My dear James, you should have insisted.'

'I did, but it was no use. You know how angry Dr. Brown gets at the least opposition. And the Bishop backed him up. They said it would excite her.'

'I never heard of such a thing. What is the matter with her?'

'Shock, Dr. Brown calls it. They have been afraid of collapse all day, but she is better this evening. They seemed to think a great deal of her knowing Regie.'

'Did the little lamb forgive her?'

'Oh yes, he kissed her and she knew him and cried. And it seems her hands are severely burnt. They have got a nurse, and they have telegraphed for Miss West. The Bishop was very good to Regie and gave him that fur rug.'

They looked at the splendid blue fox rug on the sofa.

'I am afraid,' said Mrs. Gresley after a pause, 'that Hester did run all the way to Southminster as the Bishop said. Abel said the Bishop's coachman told him that she came late last night to the Palace, and she was white with snow when the footman let her in.'

'My dear, I should have thought you were too sensible to listen to servant's gossip,' said Mr. Gresley impatiently. 'Your own common sense will tell you that

Hester never performed that journey on foot. I told Dr. Brown the same, but he lost his temper at once. It's curious how patient he is in a sick room, and how furious he can be out of it. He was very angry with me, too, because when he mentioned to the Bishop in my presence that Hester was under morphia, I said I strongly objected to her being drugged, and when I repeated that morphia was a most dangerous drug with effects worse than intoxication, in fact, that morphia was a form of intoxication, he positively before the Bishop shook his fist in my face, and said he was not going to be taught his business by me.

'The Bishop took me away into the study. Dick Vernon was sitting there, at least he was creeping about on all fours with Regie on his back. I think he must be in love with Hester, he asked so anxiously if there was any change. He would not speak to me, pretended not to know me. I suppose the Bishop had told him about the porch, and he was afraid I should come on him for repairs as he had tampered with it. The Bishop sent them away, and said he wanted to have a talk with me. The Bishop himself was the only person who was kind.'

There was a long pause. Mrs. Gresley laid her soft cheek against her husband's, and put her small hand in a protecting manner over his large one. It was not surprising that on the following Sunday Mr. Gresley said such beautiful things about women being pillows against which weary masculine athletes could rest.

'He spoke very nicely of you,' went on Mr. Gresley at last. 'He said he appreciated your goodness in letting Regie go after what had happened, and your offer to come and nurse Hester yourself. And then he spoke about *me*. And he said he knew well how devoted I was to my work, and how anything I did for the Church was a real labour of love, and that my heart was in my work.'

'It is quite true. So it is,' said Mrs. Gresley.

'I never thought he understood me so well. And he went on to say that he knew I must be dreadfully anxious about my sister, but that as far as money was concerned – I had offered to pay for a nurse – I was to put all anxiety off my mind. He would take all responsibility about the illness. He said he had a little fund laid by for emergencies of this kind, and that he could not spend it better than on Hester whom he loved like his own child. And then he went on to speak of Hester. I don't remember all he said when he turned off about her, but he spoke of her as if she were a person quite out of the common.'

'He always did spoil her,' said Mrs. Gresley.

'He went off on a long rigmarole about her and her talent, and how vain he and I should be if leading articles appeared in the *Spectator*[305] about us as they did about her. I did not know there had been anything of the kind, but he said every one else did. And then he went on more slowly that Hester was under a foolish hallucination, as groundless, no doubt, as that she had caused Regie's death, that her book was destroyed. He said, 'It is this idea which has got firm hold of her, but which has momentarily passed off her mind in her anxiety about

Regie, which has caused her illness.' And then he looked at me. He seemed really quite shaky. He held on to a chair. I think his health is breaking.'

'And what did you say?'

'I said the truth, that it was no hallucination but the fact, that much as I regretted to say so Hester had written a profane and immoral book, and that I had felt it my duty to burn it, and a very painful duty it had been. I said he would have done the same if he had read it.'

'I am glad you said that.'

'Well, the awkward part was that he said he had read it, every word, and that he considered it the finest book that had been written in his day. And then he began to walk up and down and to become rather excited, and to say that he could not understand how I could take upon myself such a responsibility, or on what grounds I considered myself a judge of literature. As if I ever did consider myself a judge! But I do know right from wrong. We had got on all right up till then, especially when he spoke so cordially of you and me, but directly he made a personal matter of Hester's book, setting his opinion against mine, for he repeated over and over again it was a magnificent book, his manner seemed to change. He tried to speak kindly, but all the time I saw that my considering the book bad while he thought it good, gravelled him, and made him feel annoyed with me. The truth is, he can't bear any one to think differently from himself.'

'He always was like that,' said the comforter.

'I said I supposed he thought it right to run down the clergy and hold them up to ridicule. He said 'Certainly not, but he did not see how that applied to anything in Hester's book.' He said, 'She has drawn us without bias towards us, exactly as we appear to three-quarters of the laity. It won't do us any harm to see ourselves for once as others see us. There is in these days an increasing adverse criticism of us in many men's minds, to which your sister's mild rebukes are as nothing. We have drawn it upon ourselves, not so much by our conduct, which I believe to be uniformly above reproach, or by any lack of zeal, as by our ignorance of our calling; by our inability to 'convert life into truth,' the capital secret of our profession, as I was once told as a divinity student. I for one believe that the Church will regain her prestige and her hold on the heart of the nation, but if she does, it will be mainly due to a new element in the minds of the clergy, a stronger realisation, not of our responsibilities – we have that – but of the education, the personal search for truth, the knowledge of human nature, which are necessary to enable us to meet them.' He went on a long time about that. I think he grows very wordy. But I did not argue with him. I let him say what he liked. I knew that I must be obedient to my Bishop, just as I should expect my clergy to be to me, if I ever am a Bishop myself. Not that I expect I ever shall be' – Mr. Gresley was over tired – 'but it seemed to me as he talked about the book, that all the time, though he put me down to the highest motives – he did me that justice – he was trying to make me own I had done wrong.'

'You didn't say so?' said the little wife hotly.

'My dear, need you ask? But I did say at last that I had consulted with Archdeacon Thursby on the matter, and he had strongly advised me to do as I did. The Bishop seemed thunderstruck. And then – it really seemed providential – who should come in but Archdeacon Thursby himself. The Bishop went straight up to him, and said 'You come at a fortunate moment, for I am greatly distressed at the burning of Miss Gresley's book, and Gresley tells me that you advised it.' And would you believe it,' said Mr. Gresley in a strangled voice, 'the Archdeacon actually denied it then and there. He said he did not know Hester had written a book, and had never been consulted on the subject.'

The tears forced themselves out of Mr. Gresley's eyes. He was exhausted and overwrought. He sobbed against his wife's shoulder.

'Wicked liar!' whispered Mrs. Gresley into his parting. 'Wicked, wicked man! Oh! James, I never thought the Archdeacon could have behaved like that!'

'Nor I,' gasped Mr. Gresley, 'but he did. I suppose he did not want to offend the Bishop. And when I expostulated with him, and reminded him of what he had advised only the day before, he said that was about a letter, not a book, as if it mattered which it was. It was the principle that mattered. But they neither of them would listen to me. I said I had offered to help to re-write it, and the Bishop became quite fierce. He said I might as well try to re-write Regie if he were in his coffin. And then he mentioned casually, as if it were quite an afterthought, that Hester had sold it for a thousand pounds. All through, I knew he was really trying to hurt my feelings in spite of his manner, but when he said *that* he succeeded.'

Mr. Gresley groaned.

'A thousand pounds!' said Mrs. Gresley, turning white. 'Oh! It isn't possible.'

'He said he had seen the publisher's letter offering it, and that Hester had accepted it by his advice. He seemed to know all about her affairs. When he said that, I was so distressed I could not help showing it, and he made rather light of it, saying the money loss was the least serious part of the whole affair, but of course it is the worst. Poor Hester, when I think that owing to me she has lost a thousand pounds! Seventy pounds a year, if I had invested it for her, and I know of several good investments, all perfectly safe, at seven per cent. – when I think of it it makes me absolutely miserable. We won't talk of it any more. The Bishop sat with his head in his hands for a long time after the Archdeacon had gone, and afterwards he was quite kindly again, and said we looked at the subject from such different points of view that perhaps there was no use in discussing it. And we talked of the Church Congress[306] until the fly came, only he seemed dreadfully tired, quite knocked up. And he promised to let us know first thing to-morrow morning how Hester was. He was cordial when we left. I think he meant well. But I can never feel the same to Archdeacon Thursby again. He was quite my greatest friend among the clergy round here. I suppose I shall learn in time not to have such a high ideal of people, but I certainly thought very highly of him until to-day.'

Mr. Gresley sat upright, and put away his handkerchief with decision.

'One thing this miserable day has taught us,' he said, 'and that is that we must part with Fraülein. If she is to become impertinent the first moment we are in trouble, such a thing is not to be borne. We could not possibly keep her after her behaviour to-day.'

CHAPTER XLIV

If two lives join, there is oft a scar.
ROBERT BROWNING.[307]

RACHEL left Westhope Abbey the day after Lord Newhaven's funeral, and returned to London. And the day after that Hugh came to see her, and proposed, and was accepted.

He had gone over in his mind a hundred times all that he should say to her on that occasion. If he had said all that he was fully resolved to say it is hardly credible that any woman, however well disposed towards him, would have accepted so tedious a suitor. But what he really said, in a hoarse inaudible voice, was, 'Rachel, will you marry me?' He was looking so intently into a little grove of Roman hyacinths that perhaps the hyacinths heard what he said; at any rate, she did not. But she supposed from long experience that he was proposing, and she said 'Yes' immediately.

She had not intended to say so, at least not at first. She had made up her mind that it would be only right to inform him that she was fourteen months older than he (she had looked him out in Burke where she herself was not to be found);[308] that she was 'old enough to be his mother'; also that she was of a cold revengeful temper not calculated to make a home happy, and several other odious traits of character which she had never dreamed of confiding to any of the regiment of her previous lovers.

But the only word she had breath to say when the time came was 'Yes.'

Rachel had shivered and hesitated on the brink of a new love long enough. Her anxiety about Hugh had unconsciously undermined her resistance. His confession had given her instantly the confidence in him which had been wanting. It is not perfection that we look for in our fellow creatures, but for what is apparently rarer, a little plain dealing.

How they rise before us! – the sweet reproachful faces of those whom we could have loved devotedly if they had been willing to be straightforward with us; whom we have lost, not by our own will, but by that paralysis of feeling which gradually invades the heart at the discovery of small insincerities. Sincerity seems our only security against losing those who love us, the only cup in which those who are worth keeping will care to pledge us when youth is past.

Rachel was not by nature *de celles qui se jettent dans l'amour comme dans un précipice*.[309] But she shut her eyes, recommended her soul to God, and threw herself over. She had climbed down once – with assistance – and she was not going to do that again. That she found herself alive at the bottom was a surprise to her, but a surprise that was quickly forgotten in the constant wonder that Hugh could love her as devotedly as it was obvious he did.

Women would have shared that wonder, but not men. There was a home ready-made in Rachel's faithful, dog-like eyes which at once appealed to the desire of expansion of empire in the heart of the free-born Briton.

Hugh had, until lately, considered woman as connected with the downward slope of life. He would have loudly disclaimed such an opinion if it had been attributed to him; but nevertheless it was the key-note of his behaviour towards them, his belief concerning them which was of a piece with his cheap cynicism and dilettante views of life. He now discovered that woman was made out of something more than man's spare rib.[310]

It is probable that if he had never been in love with Lady Newhaven Hugh would never have loved Rachel. He would have looked at her, as many men did, with a view to marriage, and would probably have dismissed her from his thoughts as commonplace. He knew better now. It was Lady Newhaven who was commonplace. His worldliness was dropping from him day by day as he learned to know Rachel better.

Where was his cynicism now that she loved him?

His love for her, humble, triumphant, diffident, passionate, impatient by turns, now exacting, now selfless, possessed him entirely. He remembered once with astonishment that he was making a magnificent match. He had never thought of it, as Rachel knew, as she knew well.

December came in bleak and dark. The snow did its poor best, laying day after day its white veil upon the dismal streets. But it was misunderstood. It was scraped into murky heaps. It melted and then froze, and then melted again. And London groaned and shivered on its daily round.

Every afternoon Hugh came, and every morning Rachel made her rooms bright with flowers for him. The flower shop at the corner sent her tiny trees of white lilac, and sweet little united families of hyacinths and tulips. The time of azaleas was not yet. And once he sent her a bunch of daffodils. He knew best how he had obtained them.

Their wild sweet faces peered at Rachel, and she sat down faint and dizzy, holding them in her nerveless hands. If one daffodil knows anything, all daffodils know it to the third and fourth generation.

'Where is he?' they said, 'that man whom you loved once? We were there when he spoke to you. We saw you stand together by the attic window. We never say, but we heard, we remember. And you cried for joy at night afterwards. We never say. But we heard. We remember.'

Rachel's secretary in the little room on the ground floor was interrupted by a tap at the door. Rachel came in laden with daffodils. Their splendour filled the grey room.

'Would you mind having them?' she said smiling, and laying them down by her. 'And would you kindly write a line to Jones telling him not to send me daffodils again. They are a flower I particularly dislike.'

'Rachel?'

'Hugh!'

'Don't you think it would be better if we were married immediately?'

'Better than what?'

'Oh! I don't know, better than breaking it off.'

'You can't break it off now. I'm not a person to be trifled with. You have gone too far.'

'If you gave me half your attention, you would understand that I am only expressing a wish to go a little further, but you have become so frivolous since we have been engaged that I hardly recognise you.'

'I suit myself to my company.'

'Are you going to talk to me in that flippant manner when we are married. I sometimes fear, Rachel, you don't look upon me with sufficient awe. I foresee I shall have to be very firm when we are married. When may I begin to be firm?'

'Are these such evil days, Hugh?'

'I am like Oliver Twist,' he said, 'I want more.'[311]

They were sitting together one afternoon in the firelight in silence. They often sat in silence together.

'A wise woman once advised me,' said Rachel at last, 'if I married, never to tell my husband of any previous attachment. She said, Let him always believe that he was the first

That ever burst

Into that silent sea.[312]

I believe it was good advice, but it seems to me to have one drawback – to follow it may be to tell a lie. It would be in my case.'

Silence.

'I know that a lie and an adroit appeal to the vanity of man are supposed to be a woman's recognised weapons. The same woman told me that I might find myself mistaken in many things in this world, but never in counting on the vanity of man. She said that was a reed which would never pierce my hand. I don't think you are vain, Hugh.'

'Not vain! Why I am so conceited at the fact that you are going to marry me that I look down on every one else. I only long to tell them so. When may I tell my mother, Rachel? She is coming to London this week.'

'You have the pertinacity of a fly. You always come back to the same point. I am beginning to be rather bored with your marriage. You can't talk of anything else.'

'I can't think about anything else.'

He drew her cheek against his. He was an ingratiating creature.

'Neither can I,' she whispered.

And that was all Rachel ever said of all she meant to say about Mr. Tristram.

A yellow fog. It made rings round the shaded electric lamp by which Rachel was reading. The fire burned tawny and blurred. Even her red gown looked dim. Hugh came in.

'What are you reading?' he said, sitting down by her.

He did not want to know, but if you are reading a book on another person's knee you cannot be a very long way off. He glanced with feigned interest at the open page, stooping a little for he was short-sighted now and then – at least now.

Rachel took the opportunity to look at him. You can't really look at a person when he is looking at you. Hugh was very handsome, especially side face, and he knew it, but he was not sure whether Rachel thought so.

He read mechanically:

> *Take back your vows.*
> *Elsewhere you trimmed and taught these lamps to burn;*
> *You bring them stale and dim to serve my turn.*
> *You lit those candles in another shrine,*
> *Guttered and cold you offer them on mine.*
> *Take back your vows.*[313]

A shadow fell across Hugh's mind. Rachel saw it fall.

'You do not think that of me, Rachel,' he said, pointing to the verse. It was the first time he had alluded to that halting confession which had remained branded on the minds of both.

He glanced up at her, and she suffered him for a moment to look through her clear eyes into her soul.

'I never thought that of you,' she said with difficulty. 'I am so foolish that I believe the candles are lit now for the first time. I am so foolish that I believe you love me nearly as much as I love you.'

'It is a dream,' said Hugh passionately, and he fell on his knees, and hid his white face against her knee. 'It is a dream. I shall wake, and find you never cared for me.'

She sat for a moment stunned by the violence of his emotion, which was shaking him from head to foot. Then she drew him into her trembling arms, and held his head against her breast.

She felt his tears through her gown.

'What is past will never come between us,' she said brokenly at last. 'I have cried over it, too, Hugh, but I have put it from my mind. When you told me about it, knowing you risked losing me by telling me, I suddenly trusted you entirely. I had not quite up till then. I can't say why, except that perhaps I had grown suspicious because I was once deceived. But I do now because you were open with me. I think, Hugh, you and I can dare to be truthful to each other. You have been so to me, and I will be so to you. I knew about *that* long before you told me. Lady Newhaven, poor thing, confided in me last summer. She had to tell some one. I think you ought to know that I know. And oh, Hugh, I knew about the drawing of lots, too.'

Hugh started violently, but he did not move.

Would she have recognised that ashen convulsed face if he had raised it?

'Lady Newhaven listened at the door when you were drawing lots, and she told me. But we never knew which had drawn the short lighter till Lord Newhaven was killed on the line. Only she and I and you know that that was not an accident. I know what you must have gone through all the summer, feeling you had taken his life as well. But you must remember it was his own doing, and a perfectly even chance. You ran the same risk. His blood is on his own head. But oh, my darling, when I think it might have been you!'

Hugh thought afterwards that if her arms had not been round him, if he had been a little distance from her, he might have told her the truth. He owed it to her, this woman who was the very soul of truth. But if she had withdrawn from him, however gently, in the moment when her tenderness had for the first time vanquished her natural reserve, if she had taken herself away then, he could not have borne it. In deep repentance after Lord Newhaven's death, he had vowed that from that day forward he would never deviate again from the path of truth and honour, however difficult it might prove. But this frightful moment had come upon him unawares. He drew back instinctively, giddy and unnerved, as from a chasm yawning suddenly among the flowers, one step in front of him. He was too stunned to think. When he rallied they were standing together on the hearthrug, and she was saying – he did not know what she was saying, for he was repeating over and over again to himself, 'The moment is past. The moment is past.'

At last her words conveyed some meaning to him.

'We will never speak of this again, my friend,' she said; 'but now that no harm can be done by it, it seemed right to tell you I knew.'

'I ought never to have drawn,' said Hugh hoarsely.

'No,' said Rachel. 'He was in fault to demand such a thing. It was inhuman. But having once drawn he had to abide by it, as you would have done if you had drawn the short lighter.'

She was looking earnestly at him, as at one given back from the grave.

'Yes,' said Hugh, feeling she expected him to speak. 'If I had drawn it I should have had to abide by it.'

'I thank God continually that you did not draw it. You made him the dreadful reparation he asked. If it recoiled upon himself you were not to blame. You have done wrong, and you have repented. You have suffered, Hugh. I know it by your face. And perhaps I have suffered, too, but that is past. We will shut up the past, and think of the future. Promise me that you will never speak of this again.'

'I promise,' said Hugh mechanically.

'The moment to speak is past,' he said to himself.

Had it ever been present?

CHAPTER XLV

Dieu n'oublie personne. Il visite tout le monde.
                                        VINET.[314]

HUGH did not sleep that night.

His escape had been too narrow. He shivered at the mere thought of it. It had never struck him as possible that Rachel and Lady Newhaven had known of the drawing of lots. Now that he found they knew, sundry small incidents, unnoticed at the time, came crowding back to his memory. That was why Lady Newhaven had written so continually those letters which he had burnt unread. That was why she had made that desperate attempt to see him in the smoking-room[315] at Wilderleigh after the boating accident. She wanted to know which had drawn the short lighter. That explained the mysterious tension which Hugh had noticed in Rachel during the last days in London before – before the time was up. He saw it all now. And, of course, they naturally supposed that Lord Newhaven had committed suicide. They could not think otherwise. They were waiting for one of the two men to do it.

'If Lord Newhaven had not turned giddy and stumbled on to the line, if he had not died by accident when he did,' said Hugh to himself, 'where should I be now?'

There was no answer to that question.

What was the use of asking it? He *was* dead. And, fortunately, the two women firmly believed he had died by his own hand. Hugh as firmly believed that the death was accidental.

But it could not be his duty to set them right, to rake up the whole hideous story again.

By an extraordinary, by a miraculous chance, he was saved, as it were, a second time. It could do no good to allude to the dreadful subject again. Besides, he had promised Rachel never to speak of it again.

He groaned, and hid his face in his hands.

'Oh, coward and wretch that I am,' he said. 'Cannot I even be honest with myself? I lied to her to-day. I never thought I could have told Rachel a lie, but I did. I can't live without her. I must have her. I would rather die than lose her now. And I should have lost her if I'd told her the truth. I felt that. I am not worthy. It was an ill day for her when she took my tarnished life into her white hands. She ought to have trodden me under foot. But she does love me, and I will never deceive her again. She does love me, and, God helping me, I will make her happy.'

The strain of conflict was upon Hugh – the old, old conflict of the seed with the earth, of the soul with love. How many little fibres and roots the seed puts out, pushed by an unrecognised need within itself, not without pain, not without a gradual rending of its being, not without a death unto self into a higher life. Love was dealing with Hugh's soul as the earth deals with the seed, and – he suffered.

It was a man who did not look like an accepted lover who presented himself at Rachel's door the following afternoon.

But Rachel was not there. Her secretary handed Hugh a little note which she had left for him, telling him that Hester had suddenly fallen ill, and that she had been sent for to Southminster. The note ended: 'These first quiet days are past. So now you may tell your mother, and put our engagement in the *Morning Post*.'[316]

Hugh was astonished at the despair which overwhelmed him at the bare thought that he should not see Rachel that day and not the next either. It was not to be borne. She had no right to make him suffer like this. Day by day, when a certain restless fever returned upon him, he had known, as an opium eater knows, that at a certain hour he should become rested and calm and sane once more. To be in the same room with Rachel, to hear her voice, to let his eyes dwell upon her, to lean his forehead for a moment against her hand, was to enter, as we enter in dreams, a world of joy and comfort, and boundless, endless, all-pervading peace.

And now he was suddenly left shivering in a bleak world without her. With her he was himself, a released, freed self, growing daily further and further away from all he had once been. Without her he felt he was nothing but a fierce wounded animal.

He tried to laugh at himself as he walked slowly away from Rachel's house. He told himself that he was absurd, that an absence of a few days was nothing. He turned his steps mechanically in the direction of his mother's lodgings. At any rate, he could tell her. He could talk about this cruel woman to her. The smart was momentarily soothed by his mother's painful joy. He wrenched himself somewhat out of himself as she wept the tears of jealous love which all mothers must weep when the woman comes who takes their son away.

'I am so glad,' she kept repeating. 'These are tears of joy, Hughie. I can forgive her for accepting you, but I should never have forgiven her if she had refused you – if she had made my boy miserable. And you have been miserable lately. I have seen it for a long time. I suppose it was all this coming on.'

He said it was. The remembrance of other causes of irritation and moodiness had slipped entirely off his mind.

He stayed a long time with his mother, who pressed him to wait till his sister, who was shopping, returned. But his sister tarried long out of doors, and at last the pain of Rachel's absence returning on him, he left suddenly, promising to return in the evening.

He did not go back to his rooms. He wandered aimlessly through the darkening streets, impatient of the slow hours. At last he came out on the Embankment. The sun was setting redly, frostily, in a grey world of sky-mist and river-mist and spectral bridge and spire. A shaking pathway of pale flame came across the grey of the hidden river to meet him.

He stood a long time looking at it. The low sun touched and forsook, touched and forsook point by point the little crowded world which it was leaving.

'My poor mother,' said Hugh to himself. 'Poor, gentle, loving soul whom I so nearly brought down with sorrow to the grave. She will never know what an escape she has had. I might have been more to her. I might have made her happier, seeing her happiness is wrapped up in me. I will make up to her for it. I will be a better son to her in future. Rachel and I together will make her last years happy. Rachel and I together,' said Hugh over and over again.

And then he suddenly remembered that though Rachel had taken herself away he could write to her, and – he might look out the trains to Southminster. He leaped into a hansom[317] and hurried back to his rooms.

The porter met him in a mysterious manner in the entrance. Lady waiting to see him. Lady said she was his sister. Had been waiting two hours. In his rooms now.

Hugh laughed and ran up the wide common staircase. His sister had heard the news from his mother and had rushed over at once.

As he stooped a little to fit the latch-key on his chain into the lock a man, who was coming down the stairs feeling in his pockets, stopped with a sudden exclamation. It was Captain Pratt, pallid, smiling, hair newly varnished, resplendent in a magnificent fur overcoat.

'What luck,' he said. 'Scarlett, I think. We met at Wilderleigh. Have you such a thing as a match about you?'

Hugh felt in his pockets. He had not one.

'Never mind,' he said, opening the door. 'I've plenty inside. Come in.'

Hugh went in first, extricating his key. Captain Pratt followed, murmuring, 'Nice little dens, these. A pal of mine lives just above – Streatham. You know Streatham, son of Lord –'

The remainder of the sentence was lost.

The door opened straight into the little sitting-room.

A woman in deep mourning rose suddenly out of a chair by the fire and came towards them.

'Hughie!' she said.

It was Lady Newhaven.

It is probable that none of the tableaux[318] she had arranged were quite so dramatic as this one, in which she had not reckoned on that elaborate figure in the doorway.

Captain Pratt's opinion of Hugh, whom he had hitherto regarded as a pauper with an involved estate, leapt from temperate to summer heat – blood heat. After the first instant he kept his eyes steadily fixed on Hugh.

'I – er – thank you, Scarlett. I have found my matches. A thousand thanks. Good night.'

He was disappearing, but Hugh, his eyes flashing in his grey face, held him forcibly by the arm.

'Lady Newhaven,' he said. 'The porter is inexcusable. These are my rooms which he has shown you into by mistake, not Mr. Streatham's, your nephew. He is just above. I think,' turning to Captain Pratt, 'Streatham is out of town.'

'He is out of town,' said Captain Pratt, looking with cold admiration at Hugh. 'Admirable,' he said to himself; 'a born gentleman.'

'This is not the first time Streatham's visitors have been shown in here,' continued Hugh. 'The porter shall be dismissed. I trust you will forgive me my share in the annoyance he has caused you. Is your carriage waiting?'

'No,' said Lady Newhaven faintly, quite thrown off the lines of her prepared scene by the sudden intrusion into it of a foreign body.

'My hansom is below,' said Captain Pratt deferentially, venturing, now that the situation was, so to speak, draped, to turn his discreet agate eyes towards Lady Newhaven. 'If it could be of the least use, I myself should prefer to walk.'

Now that he looked at her he looked very hard at her. She was a beautiful woman.

Lady Newhaven's self-possession had returned sufficiently for her to take up her fur cloak.

'Thank you,' she said, letting Captain Pratt help her on with it. 'I shall be glad to make use of your hansom, if you are sure you can spare it. I am shocked at having taken possession of your rooms,' turning to Hugh; 'I will write to Georgie Streatham to-night. I am staying with my mother, and I came across to ask him to take my boys to the pantomime, as I cannot take them myself – so soon,' with a glance at her crape.[319] 'Don't come down, Mr. Scarlett. I have given you enough trouble already.'

Captain Pratt's arm was crooked. He conducted her in his best manner to the foot of the staircase and helped her into his hansom. His manner was not so unctuous as his father's, but it was slightly adhesive. Lady Newhaven shuddered involuntarily as she took his arm.

Hugh followed.

'I hope you will both come and see my mother,' she said, with an attempt at graciousness. 'You know Lady Trentham, I think?' – to Captain Pratt.

'Very slightly. No. Delighted!' murmured Captain Pratt, closing the hansom doors in an intimate manner. 'And if I could be of the least use at any time in taking your boys to the pantomime – er – only too glad. The glass down, Richards!'

The hansom with its splendid bay horse rattled off.

Captain Pratt nodded to Hugh, who was still standing on the steps, and turned away to buy a box of matches from a passing urchin. Then he turned up his fur collar, and proceeded leisurely on his way.

'Very stand-off both of them in the past,' he said to himself, 'but they will have to be civil in future. I wonder if he will make her keep her title. Deuced awkward for them both though, only a month after Newhaven's death. I wish that sort of *contretemps* would happen to me when I'm bringing in a lot of fellows suddenly. An opening like that is all I want to give me a start, and I should get on as well as anybody. The aristocracy all hang together, whatever Selina and Ada may say. Money don't buy everything, as the governor thinks. But if you're once in with 'em you're in.'

Hugh went back to his room and locked himself in. He was a delicate man, highly strung, and he had not slept the night before. He collapsed into a chair and remained a long time, his head in his hands.

It was too horrible, this woman coming back upon him suddenly like the ghost of some one whom he had murdered. His momentary infatuation had been clean forgotten in his overwhelming love for Rachel. His intrigue with Lady Newhaven seemed so long ago that it had been relegated to the same mental shelf in his mind as the nibbling of a certain forbidden ginger-bread when he was home for his first holidays. He could not be held responsible for either offence after this immense interval of time. It was not he who had committed them, but that other embryo self, that envelope of flesh and sense which he was beginning to abhor, through which he had passed before he reached himself, Hugh, the real man, the man who loved Rachel, and whom Rachel loved.

He had not flinched when he came unexpectedly on Lady Newhaven. At the sight of her a sudden passion of anger shot up and enveloped him as in one flame from head to foot. His love for Rachel was a weapon, and he used it. He did not greatly care about his own good name, but the good name of the man whom Rachel loved was a thing to fight for. It was for her sake, not Lady Newhaven's, that he had concocted the story of the mistaken rooms. He should not have had the presence of mind if Rachel had not been concerned.

He had not finished with Lady Newhaven. He should have trouble yet with her, hideous scenes, in which the corpse of his dead lust would be dragged up, a thing to shudder at, out of its nettly grave.

He could bear it. He must bear it. Nothing would induce him to marry Lady Newhaven, as she evidently expected. He set his teeth. 'She will know the day after to-morrow,' he said to himself, 'when she sees my engagement to Rachel in the papers. Then she will get at me somehow, and make my life a hell to me, while she can. And she will try and come between me and Rachel. I deserve it. I deserve anything I get. But Rachel knows and will stick to me. I will go down to her to-morrow. I can't go on without seeing her. And she won't mind, as the engagement will be given out next day.'

He became more composed at the thought of Rachel. But presently his lip quivered. It would be all right in the end. But, oh! not to have done it! Not to have done it! To have come to his marriage with a whiter past, not to need her forgiveness on the very threshold of their life together, not to have been unfaithful to her before he knew her.

What man who has disbelieved in his youth in the sanctity of Love, and then later has knelt in its Holy of Holies, has escaped that pang?

CHAPTER XLVI

There's neither honesty, manhood, nor good fellowship in thee.

SHAKESPEARE.[320]

'MY mind misgives me, Dick!' said the Bishop, a day or two later, as Dick joined him and his sister and Rachel at luncheon at the Palace. 'I am convinced that you have been up to some mischief.'

'I have just returned from Warpington, my lord. I understood it was your wish I should ride over and tell them Hester was better.'

'It certainly was my wish. I'm very much obliged to you. But I remembered after you had gone that you had refused to speak to Gresley when he was over here, and I was sorry I sent you.'

'I spoke to him all right,' said Dick grimly. 'That was why I was so alacritous to go.'

The Bishop looked steadily at him.

'Until you are my suffragan[321] I should prefer to manage my own business with my clergy.'

'Just so,' said Dick, helping himself to mustard. 'But you see I'm his cousin, and I thought it just as well to let him know quietly and dispassionately what I thought of him. So I told him I was not particular about my acquaintances. I knew lots of bad eggs out in Australia, half of them hatched in England, chaps who'd been shaved and tubbed gratis by Government,[322] in fact I'd a large visiting list, but that I drew the line at such a cad as him, and that he might remember I wasn't going to preach for him at any more of his little cold water cures'[323] – a smile hovered on Dick's crooked mouth – 'or ever take any notice of him in future. That was what he wanted, my lord. You were too soft with him, if you'll excuse my saying so. But that sort of chap wants it giving him hot and strong. He doesn't understand anything else. He gets quite beyond himself, fizzing about on his little pocket-handkerchief of a parish, thinking he is a sort of god, because no one makes it their business to keep him in his place, and rub it into him that he is an infernal fool. That is why some clergymen jaw so, because they never have it brought home to them what rot they talk. They'd be no sillier than other men if they were only treated properly. I was very calm, but I let him have it. I told him he was a mean sneak, and that either he was the biggest fool or the biggest rogue going, and that the mere fact of his cloth did not give him the right to do dishonest things with other people's property, though it did save him from the pounding he richly deserved. He tried to interrupt, indeed he was tooting all the time like a fog-horn, but I did not take any notice, and I wound up by saying it was men like him who brought discredit on the Church and on the clergy, and who made the gorge rise of decent chaps like me.'

'Yes,' said Dick after a pause. 'When I left him he understood, I don't say entirely, but he had a distant glimmering. It isn't often I go on these errands of mercy, but I felt that the least I could do was to back you up, my lord. Of course, it is in little matters like this that lay helpers come in, who are not so hampered about their language as I suppose the clergy are.'

The Bishop tried, he tried hard, to look severe, but his mouth twitched.

'Don't thank me,' said Dick. 'Nothing is a trouble where you are concerned. It was – ahem – a pleasure.'

'That I can believe,' said the Bishop. 'Well, Dick, Providence makes use of strange instruments – the jawbone of an ass has a certain Scriptural prestige.[324]

I daresay you reached poor Gresley where I failed. I certainly failed. But if it is not too much to ask, I should regard it as a favour another time if I might be informed beforehand what direction your diocesan aid was about to take.'

Dr. Brown, who often came to luncheon at the Palace, came in now. He took off his leathern driving gloves and held his hands to the fire.

'Cold,' he said. 'They're skating everywhere. How is Miss Gresley?'

'She knows us to-day,' said Rachel, 'and she is quite cheerful.'

'Does the poor thing know her book is burnt?'

'No. She was speaking this morning of its coming out in the spring.'

The little doctor thrust out his underlip and changed the subject.

'I travelled from Pontesbury this morning,' he said, 'with that man who was nearly drowned at Beaumere in the summer. I doctored him at Wilderleigh. Tall, thin, rather a fine gentleman. I forget his name.'

Dr. Brown always spoke of men above himself in the social scale as 'fine gentlemen.'

'Mr. Redman,' said Miss Keane, the Bishop's sister, a dignified person, who had been hampered throughout life by a predilection for the wrong name, and by making engagements in illegible handwriting by last year's almanacs.

'Was it Mr. Scarlett?' said Rachel, feeling Dick's lynx eye upon her. 'I was at Wilderleigh when the accident happened.'

'That's the man. He got out at Southminster, and asked me which was the best hotel. No, I won't have any more, thanks. I'll go up and see Miss Gresley at once.'

Rachel followed the Bishop into the library. They generally waited there together till the doctor came down.

'I don't know many young men I like better than Dick,' said the Bishop. 'I should marry him if I were a young woman. I admire the way he acts up to his principles. Very few of us do. Until he has a further light on the subject he is right to knock a man down who insults him. And from his point of view he was justified in speaking to Mr. Gresley as he did. I was sorely tempted to say something of that kind to him myself, but as one grows grey one realises that one can only speak in a spirit of love. A man of Dick's stamp will always be respected because he does not assume virtues which belong to a higher grade than he is on at present. But when he reaches that higher grade he will act as thoroughly upon the convictions that accompany it as he does now on his present convictions.'

'He certainly would not turn the other cheek to the smiter.'[325]

'I should not advise the smiter to reckon on it. And unless it is turned from that rare sense of spiritual brotherhood it would be unmanly to turn it. To imitate the outward appearance of certain virtues is like imitating the clothes of a certain class. It does not make us belong to the class to dress like it. The true foundation for the spiritual life, as far as I can see it, is in the full development of our human nature with all its simple trusts and aspirations. I admire Dick's solid foundation. It will carry a building worthy of him some day. But my words of wisdom appear to be thrown away upon you. You are thinking of something else.'

'I was thinking that I ought to tell you that I am engaged to be married.'

The Bishop's face lit up.

'I am engaged to Mr. Scarlett. That is why he has come down here.'

The Bishop's face fell. Rachel had been three days at the Palace. Dick had not allowed the grass to grow under his feet. 'That admirable promptitude,' the Bishop had remarked to himself, 'deserves success.'

'Poor, dear Dick,' he said softly.

'That is what Hester says, I told her yesterday.'

'I really have a very high opinion of Dick,' said the Bishop.

'So have I. If I might have two I would certainly choose him second.'

'But this superfluous Mr. Scarlett comes first, eh?'

'I am afraid he does.'

'Well,' said the Bishop with a sigh, 'if you are so ungrateful as to marry to please yourself instead of to please me there is nothing more to be said. I will have a look at your Mr. Scarlett when he comes to tea. I suppose he will come to tea. I notice the most *farouche*[326] men do when they are engaged. It is the first step in the taming process. I shall of course bring an entirely unprejudiced mind to bear upon him, as I always make a point of doing, but I warn you beforehand I shan't like him.'

'Because he is not Mr. Dick.'

'Well, yes, because he is not Dick. I suppose his name is Bertie.'

'Not Bertie,' said Rachel indignantly, 'Hugh.'

'It's a poor inefficient kind of name, only four letters, and a duplicate at each end. I don't think, my dear, he is worthy of you.'

'Dick has only four letters.'

'I make it a rule never to argue with women. Well, Rachel, I'm glad you have decided to marry. Heaven bless you, and may you be happy with this man. Ah! Here comes Dr. Brown.'

'Well!' said the Bishop and Rachel simultaneously.

'She's better,' said the little doctor angrily, he was always angry when he was anxious. 'She's round the first corner. But how to pull her round the next corner, that is what I'm thinking.'

'Defer the next corner.'

'We can't now her mind is clear. She's as sane as you or I are, and a good deal sharper. When she asks about her book she'll have to be told.'

'A lie would be quite justifiable under the circumstances.'

'Of course, of course, but it would be useless. You might hoodwink her for a day or two, and then she would find out, first that the *magnum opus*[327] is gone, and secondly, that you and Miss West, whom she does trust entirely at present, have deceived her. You know what she is when she thinks she is being deceived. She abused you well, my lord, until you reinstated yourself by producing Regie Gresley. But you can't reinstate yourself a second time. You can't produce the book.'

'No,' said the Bishop. 'That is gone for ever.'

Rachel could not trust herself to speak. Perhaps she had realised more fully than even the Bishop had done what the loss of the book was to Hester, at least, what it would be when she knew it was gone.

'Tell her, and give her that if she becomes excitable,' said Dr. Brown, producing a minute bottle out of a voluminous pocket. 'And if you want me I shall be at Canon Wylde's at five o'clock. I'll look in anyhow before I go home.'

Rachel and the Bishop stood a moment in silence after he was gone, and then Rachel took up the little bottle, read the directions carefully, and turned to go upstairs.

The Bishop looked after her but did not speak. He was sorry for her.

'You can go out till tea-time,' said Rachel to the nurse. 'I will stay with Miss Gresley till then.'

Hester was lying on a couch by the fire in a rose-coloured wrapper. Her small face set in its ruffle of soft lace looked bright and eager. Her hair had been cut short, and she looked younger and more like Regie than ever.

Her thin hands lay contentedly in her lap. The principal bandages were gone. Only three fingers of the right hand were in a chrysalis state.

'I shall not be in too great a hurry to get well,' she said to Rachel. 'If I do you will rush away to London and get married.'

'Shall I?' Rachel set down the little bottle on the mantel-piece.

'When is Mr. Scarlett coming down?'

'He came down to-day.'

'Then possibly he may call.'

'Such things do happen.'

'I should like to see him.'

'In a day or two, perhaps.'

'And I want to see dear Dick, too.'

'He sent you his love. Mr. Pratt was here at luncheon yesterday, and he asked me who the old chap was who put on his clothes with a shoe-horn.'[328]

'How like him! Has he said anything more to the Bishop on the uses of swearing?'

'No. But the Bishop draws him on. He delights in him.'

'Rachel, are you sure you have chosen the best man?'

'Quite sure, I mean I never had any choice in the matter. You see I love Hugh, and I'm only fond of Mr. Dick.'

'I always liked Mr. Scarlett,' said Hester. 'I've known him ever since I came out, and that wasn't yesterday. He is so gentle and refined, and one need not be on one's guard in talking to him. He understands what one says, and he is charming looking.'

'Of course, I think so.'

'And this is the genuine thing, Rachel? Do you remember our talk last summer?'

Rachel was silent a moment.

'All I can say is,' she said brokenly, 'that I thank God day and night that Mr. Tristram did not marry me – that I'm free to marry Hugh.'

Hester's uncrippled hand stole into Rachel's.

'Everybody will think,' said Rachel, 'when they see the engagement in tomorrow's papers that I give him everything, because he is poor and his place involved, and of course I am horribly wealthy. But in reality it is I who am poor and he who is rich. He has given me a thousand times more than I could ever give him, because he has given me back the power of loving. It almost frightens me that I can care so much a second time. I should not have thought it possible. But I seem to have got the hang of it now, as Mr. Dick would say. I wish you were downstairs, Hester, as you will be in a day or two. You would be amused by the way he shocks Miss Keane. She asked if he had written anything on his travels, and he said he was on the point of bringing out a little book on 'Cannibal Cookery,' for the use of Colonials. He said some of the recipes were very simple. He began: 'You take a hand and close it round a yam.' But the Bishop stopped him.'

The moment Rachel had said, 'He is on the point of bringing out a book,' her heart stood still. How could she have said such a thing? But apparently Hester took no notice.

'He must have been experimenting on my poor hand,' she said. 'I'm sure I never burnt it like this myself.'

'It will soon be better now.'

'Oh! I don't mind about it now that it doesn't hurt all the time.'

'And your head does not ache to-day, does it?'

'Nothing to matter. But I feel as if I had fallen on it from the top of the cathedral. Dr. Brown says that is nonsense, but I think so all the same. When you believe a thing, and you're told it's nonsense, and you still believe it, that is an hallucination, isn't it?'

'Yes.'

'I have had a great many,' said Hester slowly. 'I suppose I have been more ill than I knew. I thought I saw, I really did see, the spirits of the frost and the snow looking in at the window. And I talked to them a long time, and asked them what quarrel they had with me, their sister, that since I was a child they had always been going about to kill me. Aunt Susan always seemed to think they were enemies who gave me bronchitis. And I told them how I loved them and all their works. And they breathed on the pane and wrote beautiful things in frost-work, and I read them all. Now, Rachel, is that an hallucination about the frost-work, because it seems to me still, now that I am better, though I can't explain it, that I do see the meaning of it at last, and that I shall never be afraid of them again.'

Rachel did not answer.

She had long since realised that Hester, when in her normal condition, saw things which she herself did not see. She had long since realised that Hester always accepted as final the limit of vision of the person she was with, but that that limit changed with every person she met. Rachel had seen her adjust it to persons more short-sighted than herself, with secret self-satisfaction, and then with sudden bewilderment had heard Hester accept as a commonplace from some one else what appeared to Rachel fantastic in the extreme. If Rachel had considered her own mind as the measure of the normal of all other minds, she could not have escaped the conclusion that Hester was a victim of manifold delusions. But, fortunately for herself, she saw that most ladders possessed more than the one rung on which she was standing.

'That is quite different, isn't it?' said Hester, 'from thinking Dr. Brown is a grey wolf.'

'Quite different. That was an hallucination of fever. You see that for yourself now that you have no fever.'

'I see that, of course, now that I have no fever,' repeated Hester, her eyes widening. 'But one hallucination quite as foolish as that is always coming back, and I can't shake it off. The wolf was gone directly, but this is just the same now I am better, only it gets worse and worse. I have never spoken of it to any one, because I know it is so silly. But, Rachel – I have no fever now – and yet – I know you'll laugh at me – I laugh at my own foolish self – and yet all the time I have a horrible feeling that' – Hester's eyes had in them a terror that was hardly human – 'that my book is burnt.'

CHAPTER XLVII

The soul of thy brother is a dark forest.
                                        Russian Proverb.

'A MARRIAGE has been arranged, and will shortly take place, between Hugh St. John Scarlett, of Kenstone Manor, Shropshire, only son of the late Lord Henry Scarlett, and Rachel, only child of the late Joshua Hopkins West, of Birmingham.'

This announcement appeared in the *Morning Post* a few days after Christmas, and aroused many different emotions in the breasts of those who read it.

'She has done it to spite me,' said Mr. Tristram to himself over his morning rasher, in the little eating-house near his studio. 'I knew there was some one else in her mind when she refused me. I rather thought it was that weedy fellow with the high nose. Will he make her happy because he is a lord's son? That is what I should like to ask her. Poor Rachel, if we had been able to marry five years ago we should never have heard of this society craze. Well, it's all over now.' And Mr. Tristram henceforward took the position of a man suffering from an indelible attachment to a woman who had thrown him over for a title.

The Gresleys were astonished at the engagement. It was so extraordinary that they should know both persons. Now that they came to think of it, both of them had been to tea at the Vicarage only last summer.

'A good many people pop in and out of this house,' they agreed.

'I am as certain as that I stand here,' said Mr. Gresley, who was sitting down, 'that that noisy boor, that underbred, foul-mouthed Dick Vernon wanted to marry her.'

'Don't mention him,' said Mrs. Gresley. 'When I think of what he dared to say –'

'My love,' said Mr. Gresley, 'I have forgiven him. I have put from my mind all he said, for I am convinced he was under the influence of drink at the time. We must make allowance for those who live in hot climates. I bear him no grudge. But I am glad that a man of that stamp should not marry Miss West. Drunkenness makes a hell of married life. Mr. Scarlett, though he looked delicate, had at least the appearance of being abstemious.'

Fräulein heard the news as she was packing her boxes to leave Warpington Vicarage. She was greatly depressed. She could not be with her dear Miss Gresley in this mysterious illness which some secret sorrow had brought upon her; but at least Miss West could minister to her. And now it seemed Miss West was think-ing of 'Brautigams'[329] more than of Hester.

Fräulein had been very uncomfortable at the Vicarage, but she wept at leav-ing. Mrs. Gresley had never attained to treating her with the consideration which she would have accorded to one whom she considered her equal. The servants were allowed to disregard with impunity her small polite requests. The nurse was consistently, ferociously jealous of her. But the children had made up for all, and now she was leaving them; and she did not own it to herself, for she was but five and thirty and the shyest of the shy; but she should see no more that noble-hearted, that musical Herr B-r-r-rown.

'Doll,' said Sybell Loftus to her husband at breakfast, 'I've made another match. I thought at the time he liked her. You remember Rachel West, not pretty, but with a nice expression – and what does beauty matter? She is engaged to Mr. Scarlett.'

'Quiet, decent chap,' said Doll; 'and I like *her*. No nonsense about her. Good thing he wasn't drowned.'

'Mr. Harvey will feel it. He confided to me that she was his ideal. Now Rachel is everything that is sweet and good and dear, and she will make a most excellent wife, but I should never have thought, would you, that she could be anybody's ideal?'

Doll opened his mouth to say, 'That depends,' but remembered that his wife had taken an unaccountable dislike to that simple phrase, and remained silent.

Captain Pratt, who was spending Christmas with his family, was the only person at Warpington Towers who read the papers. On this particular morning he came down to a late breakfast after the others had finished. His father, who was always down at eight, secretly admired his son's aristocratic habits while he affected to laugh at them. 'Shameful luxurious ways, these young men in the Guards.[330] Fashionable society is rotten, sir, rotten to the core. Never get up till noon. My boy is as bad as any of them.'

Captain Pratt propped up the paper open before him while he sipped his coffee and glanced down the columns. His travelling eye reached Hugh's engagement.

Captain Pratt rarely betrayed any feeling except *ennui*,[331] but as he read, astonishment got the better of him.

'By George,' he said below his breath.

The bit of omelette on its way to his mouth was slowly lowered again, and remained sticking on the end of his fork.

What did it mean? He recalled that scene in Hugh's rooms *only last week*. He had spoken of it to no one, for he intended to earn gratitude by his discretion. Of course, Scarlett was going to marry Lady Newhaven after a decent interval. She was a very beautiful woman, with a large jointure, and she was obviously in love with him. The question of her conduct was not considered. It never entered Captain Pratt's head, any more than that of a ten-year-old child. He was aware that all the women of the upper classes were immoral, except newly come-out girls. That was an established fact. The only difference between the individuals, which caused a separation as of the sheep from the goats,[332] was whether they were compromised or not. Lady Newhaven was not, unless he chose to compromise her. No breath of scandal had ever touched her.

But what was Scarlett about? Could they have quarrelled? What did it mean? *And what would she do now?*

'By George!' said Captain Pratt again, and the agate eyes narrowed down to two slits.

He sat a long time motionless, his untasted breakfast before him. His mind was working, weighing, applying now its scales, now its thermometer.

Rachel and Hugh were sitting together looking at a paragraph in the *Morning Post*.

'Does Miss Gresley take any interest?' said Hugh.

He was a little jealous of Hester. This illness, the cause of which had sincerely grieved him, had come at an inopportune moment. Hester was always taking Rachel from him.

'Yes,' said Rachel, 'a little when she remembers, But she can only think of one thing.'

'That unhappy book.'

'Yes. I think the book was to Hester something of what you are to me. Her whole heart was wrapped up in it – and she has lost it. Hugh, whatever happens, you must not be lost now. It is too late. I could not bear it.'

'I can only be lost if you throw me away,' said Hugh,

There was a long silence.

'Lady Newhaven will know to-day,' said Rachel at last, 'I tried to break it to her, but she did not believe me.'

'Rachel,' said Hugh, stammering, 'I meant to tell you the other day, only we were interrupted, that *she* came to my rooms the evening before I came down here. I should not have minded quite so much, but Captain Pratt came in with me and – found her there.'

'Oh Hugh, that dreadful man! Poor woman!'

'Poor woman!' said Hugh, his eyes flashing. 'It was poor you I thought of. Poor Rachel! to be marrying a man who –'

There was another silence.

'I have one great compensation,' said Rachel, laying her cool, strong hand on his. 'You are open with me. You keep nothing back. You need not have mentioned this unlucky meeting, but you did. It was like you. I trust you entirely, Hugh. I bless and thank you for loving me. If my love can make you happy, oh Hughie, you will be happy.'

Hugh shrank from her. The faltered words were as a two-edged sword.

She looked at the sensitive, paling face with tender comprehension. The mother-look crept into her eyes.

'If there is anything else that you wish to tell me, tell me now.'

A wild overwhelming impulse to fling himself over the precipice out of the reach of those stabbing words! A horrible nauseating recoil that seemed to rend his whole being.

Somebody said hoarsely:

'There is nothing else.'

It was his own voice, but not his will, that spoke. Had any one ever made him suffer like this woman who loved him?

Lady Newhaven had returned to Westhope ill with suspense and anxiety. She had felt sure she should successfully waylay Hugh in his rooms, convinced that if they could but meet the clouds between them (to borrow from her vocabulary) would instantly roll away. They had met, and the clouds had not rolled away. She vainly endeavoured to attribute Hugh's evident anger at the sight of her to her want of prudence, to the accident of Captain Pratt's presence. She would not admit the thought that Hugh had ceased to care for her, but it needed a good deal of forcible thrusting away. She could hear the knock of the unwelcome guest upon her door, and though always refused admittance he withdrew only to return. She had been grievously frightened, too, at having been seen in equivocal circumstances by such a man as Captain Pratt. The very remembrance made her shiver.

'How angry Edward would have been,' she said to herself. 'I wonder whether he would have advised me to write a little note to Captain Pratt, explaining how I came there, and asking him not to mention it. But, of course, he won't repeat it. He won't want to make an enemy of me and Hugh. The Pratts think so much of me. And when I marry Hugh' – (knock at the mental door) – '*if ever* I marry Hugh, we will be civil to him and have him to stay. Edward never would, but I don't think so much of good family, and all that, as Edward did. We will certainly ask him.'

It was not till after luncheon that Lady Newhaven, after scanning the *Ladies' Pictorial*,[333] languidly opened the *Morning Post*.

Suddenly the paper fell from her hands on to the floor. She seized it up and read again the paragraph which had caught her eye.

'No. No,' she gasped; 'it is not true. It is not possible.' And she read it a third time.

The paper fell from her nerveless hands again, and this time it remained on the floor.

It is doubtful whether until this moment Lady Newhaven had known what suffering was. She had talked freely of it to others. She had sung, as if it were her own composition, 'Cleansing Fires.'[334] She often said it might have been written for her.

> In the cruel fire of sorrow,
>> [*slow, soft pedal.*
> Cast thy heart, do not faint or wail,
>> [*both pedals down, quicker.*
> Let thy hand be firm and steady,
>> [*loud, and hold on to last syllable.*
> Do not let thy spi-rit quail,

[bang! B natural. With resolution.
Bu-ut ....
[hurricane of false notes, &c. &c.

But now, poor thing, the fire had reached her, and her spirit quailed immediately. Perhaps it was only natural that as her courage failed something else should take its place; an implacable burning resentment against her two betrayers, her lover and her friend. She rocked herself to and fro. Lover and friend. 'Oh! never, never trust in man's love or woman's friendship henceforth for ever.'[335] So learned Lady Newhaven the lesson of suffering.

'Lover and friend hast Thou put far from me,' she sobbed, 'and mine acquaintance out of my sight.'[336]

A ring at the door-bell proved that the latter part of the text at any rate was not true in her case.

A footman entered.

'Not at home. Not at home,' she said impatiently.

'I said not at home, but the gentleman said I was to take up his card,' said the man, presenting a card.

When Captain Pratt tipped he tipped heavily.

Lady Newhaven read it.

'No. Yes. I will see him,' she said. It flashed across her mind that she must be civil to him, and that her eyes were not red. She had not shed tears.

The man picked the newspaper from the floor, put it on a side table, and withdrew.

Captain Pratt came in, bland, deferential, orchid in buttonhole.

It was not until he was actually in the room, his cold appraising eyes upon her, that the poor woman realised that her position towards him had changed. She could not summon up the nonchalant distant civility which, according to her ideas, was sufficient for her country neighbours in general, and the Pratts in particular.

Captain Pratt opined that the weather, though cold, was seasonable.

Lady Newhaven agreed.

Captain Pratt regretted the hard frost on account of the hunting. Four hunters eating their heads off, &c.

Lady Newhaven thought the thaw might come any day.

Captain Pratt had been skating yesterday on the parental flooded meadow. Flooded with fire engine. Men out of work. Glad of employment, &c.

How kind of Captain Pratt to employ them.

Not at all. It was his father. Duties of the landed gentry, &c. He believed if the frost continued they would skate on Beaumere.

No, no one was allowed to skate on Beaumere. The springs rendered the ice treacherous.

Silence.

Captain Pratt turned the gold knob of his stick slowly in his thick white fingers. He looked carefully at Lady Newhaven, as a connoisseur with intent to buy looks at a piece of valuable china. She was accustomed to being looked at, but there was something in Captain Pratt's prolonged scrutiny which filled her with vague alarm. She writhed under it. He observed her uneasiness, but he did not remove his eyes.

Were the boys well?

They were quite well, thanks. She was cowed.

Were they fond of skating?

Very fond.

Might he suggest that they should come over and skate at Warpington Towers tomorrow. He himself would be there, and would take charge of them.

He rose slowly as one who has made up his mind. Lady Newhaven feared it would be troubling Captain Pratt too much.

It would be no trouble to Captain Pratt; on the contrary, a pleasure.

His hand was now extended. Lady Newhaven had to put hers into it.

Perhaps next week if the frost held. She tried to withdraw her hand. Oh, well, then, to-morrow; certainly, to-morrow.

'You may rely on me to take care of them,' said Captain Pratt, still holding her hand. He obliged her to look at him. His hard eyes met her frightened blue ones. 'You may rely on my discretion entirely – in all matters,' he said meaningly.

Lady Newhaven winced, and her hand trembled violently in his.

He pressed the shrinking little hand, let it go, and went away.

CHAPTER XLVIII

Le temps apporte, emporte, mais ne rapporte pas.[337]

'MAY I come in?' said the Bishop, tapping at Hester's door.

'Do come in.'

Hester was lying propped up by many cushions on a sofa in the little sitting-room leading out of her bedroom. She looked a mere shadow in the firelight.

She smiled at him mechanically, but her face relapsed at once into the apathetic expression which sat so ill upon it. Her lustreless eyes fixed themselves again on the fire.

'And what are you going to do this afternoon?' she said politely. It was obvious she did not care what he did.

'I am going to Westhope on business,' he said, looking narrowly at her. It was all very well for Dr. Brown to say she must be roused; but how were his instructions to be carried out?

'I am a great deal of trouble to you,' said Hester. 'Could not I be sent to a home, or a place where you go through a cure, where I should be out of the way till I'm well.'

'Have I deserved that, Hester?'

'No; but you know I always try to wound my best friends.'

'You don't succeed, my child, because they know you are in heavy trouble.'

'We will not speak of that,' said Hester quickly.

'Yes, the time has come to speak of it. Why do you shut us out of this sorrow? Don't you see that you make our burdens heavier by refusing to let us share yours?'

'You can't share it,' said Hester, 'no one can.'

'Do you think I have not grieved over it?'

'I know you have, but it was waste of time. It's no good – no good. Please don't cheer me, and tell me I shall write better books yet, and that this trial is for my good. Dear Bishop, don't try and comfort me. I can't bear it.'

'My poor child, I firmly believe you will write better books than the one which is lost, and I firmly believe that you will one day look back upon this time as a step in your spiritual life, but I had not intended to say so. The thought was in my mind, but it was you who put the words into my mouth.'

'I was so afraid that –'

'That I was going to improve the occasion?'

'Yes. Dr. Brown and the nurse are so dreadfully cheerful now, and always talking about the future, and how celebrated I shall be some day. If you and Rachel follow suit I shall – I think I shall go out of my mind.'

The Bishop did not answer.

'Dr. Brown may be right,' Hester went on. 'I may live to seventy, and 1 may become – what does he call it – a distinguished author. I don't know and I don't care. But whatever happens in the future, nothing will bring back the book which was burnt.'

The Bishop did not speak. He dared not.

'If I had a child,' Hester continued in the exhausted voice with which he was becoming familiar, 'and it died, I might have ten more, beautiful and clever and affectionate, but they would not replace the one I had lost. Only if it were a child,' a little tremor broke the dead level of the passionless voice, 'I should meet it again in heaven. There is the resurrection of the body for the children of the body, but there is no resurrection that I ever heard of for the children of the brain.'[338]

Hester held her thin right hand with its disfigured first finger to the fire.

'A great writer who had married and had children whom she worshipped, once told me that the pang of motherhood is that even your children don't seem your very own. They are often more like some one else than their parents, perhaps the spinster sister-in-law, whom every one dislikes, or some entire alien. Look at Regie. He is just like me, which must be a great trial to Minna. And they grow up bewildering their parents at every turn by characteristics they don't understand. But she said the spiritual children, the books, are really ours.'

'If you were other than you are,' said Hester, after a long pause, 'you would reprove me for worshipping my own work. I suppose love is worship. I loved it for itself, not for anything it was to bring me. That is what people like Dr. Brown don't understand. It was part of myself. But it was the better part. The side of me which loves success, and which he is always appealing to, had no hand in it. My one prayer was that I might be worthy to write it, that it might not suffer by contact with me. I spent myself upon it.' Hester's voice sank. 'I knew what I was doing. I joyfully spent my health, my eyesight, my very life upon it. I was impelled to do it by what you perhaps will call a blind instinct, what I, poor simpleton and dupe, believed at the time to be nothing less than the will of God.'

'You will think so again,' said the Bishop, 'when you realise that the book has left its mark and influence upon your character. It has taught you a great deal. The mere fact of writing it has strengthened you. The outward and visible form is dead, but its spirit lives on in you. You will realise this presently.'

'Shall I? On the contrary, the only thing I realise is that it is not God who is mocked, but His foolish children who try to do His bidding. It seems He is not above putting a lying spirit in the mouth of his prophets.[339] Do you think I still blame poor James for his bonfire, or his jealous little wife who wanted to get rid of me? Why should I? They acted up to their lights as your beloved Jock did when he squeezed the life out of that rabbit in Westhope Park. In all those days when I did not say anything, it was because I felt I had been deceived. I had done my part. God had not done His. He should have seen to it that the book was not destroyed. You prayed by me once when you thought I was unconscious. I heard all right. I should have laughed if I could, but it was too much trouble.'

'These thoughts will pass away with your illness,' said the Bishop. 'You are like a man who has had a blow, who staggers about giddy and dazed, and sees the pavement rising up to strike him. The pavement is firm under his feet all the time.'

'Half of me knows in a dim blind way that God is the same always,' said Hester, 'while the other half says "Curse God and die."'

'That is the giddiness, the vertigo after the shock.'

'Is it? I dare say you are right. But I don't care either way.'

'Why trouble your mind about it, or about anything?'

'Because I have a feeling, indeed it would be extraordinary if I had not, for Dr. Brown is always rubbing it in, that I ought to meet my trouble bravely, and not sink down under it, as he thinks I am doing now. He says others have suffered more than I have. I know that, for I have been with them. It seems,' said

Hester, with the ghost of a smile, 'that there is an etiquette about these things, just as the blinds are drawn up after a funeral. The moment has come for me, but I have not drawn up my blinds.'

'You will draw them up presently.'

'I would draw them up now,' said Hester, looking at him steadily, 'if I could. I owe it to you and Rachel to try, and I have tried, but I can't.'

The Bishop's cheek paled a little.

'Take your own time,' he said, but his heart sank.

He saw a little boat with torn sail and broken rudder, drifting on to a lee shore.

'I seem to have been living at a great strain for the last year,' said Hester. 'I don't know one word from another now, but I think I mean concentration. That means holding your mind to one place, doesn't it? Well, now, something seems to have broken, and I can't fix it to anything any more. I can talk to you and Rachel for a few minutes if I hold my mind tight, but I can't really attend, and directly I am alone or you leave off speaking, my mind gets loose from my body and wanders away to an immense distance, to long dreary desert places. And then if you come in I make a great effort to bring it back, and to open my eyes, because if I don't you think I'm ill. You don't mind if I shut them now, do you, because I've explained about them, and holding them open does tire me so. I wish they could be propped open. And – my mind gets further and further away every day. I hope you and Rachel won't think I am giving way if – sometime – I really can't bring it back any longer.'

'Dear Hester, no.'

'I will not talk any more then. If you and Rachel understand, that is all that matters. I used to think so many things mattered, but I don't now. And don't think I'm grieving about the book while I'm lying still. I have grieved, but it is over. I'm too tired to be glad or sorry about anything any more.'

Hester lay back spent and grey among her pillows.

The Bishop roused her to take the stimulant put ready near at hand, and then sat a long time watching her. She seemed unconscious of his presence. At last the nurse came in, and he went out silently, and returned to his study. Rachel was waiting there to hear the result of the interview.

'I can do nothing,' he said. 'I have no power to help her. After forty years ministry I have not a word to say to her. She is beyond human aid, at least she is beyond mine.'

'You think she will die?'

'I do not see what is going to happen to prevent it, but I am certain it might be prevented.'

'You could not rouse her?'

'No, she discounted anything I could have said, by asking me not to say it. That is the worst of Hester. The partition between her mind and that of other people is so thin that she sees what they are thinking about. Thank God, Rachel, that you are not cursed with the artistic temperament! That is why she has never married. She sees too much. I am not a matchmaker, but if I had had to take the responsibility, I should have married her at seventeen to Lord Newhaven.'

'You know he asked her?'

'No, I did not know it.'

'It was a long time ago, when first she came out. Lady Susan was anxious for it, and pressed her. I sometimes think if she had been given time, and if her aunt had let her alone – but he married within the year. But what are we to do about Hester? Dr. Brown says something must be done, or she will sink in a decline. I would give my life for her, but I can do nothing. I have tried.'

'So have I,' said the Bishop. 'But it has come to this. We have got to trust the one person whom we always show we tacitly distrust by trying to take matters out of His hands. We must trust God. So far we have strained ourselves to keep Hester alive, but she is past our help now. She is in none the worse case for that. We are her two best friends save one. We must leave her to the best Friend of all. God has her in His hand. For the moment the greater love holds her away from the less, like the mother who takes her sick child into her arms, apart from the other children who are playing round her. Hester is in God's keeping, and that is enough for us. And now take a turn in the garden, Rachel. You are too much indoors. I am going out on business.'

When Rachel had left him the Bishop opened his despatch box, and took out a letter.

It was directed to Lady Newhaven.

'I promised to give it into her own hand a month after his death, whenever that might happen to be,' he said to himself. 'There was some trouble between them. I hope she won't confide it to me. Anyhow, I must go and get it over. I wish I did not dislike her so much. I shall advise her not to read it till I am gone.'

CHAPTER XLIX

The mouse fell from the ceiling, and the cat cried 'Allah!'
                                                              Syrian Proverb.

THAT help should come through such a recognised channel as a Bishop could surprise no one, least of all Lady Newhaven, who had had the greatest faith in the clergy all her life, but, nevertheless, so overwhelmed was she by despair and its physical sensations, that she very nearly refused to see the Bishop when he called. Her faith even in lawn sleeves momentarily tottered. Who would show her any good? Poor Lady Newhaven was crushed into a state of prostration so frightful that we must not blame her if she felt that even an Archbishop would have been powerless to help her.

She had thought, after the engagement was announced, of rushing up to London and insisting on seeing Hugh; but always, after she had looked out the trains, her courage had shrunk back at the last moment. There had been a look on Hugh's face during that last momentary meeting which she could not nerve herself to see again. She had been to London already once to see him without success.

She knew Rachel was at the Palace at Southminster nursing Hester, and twice she had ordered the carriage to drive over to see her, and make a desperate appeal to her to give up Hugh. But she knew that she should fail. And Rachel would triumph over her. Women always did over a defeated rival. Lady Newhaven had not gone.

The frightful injustice of it all wrung Lady Newhaven's heart to the point of agony. To see her own property deliberately stolen from her in the light of day, as it were in the very market place, before everybody, without being able to raise a finger to regain him! It was intolerable. For she loved Hugh as far as she was capable of loving anything. And her mind had grown round the idea that he was hers as entirely as a tree will grow round a nail fastened into it.

And now he was to marry Rachel, and soon.

Let no one think they know pain until they know jealousy.

But when the Bishop sent up a second time, asking to see her on business, she consented.

It was too soon to see callers, of course. But a Bishop was different. And how could she refuse to admit him when she had admitted that odious Captain Pratt only four days before. She hoped no one would become aware of that fact. It was as well for her that she could not hear the remarks of Selina and Ada Pratt, as they skated on the frozen meadows with half, not the better-half, of Middleshire.

'Poor Vi Newhaven. Yes, she won't see a creature. She saw Algy for a few minutes last week, but then he is an old friend, and does not count. He said she was quite heartbroken. He was quite upset himself. He was so fond of Ted Newhaven.'

The Bishop would not even sit down. He said he was on the way to a confirmation, and added that he had been entrusted with a letter for her, and held it towards her.

'It is my husband's handwriting,' she said, drawing back with instinctive fear.

'It is from your husband,' said the Bishop gently, softening somewhat at the sight of the ravages which despair had made in the lovely face since he had last seen it. 'He asked me to give it into your own hand a month after his death.'

'Then he told you that –'

'He told me nothing, and I wish to hear nothing.'

'I should like to confess all to you, to feel myself absolved,' said Lady Newhaven in a low voice, the letter in her trembling hand.

He looked at her, and he saw that she would not say all. She would arrange details to suit herself, and would omit the main point altogether, whatever it might be, if, as was more than probable it told against herself. He would at least save her from the hypocrisy of a half-confession.

'If in a month's time you wish to make a full confession to me,' he said, 'I will hear it. But I solemnly charge you in the meanwhile to speak to no one of this difficulty between you and your husband. Whatever it may have been, it is past. If he sinned against you, he is dead, and the least you can do is to keep silence. If you wronged him' – Lady Newhaven shook her head vehemently – 'If you wronged him,' repeated the Bishop, his face hardening, 'be silent for the sake of the children. It is the only miserable reparation you can make him.'

'You don't understand,' she said feebly.

'I know that he was a kindly, gentle-natured man, and that he died a hard and bitter one,' said the Bishop. 'God knows what is in that letter, but your husband said it would be of the greatest comfort and assistance to you in a difficulty which he foresaw for you. I will leave you to read it.'

And he left the room.

The early December twilight was creeping over everything. Lady Newhaven took the letter to the window, and after several futile attempts succeeded in opening it.

It ran as follows:

'It is irreligious to mourn too long for the dead. "I shall go to him, but he shall not return to me," II. Sam. xii. 23.[340] In the meanwhile, until you rejoin me, I trust you will remember that it is my especial wish that you should allow one who is in every way worthy of you to console you for my loss, who will make you as happy as you both deserve to be. That I died by my own hand you and your so-called friend Miss West are of course aware. That "the one love of your life" drew the short lighter you are perhaps not aware. I waited two days to see if he would fulfil the compact, and as he did not – I never thought he would – I retired in his place. I present to you this small piece of information as a wedding-present, which, if adroitly handled, may add to the harmony of domestic life. And if by any chance he should have conceived the dastardly, the immoral idea of deserting you in favour of some mercenary marriage – of which I rather suspect him – you will find this piece of information invaluable in restoring his allegiance at once. He is yours by every sacred tie, and no treacherous female friend must wrest him from you.

'Your late husband,

'NEWHAVEN.'

Lady Newhaven put the letter in her pocket, and then fainted away, with her fair head on the window-ledge.

CHAPTER L

There cannot be a pinch in death more sharp than this is.[341]

THE Bishop's sister, Miss Keane, whose life was a perpetual orgy of mothers' meetings and G.F.S. gatherings, was holding a district visitors' working party in the drawing-room at the Palace. The ladies knitted and stitched, while one of their number heaped fuel on the flame of their enthusiasm by reading aloud the 'History of the Diocese of Southminster.'

Miss Keane took but little heed of the presence of Rachel and Hester in her brother's house. Those who work mechanically on fixed lines seem as a rule to miss the pith of life. She was kind when she remembered them, but her heart was where her treasure was – namely, in her escritoire,[342] with her list of Bible classes, and servants' choral unions, and the long roll of contributors to the guild of work which she herself had started.

When she had been up to Hester's room, invariably at hours when Hester could not see her, and when she had entered Rachel's sledge-hammer subscriptions in her various account-books, her attention left her visitors. She considered them superficial, and wondered how it was that her brother could find time to spend hours talking to both of them, while he had rarely a moment in which to address her chosen band in the drawing-room. She was one of those persons who find life a very prosaic affair, quite unlike the fiction she occasionally read.

She often remarked that nothing except the commonplace happened. Certainly she never observed anything else.

So Hester lay in the room above halting feebly between two opinions, whether to live or to die, and Rachel sat in the Bishop's study beneath, waiting to make tea for him on his return from the confirmation.

If she did not make it, no one else did. Instead of ringing for it he went without it.

Rachel watched the sun set – a red ball dropping down a frosty sky. It was the last day of the year. The new year was bringing her everything.

'Good-bye, good-bye,' she said, looking at the last rim of the sun as he sank. And she remembered other years when she had watched the sun set on the last day of December, when life had been difficult – how difficult!

'If Hester could only get better I should have nothing left to wish for,' she said, and she prayed the more fervently for her friend, because she knew that even if Hester died, life would still remain beautiful; the future without her would still be flooded with happiness.

'A year ago if Hester had died I should have had nothing left to live for,' she said to herself. 'Now this newcomer, this man whom I have known barely six months, fills my whole life. Are other women as narrow as I am? Can they care only for one person at a time like me? Ah, Hester! forgive me, I can't help it.'

Hugh was coming in presently. He had been in that morning, and the Bishop had met him, and had asked him to come in again to tea. Rachel did not know what the Bishop thought of him, but he had managed to see a good deal of Hugh.

Rachel waited as impatiently as most of us, when our happiness lingers by us, loth to depart.

At last she heard the footman bringing some one across the hall.

Would Hugh's coming ever become a common thing? Would she ever be able to greet him without this tumult of emotion, ever be able to take his hand without turning giddy on the sheer verge of bliss.

The servant announced, 'Lady Newhaven.'

The two women stood looking at each other. Rachel saw the marks of suffering on the white face, and her own became as white. Her eyes fell guiltily before Lady Newhaven's.

'Forgive me,' she said.

'Forgive you?' said Lady Newhaven in a hoarse voice. 'It is no use asking me for forgiveness.'

'You are right,' said Rachel, recovering herself, and meeting Lady Newhaven's eyes fully. 'But what is the use of coming here to abuse me? You might have spared yourself and me this at least. It will only exhaust you and – wound me.'

'You must give him up,' said Lady Newhaven, her hands fumbling under her crape cloak. 'I've come to tell you that you must let him go.'

The fact that Hugh had drawn the short lighter, and had not taken the consequences, did not affect Lady Newhaven's feelings towards him in the least, but she was vaguely aware that somehow it would affect Rachel's, and now it would be Rachel's turn to suffer.

Rachel paused a moment, and then said slowly:

'He does not wish to be let go.'

'He is mine.'

'He was yours once,' said Rachel, her face turning from white to grey. That wound was long in healing. 'But he is mine now.'

'Rachel, you cannot be bad all through.' Lady Newhaven was putting the constraint upon herself which that tightly clutched paper, that poisoned weapon in reserve, enabled her to assume. For Hugh's sake she would only use it if other means failed. 'You must know that you ought to look upon him as a married man. Don't you see?' – wildly – 'that we *must* marry, to put right what was wrong. He owes it to me. People always do.'

'Yes, they generally do,' said Rachel; 'but I don't see how it makes the wrong right.'

'I look upon Hugh as my husband,' said Lady Newhaven.

'So do I.'

'Rachel, he loves me. He is only marrying you for your money.'

'I will risk that.'

'I implore you on my knees to give him back to me.'

And Lady Newhaven knelt down with bare white outstretched hands. (Tableau number one. New Series.)

Rachel shrank back involuntarily.

'Listen, Violet,' she said, 'and get up. I will not speak until you get up.' Lady Newhaven obeyed. 'If I gave back Hugh to you a hundred times it would not make him love you any more, or make him marry you. I am not keeping him from you. This marriage is his own doing. Oh! Violet, I'm not young and pretty. I've no illusions about myself; but I believe he really does love me, in spite of that, and I know I love him.'

'I don't believe it,' said Lady Newhaven. 'I mean about him. Not about you, of course.'

'Here he is. Let him decide,' said Rachel.

Hugh came in unannounced. Upon his grave face there was that concentrated look of happiness which has settled in the very deep of the heart, and gleams up into the eyes.

His face changed painfully. He glanced from one woman to the other. Rachel was sorry for him. She would fain have spared him, but she could not.

'Hugh,' she said gently, her steadfast eyes resting on him, 'Lady Newhaven and I were talking of you. I think it would be best if she heard from your own lips what she naturally will not believe from mine.'

'I will never believe,' said Lady Newhaven, 'that you will desert me now, that all the past is nothing to you, and that you will cast me aside for another woman.'

Hugh looked at her steadily. Then he went up to Rachel, and taking her hand, raised it to his lips. There was in his manner a boundless reverent adoration that was to Lady Newhaven's jealousy as a match to gunpowder.

Rachel kept his hand.

'Are you sure you want him, Rachel?' gasped Lady Newhaven, holding convulsively to a chair for support. 'He has cast me aside. He will cast you aside next, for he is a coward and a traitor. Are you sure you want to marry him? His hands are red with blood. He murdered my husband.'

Rachel's hand tightened on Hugh's.

'It was an even chance,' she said. 'Those who draw lots must abide by the drawing.'

'It was an even chance,' shrieked Lady Newhaven. 'But who drew the short lighter, tell me that? Who refused to fulfil his part when the time was up? Tell me that.'

'You are mad,' said Rachel.

'I can prove it,' said Lady Newhaven, holding out the letter in her shaking hands. 'You may read it, Rachel. I can trust you. Not him, he would burn it. It is from Edward; look, you know his writing, written to tell me that he,' pointing at Hugh, 'had drawn the short lighter, but that, as he had not killed himself when the time came, he, Edward, did so instead. That was why he was late. We always wondered, Rachel, why he was two days late. Read it. Read it.'

'I will not read it,' said Rachel, pushing away the paper. 'I do not believe a word of it.'

'You shall believe it. Ask him to deny it, if he can.'

'You need not trouble to deny it,' said Rachel, looking full at Hugh.

The world held only her and him. And as Hugh looked into her eyes his soul rose up and scaled the heights above it till it stood beside hers.

There is a sacred place where, if we follow close in love's footsteps, we see him lay aside his earthly quiver and his bitter arrows, and turn to us as he is, with the light of God upon him, one with us as one with God. In that pure light lies cease to be. We know them no more, neither remember them, for love and truth are one.

Hugh strode across to Lady Newhaven, took the letter from her, and threw it into the heart of the fire. Then he turned to Rachel.

'I drew the short lighter,' he said. 'I meant to take the consequences at first, but when the time came – I did not. Partly I was afraid, and partly I could not leave you.'

If Lady Newhaven yearned for revenge she had it then. They had both forgotten her. But she saw Rachel's eyes change as the eyes of a man at the stake might change when the fire reached him.[343] She shrank back from the agony in them. Hugh's face became pinched and thin as a dead man's. A moment ago he saw no consequences. He saw only that he could not lie to her. His mind fell headlong from its momentary foothold. What mad impulse had betrayed him to his ruin?

'You drew the short lighter, and you let me think all the time that he had,' said Rachel, her voice almost inaudible in its fierce passion. 'You drew it, and you let him die instead of you, as any one who knew him would know he would. And when he was dead you came to me, and kept me in ignorance even – that time – when I said I trusted you.'

The remembrance of that meeting was too much.

Rachel turned her eyes on Lady Newhaven who was watching her terror-stricken.

'I said I would not give him up, but I will,' she said violently. 'You can take him if you want him. What was it you said to me, Hugh? That if you had drawn the short lighter you would have had to abide by it. Yes, that was it. Your whole intercourse with me has been one lie from first to last. You were right, Violet, when you said he ought to marry you. It will be another lie on the top of all the others.'

'It was what Edward wished,' faltered his widow. 'He says so in the letter that has just been burnt.'

'Lord Newhaven wished it,' said Rachel, looking at the miserable man between them. 'Poor Lord Newhaven! First his honour. Then his life. You have taken everything he had. But there are still his shoes.'[344]

'Rachel!' said Hugh suddenly, and he fell on his knees before her, clasping the hem of her gown.

She pushed him violently from her, tearing her gown in releasing it from his frenzied grasp.

'Leave me,' she whispered. Her voice was almost gone. 'Coward and liar, I will have nothing more to do with you.'

He got upon his feet somehow. The two grey desperate faces spent with passion faced each other. They were past speech.

He read his death warrant in her merciless eyes. She looked at the despair in his without flinching.

He stood a moment, and then feeling his way, like one half blind, left the room, unconsciously pushing aside Lady Newhaven whom both had forgotten.

She gave one terrified glance at Rachel, and slipped out after him.

CHAPTER LI

I thought, 'Now, if I had been a woman, such
As God made women, to save men by love –
By just my love I might have saved this man.'
ELIZABETH BARRETT BROWNING.[345]

'HAS Lady Newhaven been here?' said the Bishop, coming into the study, his hands full of papers. 'I thought I saw her carriage driving away as I came up.'

'She has been here.'

The Bishop looked up suddenly, his attention arrested by Rachel's voice. There is a white heat of anger that mimics the pallor of a fainting fit. The Bishop thought she was about to swoon, until he saw her eyes. Those gentle faithful eyes were burning. He shrank as one who sees the glare of fire raging inside familiar windows.

'My poor child,' he said, and he sat down heavily in his leather armchair.

Rachel still stood. She looked at him, and her lips moved, but no sound came forth.

The Bishop looked intently at her.

'Where is Scarlett?' he said.

'Hugh is gone,' she said stammering. 'I have broken off my engagement with him. He will never come back.'

And she fell suddenly on her knees, and hid her convulsed face against the arm of a chair.

The Bishop did not move. He waited for this paroxysm of anger to subside. He had never seen Rachel angry before in all the years he had known her, but he watched her without surprise. Only stupid people think that coal cannot burn as fiercely as tow.

She remained a long time on her knees, her face hidden. The Bishop did not hurry her. At last she began to sob silently, shuddering from head to foot.

Then he came and sat down near her, and took the cold clenched hands in his.

'Rachel, tell me,' he said gently.

She tried to pull her hands away; but he held them firmly. He obliged her to look up at him. She raised her fierce disfigured face for a moment, and then let it fall on his hands and hers.

'I am a wicked woman,' she said. 'Don't trouble about me. I'm not worth it. I thought I would have kept all suffering from him, but now – if I could make him suffer – I would.'

'I have no doubt he is suffering.'

'Not enough. Not like me. And I loved him and trusted him. And he is false, too, like that other man I loved, like you, only I have not found you out yet, like Hester, like all the rest. I will never trust any one again. I will never be deceived again. This is – the – second time.'

And Rachel broke into a passion of tears.

The Bishop released her hands, and felt for his own handkerchief.

Then he waited, praying silently. The clock had made a long circuit before she raised herself.

'I am very selfish,' she said looking with compunction at the kind tried face. 'I ought to have gone to my room instead of breaking down here. Dear Bishop, forgive me. It is past now. I shall not give way again.'

'Will you make me some tea?' he said.

She made the tea with shaking hands, and awkward half-blind movements. It was close on dinner time, but she did not notice it. He obliged her to drink some, and then he settled himself in his leather armchair. He went over his engagements for the evening. In half an hour he ought to be dining with Canon Glynn to meet an old college friend. At eleven he had arranged to see a young clergyman whose conscience was harrying him. He wrote a note on his knee without moving saying he could not come, and touched the bell at his elbow. When the servant had taken the note, he relapsed into the depths of his armchair, and sipped his tea.

'I think, Rachel,' he said at last, 'that I ought to tell you that I partly guess at your reason for breaking off your engagement. I have known for some time that there was trouble between the Newhavens. From what Lady Newhaven said to me to day, and from the fact that she has been here, and that immediately after seeing her you broke your engagement with Scarlett, I must come to the conclusion that Scarlett had been the cause of this trouble.'

Rachel had regained her composure. Her face was white and hard.

'You are right,' she said. 'He was at one time – her lover.'

'And you consider, in consequence, that he is unfit to become your husband?'

'No. He told me about it before he asked me to marry him. I accepted him, knowing it.'

'Then he was trying to retrieve himself. He acted towards you, at any rate, like an honourable man.'

Rachel laughed. 'So I thought at the time.'

'If you accepted him, knowing about his past, I don't see why you should have thrown him over. One dishonourable action sincerely repented does not make a dishonourable man.'

'I did not know all,' said Rachel. 'I do now.'

The Bishop looked into the fire.

Her next words surprised him.

'You really cared for Lord Newhaven, did you not?'

'I did.'

'Then as you know the one thing he risked his life to conceal for the sake of his children, namely, his wife's misconduct, I think I had better tell you the rest.'

So Rachel told him in harsh bald language the story of the drawing of lots, and how she and Lady Newhaven had remined ignorant as to which had drawn the short lighter. How Hugh had drawn it; how when the time came he had failed to fulfil the agreement; how two days later Lord Newhaven had killed himself; and how she and Lady Newhaven had both, of course, concluded that Lord Newhaven must have drawn the short lighter.

Rachel went on, her hard voice shaking a little.

'Hugh had told me that he had had an entanglement with a married woman. I knew it long before he spoke of it, but just because he risked losing me by owning it I loved and trusted him all the more. I thought he was, at any rate, an upright man. After Lord Newhaven's death he asked me to marry him, and I accepted him. And when we were talking quietly one day' – Rachel's face became, if possible, whiter than before – 'I told him that I knew of the drawing of lots. (He thought no one knew of it except the dead man and himself.) And I told him that he must not blame himself for Lord Newhaven's death. He had brought it on himself. I said to him' – Rachel's voice trembled more and more – '"It was an even chance. You might have drawn the short lighter yourself." And – he – said that if he had, he should have had to abide by it.'

The Bishop shaded his eyes with his hand. It seemed cruel to look at Rachel, as it is cruel to watch a man drown.

'And how do you know he did draw it?' he said.

'It seems Lord Newhaven left his wife a letter, which she has only just received, telling her so. She brought it here to-day to show me.'

'Ah! A letter! And you read it?'

'No,' said Rachel, scornfully, 'I did not read it. I did not believe a word she said about it. Hugh was there, and I told him I trusted him; and he took the letter from her, and put it in the fire.'

'And did he not contradict it?'

'No. He said it was true. He has lied to me over and over again, but I saw he was speaking the truth for once.'

There was a long silence.

'I don't know how other people regard those things,' said Rachel at last, less harshly – she was gradually recovering herself – 'but I know to me it was much worse that he could deceive me than that he should have been Lady Newhaven's lover. I did feel that dreadfully. I had to choke down my jealousy when he kissed me. He had kissed her first. He had made that side of his love common and profane;[346] but the other side remained. I clung to that. I believed he really loved me, and that supported me and enabled me to forgive him, though men don't know what that forgiveness costs us. Only the walls of our rooms know that. But it seems to me much worse to have failed me on that other side as well – to have deceived me – to have told me a lie – just when – just when we were talking intimately.'

'It was infinitely worse,' said the Bishop.

'And it was the action of a coward to draw lots in the first instance if he did not mean to abide by the drawing, and the action of a traitor, once they were drawn, not to abide by them. But yet, if he had told me – if he had only told me the whole truth – I loved him so entirely that I would have forgiven – *even that*. But whenever I alluded to it, he lied.'

'He was afraid of losing you.'

'He has lost me by his deceit. He would not have lost me if he had told me the truth. I think – I know – that I could have got over anything, forgiven anything, even his cowardice, if he had only admitted it and been straightforward with me. A little plain dealing was all I asked, but – I did not get it.'

The Bishop looked sadly at her. Straightforwardness is so seldom the first requirement a woman makes of the man she loves. Women, as a rule, regard men and their conduct only from the point of view of their relation to women – as sons, as husbands, as fathers. Yet Rachel, it seemed, could forgive Hugh's sin against her as a woman, but not his further sin against her as a friend.

'Yet it seems he did speak the truth at last,' he said.

'Yes.'

'And after he had destroyed the letter, which was the only proof against him.'

'Yes.'

Another silence.

'I am glad you have thrown him over,' said the Bishop slowly, 'for you never loved him.'

'I deceived myself in that case,' said Rachel bitterly. 'My only fear was that I loved him too much.'

The Bishop's face had become fixed and stern.

'Listen to me, Rachel,' he said. 'You fell desperately in love with an inferior man. He is charming, refined, well-bred, and with a picturesque mind, but that is all. He is inferior. He is by nature shallow and hard (the two generally go together), without moral backbone, the kind of man who never faces a difficulty, who always flinches when it comes to the point, the stuff out of which liars and cowards are made. His one redeeming quality is his love for you. I have seen men in love before. I have never seen a man care more for a woman than he cares for you. His love for you has taken entire possession of him, and by it he will sink or swim.'

The Bishop paused. Rachel's face worked.

'He deceived you,' said the Bishop, 'not because he wished to deceive you, but because he was in a horrible position, and because his first impulse of love was to keep you at any price. But his love for you was raising him even while he deceived you. Did he spend sleepless nights because for months he vilely deceived Lord Newhaven? No. Rectitude was not in him. His conscience was not awake. But I tell you, Rachel, he has suffered like a man on the rack from deceiving you. I knew by his face as soon as I saw him that he was undergoing some great mental strain. I did not understand it, but I do now.'

Rachel's mind, always slow, moved, stumbled to its bleeding feet.

'It was remorse,' she said, turning her face away.

'It was not remorse. It was repentance. Remorse is bitter. Repentance is humble. His love for you has led him to it. Not your love for him, Rachel, which breaks down at the critical moment; his love for you which has brought him for the first time to the perception of the higher life, to the need of God's forgiveness, which I know from things he has said, has made him long to lead a better life, one worthier of you.'

'Don't,' said Rachel. 'I can't bear it.'

The Bishop rose, and stood facing her.

'And at last,' he went on,' at last, in a moment, when you showed your full trust and confidence in him, he shook off for an instant the clogs of the nature which he brought into the world, and rose to what he had never been before – your equal. And his love transcended the lies that love itself on its lower plane had prompted. He reached the place where he could no longer lie to you. And then, though his whole future happiness depended on one more lie, he spoke the truth.'

Rachel put out her hand as if to ward off what was coming.

'And how did you meet him the first time he spoke the truth to you?' continued the Bishop inexorably. 'You say you loved him, and yet – you spurned him from you, you thrust him down into hell. You stooped to him in the beginning. He was nothing until your fancied love fell upon him. And then you break him. It is women like you who do more harm in the world than the bad ones. The harm that poor fool Lady Newhaven did him is as nothing compared to the harm you have done him. You were his god, and you have deserted him. And you say you loved him. May God preserve men from the love of women if that is all that a good woman's love is capable of.'

'I can do nothing,' said Rachel hoarsely.

'Do nothing!' said the Bishop fiercely. 'You can do nothing when you are responsible for a man's soul! God will require his soul at your hands. Scarlett gave it into your keeping, and you took it. You had no business to take it if you meant to throw it away. And now you say you can do nothing!'

'What can I do?' said Rachel faintly.

'Forgive him.'

'Forgiveness won't help him. The only forgiveness he would care for is to marry me.'

'Of course. It is the only way you can forgive him.'

Rachel turned away. Her stubborn quivering face showed a frightful conflict. The Bishop watched her.

'My child,' he said gently, 'we all say we follow Christ, but most of us only follow Him and His cross – part of the way. When we are told that our Lord bore our sins, and was wounded for our transgressions, I suppose that meant that He felt as if they were His own in His great love for us.[347] But when you shrink from bearing your fellow creature's transgressions, it shows that your love is small.'

Rachel was silent.

'If you really love him you will forgive him.'

Rachel clenched and unclenched her hands.

'You are appealing to a nobility and goodness which are not in me,' she said stubbornly.

'I appeal to nothing but your love. If you really love him you will forgive him.'

'He has broken my heart.'

'I thought that was it. It is yourself you are thinking of. But what is he suffering at this moment? You do not know or care. Where is he now, that poor man who loves you? Rachel, if you had ever known despair, you would not thrust a fellow creature down into it.'

'I have known it,' said Rachel hoarsely.

'Were not you deserted once? You were deserted to very little purpose, if after that you can desert another. Go back in your mind, and – remember. Where you stood once he stands now. You and his sin have put him there. You and his sin have tied him to his stake. Will you range yourself for ever on the side of his sin? Will you stand by and see him perish?'

Silence; like the silence round a death-bed.

'He is in a great strait. Only love can save him.'

Rachel flung out her arms with an inarticulate cry.

'I will forgive him,' she said. 'I will forgive him.'

CHAPTER LII

Les âmes dont j'aurai besoin,
Et les étoiles sont trop loin;
Je mourrai dans un coin.[348]

How Hugh shook off Lady Newhaven when she followed him out of the Palace he did not know. There had been some difficulty. She had spoken to him, had urged something upon him. But he had got rid of her somehow, and had found himself sitting in his bedroom at the Southminster Hotel. Anything to be alone! He had felt that was the one thing in life to attain. But now that he was alone solitude suddenly took monstrous and hideous proportions, and became a horror to flee from. He could not bear the face of a fellow creature. He could not bear this ghoul of solitude. There was no room for him between these great millstones. They pressed upon him till he felt they were crushing him to death between them. In vain he endeavoured to compose himself, to recollect himself. But exhaustion gradually did for him what he could not do for himself.

Rachel had thrown him over. He had always known she would, and – she had.

They were to have been married in a few weeks; three weeks and one day. He marked a day off every morning when he waked. He had thought of her as his wife till the thought had become part of himself. Its roots were in his inmost being. He tore it out now, and looked at it apart from himself, as a man bleeding and shuddering looks upon a dismembered limb.

The sweat broke from Hugh's forehead. The waiting and daily parting had seemed unbearable, that short waiting of a few weeks. Now she would never be his. That long, evergrowing hunger of the heart would never be appeased. She had taken herself away, taking away with her her dear hands and her faithful eyes and the low voice, the very sound of which brought comfort and peace. They were his hands and eyes. She had given them to him. And now she had wrenched them away again, those faithful eyes had seared him with their scorn, those white hands against which he had leaned his forehead, had thrust him violently from her. He could not live without her. This was death, to be parted from her.

'I can't, Rachel, I can't,' said Hugh, over and over again. What was any lesser death, compared to this, compared to her contempt?

She would never come back. She despised him. She would never love him any more. He had told her that it must be a dream that she could love him, and that he should wake. And she had said it was all quite true. How sweetly she had said it. But it was a dream after all, and he *had* waked – in torment. Life as long as he lived would be like this moment.

'I will not bear it,' he said suddenly, with the frantic instinct of escape which makes a man climb out of a burning house over a window ledge. Far down is the pavement, quiet, impassive, deadly. But behind is the blast of the furnace. Panic staggers between the two and – jumps.

'I will not bear it,' said Hugh, tears of anguish welling up into his eyes.

He had not only lost her, but he had lost himself. That better humble earnest self had gone away with Rachel, and he was thrust back on the old false cowardly self whom since she had loved him he had abhorred. He had disowned it. He had cast it off. Now it enveloped him again like a shirt of fire, and a voice within him said, 'This is the real you. You deceived yourself for a moment. But this is the real you, the liar, the coward, the traitor, who will live with you again for ever.'

'I am forsaken,' said Hugh. He repeated the words over and over again. 'Forsaken. Forsaken.' And he looked round for a way of escape.

Somewhere in the back of his mind a picture hung which he had seen once and never looked at again. He turned and looked at it now, as a man turns and looks at a picture on the wall behind him.

He saw it again, the still upturned face of the little lake among its encircling trees, as he had seen it that day when he and Doll came suddenly upon it in the woods. What had it to do with him? He had escaped from it once. *He understood now.*

Who, that has once seen it, has ever forgotten it, the look that deep water takes when life is unbearable! 'Come down to me among my tall water plants,' it says. 'I am a refuge, a way of escape. This horror and nightmare of life cannot reach you in my bosom. Come down to me. I promise nothing but to lay my cool hand upon the fire in your brain, and that the world shall release its clutch upon you, the world which promises and will not keep its promises. I will keep mine.'

Hugh's mind wavered, as the flame of a candle wavers in a sudden draught. So had it wavered once in the fear of death, and he had yielded to that fear. So it wavered now in a greater fear, the fear of life, and he yielded to that fear.

He caught up his hat, and went out.

It was dark, and he hit against the people in the feebly lighted streets as he hurried past. How hot it was! How absurd to see those gathered heaps of snow, and the muffled figures of men and women.

Presently he had left the town, and was in the open country. Where was he going along this interminable road in this dim snow light?

The night was very still. The spirit of the frost stooped over the white face of the earth. The long homely lines of meadow and wold and hedgerow showed like the austere folds of a shroud.

Hugh walked swiftly, looking neither to right nor left. The fire in his brain mounted, mounted. The moon, entangled in a dim thicket, got up behind him.

At last he stopped short. That farm on the right! He had seen it before. Yes. That was Greenfields. Doll had pointed it out to him when they had walked on that Sunday afternoon to Beaumere. They had left the road here, and had taken to the fields. There was the gate. Hugh opened it. Crack had been lost here and had rejoined them in the wood. The field was empty. A path like a crease ran across it.

He knew the way. It was the only way of escape from this shadow in front of him, this other self who had come back to him, and torn Rachel from him, and made her hate him. She loved him really. She was faithful. She would never have forsaken him. But she had mistaken this evil creeping shadow for him, and he had not been able to explain. But she would understand presently. He would make it all very clear and plain, and she would love him again, when he had got rid of this other Hugh. He would take him down and drown him in Beaumere. It was the only way to get rid of him. And he, the real Hugh, would get safely through. He had done it once, and he knew. He should stifle and struggle for a little while. There was a turn exceeding sharp to be passed, but he should reach that place of peace beyond, as he had done before, and find Rachel waiting for him, her arms round him again.

'It is the only way,' he said over and over again, 'the only way.'

He reached the wood. The moon was up now, and smote white and sharp down the long winding aisle of the cathedral which God builds Him in every forest glade, where the hoar frost and the snow held now their solemn service of praise.

Hugh saw the little light of the keeper's cottage, and instinctively edged his way to the left. He was pressed for time. A wheel was turning in his head, so quickly, so quickly in this great heat that, unless he were quicker than it, it would out-distance him altogether.

At last he saw the water, and ran down swiftly towards it. The white tree-trunks were in league against him, and waylaid him, striking him violently. But he struck back, and got through them. They fell behind at last. His shadow was beside him now, short and nimble. He looked round once or twice to make sure it was still with him.

He reached the water's edge and then stopped short, aghast. Where was the water gone? It had deceived him and deserted him, like everything else. It was all hard as iron, one great white sheet of ice stretching away in front of him. He had thought of the little lake as he had last seen it, cool and deep, and with the shadows of the summer trees in it. It was all changed and gone. There was no help here. The way of escape was closed. With a hoarse cry he set off, running across the ice in the direction of the place where he had been nearly drowned before.

It was here, opposite that clump of silver birch. The ice was a different colour here. It tilted and creaked suddenly beneath his feet. He flung himself down upon it and struck it wildly with his fist. 'Let me through,' he stammered. But the ice resisted him. It made an ominous dry crackling as if in mockery. It barely resisted him, but it did resist him. And he had no time, no time. He scrambled to his feet again, and it gave way instantly. The other self pounced suddenly upon him and came through with him, and they struggled furiously together in deep water.

'I must, I must,' gasped Hugh between his clenched teeth.

'You shall not,' said the other self, mad with terror. 'Hold on to the ice.'

Hugh saw his bleeding hands holding tightly to the jagged edge. It broke. He clutched another piece. It broke again. The current was sucking him slowly under the ice. The broken pieces pushed him. One arm was under already, and he could not get it out. The animal horror of a trap seized him. He had not known it would be like this. He was not prepared for this.

The other self fought furiously for life, clutching and tearing at the breaking ice.

'Call,' it said to him, 'while there is still time.'

Hugh set his teeth.

The ice broke in a great piece and tilted heavily against him. It was over one shoulder.

'Call,' said the other self sharply again, 'or you will be under the ice.'

And up to the quiet heaven rose once and again a hoarse wild cry of human agony and despair.

CHAPTER LIII

Ueber allen gipfeln
Ist Ruh;
In allen Wipfeln
Spürest Du
Kaum einen Hauch;
Die Vögelein schweigen im Walde.
Warte nur, balde
Ruhest Du auch.
                    GOETHE.[349]

THE doctor was very late. Rachel, who was going to the Watch Service,[350] waited for the Bishop in the hall till he came out of his study with the curate,[351] who had doubts.

When the young man had left, Rachel said, hesitating:

'I shall not go to the service if Dr. Brown does not arrive before then. Hugh was to have come with us. I don't want him to go all through the night thinking – perhaps if I am prevented going you will see him, and speak a word to him.'

'My dear,' said the Bishop, 'I went across to his rooms two hours ago, directly you went up to Hester.'

He loved Rachel, but he wondered at her lack of imagination.

'Two hours ago! And what did you say to him?'

'I did not see him. I was too late. He was gone.'

'Gone!' said Rachel faintly. 'Where?'

'I do not know. I went up to his rooms. All his things were still there.'

'Where is he now?'

'I do not know.'

The Bishop looked at her compassionately. She had been a long time forgiving him. While she hesitated he had said to her, 'Where is he now?' and she had not understood.

Her face became pinched and livid. She understood now, after the event.

'I am frightened for him,' she said.

The Bishop had been alarmed while she poured out his tea before they began to talk.

'Perhaps he has gone back to London,' she said, her eyes widening with a vague dread.

The Bishop had gone on to the station, and had ascertained that Hugh had not left by the one train which had stopped at Southminster between seven and nine. But he did not add to her anxiety by saying so.

The doctor's brougham,[352] coming at full speed, drew up suddenly at the door.

'There he is at last,' said the Bishop, and before the bell could be rung he opened the door.

A figure was already on the threshold, but it was not Dr. Brown. It was Dick.

'Where is Dr. Brown?' said Rachel and the Bishop simultaneously, looking at the doctor's well known brougham and smoking horses.

'He asked me to come,' said Dick, measuring Rachel with his eye. Then he did as he would be done by, and added slowly. 'He was kept. He was on his way here from Wilderleigh, where one of the servants is ill, and as I was dining there he offered me a lift back. And when we were passing that farm near the wood a man stopped us. He said there had been an accident – some one nearly drowned. I went, too. It turned out to be Scarlett. Dr. Brown remained with him, and sent me to take you to him.'

'Is he dead?' asked Rachel, her eyes never leaving Dick's face.

'No, but he is very ill.'

'I will come now.'

The chaplain[353] came slowly across the hall, laden with books and papers.

'Let Canon Sebright know at once that I cannot take part in the service,' said the Bishop sharply; and he hurried down the steps after Rachel, and got into the carriage with her. Dick turned up the collar of his fur coat, and climbed up beside the coachman.

The carriage turned warily, and then set off at a great pace.

The cathedral loomed up suddenly, all aglow with light within. Out into the night came the dirge of the organ for the dying year.

The Bishop kept his eyes fixed on the pane. The houses were left behind. They were in the country.

'Who is that?' said Rachel suddenly, as a long shadow ran beside them along the white hedgerow.

'It is only Dick. There is a rise in the ground here, and he is running to ease the horses.'

There was a long silence.

'I believe he did it on purpose,' said Rachel at last. 'I forsook him in his great need, and now he has forsaken me.'

'He would never forsake you, Rachel.'

'Not knowingly,' she said. 'I did it knowing. That is the difference between him and me.'

She did not speak again.

For a lifetime, as it seemed to the Bishop, the carriage swayed from side to side of the white road. At last, when he had given up all hope, it turned into a field and jolted heavily over the frozen ruts. Then it came to a standstill.

Rachel was out of the carriage before Dick could get off the box.

She looked at him without speaking, and he led the way swiftly through the silent wood under the moon. The Bishop followed.

The keeper's cottage had a dim yellow glimmer in it. Man's little light looked like a kind of darkness in the great white, all-pervading splendour of the night. The cottage door was open. Dr. Brown was looking out.

Rachel went up to him.

'Where is he?' she said.

He tried to speak; he tried to hold her gently back while he explained something. But he saw she was past explanation, blind and deaf except for one voice, one face.

'Where is he?' she repeated, shaking her head impatiently.

'Here,' said the doctor, and he led her through the kitchen. A man and woman rose up from the fireside as she came in. He opened the door into the little parlour.

On the floor on a mattress lay a tall figure. The head, supported on a pillow, was turned towards the door, the wide eyes were fixed on the candle on the table. The lips moved continually. The hands were picking at the blankets.

For the first moment Rachel did not know him. How could this be Hugh? How could these blank, unrecognising eyes be Hugh's eyes, which had never until now met hers without love?

But it was he. Yes, it was he. She traced the likeness as we do in a man's son to the man himself.

She fell on her knees beside him and took the wandering hands and kissed them.

He looked at her, through her, with those bright unseeing eyes, and the burning hands escaped from hers back to their weary work.

Dick, whose eyes had followed Rachel, turned away biting his lip, and sat down in a corner of the kitchen. The keeper and his wife had slipped away into the little scullery.

The Bishop went up to Dick and put his arm round his shoulders. Two tears of pain were standing in Dick's hawk-eyes. He had seen Rachel kiss Hugh's hands. He ground his heel against the brick floor.

The Bishop understood, and understood, too, the sudden revulsion of feeling.

'Poor chap!' said Dick huskily. 'It's frightful hard luck on him to have to go just when she was to have married him. If it had been me I could not have borne it; but then I would have taken care I was not drowned. I'd have seen to that. But it's frightful hard luck on him, all the same.'

'I suppose he was taking a short cut across the ice.'

'Yes,' said Dick, 'and he got in where any one who knew the look of ice would have known he would be sure to get in. The keeper watched him cross the ice. It was some time before they could get near him to get him out, and it seems there is some injury.'

Dr. Brown came slowly out, half closing the parlour-door behind him.

'I can do nothing more,' he said. 'If he lived he would have brain fever. But he is dying.'

'Does he know her?'

'No. He may know her at the last, but it is doubtful. I can do nothing, and I am wanted elsewhere.'

'I will stop,' said the Bishop.

'Shall I take you back?' said Dr. Brown, looking at Dick. But Dick shook his head.

'I might be of use to her,' he said when the doctor had gone.

So the two men who loved Rachel sat in impotent compassion in the little kitchen through the interminable hours of the night. At long intervals the Bishop went quietly into the parlour, but apparently he was not wanted there. Once he went out and got a fresh candle, and put it into the tin candlestick, and set it among the china ornaments on wool-work mats.

Hugh lay quite still now with his eyes half closed. His hands lay passive in Rachel's. The restless fever of movement was past. She almost wished it back, so far, so far was his life ebbing away from hers.

'Hughie,' she whispered to him over and over again. 'I love you. Do not leave me.'

But he muttered continually to himself and took no heed of her.

At last she gave up the hopeless task of making him hear, and listened intently. She could make no sense of what he said. The few words she could catch were repeated a hundred times amid an unintelligible murmur. The boat, and Loftus, and her own name – and Crack. Who was Crack? She remembered the little dog which had been drowned. And the lips which were so soon to be silent talked on incoherently while Rachel's heart broke for a word.

The night was wearing very thin. The darkness before the dawn, the deathly chill before the dawn were here. Through the low uncurtained window Rachel could see the first wan light of the new day and the new year.

Perhaps he would know her with the daylight.

The new day came up out of the white east in a great peace, pale as Christ newly risen from the dead, with the splendour of God's love upon Him.

A great peace and light stole together into the little room.

Hugh stirred, and Rachel saw a change pass over his pinched, sunken face.

'It was the only way to reach her,' he said slowly and distinctly; 'the only way. I shall get through, and I shall find her upon the other side, as I did before. It is very cold, but I shall get through. I am nearly through now.'

He sat up, and looked directly at her. He seemed suddenly freed, released. A boyish look that she had never seen came into his face, a look which remained in Rachel's heart while she lived.

Would he know her?

The pure light was upon his face, more beautiful than she had ever seen it. He looked at her with tender love and trust shining in his eyes, and laughed softly.

'I have found you,' he said, stretching out his arms towards her. 'I lost you, I don't remember how, but I came to you through the water. I knew I should find you, my Rachel, my sweet wife.'

He was past the place of our poor human forgiveness. He might have cared for it earlier, but he did not want it now. He had forgotten that he had any need of it, for the former things had passed away. Love only remained.

She took him in her arms. She held him to her heart.

'I knew you would,' he said, smiling at her. 'I knew it. We will never part again.'

And with a sigh of perfect happiness he turned wholly to her, his closed eyes against her breast.

CONCLUSION

IT was autumn once more. The brambles were red in the hollow below Warpington Vicarage. Abel was gathering the apples in the orchard.

Mr. and Mrs. Gresley were sitting together in the shade of the new porch, contemplating a triumphal arch which they had just erected across the road. 'Long life and happiness' was the original motto inscribed thereon.

Mrs. Gresley, in an alarming new hat, sank back exhausted in her garden-chair.

'The Pratts are having six arches, all done with electric-light designs of hearts with their crest on the top,' she said. 'They are to be lit up at nine o'clock. Mr. Pratt said he did not mind any expense on such an occasion. He said it made an epoch in the life of the county.'

'Well,' said Mr. Gresley, 'I lead too busy a life to be always poking my nose into other people's affairs, but I certainly never did expect that Lady Newhaven would have married Algy Pratt.'

'Ada and Selina say Algy and she have been attached for years: that is why the wedding is so soon – only nine months – and she is to keep her title, and they are going to live at Westhope. I told Ada and Selina I hoped they did not expect too much from the marriage, for sometimes people who did were disappointed, but they only laughed and said Vi had promised Algy to take them out next season.'

'We seem to live in an atmosphere of weddings,' said Mr. Gresley. 'First, Dr. Brown and Fraülein, and now Algy Pratt and Lady Newhaven.'

'I was so dreadfully afraid that Fraülein might think our arch was put up for her and presume upon it,' said Mrs. Gresley, 'that I thought it better to send her a little note, just to welcome her cordially, and tell her how busy we were about the Pratt festivities, and what a *coincidence* it was her arriving on the same day. I told her I would send down the children to spend the morning with her to-morrow. I knew that would please her, and it is Miss Baker's day in Southminster with her aunt, and I shall really be too busy to see after them. In some ways I don't like Miss Baker as much as Fraülein. She is paid just the same, but she does much less, and she is really quite short sometimes if I ask her to do any little thing for me, like copying out that church music.'

'Hester used to do it,' said Mr. Gresley.

'Miss Brown told me she had heard from Hester, and that she and Miss West are still in India. And they mean to go to Australia and New Zealand, and come home next spring.'

'Was Hester well?'

'Quite well. You know, James, I always told you that hers was not a genuine illness. That was why they would not let us see her. It was only hysteria,[354] which girls get when they are disappointed at not marrying, and are not so young as they were. Directly poor Mr. Scarlett died, Hester left her room, and devoted herself to Miss West, and Dr. Brown said it was the saving of her. But for my part I always thought Hester took in Dr. Brown and the Bishop about that illness.'

'I should not wonder if Hester married Dick Vernon,' said Mr. Gresley. 'It is rather marked their going to Australia when he went back there only a few months ago. If she had consulted me I should have advised her not to follow him up.'

A burst of cheering, echoed by piercing howls from Boulou locked up in the empty nursery.

'I hope Miss Baker has put the children in a good place. She is sure to be in a good one herself,' said Mrs. Gresley, as she and her husband took up their position by the gate.

More cheering! A sudden flourish of trumpets and a trombone from the volunteer band at the corner, of which Mr. Pratt was Colonel.[355]

A clatter of four white horses and an open carriage. A fleeting vision of Captain Pratt, white waistcoat, smile, teeth, eye-glass, hat waved in lavender-kid hand! A fleeting vision of a lovely woman in white, with a wonderful white-feathered hat, and a large diamond heart, possibly a love token from Captain Pratt, hanging on a long diamond chain, bowing and smiling beside her elaborate bridegroom.

In a moment they were past, and a report of cannon and field artillery showed that the east lodge of Warpington Towers had been reached, and the solemn joy of the Pratts was finding adequate expression.

'She looked rather frightened,' said Mrs. Gresley.

'Such a magnificent reception is alarming to a gentle, retiring nature,' said Mr. Gresley.

More cheering! this time much more enthusiastic than the last – louder, deafening.

Dr. Brown's dog-cart came slowly in sight, accompanied by a crowd.

'They have taken out the horse and are dragging them up,' said Mrs. Gresley in astonishment. 'Look at Dr. Brown waving his hat, and Fraülein bowing in that silly way. Well, I only hope her head won't be turned by the arches and everything. She will find my note directly she gets in. Really, James! two brides and bridegrooms in one day! It is like the end of a novel.'

POSTSCRIPT

WE turn the pages of the Book of Life with impatient hands. And if we shut up the book at a sad page we say hastily 'Life is sad.' But it is not so. There are other pages waiting to be turned. I, who have copied out one little chapter of the lives of Rachel and Hester, cannot see plainly, but I catch glimpses of those other pages. I seem to see Rachel with children round her, and Dick not far off, and the old light rekindled in Hester's eyes. For Hope and Love and Enthusiasm never die. We think in youth that we bury them in the graveyards of our hearts, but the grass never yet grew over them. How, then, can life be sad, when they walk beside us always in the growing light towards the Perfect Day.

October, 1899.[a]

EDITORIAL NOTES

1. *'After the Red Pottage ... bitter cry'*: Dean Farrar, 'Selling the Birthright', in *Everyday Christian Life* (Whitefish, MT: Kessinger Publishing, 2004), p. 183, originally published (London: William Ibister, 1887).

2. *I have not lack'd ... thy praise*: Tennyson, 'To —', ll. 4–5, in 'Juvenilia', in *The Complete Works of Alfred Tennyson*, ed. A. C. Loffelt (Rotterdam, 1871).

3. *In tragic life ... GEORGE MEREDITH*: from Meredith's sonnet sequence *Modern Love* (London: Chapman & Hall, 1862), no. 43, ll. 12–14.

4. *Sterne's starling ... bars of his cage*: an allusion to Laurence Sterne, *A Sentimental Journey* (London: Becket & Hondt, 1767), p. 24.

5. *hansom*: a light two wheeled cab , precursor of the modern taxi.

6. *'the glass of fashion'*: *Hamlet*, III.i.150–4.

7. liaison: French: 'a meeting'. In English the word is generally used to suggest a specifically romantic encounter.

8. *brougham*: a closed four-wheeled carriage drawn by one horse.

9. *chromo-lithograph*: a picture lithographed in colours.

10. sobriquet: French: 'nickname'.

11. *ought I to put my gloves on?*: Dick reveals his indifference to etiquette despite his social standing; he is in any case out of touch, having been abroad for some years. This small incident is part of Cholmondeley's point that genuinely upper-class figures such as Dick have less need to observe rigid etiquette than newcomers such as Captain Pratt, who will appear in a later chapter.

12. *But as he groped ... RUDYARD KIPLING*: 'The Ballad of the King's Mercy', stanza 8, ll. 1–2, in *Barrack-Room Ballads and Other Verses* (London: Methuen, 1892).

13. *the temptation in the wilderness*: a reference to Christ's temptation by Satan after forty days in the wilderness. For an account of Christ's rejection of Satan see Matthew 4; Luke 4.

14. *blasé*: French: 'insouciant', 'indifferent'.

15. *carbines*: a type of rifle.

16. *pistols for two and coffee for four*: duelling had been illegal since the eighteenth century but persisted in England until the start of Victoria's reign. As late as 1839 Dickens included an aristocratic duel in *Nicholas Nickleby*.

17. *the pheasant shooting*: The season for pheasant shooting officially runs 1 October–1 February.

18. *Had David qualms ... the ewe lamb*: 2 Samuel 11:1–16. During the siege of Rabbah, David slept with Bathsheba, wife of Uriah the Hittite, and then arranged for Uriah to be placed in a vulnerable front-line position, this causing his death. The story continues in 2 Samuel 12:1–7. God sent Nathan the prophet to confront David, telling a parable about a rich man who stole a ewe lamb from a poor man; David however failed to understand that he was the rich man of the story, Bathsheba the ewe lamb and Uriah the poor man.

19. *'Thou art the man'*: 2 Samuel 12:7.
20. *'Imitation of Christ'*: written by the Augustinian monk Thomas á Kempis (1380–1471), *De Imitatione Christi* was translated into English in the fifteenth century and was still widely read in the nineteenth.
21. *For the sin ye do ... RUDYARD KIPLING*: 'Tomlinson', l. 163, in *Barrack-Room Ballads*.
22. *What the* Bandar-log *think ... RUDYARD KIPLING*: *The Jungle Book* (London: Macmillan, 1894), Kaa's Hunting.
23. *raté*: French: 'failure'.
24. *'new woman'*: following the various feminist recovery programmes of the late twentieth century, Cholmondeley has been known principally as a New Woman writer. However this direct reference to the New Woman is almost unique in her work.
25. *agnostic*: the term is most widely associated with the scientist T. H. Huxley (1825–95), an early supporter of Darwin's evolutionary theories and opponent of biblical literalism.
26. *muff-chain*: worn round the neck and passed through a muff, or hand-warmer, to prevent it from falling when the wearer withdrew their hands.
27. *an exile something like Nebuchadnezzar's*: 'Jehozadak was deported when the Lord sent Judah and Jerusalem into exile by the hand of Nebuchadnezzar.' 1 Chronicles 6:15.
28. *Kipling's 'silly sailors ... twanged unhandily'*: 'Loud sang the souls of the jolly, jolly Mariners, / Plucking at their harps, and they plucked unhandily'. 'The Last Chantrey' (1893), stanza 8, ll. 1–2.
29. *pince-nez*: French: reading glasses designed to grip the nose.
30. *district visitor*: a representative of a charitable, often religious body, who visited the poor within an appointed area. The ineffectiveness of district visitors is satirized by Dickens in *Bleak House* (1853) in the figure of Mrs Pardiggle.
31. *Içi bas tous ... BOURGET*: 'Here below all men cry after / Their friendships and their loves.' In fact this poem, 'Ici bas', is by René François Sully Prudhomme, from *Stances et Pöemes* (Paris: Fauré, 1865).
32. *Hester, in blue serge, told Rachel, in crimson velvet*: again, Cholmondeley stresses that social standing cannot be acquired, by making the middle-class Rachel better dressed than her upper-class counterpart Hester.
33. *everything I touched ... the result of sweated labour*: contemporary sources suggest that after the strike at Bryant and May's match factory in 1880, conditions improved somewhat for the girls and women employed in making matches in the factories. However the related work of matchbox making, undertaken at home, was still recognized as a form of sweated labour in the 1890s.
34. *sea of shame ... gave up its awful dead*: From the prayer for the burial of the dead at sea: 'We therefore commit their body to the deep, looking for the general Resurrection in the last day, and the life of the world to come, through our Lord Jesus Christ; at whose second coming in glorious majesty to judge the world, the sea shall give up her dead'.
35. *frieze*: a coarse woollen cloth.
36. *flittings*: disappearances to avoid payment of outstanding rent.
37. *Cure the drunkard ... EMERSON*: Ralph Waldo Emerson, 'Social Aims', in *Letters and Social Aims* (Boston, MA: Osgood, 1876), p. 94. Cholmondeley maintained that no other writer, George Eliot not excepted, had influenced her as much as Emerson.
38. tableaux vivants: French: 'living pictures'. A popular form of entertainment in the nineteenth century; a small number of people would group together to form a recognizable, often historical, scene.
39. *A square-set man and honest. TENNYSON*: *The Holy Grail* (London: Strahan & Co., 1869), p. 75.

40. incog: abbreviation of the Italian incognito: in disguise, literally 'unknown'.

41. *A.D.C.*: aide de camp; confidential secretary to a high-ranking military commander.

42. *Pour vivre tranquille ... gens d'église*: French: 'to live in peace one must live far from men of the Church'. Source untraced.

43. *G.F.S.*: Girls Friendly Society; a religious youth organization formed in 1875 with a number of local branches.

44. *morning service*: taken from the Book of Common Prayer, this is traditionally the best attended of the Sunday services.

45. *now against Lazarus ... in a distant desert*: John 11 gives an account of the death and resurrection of Lazarus; the story of John the Baptist is relayed in all four Gospels. It is unclear which desert Cholmondeley is referring to.

46. *dinner parties all through Lent, and Sunday luncheons*: as a High-Church vicar, Gresley would not approve of such indulgence during Lent, traditionally a time of self-denial. As a Sabbatarian he would also disapprove of cooking on a Sunday. As if in answer to this, the narrator repeatedly draws attention to the poor standard of cooking in the Gresleys' own house.

47. *freethinking*: the doubt or denial of religious tenets based on rational argument.

48. *Hester 'laced in'*: pulled the laces of her corset tight in order to reduce the span of her waist. Minna, the mother of an expanding family, reveals her jealousy of Hester's slim physique.

49. *succés fou*: French: 'wild success'.

50. *the Indian tribal rising*: Cholmondeley probably has in mind a clash between indigenous and American troops at Leech Lake in the Chippewa Reservation, Minnesota, in October 1898. Heavy American losses were reported in the English press.

51. *'Modern Dissent'*: Non-Anglican Protestants were known as Dissenters from the time of their secession from the Church of England in the late eighteenth century. As a High Churchman Gresley is implacably opposed to all such denominations.

52. *Chapter meeting*: the Chapter is made up of the canons and presided over by the dean or provost of the cathedral.

53. *sale of work*: a charitable sale of craftwork produced by the ladies of the parish.

54. *Wonderful power to benumb ... EMERSON: The Conduct of Life* (Boston, MA: Ticknor & Fields, 1860), p. 236.

55. *Veritas*: Latin: 'truth'. Hester is disturbed by Gresley's assumption of this position as the sole arbiter of truth.

56. nom de guerre: French: 'war name'.

57. *'The Blue Bells of Scotland'*: sung by Mrs Jordan, first printed in *The New Whim of the Night, or The Town and Country Songster for 1801* (London: C. Sheppard, [1801]). Author unknown.

58. Klavier Stück: German: a piece played on piano, correctly written as one word (Klavierstück).

59. tu quoque: Latin: 'you too', a retort rebounding on the accuser.

60. *'au revoir'*: French: 'goodbye'.

61. *'The light shineth ... darkness comprehendeth it not*: John 1:5.

62. *red rag*: proverbial, based on the assumption that bulls are enraged by the colour red. In fact they are colour-blind.

63. *Broad Church*: not a cohesive church party, rather a unifying name given to liberal Christians.

64. *run with the hare and hunt with the hounds*: proverbial; to keep in with both sides.

65. *'runners' or 'suckers'*: long thin shoots coming from the damaged roots of fruit trees.
66. *'curly kebbidge,' or 'salary', or 'sparrow-grass'*: curly cabbage, celery or asparagus.
67. *our policy in China*: through the nineteenth century China had effectively been forced to accept British trade and culture. Tension surfaced periodically, notably in the Opium Wars of 1839–42, and at the end of the century British missionaries were still a cause of resentment and anti-British feeling.
68. *'How dreadful is ... the house of God'*: Genesis 28:17.
69. *Thy will be done*: from the Lord's Prayer. The line continues, 'on earth as it is in heaven'.
70. *It is as useless ...* GEORGE ELIOT: *Middlemarch* (1870), Book V, ch. 45. 'But even [Lydgate's] proud outspokenness was checked by the discernment that it was as useless to fight against the interpretations of ignorance as to whip the fog'.
71. *ardent total abstainers*: i.e. they abstain from all alcohol on religious grounds.
72. *he never hit off fair*: this seems to be a misunderstanding on Cholmondeley's part. In hockey it is impossible to hit off fairly or unfairly.
73. *aber Sie vergessen*: German: 'But you (second person, polite form) forget'.
74. *grace*: a brief prayer said before a meal.
75. *ruri-diaconal Chapter meeting*: chapter meeting in the area of a rural dean.
76. *for better for worse*: an ironic allusion to the marriage service.
77. choyée: French: 'pampered', 'cherished'.
78. *'tuft-hunters'*: a term much used by mid-century writers such as Thackeray to describe those who seek acquaintance with titled people.
79. *'swells'*: originally derived from the idea of the dandy, a swell was sometimes presented as a less aristocratic figure who aspired unsuccessfully to the same status. Cholmondeley appears to be mocking both Minna's old fashioned slang and her conflation of genuine county families with their imitators (such as Minna's own friends the Pratts).
80. *The depth and dream ...* RUDYARD KIPLING: 'L'Envoi' to *Life's Handicap* (London: Macmillan, 1891), l. 17.
81. *'not wisely but too well'*: *Othello*, V.ii.344. Also the title of an 1867 novel by Cholmondeley's friend Rhoda Broughton.
82. *He used to come to our 'At Homes,' but he was never asked to dinner*: Captain Pratt takes advantage of the open invitation implicit in the 'at home' afternoon of the aristocratic Lady Susan. She, however, will not gratify him by proffering a personal invitation.
83. *'parti'*: French: an obsolete term for an eligible bachelor.
84. *she is not strong just now*: Minna is expecting another baby.
85. *that large class whose eyes are holden*: Luke 24:16.
86. façon de parler: French: 'figure of speech'.
87. *Originality irritates ...* W. W. PEYTON: *The Memorabilia of Jesus: Commonly Called the Gospel of St. John* (London: A. & C. Black, 1892), p. 275.
88. *Jowett ... 'A Bishop without a sense of humour is lost'*: an approving allusion to the Broad Church contributor to *Essays and Reviews* (London: J. W. Parker & Son, 1860) Benjamin Jowett (1817–93), Master of Balliol College, Oxford. Allusion untraced.
89. *Low Church parish and High Church parson*: Gresley's inept handling of religious differences is repeatedly shown as exacerbating what would be already a tense situation. Cholmondeley's own father was noted for his good relationship with the dissenters of Hodnet, and in a letter of 1897 she complained of the view that anyone not attacking Dissent must secretly belong to it.
90. *a son of Anak*: Deuteronomy 9:2. 'You know about them and have heard it said: "Who can stand up against the Anakites?"'

91. *broke all previous records of birch rods at Eton*: Public schools such as Eton were notorious for their routine use of corporal punishment at this time. To endure a caning or 'licking' without flinching conferred prestige on the sufferer; this comment shows the Bishop boasting of Dick's physical courage as well as his maverick nature.
92. *his strictly phonetic spelling*: by sound rather than rule. The Bishop is politely indicating that Dick's spelling is inadequate.
93. esprit de corps: French: 'team spirit'.
94. á propos *of nothing*: French: not relevant to the previous conversation, i.e. a *non sequitur*.
95. *an apostate*: a religious backslider.
96. *goody-goody books*: moral or religious stories, possibly derived from the 1765 tale *The History of Little Goody Two-Shoes*.
97. cordon: French: a defensive ring.
98. *Only those who know ...* GEORGE ELIOT: *Middlemarch*, Book VII, ch. 73.
99. *'bulls'-eyes'*: sticky, round, hard, black and white sweets coloured to resemble a large eye.
100. *on stepping stones – not of our dead selves*: an allusion to the first stanza of Tennyson's *In Memoriam* (1850). 'I held it truth, with whom who sings / To once clear harp in divers tones, / That men may rise on stepping-stones / Of their dead selves to higher things'.
101. *monthly nurses*: nurses who attended to a woman and her new baby.
102. *brown holland gown*: Holland was a weave of linen or cotton, for everyday use.
103. *hard collars and cuffs and imitation tie*: with the one exception of Dick Vernon the upper-class figures, such as Hugh and Hester, all dress well; Cholmondeley is therefore reminding the reader of Minna's provincialism. Ironically, given her submission to her husband, this 'masculine' costume is also reminiscent of caricatures of the New Woman as circulated by Punch.
104. *smart*: a term that Cholmondeley suggests is only used by the middle or parvenu class; in this formulation it has connotations of ostentation or a lack of taste, unperceived by a speaker who lacks the breeding to distinguish between good taste and bad.
105. *morning service*: see note 44 above.
106. *Apostolic Succession*: this doctrine holds that the first bishops were appointed by Christ's apostles, and that bishops alone have the power to appoint successors in an unbroken line.
107. *Beware of a silent dog and of still water*: Latin proverb.
108. *chaste stucco Gothic erections with church windows*: The Mock Gothic style, largely inspired by medieval church architecture, enjoyed an enormous popularity in the nineteenth century. Cholmondeley mocks Pratt's tasteless excess in this description of false 'church windows', implicitly contrasted with the authenticity of Westhope Abbey, the residence of Lord Newhaven.
109. *unknown Saharas*: The African Sahara is the world's largest desert.
110. *It's like keeping a dog and barking yourself*: proverbial, meaning to undertake a task already allocated to another.
111. *It's a way worms have*: proverbial: 'Tread on a worm and it will turn'. Reworked by Shakespeare in *3 Henry VI*, II.ii.17, as 'The smallest worm will turn being trodden on'; the modern expression is 'the worm has turned' or 'the worm will turn'.
112. *the post-office ... once anything is in, in it is*: by the terms of the 1837 Act for the Management of the Post, post office officials were banned from opening post or causing it to be delayed.
113. *Une grande passion ... moyen de sagesse*: 'an unhappy grand passion is a great teacher of wisdom'. J.-J. Rousseau, *Julie, ou la Nouvelle Héloïse* (1761), Part 6, letter 7.

114. *'Whether it be ... other men's lives'*: Apocrypha, Sirach 19:8.
115. *the book, not of life, but of Burke*: In other words, not the Bible, but Burke's *History of the Landed Gentry* (first published in 1826), to feature in which was a token of family status. Cholmondeley's satirical use of religious terms sometimes led to her being accused of treating religion with inappropriate flippancy, a charge she always denied.
116. Tableau: see note 38 above.
117. *On s'ennuie presque toujours avec ceux qu'on ennuie*: French: 'one is almost always bored in the company of those who find one boring also'. Source untraced.
118. *parochial rounds*: visits to parishioners. Gresley is conscientious in setting aside appropriate amounts of time for this duty.
119. *crewel-work antimacassars ... tussore silk ones*: antimacassars were decorative pieces of material placed against the backs of chairs and sofas to protect them against macassar hair oil. Again Cholmondeley pokes fun at Minna's lack of taste.
120. *it is more blessed to give than to receive*: Acts 20:35.
121. *a curate*: A curate, who may or may not have been already ordained, acts as assistant to the vicar of a parish, usually as preparation for taking on a more responsible role as parish priest at a later date.
122. *muff-chains*: see note 26 above.
123. *the most distressing traits of its latest recruits*: Cholmondeley was deeply concerned by the expansion of the aristocracy and gentry at this time, through the creation of new titles and the acquisition of trade fortunes. She continually stressed the value of traditional families as opposed to newly created landowning powers, as represented by the Pratts.
124. *I never bike in London*: Throughout the 1890s the female cyclist was controversially associated with rational dress and the New Woman. One journal to run a series of articles on this debate was Jerome K. Jerome's weekly *To-day*. Ada reveals her own lack of social refinement in making such a rude comment at Rachel's expense.
125. *She is only Birmingham ... The Pratts were 'Liverpool'*: possibly a reference to the means in which their respective fortunes have been accrued. Rachel's father is likely to have manufactured cheap goods in Birmingham, whereas Liverpool merchants might be involved in the more prestigious foreign trade. However, see Lord Newhaven's later association of Rachel with 'coal-mines', above, p. 134.
126. *Le monde est plein ... LA FONTAINE*: 'The world is full of people who are no wiser.' From 'La grenouille qui veut se faire aussi grosse que le boeuf' ('The Frog who Wanted to be as Big as a Ox'), in *Fables choisies* (Anvers: Henry van Dunewalt, 1688).
127. *temperance meeting*: often with a religious bias, such meetings were aimed at promoting the responsible use of alcohol – or in this case, abstention – among the working classes in particular.
128. *Parish Room*: a room used for local and church activities.
129. *Oxford shoe*: a traditional men's shoe, either laced through several holes or fastened with buttons.
130. *'school forms'*: long benches, designed to allow children to sit in rows in front of their desks.
131. *Archdeacon*: a church dignitary next in standing to a bishop.
132. *'Evolution! ... rocked the cradle*: Gresley's fatuous dismissal of Darwin by the time of writing reveals his attitudes as long out of date, allowing Cholmondeley to suggest by extension that his opposition to women's rights is equally absurd.
133. *temperance, by which he meant total abstinence*: from alcohol. Total abstainers often defended their position on religious grounds.

134. *evil one*: the devil.

135. *take the pledge*: Members of the religious Band of Hope signed a pledge to abstain from alcohol in perpetuity.

136. *There is a text in the Bible about wine making glad the heart of man*: Psalm 104:15.

137. *we hear of new wine bursting old bottles*: Mark 2:22.

138. *Nothing but 'pop'*: a children's drink such as ginger beer.

139. *to pour oil ... on the troubled waters*: proverbial. As the Pratt fortune has been made from oil, Cholmondeley is satirizing both Pratt's parvenu status and his personal manner.

140. *'seat'*: country estate; again Cholmondeley references the Pratt family's pretensions.

141. *nesh*: a northern dialect expression meaning to fear the cold. Here Vernon is unafraid of the reaction he may get.

142. *just silly to go back to Australy with 'im*: desperate to go back to Australia with him.

143. *fetched 'em all most*: almost won them all over.

144. *Le bruit est pour ... M. DELANONI*: 'Noise is for the fool. Complaint is for the silly. The honest man wronged goes without a word.' Source untraced.

145. *a detective in plain clothes*: The Criminal Investigations Department was founded in 1878, and its plain clothes officers were of a higher status than their uniformed colleagues.

146. *I'm no forwarder than I was*: I am no nearer to reaching my goal.

147. *the mob of women ... marriage for their very existence*: Women of the upper classes were still not encouraged to earn their own living at this period. Newhaven artfully captures the ambivalent position of this threatening 'mob' who are themselves threatened with penury if they fail to marry.

148. *piling everything on to the eldest son ... almost penniless*: a reference to the tradition of primogeniture, that made inadequate provision for unmarried women in the family after the death of their father.

149. *galantine*: white meat boned, spiced and served cold.

150. *a Bradshaw*: *Bradshaw's Monthly Railway Guide* had been appearing since 1838; the standard railway timetable, it was familiarly referred to as a Bradshaw.

151. *an express to London*: an express train to London at this time would have travelled at 40mph.

152. *Si l'on vous a trahi ... MAETERLINCK*: 'If you have been betrayed, it is not the treachery that matters. It is the forgiveness to which it has given rise in your heart ... but if the treachery has not fostered simplicity, a higher trust, willingness to love, you have been betrayed indeed in vain, and you can say that you have gained nothing.' *La Sagesse et la Destinée* (Paris: Bibliothèque Charpentier, 1898), p. 27.

153. *'practised to deceive'*: Sir Walter Scott, *Marmion* (1808), VI.17.27–8: 'Oh what a tangled web we weave, / When first we practise to deceive.'

154. vivâ voce *invitations*: Latin: invitations delivered by word of mouth.

155. *socialism*: prominent socialists of the late nineteenth century included a number of writers and feminists, such as George Bernard Shaw and Annie Besant. In his vague reference to socialism as a 'community of goods' Gresley again reveals his failure to grasp complex ideas.

156. *patent safe*: the first patent safes were made in the 1830s, allowing papers to be stored in fireproof chests for the first time.

157. *"let out all the length of all the reins"*: R. W. Emerson to Thomas Carlyle, 30 April 1835, in *The Correspondence of Thomas Carlyle and Ralph Waldo Emerson, 1834–1872*, 2 vols (London: Chatto & Windus, 1883), vol. 1.

158. *'Experience is converted ... into satin'*: Ralph Waldo Emerson, *The American Scholar. Self Reliance. Compensation* (New York: American Book Co., 1893), p. 6.

159. *"Love knows the secret of grief"*: Elizabeth Barrett Browning, 'Only a Curl', stanza 3, l. 5, in *Last Poems* (New York: James Miller, 1862).

160. *Like 'Celia Chettam'*: the sister of the heroine Dorothea Brooke in *Middlemarch*. Celia's new gravitas following her marriage and particularly the birth of her first child is treated satirically both by Eliot and by inference in *Red Pottage*.

161. *Christ's power to touch those blind eyes to sight*: a metaphorical use of the biblical stories concerning Christ's ministry. Hester suggests that despite his assumption of religious authority, Gresley is himself spiritually blind.

162. *Brother, thy tail ...* Song of the Bandar-log: Road-Song of the Bandar-Log, in Kipling, *The Jungle Book*, Kaa's Hunting.

163. *a great French milliner ... marvellous carnations*: Rachel's dress is at the height of fashion, but she is aware of the long hours and difficult working conditions associated with the millinery trade. In particular spending hours on fine needlework in poor light would be detrimental to the health of the seamstress. Rachel has sufficient social conscience to think about the worker rather than the designer.

164. *'Superfine'*: Like 'smart', this expression is specifically associated by Cholmondeley with the middle class.

165. *proved the gong*: The butler is summoning the guests to dinner.

166. *'High hopes faint on a warm hearth-stone'*: Rudyard Kipling, 'L'Envoi' to *The Story of the Gadsbys* (Allahabad: Wheeler & Co., 1888), p. 101.

167. *I was a "fill up"*: Hugh is standing in at the last minute.

168. *'little more and how much it is'*: Robert Browning, 'By the Fire-Side', stanza 39, l. 1, in *Men and Women* (London: Barnes & Noble, 1855).

169. *they were gentlemen ... only 'a perfect gentleman'*: the Victorian preoccupation with defining the term 'gentleman' is ably deployed by the narrator, who suggests that Rachel is now able to discern the difference because she has been moving in refined circles. Newhaven will later meditate that Hugh, despite his moral shortcomings, is a 'gentleman' in his ability to keep a secret.

170. *"The Princess," by our lion-hearted Laureate*: Tennyson's poem (1847) is in fact more ambivalent than Mr Harvey suggests in his treatment of higher education for women.

171. *With aching hands ... Matthew Arnold*: 'Morality' (1852), stanza 2.

172. *Christ comes ... troubled waves of art*: John 6:18–20 tells the story of Jesus walking on the water, immediately after the feeding of the five thousand. Cholmondeley is using the story both to sanctify the artistic vocation, and to urge trust in its promptings.

173. *sacraments*: the Anglican Church acknowledges two sacraments or holy rituals conferring grace: baptism and the Eucharist.

174. *found expression in stake and faggot*: During the Tudor dynasty a large number of 'heretics' were notoriously burned at the stake. Cholmondeley is attacking Gresley's fanaticism as much as his lack of comprehension.

175. *Il le fit avec des ... Guy De Maupassant*: 'He did it with inconsistent and irrefutable arguments which melted in the face of reason like snow, at which one cannot grasp, absurd and triumphant arguments of a country curate revealing God.' *Fort comme la mort* (*Strong as Death*; 1889), ch. 3.

176. assez beau garcon: French: 'fairly good-looking young man'.

177. *Jesu, lover of my soul*: Charles Wesley, *Hymns and Sacred Poems* (1740), no. 93.

178. *'Can the blind lead ... into the ditch?'*: Luke 6:39.

179. *Bowdlerised*: prudish censorship, after Thomas Bowdler's 1818 expurgated edition of the works of Shakespeare.
180. *peptonised beef-tea*: minced lean beef mixed with water and bicarbonate of soda and a tablespoon of the liquor pancreaticus. See *British Medical Journal* (1 May 1880), p. 649, for an account of this recipe and its suitability for invalids.
181. *Tennyson ... 'when it alteration finds'*: in fact the quotation is from Shakespeare, Sonnet 116. Mr Tristram is revealing his superficial acquaintance with English literature.
182. *stick to our colours*: proverbial, derived from the practice of rallying to the regimental flag in battle.
183. *No one was announced as an Honourable ... on cards*: strictly speaking, 'Honourable' is not a title in the same way as 'Sir' or 'Lady'. It precedes rather than replaces the usual title of Mr or Miss.
184. *"Other refuge ... soul on Thee"*: 'Jesu, Lover of my Soul', verse 2, l. 1. See note 177 above.
185. *that Judge in the black cap*: in murder cases, the judge donned a black cap to pronounce a sentence of death.
186. *chancel wall*: the wall where the clergy and choir sit, situated in the east area of the church.
187. *Look in my face ... DANTE GABRIEL ROSSETTI*: 'A Superscription', ll. 1–2, in *The House of Life* (London: Ellis & White, 1881).
188. *a life-belt*: a precursor of the modern life jacket.
189. tête-á-tête: French: a one-to-one conversation.
190. *'had been imported into his case'*: brought to bear on the matter or made a consideration.
191. *warm hearthstones*: see note 166 above.
192. *flunkey*: Like 'lackey' this is an opprobrious term for a liveried servant.
193. hauteur: French: 'haughtiness'.
194. *red rag on a bull*: see note 62 above.
195. *a little poem ... 'We rushed into each other's arms'*: Tennyson, 'The Letters', stanza 5, l. 8, in *Maud and Other Poems* (London: Edward Moxon, 1855).
196. *'love's labour lost'*: the title of a play by Shakespeare.
197. *'Only that which is replaced is destroyed'*: *Amiel's Journal: The Journal in Time of Henri-Frédéric Amiel*, trans. Mrs H. Ward (Whitefish, MT: Kessinger Publishing, n.d.), p. 36, originally published (London: Macmillan, 1889).
198. *another king in richer purple*: purple is the traditional colour of British royalty.
199. *Scales seemed to fall from her eyes*: proverbial, derived from the conversion of Saul, who was blinded during his persecution of Christians but restored to sight by Ananias. See Acts 9:16–18: 'something like scales fell from Saul's eyes, and he could see again'.
200. *'Tis not for everyone to catch a salmon*: German proverb.
201. *'the ricks stood grey to the sun'*: an adaptation of 'the ricks stand grey to the sun', in Rudyard Kipling, 'The Long Trail' (1891), l. 2.
202. *'We can't be catching pike on a Sunday'*: Doll is comically splitting hairs in this comment. Orthodox observance of the Sabbath would preclude their fishing at all.
203. *a landing-net*: for landing large fish once they have been caught.
204. *gunwale*: the upper edge of the boat's side.
205. *The main difference ... EMERSON*: *The Conduct of Life* (Boston, MA: Ticknor & Fields, 1860), p. 243.
206. *knickerbockers*: loose trousers fastening at the knee, worn for riding and walking.
207. *The less wit a man has ... he wants it*: Dutch proverb.
208. *six o'clock service*: the evening service.
209. *morning service*: see note 44 above.

210. *as worms ... church and school rates*: further to the Compulsory Church Rate Abolition Act of 1868 Dissenters no longer had to pay Church rates. Hester is making a joke based on the proverb 'the worm will turn' (see note 111 above).
211. *Irish stew*: a stew made with mutton, onions and potatoes.
212. *'grande passion'*: French: 'a grand passion'.
213. *our old garden of Eden*: Cholmondeley makes a traditional connection between childhood and pre-lapsarian innocence through invoking the biblical Garden of Eden.
214. ribes: an arching shrub.
215. *a certain scarlet berry ... deadly poison*: most likely a reference to the scarlet yew berry.
216. *'Home, Sweet Home'*: in John Howard Payne's *Clari, or The Maid of Milan* (1823), an opera in two acts.
217. *I don't see any harm myself in drawing on Sunday*: another satire on social norms. In this instance Sybell is thinking for herself because it suits her convenience, despite her professed regard for Mr Gresley's opinions.
218. *So fast does a little ... GEORGE ELIOT*: *Felix Holt the Radical* (1866), vol. 2, ch. 22.
219. *away at his County Council*: a meeting of the County Council, responsible for local government at county level.
220. *A fool's mouth is his destruction*: Proverbs 18:7.
221. *'bed-spreads'*: eiderdowns.
222. *'sheet-sham'*: an embroidered or otherwise decorated piece of material placed over the pillows when the bed was not in use.
223. empressement. French: 'eagerness'.
224. *I have never known him to go to a garden party in his life*: while Newhaven makes adroit use of polite conversation to manipulate events at several points in the novel, he does not enjoy tedious small talk with his Middleshire neighbours.
225. *tea-cosy*: a decorative cover for a tea pot, designed to keep the tea hot.
226. *death-duties*: first introduced in 1796 for estates over a certain value, and by the mid-nineteenth century payable by all beneficiaries whatever their relationship to the deceased.
227. *Bible-markers*: ornamental bookmarks designed specifically for use with Bibles.
228. *The landed interest is not going to be beaten by coal-mines*: Newhaven humorously invokes his superior status as a member of the landed gentry, to which Rachel does not belong by birth.
229. *Miss West, your burden is greater than you can bear*: Newhaven unwittingly underscores Rachel's mental agony, based on the secret he is keeping from her, despite their friendly badinage.
230. *'All's well that ends well'*: The title of a play by William Shakespeare.
231. *from the madding crowd*: from Thomas Gray's 'Elegy Written in a Country Churchyard' (1751), l. 73; perhaps also a subtly ironic allusion to Thomas Hardy's *Far from the Madding Crowd*, first published in 1874. The novel features a recklessly flirtatious heroine in the person of Bathsheba Everdene.
232. *The Bird of Time ... OMAR KHAYYIM*: *Rubaiyat of Omar Khayyam*, trans. Edward Fitzgerald (1859), stanza 7, ll. 3–4.
233. *pillar-box*: letter box.
234. *He had sold his birthright for a mess of red pottage*: Genesis 25; the story in which Esau, son of Isaac, sells his birthright to his brother Jacob for a mess of red pottage.
235. *On ne peut jamais ... boirai de ton eau*: French: 'it is impossible to assert "Fountain I will never drink of your water"'. Source untraced.

236. 'Les esprits faibles ne sont jamais sincères': French: 'weak spirits are never sincere'. Source untraced but attributed to Rochefoucauld.

237. *And he went out ... it was night*: John 13:30. 'So Judas, having taken the bit of bread, straight away went out: and it was night.'

238. *I would marry a Becky Sharp*: the scheming adventuress of W. M. Thackeray's novel *Vanity Fair* (1848).

239. *an access of moral spring cleaning*: Newhaven plays on the idea of ridding the house of dust and dirt by undertaking a thorough clean after the winter has passed.

240. *The fool saith, Who would have thought it*; collected in R. Christy, *Proverbs, Maxims and Phrases of all Ages: Classified Subjectively and Arranged Alphabetically*, 2 vols (G. P. Putnam's Sons, 1887), vol. 2.

241. *the valley of the shadow*: a traditional metaphor for death. See Psalm 23:4. 'Even though I walk through the valley of the shadow of death, I will fear no evil, for you are with me; your rod and your staff, they comfort me.'

242. *'after-dinner Christians'*: Gresley is questioning the religious commitment of parishioners who only attend later services.

243. *Might as well put a respirator on a South Sea Islander*: a respirator was a precursor to what we would now term an inhaler, used by asthmatics. Cholmondeley is presumably associating tropical weather with a freedom from this condition.

244. *curates*: see note 121 above.

245. *when they break out in buttons and gaiters*: leg-wear, buttoned down the outside. Dick is referring to the Bishop's clerical dress.

246. *a framed testimonial*: a letter from the parishioners expressing their sense of gratitude for the priest's ministry.

247. *into which she seemed to have grown like a Buddhist into his tree*: Siddhartha Gautama, the founder of Buddhism (b. *c.* 560 BC), found enlightenment while meditating under a bhodi tree.

248. *tea-gowns*: first appearing in the early 1870s as a 'robe de chambre', the tea gown became increasingly elaborate. In 1899 short-waisted 'Empire' tea gowns were in vogue.

249. *that little one-horse church*: Dick is comparing the church to a small carriage, an appropriate reference in that is both poorly attended and presided over by a single priest without the help of a curate.

250. *When the sun sets ... SHAKESPEARE*: *Richard III*, II.iii.34.

251. *Warte nur, balde Ruhest du auch*: Just wait, soon / you will rest too', Goethe, 'Wayfarer's Night Song II' (1815), ll. 7–8. See also note 349 below.

252. *writhing in your shirt of fire*: Cholmondeley may have in mind the phrase 'Like a pale martyr in his shirt of fire', from Alexander Smith's verse drama *A Life-Drama* (1857), scene ii.

253. *her French maid*: an indication of Lady Newhaven's fashion and status.

254. *Archdeacon*: see note 131 above.

255. *the Lord gave ... name of the Lord*: Job 1:21. These words form part of the funeral service.

256. *And Nicanor lay dead ... 1 MACCABEES, xv. 28*: actually 2 Maccabees 15:28.

257. *portmanteaux and dressing-bag*: trunks opening into two equal parts and a small bag to carry clean clothes or laundry, fitting into a trunk or other luggage.

258. *Le nombre des* êtres ... *AMIEL*: 'The number of people who want to see clearly is extraordinarily small. What rules mankind is a fear of the truth, or at least when the truth is of no use.' *Journal intime, 1868–1870 (Private Journal)* (Lausanne: Editions l'age de l'homme, 1987), p. 638.

259. *after the funeral the strictest etiquette ... part of the bereaved*: Victorian mourning rituals were highly ordered, and manuals such as *Cassell's Household Guide* (1880) contained advice on both practicalities and etiquette for the bereaved. Cholmondeley is here satirizing Lady Newhaven's willingness to enjoy her position, as well as her empty adherence to forms.

260. *D.V.*: from the Latin *Deo volente*: 'God willing'.

261. *mantelshelf*: mantelpiece, the decorative shelf above a fireplace.

262. pour passes le temps: French: 'to pass the time'. Lady Newhaven's use of French as the language of flirtation both suggests Hugh's sophisticated but dissolute habits, and slightly softens the brutality of the insult.

263. *To every coward safety, and afterwards his evil hour*: Spanish proverb.

264. *Victoria Cross*: the highest award of British medals, awarded for outstanding bravery.

265. *'the dim persistent rain'*: source untraced.

266. *'Julius Cæsar'*: one of Shakespeare's best-known plays, concerning the assassination of the Emperor Caesar by Cassius and Brutus.

267. *Les sots sont plus á craindre que les méchans*: French: 'fools are more to be feared than the wicked'. Source untraced.

268. *'Douglas, Douglas, tender and true'*: a poem by Dinah Craik (1859).

269. *Mr. Bentham*: Jeremy Bentham (1748–1832), a famously controversial proponent of Utilitarian philosophy.

270. *But as long as the public ... these large harvests*: for a detailed account of the more populist New Woman novels Gresley is presumably attacking here, see C. Willis, '"Heaven Defend me from Political or Highly Educated Women!"': Packaging the New Woman for Mass Consumption', in A. Richardson and C. Willis (eds), *The New Woman in Fiction and in Fact: Fin de Siècle Feminisms* (Basingstoke: Palgrave Macmillan, 2002), pp. 53–65.

271. *'Bedfordshire'*: a county in the south of England.

272. *St. Augustine*: St Augustine reintroduced Christianity in the south of England in AD 597, shortly afterwards becoming the first Archbishop of Canterbury.

273. *the parish magazine*: a monthly magazine concerned with the affairs of the parish, to which the local clergy would be likely to contribute religious or other passages.

274. *Apostolic Succession*: see note 106 above.

275. *Husks that the swine did eat*: Luke 15:15–16. 'And he would fain have filled his belly with the husks that the swine did eat: and no man gave unto him.'

276. *his Father's house*: the church.

277. *'I have dismissed ... use for him'*: This is partly based on a conversation between Cholmondeley's father and his friend the Rev. Rowland Corbet, recorded by Cholmondeley in *Under One Roof: A Family Memoir* (London: J. Murray, 1918), p. 16.

278. *dead self*: an allusion to Tennyson. See note 100 above.

279. *French novels ... improprieties contained in them*: the moral reaction against French realism was still widespread in late Victorian England. In a letter of 1895 Cholmondeley assures her father that she will allow only her oldest brother to read a consignment of French novels she has been lent by a friend. Private archive.

280. *the Evil One*: see note 134 above.

281. *The only sin ... EMERSON*: 'Clubs' in *Society and Solitude* (Cambridge: Welch, Bigrelow & Co, 1870), p. 209.

282. *the justice of eternal punishment*: the question of eternal damnation was extremely controversial among both Christians and non-believers in the nineteenth century, and was an important force behind many stories of loss of faith.

283. *agnosticism*: see note 25 above.

284. *almshouses*: charitable housing for the poor, inaugurated through the giving of alms as early as medieval times.

285. risqué: French: 'titillating', used about a story or piece of gossip based on a sexual scandal.

286. *goffered frills*: crimped with hot irons.

287. douche: French: 'shower'.

288. *not 'on all fours' with the real one*: comparable to, on a level with it.

289. *bandbox*: a decorative stiff box something like a modern hat box and designed for packing articles such as bonnets or other light items to protect them from crushing.

290. *And we are punished ... OWEN MEREDITH*: 'A Love Letter', stanza 28, in *The Wanderer* (London: Chapman & Hall, 1858). Owen Meredith was the pseudonym of Edward Bulwer-Lytton (1831–91), the son of Dickens's friend of the same name.

291. menu: French: 'slight', 'small', but adopted into English and used here in the modern sense of selected meal.

292. *G.F.S.*: see note 43 above.

293. *four enormous volumes of Pusey*: Edward B. Pusey (1800–82), a leader of the Oxford (Tractarian) Movement in the 1830s. His High-Church principles would appeal to Gresley.

294. *foot-warmer*: a stoppered pottery jar, precursor of the modern hot water bottle.

295. *watch chain*: a small chain used as a watch guard for a pocket rather than wrist watch.

296. *Is it well with the child?*: an allusion to 2 Kings 4:26–34, the story of the Shunnamite's son, who is miraculously restored to life.

297. *morning service*: see note 44 above.

298. *parlourmaid*: The duties of a parlour maid might include cleaning, attending to the bedrooms and serving at meal times.

299. *'little rifts within the lute'*: proverb meaning a token of impending disharmony, taken from Tennyson's 'Merlin and Vivien', l. 391, in *Idylls of the King* (1859), first published as 'Vivien' (London: Moxon & Co, 1859).

300. *The Devil has no ... PHILIP H. WICKSTEED*: in fact this is a quotation from Henrik Ibsen's *Peer Gynt* (1867). The Unitarian minister Wicksteed quotes it in a lecture on the play. See 'Peer Gynt', in *Four Lectures on Henrik Ibsen: Dealing Chiefly with his Metrical Works* (London: Swann Sonnenschein & Co., 1892), p. 54.

301. *It takes two ... THOREAU*: *A Week on the Concord and Merrimack Rivers* (London: Penguin, 1849), p. 215.

302. *They do say as too much learning flies to the 'ead*: The debate over the limits of female education was particularly fraught at this time, given the emergence of the knowledge-seeking New Woman. Conservative social commentators and some doctors insisted that over-educated women were prone to hysteria and other nervous complaints.

303. débris: French: bits of rubbish.

304. *fly*: a one-horse hackney carriage.

305. *leading articles appeared in the* Spectator: Two of Cholmondeley's previous novels, *Sir Charles Danvers* (1889) and *Diana Tempest* (1893), had been reviewed by the *Spectator*; this allusion to Hester's fame may therefore be aimed at Cholmondeley's own relations and acquaintance, some of whom she felt were dismissive of her work.

306. *Church Congress*: used to describe meetings above the parish level before the structuring of synods in the 1930s.
307. *If two lives join ...* ROBERT BROWNING: 'By the Fire Side', stanza 47, l. 3, in *Men and Women* (1863).
308. *she had looked him out in Burke where she herself was not to be found*: again Cholmondeley draws the reader's attention to the difference in social status between Rachel and Hugh. As an iron manufacturer and self-made man, Rachel's father would not appear in Burke's. See note 115 above.
309. *de celles qui ... dans un precipice*: French: 'of those who throw themselves into love as if off a precipice'.
310. *woman was made ... man's spare rib*: according to the Old Testament, Eve was made from Adam's spare rib.
311. *like Oliver Twist ... I want more*: in Dickens's 1837 novel *Oliver Twist*, Oliver famously asks for more to eat in the workhouse, to the horror of the Poor Law guardians.
312. *That ever burst Into that silent sea*: S. T. Coleridge, 'The Rime of the Ancient Mariner', ll. 101–2, first published in the *Lyrical Ballads*, co-authored with Wordsworth (Bristol: Joseph Cottle, 1798).
313. *Take back your vows ... Take back your vows*: John Leicester Warren, 'A Song of Faith Forsworn', ll. 19–24, in *Poems Dramatic and Lyrical* (1895). Reproduced in *Decadent Verse: An Anthology of Late-Victorian Poetry* (London: Anthem Press, 2009), p. 391.
314. *Dieu n'oublie personne ...* VINET: 'God forgets no one. He visits everyone.' Alexandre Rodolphe Vinet, *Méditations évangéliques* (Paris, 1849), p. 28.
315. *smoking-room*: a traditionally male preserve, used both for smoking and conversation in which women could not appropriately participate.
316. *put our engagement in the* Morning Post: a surprising choice also made by Madeleine Verelst in *Diana Tempest*. The *Morning Post* had a predominantly middle-class readership, and in a novel so concerned with class status, Cholmondeley's upper-class figures such as Hugh might be expected to favour *The Times*.
317. *hansom*: see note 5 above.
318. *tableaux*: see note 38 above.
319. *I cannot take them myself ... her crape*: Lady Newhaven is still in mourning for Lord Newhaven. Black crape would be worn for the first twelve months and during this time she would be expected to circumscribe her social activities to a great extent.
320. *There's neither honesty ...* SHAKESPEARE: *1 Henry IV*, I.ii.139–40.
321. *suffragan*: an assistant or subordinate bishop of a diocese.
322. *shaved and tubbed gratis by Government*: the last convicts were transported from England to Australia in 1868.
323. *little cold water cures*: a play on the fashionable 'water cures' popular with invalids throughout the century.
324. *the jawbone of an ass has a certain Scriptural prestige*: in Numbers 22:21–38 Balaam's ass refuses to pass an angel with a sword in his hand. When Balaam smites the ass three times, the ass rebukes him.
325. *'He certainly would not turn the other cheek to the smiter'*: an allusion to Christ's injunction 'But I tell you, Do not resist an evil person. If someone strikes you on the right cheek, turn to him the other also.' See Matthew 5:39; Luke 6:29.
326. farouche: French: 'wild', 'fierce'.
327. magnum opus: Latin: 'great work'.
328. *shoe-horn*: a device used for easing the back of the ankle into shoes.

329. *'Brautigams'*: German: 'lovers'.
330. *Shameful luxurious ways, these young men in the Guards*: The Guards were notorious for their extravagance and luxurious living. Pratt is both displaying the family wealth and aggressively claiming status.
331. ennui: French: 'boredom'.
332. *a separation as of the sheep from the goats*: proverbial, based on Matthew 35:22.
333. Ladies' Pictorial: otherwise *Lady's Pictorial*, a woman's magazine containing both fiction and fashion articles from the early 1880s.
334. *'Cleansing Fires'*: Adelaide Anne Proctor, 'Cleansing Fires', ll. 9–12, in *Legends and Lyrics* (New York: Appleton, 1858): 'In the cruel fire of sorrow, / Cast thy heart, do not faint or wail/ Let they hand be firm and steady, / Do not let thy spirit quail'.
335. *'Oh! never, never ... henceforth for ever'*: source untraced.
336. *'Lover and friend ... out of my sight'*: Psalms of David, Psalm 88, 'Domine Deus'.
337. *Le temps ... ne rapporte pas*: French: 'time brings, takes away but does not give back'. Source untraced.
338. *There is the resurrection ... of the brain*: Hester alludes to the orthodox Christian belief in the physical resurrection of the body on the Day of Judgement, in order to lament by contrast the irrevocable loss of her literary work.
339. *It seems He is not ... mouth of his prophets*: In 1 Kings 22:20–2 a spirit stands before God and offers to entice Ahab into attacking Ramoth Gilead by being a lying spirit in the mouths of his prophets. See also Chronicles 18:21–3.
340. *'I shall go ... to me,' II. Sam. xii. 23*: 2 Samuel 12:23.
341. *There cannot be a pinch in death more sharp than this is*: source unknown.
342. *escritoire*: from the French, small writing desk.
343. *as the eyes of a man ... fire reached him*: fire is used as a metaphor for suffering throughout the novel.
344. *But there are still his shoes*: proverbial; to fill a dead man's shoes is to step into his vacant place.
345. *I thought ... ELIZABETH BARRETT BROWNING: Aurora Leigh* (1859), Book VII, ll. 184–6.
346. *He had kissed her first ... common and profane*: like other New Women, Rachel is a social purist who believes in premarital chastity for both sexes. This is a rare allusion in Cholmondeley's work.
347. *When we are told that our Lord ... great love for us*: the Bishop resembles both Cholmondeley herself and the Broad Church Benjamin Jowett (see note 88 above) in his willingness to reinterpret Christian doctrine. Here he explains the most contentious of doctrines, the Vicarious Atonement, in liberal terms.
348. *Les âmes dont ... dans un coin*: French: 'The hearts of which I have need, / And the stars are too far off; I will die in a corner'. Source untraced.
349. *Ueber allen gipfeln ... GOETHE*: 'Over all the hilltops / is calm. / In all the treetops / you feel hardly / a breath of air. / The little birds fall silent in the woods. / Just wait. Soon / you will rest too.' Goethe, 'Wayfarer's Night Song II' (1815).
350. *Watch Service*; a late-night service held on 31 December.
351. *curate*: see note 121 above.
352. *brougham*: see note 8 above.
353. *chaplain*: a clergyman attached to a private chapel or institution.
354. *It was only hysteria*: hysteria was often associated with both spinsters and the New Woman in the public imagination.

355. *volunteer band ... Mr Pratt was Colonel*: Mr Pratt's involvement with the Salvation Army
allows him simultaneously to parade his religion (as he has already been seen to do at the
temperance meeting), exercise his love of power and, on this occasion, add to the osten-
tatious celebrations surrounding Captain Pratt's marriage to Violet Newhaven.

TEXTUAL NOTES

The copy-text is the first edition of 1899, published in London by Edward Arnold, referred to as *1899a* in the notes below. This has been compared to the second edition, also published in London by Edward Arnold in 1899, referred to as *1899b* in the notes below. Two editions were published in New York by Harper & Brothers in 1900, referred to as *1900a* and *1900b* in the notes below, although the editions are not given in the original texts. Several subsequent editions were published by Edward Arnold in 1900 and one in 1905. Only major textual variants have been noted below, including major variations from the manuscript version, referred to below as *MS*.

Textual Variants

1a   Author of 'Diana Tempest'] Author of 'The Danvers Jewels' *1900a*
3a   Sterne's starling,] *1899b, 1900a, 1900b*; Swift's starling *1899a*; silently corrected here
22a   MANY sarcastic but true ... till they do come.] Few women are capable of friendship and those few not seldom attract each other. This faith is given to those who value it. Till a more exciting emotion comes their way. *MS*
243a   *October*, 1899.] *1899b omits*

Silent Corrections

37   who only see side issues.] who who only see side issues. *1899a, 1899b*
57   better than I expected.'] better than he expected.' *1899a, 1899b*
83   point is, remember] point is, Remember *1899a, 1899b*
104   the veiled trees] the the veiled trees *1899a, 1899b*
158   regarded him. Rachel did not] regarded him Rachel did not *1899a, 1899b*

For Product Safety Concerns and Information please contact our EU
representative GPSR@taylorandfrancis.com
Taylor & Francis Verlag GmbH, Kaufingerstraße 24, 80331 München, Germany